ORGANIZATION CHANGE AND DEVELOPMENT

IMI *infor:*
Sandvf

ORGANIZATION CHANGE AND DEVELOPMENT

A Systems View

MICHAEL BEER
Graduate School of Business Administration
Harvard University

Goodyear Publishing Company, Inc.
Santa Monica, California

Library of Congress Cataloging in Publication Data

Beer, Michael.
    Organization change and development.

    Includes index.
    1. Organizational change. I. Title.
HD58.8.B44   658.4'06   79-25855
ISBN 0-8302-6416-7

Current printing (last digit):
10 9 8 7 6 5 4 3 2 1

ISBN: 0-8302-6416-7
Y- 6416-5

Printed in the United States of America

Designer: Linda M. Robertson

In memory of my friend and colleague,
Dr. Alan T. Hundert

CONTENTS

PREFACE

It has been approximately three decades since organization development (OD) emerged as a field. From a very small beginning has sprung a field in which there is a substantial body of theory and practice. It was not long ago that there were no courses in OD at schools of business, education, or public administration. Today there are not only courses but whole programs devoted to training practitioners in this field. Furthermore, organization development has been integrated into other courses of study as its theory and practice became more relevant to contemporary organizational problems. Similarly the relatively isolated application of OD at companies like Exxon, Union Carbide, TRW, and Corning Glass Works in the 1950s and 1960s has spread to both small and large companies. Research in OD has also increased in recent years and out of it has emerged better theory, concepts, and social technology. OD is establishing itself as a legitimate field of inquiry for academics.

Despite its strong beginning and promising future, OD is still widely misunderstood. For every example of a successful application, there is an example of its misapplication. For every manager and academic who has come to see the potential of OD, there are managers and academics who regard OD as a dangerous or soft-minded fad. OD still seems to be plagued by some very real questions about its legitimacy. At the root of these questions is considerable misunderstanding about the nature of OD. It is often confused with sensitivity training. Or it may be seen as impractical to apply in organizations where power and politics are a reality. In short, some see it as soft and idealistic and, therefore, a luxury they cannot afford.

It is the objective of this book to try to clarify the nature of organization development as an increasingly precise body of knowledge and practice which has great potential for improving the effectiveness of organizations. While one of OD's roots is undeniably the T group movement, there is a substantial body of organization theory and management practice which can now be integrated into the field. In writing this book, I have tried to convey OD as a discipline and practice which managers, particularly general managers, need to understand. At the heart of this attempt is the *systems view* of organizations. Effective general managers have a broad perspective which allows them to see the **ix** organization as interacting with its environment. This perspective helps them integrate the efforts of people and groups and to responsibly lead them toward the achievement of organizational purpose. Organization development theory and practice is presented here as an important research based field for managing organizational effectiveness. This managerial perspective is substantially different from a number of other texts in OD and from the perception of many managers that OD is a narrow specialty best relegated to one or two professionals somewhere in Personnel.

The reader might ask how I have come by my view that OD is important for general managers. First, my own experience as an internal and external consultant to general managers has convinced me that OD can make a difference in improving organizational effectiveness. The effective general manager is already intuitively using many of the ideas and practices associated with OD. Organization development has also been helpful to those managers who are trying to learn how to manage behavior in a large organization. Secondly, my teaching experience at the Harvard Graduate School of Business Administration in both the MBA and the executive programs, has eradicated any doubt I might have had about the potential usefulness of the ideas and methods associated with OD. There is no school that I know of which is more managerially oriented than the Harvard Graduate School of Business. Yet, I have found no difficulty meshing my own ideas with those of my colleagues; I have found them quite compatible. Furthermore, I have found that ideas and methods associated with OD are of use to executives in understanding management problems and dealing with them. Indeed, many of the ideas discussed in this text are used in the Managing Organizational Effectiveness (MOE) program, a two-week program aimed at helping senior executives diagnose and improve their organizations.

That OD can claim to be a precise and "hard" discipline is supported by an increasingly large body of research and experience. It has not been my goal to present all this research. To the contrary, few studies are described per se. Rather I have integrated research and theory into concepts that I have found useful in the teaching and practice of organization change and development. The ideas presented have a strong research and experience base. In this regard, I should clarify that where formal investigations support certain assertions I have used the term *research*. Where my own or others' experience in OD is the primary support for an assertion, I have used the term *experience*.

The generalist rather than specialist orientation of the book is reflected in several aspects. The systems model is presented early in the book and is used as an organizing theme throughout. The discussion of how organizations change presents ideas which should be useful to general managers. The term "change agent" is used frequently and is meant to denote an OD consultant or manager or a team of both. The reader may find this confusing at times but it is done in the firm belief that managers can insert themselves into the OD process as easily and probably more effectively than OD professionals. The emphasis on structural innovations and interventions and the discussion of open systems planning are also aimed at conveying the breadth and scope of OD. Finally, the last part of the book presents a strategic perspective of OD which in my view is essential to the general manager and all too often is left out of OD books.

With this approach, it should be clear that the book is primarily aimed at an introduction to organization change and development for both managers and prospective managers. Since MBA's are the primary audience, I have included many short cases in boxes throughout the text. These provide illustrative examples of OD in action. I have also included several teaching cases. These cases can be used in several classes to help students grapple with the problems of change. Other cases can be obtained from the **x** Intercollegiate Case Clearing House. The book can also be used in an executive education program concerned with teaching the management of organizational change and improvement. Finally, the book could serve the personnel or OD specialist who would like to sharpen his or her understanding of the practice, strategy, and politics of OD. In general, the book tries to combine a conceptual sophistication with a practice orientation on the assumptions that these are the backbone of OD.

The task of writing this book has spanned a long period of time. I started writing when I was Director of Organizational Research and Development at Corning Glass Works. A career change which brought me to Harvard slowed down progress but also added a new perspective which I believe has contributed to the usefulness of the book for MBA's and managers.

No venture like this could be completed without the help of many people. It is impossible to mention them all, but I would like to thank those who played an important role directly or indirectly. First and foremost, I am indebted to Corning Glass Works and its managers for sponsoring an OD effort over the eleven years I was there. When I first came I did not know about OD and neither did they! By the time I left, I had the opportunity to formulate ideas and innovate in the development of OD at Corning. These formative years had a major impact on my view of OD. I would particularly like to thank Mr. Julian Allen and Dr. Thomas MacAvoy, president of Corning, for their early interest and support as boss and client respectively. Naturally I am indebted to all the members of Corning's OD department over the years. The colleagueship and intellectual excitement we shared was invaluable to the development of many ideas in this book.

I would also like to acknowledge several people who did not help me on this book directly, but whose work strongly influenced me. The late Ralph Stogdill, with his systems thinking, was influential during my graduate studies at Ohio State University and so was Bob House. Bob Blake's and Jane Mouton's Managerial Grid served as my introduction to OD. The research and theories of Paul Lawrence and Jay Lorsch coincided with OD agendas at Corning and helped me break into new ways of thinking.

I sincerely appreciate the help of many others. Tom Cummings, Dave Brown, John Kotter, and Len Schlesinger all read the manuscript and gave me many helpful comments. I want to single out Lyman Porter, Goodyear's editorial consultant, for his enormous patience, encouragement, and constructive criticism. Eliza Collins' editorial help, supported by the Division of Research at the Harvard Graduate School of Business, was immensely useful. Of course, no book could be completed without the help of numerous secretaries. I want to thank Vivian Dexter for help on a much earlier version of the manuscript. In particular I want to express my appreciation to Rita McSweeney, who has worked on several revisions of this manuscript and has helped pull it all together. Without her dedication and competent assistance this book could not have been completed.

In the final analysis, no project of this kind can be completed without substantial sacrifice by one's family. I am deeply thankful to my wife, Cynthia, for understanding, providing emotional support, and some editorial help. To my son, Tom, and daughter, Shannon, I am grateful for being mature beyond their years and in sacrificing time with me which they would have dearly liked to have had.

MICHAEL BEER
Lecturer on Business Administration
Harvard Graduate School of Business
Boston, Mass.

THE EMERGING FIELD OF OD 1

We live in a world where organizations are an increasingly dominant force. Individuals spend a large percentage of their working lives in some form of organization. They are dependent on them for their livelihood as well as for satisfaction of many of their psychological needs. In a very real sense, a person's quality of life is dependent on conditions within his[1] organization—the job he is given to do, the nature of his supervision, the policies and procedures that define his freedom of action. How organizations function, therefore, is of great personal significance to all of us.

But the capacity of an organization to meet individual needs is heavily dependent on its ability to survive and prosper in its environment. The organization is dependent on its members for motivation to apply skills, knowledge, and creativity to their assigned tasks. When the organization cannot harness enough of its members' energy and direct them toward organizational goals, it may not be able to deliver its product or service at a competitive price. Individuals who work in organizations that cannot compete, will not long be able to achieve their personal goals through the organization.

The well-being of society is dependent on effective exchanges between (1) individuals and their organization, and (2) between organizations and their environment. If the first exchange is ineffective, the psychological well-being of the employees is in danger. Labor strife, dissatisfaction, turnover, and absenteeism are continued reminders that this exchange is a difficult one to manage.

If the second exchange, that between the organization and its environment, is ineffective, the economic viability of a society is threatened. Nowhere is this more apparent today than in Great Britain where difficulties in being productive and competitive in international markets have become central concerns not only for organizations but for society as a whole. How is it possible for organizations, indeed, for a society to arrive at this point? Let us start with an illustrative example:

Nearly everyone in business talks about improving productivity in U.S. manufacturing but notable breakthroughs are rare. Lately, the workers at a continuous weld pipe mill of a large U.S. steel manufacturer have shown that dramatic gains can be made   **1** without major capital expenditures. In three months of 1972, they raised their productivity by a Herculean 32 percent.

The workers had a powerful incentive. In October, corporate officials announced that the 4000-ton-a-month plant was being shut down, a victim of rising costs and stiffening foreign competition: A ton of two-inch pipe that sold for $300 was being offered by Japanese mills for $240. Dino Paponeto, the President of United Steel Workers local recalls, "We asked management to give us a chance to make the mill pay."

Mill executives agreed to postpone the closing and adopt a few suggestions which workers had been requesting for years. A traveling saw that cut pipe into sections after it left the furnace was repaired for only $3,000. As a result, spoilage dropped from 29 percent of output to 9 percent. A few storage racks and inspection tables were also rearranged to permit a smoother flow of work. Two crucial but low-paid employees who operated a pipe straightening machine were given raises from $3.70 to $4.07 an hour. The workers made a relatively minor change in their production schedule to prevent some machines lying idle while different sizes of pipe were being processed on others. The plant's maintenance staff took only a day to repair breakdowns that formerly took a week to fix. Operators of straightening and threading machines began catching mistakes that they had previously let pass.

"There is a new spirit in the mill," says Assistant Works Manager Ray Robinson. Observes the union's Paponeto: Being recognized as people who can make creative suggestions has given the men a certain dignity (Time, 1973).

This example illustrates the problem of exchange between the individual and the organization as well as between the organization and its environment. The survival of the steel mill depended on management's ability to sense change in its market, develop goals to meet these changes, and unleash the energy of its members (workers and managers) to achieve these goals. The needs of the workers for a secure job and job satisfaction depended on the mill's capacity to survive. Yet, despite this, they apparently withheld a good deal of their potential productive effort until it was almost too late. Why?

One can see from the rapid turnaround that potential energy for operating the mill at higher productivity was available, but the steel mill management did not unleash worker motivation nor did it provide the kind of "dignity" the workers wanted. Only the threats of job loss and organizational death were able to energize employees, unions, and management to develop patterns of motivation, innovation, and collaboration required for survival. Had those patterns been adopted earlier the corporation would not have lost years of potentially higher profitability, and the employees would not have lost years of potential satisfaction from a secure job and a sense of accomplishment.

This example demonstrates what is probably true of most organizations—the energy to maintain an effective organization is present. Often not present are the knowledge, skill, and will on the part of management to create conditions that will avert the crisis.

This book will be examining organization development (OD), a rapidly emerging field of applied behavioral science concerned with helping contemporary organizations deal with problems of commitment and adaptability. Organization development offers organizations and their members the means to discover innovative organizational solutions which will unleash commitment and develop adaptiveness. It also provides a growing theory and social technology for catalyzing the process of change itself. Obviously, the position of this book is that OD theory and technology is a fresh approach which can be helpful to organizations in accomplishing this goal.

The remainder of this chapter will deal with: the historical antecedents of the problem in commitment and adaptability that exist in many contemporary organizations; a framework for understanding organizations and their development; why OD is emerging and is likely to play an important role in organizations of the future; and finally, the definition of OD itself.

THE RISE AND DECLINE OF THE BUREAUCRATIC ORGANIZATION

The twentieth century has seen the emergence of "bureaucratic" organizations as the primary means of bringing together and utilizing labor, capital, and technology for the accomplishment of organizational purposes. The most prominent of these is the corporation.

Born of the industrial revolution, the corporation has emerged with some modification along the lines suggested by the German sociologist, Max Weber (1947). It is hierarchical in nature, has centralized decision making, achieves coordination through tight rules and controls, divides work according to functional specialization, and emphasizes standardization and control as a means for achieving reliability, rationality, and efficiency. Its primary means for attracting, keeping, and obtaining performance from people is economic.

If one examines conditions at the beginning of the industrial revolution, it is not difficult to understand why this form emerged. In what we would call an economically underdeveloped society, the labor force was uneducated, unskilled, and primarily interested in security and survival. Because of the nature of the work force, tasks were specialized and decision making was centralized, creating an organization form that did not rely on high levels of individual competence and internal motivation.

However, the environment in which organizations were operating did not require high levels of commitment. During this stage of economic development, markets and technology were stable and there were few demands for the corporation to adapt. What was needed was an organization that reliably performed a relatively simple and routine task. Bureaucratic organizations with their emphasis on standardization and control fit these requirements quite well.

The most important reality of today is a world of ever accelerating change in markets, technology, science, information, and values which place severe stress on bureaucratic organization (Toffler, 1970). For many organizations, the conditions which helped shape this form of organization and which made it effective have changed, creating problems not only in the steel mill we just examined, but all around us.

The Crisis in Commitment

The emergence of the union movement in the 1800s was an early indication of the human costs associated with bureaucratic organizations. Workers challenged their economic and "psychological contract" with the organization and renegotiated it through collective bargaining. For a time, more money and security allowed organizations to function without significant changes. Then the rapid pace of economic development in many countries released workers from their primary concern for security and survival. Freedom, esteem, personal growth, and self-realization have now emerged as more important needs (Herzberg, 1966; Maslow, 1954). The primary mechanism of bureaucratic organizations for attracting, motivating, and holding workers—the "economic contract"—has slowly eroded.

Specialized jobs that do not challenge employees, poor communication of goals, and increasingly centralized control systems are causing industrial workers to invest less of themselves in their jobs and the organization. More and more costly labor settlements are required to obtain minimum levels of commitment.

These problems are not restricted to the production floor. Problems of commitment, and the resultant turnover or unionization, are also beginning to be seen among white collar clerical employees, professional employees, and even managers.

The Crisis in Adaptability

It is not surprising that the organization whose main virtue was predictability and reliability should have difficulty adapting to increasingly dynamic environments. Hierarchical structure and centralized decision making can hinder the processing of huge volumes of complex information with which contemporary organizations are being inundated and delay the organization's ability to respond. Division of labor and functional specialization complicate the need to coordinate tasks. When this task must be completed within tight time limits, the problems of integrating across functional departments becomes enormous. Rules, procedures, and other centralized controls make it difficult for individuals to respond to changing conditions without taking great personal risks. When workers don't respond, the organization does not change appropriately.

The same rules, procedures, and policies also create social norms (implict or explicit expectations) which block innovation as well as responsiveness to new values. As Beckhard (1970) has pointed out "American, Anglo-Saxon, Judeo-Christian, and other values are and will be deeply challenged by the young, by ethnic and other minorities, and by emerging people who see the possibility of fundamental organizational and societal change as a real and realistic goal."

As we have seen, the crisis in commitment and adaptability is symptomatic of the increasing stress on bureaucratic organizations. To better understand why organizations are experiencing stress, why organization development has emerged from these conditions, and what organization development is, a framework for thinking about organizations and change is necessary.

CONGRUENCE AND ORGANIZATIONAL EFFECTIVENESS

Organizations are social inventions designed to achieve economc or other purposes while at the same time fulfilling member needs. The problem of contemporary organizations, discussed in the previous section, show that social structures and processes developed by managers to operate in one environment and to motivate certain employees may not be sufficient for another environment and a different set of employees. Thus, organizations may be viewed as dynamic entities that must take on structures and processes required by changing conditions and people. This means that no one organizational form or set of management principles can be used as firm guidelines for organizational design. Instead, the effectiveness of a given organizational design is contingent on the situation. It must be judged by the congruence or fit of social structures and processes with the individuals being recruited and the environment being served. The following four organizational components must be congruent.

1. *People:* Abilities, needs, values, and expectations of employees.
2. *Process:* The behaviors, attitudes, and interactions that occur within the organization at the individual, group, and intergroup level.

FIGURE 1-1   Four Organization Components Which Must Be Congruent

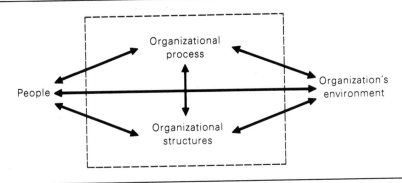

3. *Structures:* The formal mechanisms and systems of the organization that are designed to channel behavior toward organizational goals and fulfill member needs.
Examples of these include job description, job evaluation systems, organization
structure, policies, selection systems, control systems, and reward systems.

4. *Environment:* The external conditions with which the organization must deal including
its market, customers, technology, stockholders, government regulations, and the
social culture and values in which it operates.

Figure 1-1 shows these four major components. The types of people in an organization can be influenced by management through employee selection and development
policies. But the impact of these policies is likely to be felt only over a very long time
frame. Environment, though partially influenced by management, is not within their control. Past strategic choices can't be reversed easily and successive strategic choices take
a long time to change the environment. Nevertheless, strategy is crucial in that it defines
the task of the organization and, thus, the market environment in which the organization
will operate.

On the other hand, the structures of the organization and the process by which it
functions are much more within control of management through organization design and
leadership patterns. For organizations to adapt successfully, changes in structure and
process have been found critical. Indeed, they sometimes precede new strategic thrusts
(Miles & Snow, 1978). In Figure 1-1 dashed lines have been placed around these two
elements for this reason.

There is growing evidence (Friedlander, 1971; Lawrence & Lorsch, 1967; Lorsch &
Morse, 1974; Miles & Snow, 1978) that an organization's capacity to achieve its goals and
fulfill member needs is a function of the extent to which there is congruence between
people, process, structures, and environment. When these are not congruent, organizational members show frustration which may be a function of their inability to meet personal
needs, satisfy their expectations, or utilize their skills. The frustrations may also be a
function of their inability to get the job done easily and efficiently. When congruence
between these four key variables does not exist, people in the organization will perceive
barriers to the accomplishment of the task and fulfillment of their personal needs.

Managers redesign structure and process in *response* to changes in people or the
environment so that congruence and effectiveness can be maintained. They may also **5**

initiate efforts to design new organizational forms, adopt new management practices, and develop people in an effort to create a congruent pattern of people, structure, process, and environment which is more effective than a former pattern. A good example of this is the experimentation with radically different management practices and ways of organizing work in a growing number of new manufacturing plants in the U.S. (Lawler, 1977).

The manager's job has always been the development and maintenance of congruence. What now highlights this as a crucial managerial process is that rapid change in markets, technology, knowledge, society, and people, has created greater pressure on managers to find new structures and processes that will allow the maintenance of congruence. Even more importantly, the rapid rate of change is placing a premium on managers' capacity to develop organizations with a continuing capacity for sensing poor fit between organizational components, and responding with planned change. This capacity to adapt will be referred to in this book as *organizational health.* Its increasing importance is one of the main reasons that OD is now emerging as a field of inquiry and practice.

WHY ORGANIZATIONAL DEVELOPMENT IS EMERGING NOW

The need for new organizational forms, brought on by the crisis in commitment and adaptability, was only one force which stimulated the early applications of organization development in the 1950s and 1960s. The other major force has been the development of applied behavioral science knowledge.

In the last twenty years basic knowledge in the social sciences, particularly psychology and sociology, has slowly found its way into applied fields such as business administration. This was stimulated in part by the Ford and Carnegie Foundations commissions on business education whose reports in the late '50s and '60s resulted in significant expansion of organizational behavior as an area of research and teaching in business schools.

Equally important has been the innovative application of behavioral science to practical human and organizational problems which took place in the same time period. The application of "group dynamics" theory by Kurt Lewin and his associates resulted in an innovative training method known as "T" groups. In these unstructured gatherings, people learned more about themselves as well as how to work in groups in new and powerful ways.[2] Soon these methods were being applied to industrial problems (Argyris, 1964). For example, at TRW, an aerospace company, "T" groups were used to help large numbers of people adapt to a complicated matrix structure requiring collaboration. Somewhat earlier, these and other methods were applied at Exxon and Union Carbide. The success rate of these new methods was mixed.

Failures led to the development of new methods for helping not only work teams but whole organizations improve their effectiveness. For example, Floyd Mann and his associates, at the Institute for Social Research of the University of Michigan, developed a process for administering attitude surveys and feeding back results to help managers throughout an organization surface and deal with organizational problems, a method known as survey feedback. Robert Blake and Jane Mouton developed a five-year program known as the Managerial Grid by which all managers and groups throughout an organization can examine their effectiveness and take action where needed (Blake and Mouton, 1964, 1968). In England at the Tavistock Institute researchers were learning about the interaction between technology and social systems and were translating this knowledge into new ideas about the design of work (Trist et al., 1963).

The development of more useful methods and theories about organizations together with the need to solve pressing problems has resulted in the emergence of organization

6

development. Sufficient knowledge now exists for organizations in the private and public sector to utilize organization development theory, process, and methods to improve organization effectiveness (Rush, 1973).

WHAT IS ORGANIZATION DEVELOPMENT[3]

Using the conceptual framework of congruence, organization development may be seen as a process for diagnosing organizational problems by looking for incongruencies between environment, structures, processes, and people. Following are some examples of how lack of fit arises between these components and how organization development deals with it.

An organization that has enjoyed a technological edge and a secure position in its market finds that, owing to decisions made by its competitors to introduce new products, it is operating in a more competitive environment. Previously the organization had been able to function effectively within a bureaucratic framework of centralized decision making and authority, fairly explicit rules and regulations, tight financial control, and a traditional hierarchical structure. Now the organization finds its structures, procedures, policies, and top-down management approach do not seem to work as well.

Poor fit exists between the organization's structures, processes, and its external business environment. For the first time, the organization needs to be more innovative, respond more quickly to changes in its market, and develop new products and technology. There is general frustration in the organization over an inability to get decisions made quickly. As they attempt to develop new products, top management is frustrated by continued and unexpected problems. There is conflict between groups who need to coordinate their activities. Top management finds too much of its time taken up by these conflicts.

Top management seeks the help of an OD specialist to perform a diagnosis of the organization. This specialist suggests that top management commission a task force to help with conducting interviews and administering a questionnaire. Information from these sources reveals that many of the frustrations are due to an inappropriate focus for decision making. All decisions being made at the top by a few individuals does not fit with the need for more rapid decisions. The task force's feedback of its findings and the resulting discussions lead to a plan by top management to change the formal structure of the organization to achieve more coordinated decision making at lower levels on new product development. Project teams are formed to coordinate new product development at lower levels.

These groups report directly to the top of the organization. People on the teams are evaluated by both the team leader and their functional bosses. The top group sets time aside for sharpening its strategic plan. All of these changes are announced widely and are followed by numerous meetings of the new project teams. Functional groups which must work together but are currently in conflict meet to resolve differences, and top management spends some time away from work with the OD consultant to discuss their roles in the new organization.

The organization has changed its more traditional functional structure to one which allows more coordination and decision making at the level where information exists. The new structure requires that individuals in the organization adopt less formalistic attitudes about management and that they be able to confront conflict more fully. New structures and processes are adopted despite the fact that many people in the organization cannot yet function in these new ways. Meetings, training, and other intervention methods are all aimed at helping them change or helping them find other positions if they do not want to change. These activities associated with managing the organizational change take place over a two-year period.

While we would expect OD efforts to move organizations to less bureaucratic structures because of the more dynamic environment in which organizations find themselves, OD can legitimately lead to centralization of decisions, more traditional organizational forms, and more directive management styles.

A small company headed by an inventor has developed a new product that it has just begun to manufacture. As the company enters the manufacturing phase, problems develop. The people in manufacturing become extremely frustrated as their manufacturing schedules and plans are changed by the engineering department. These changes are made without discussion with the purchasing department or the production manager. Customers become dissatisfied as promised delivery dates for the new product are missed. Manufacturing people are frustrated by their inability to get the work done efficiently and to deliver the products on time. They are particularly upset by the president's support of engineering and his unwillingness to provide structure and direction for the fledgling organization.

At a series of meetings in which interview findings are fed back to management by an OD consultant, decisions are made. These include: formalized procedures for product changes and for coordinating changes with purchasing and customer service, clarification of how decisions on new products are to be made, and finally a series of personal counseling sessions between the OD consultant and the president regarding the need for clear direction. These and other changes move the organization from a loosely run R&D organization to a more highly structured manufacturing organization with more firm procedures, rules, and chains of command.

Organization development can also deal with problems at lower levels in the organizations where technology, guided by traditional industrial engineering principles, has created a work environment that is not congruent with the needs of more highly educated workers.

A plant manager asks for help from an OD consultant in solving turnover and absenteeism problems on the plant floor. Discussion indicates that morale is low and productivity is down. A task force of union and management people is formed with the help of a behavioral scientist to diagnose the problems and propose solutions. Interviews show that people find their work dissatisfying and unchallenging. With the involvement of additional task forces and help from professionals, jobs are redesigned to include more responsibility and information about quality and productivity. In some cases, groups of workers are given the responsibility for running a production line on their own. The span of control for each supervisor is increased and his role changes. To support these changes, supervisors receive training, coaching, and counseling in how to manage this new situation.

These examples of OD applications illustrate the diversity of directions an OD effort can take, the variety of techniques that fall under the umbrella of OD, and the many situations in which it can be applied. But the aim is always to surface concerns, attitudes, and views not normally discussed. Plans for action and change, based on the information surfaced and the problems identified, follow. This process is aimed at bridging the gap in communication and influence between those with less power and those with more, and between people who do not normally collaborate though they have common goals. The result is a more open organization in which effectiveness is under continuing scrutiny.

Organization development may begin because a manager senses problems that block organizational performance or employee satisfaction. Or it may begin because a manager wants to further improve his organization. Sometimes, organization development begins when a new organization is formed and there exists an opportunity to shape it in advance. Regardless of how it begins, the process described above ideally encompasses the organization as a total system. This means a variety of dimensions—individual performance, interpersonal relations, policies, supervision, organization and job structure, planning, communication, pay systems, and decision making—may all be examined and changed.

Organization development is ideally implemented by a manager knowledgeable and skillful in its use. Often, however, an organization may call in an OD consultant for help. He may be from inside or outside the firm, but he usually has had training in the behavioral sciences and in techniques of OD.[3]

The consultant acts as a catalyst in helping organizational members define problems, develop alternative solutions, implement changes, and evaluate the effects. He supplies techniques for carrying out the process of change while at the same time providing the expertise needed to solve human problems. The consultant moves change along but does *not* control the change process. Indeed, he also trains members to do their own OD so that the organization can carry on without him.

To develop an organization, a number of roles are required. Someone must recognize the need for change and initiate the process. Someone must collect data and diagnose the organization. Someone must have expertise about organizational structures and processes which could increase effectiveness. Someone must be knowledgeable about various strategies and approaches to change. Someone must implement meetings, training programs, and other interventions needed to move change along. Someone must lead by setting expectations and modeling new behaviors.

While in some instances one person, the manager, carries out all these roles, in most organization development efforts the roles are mixed in different ways between two or more people. For example, recognizing the need for change and catalyzing the process itself is often the role of the manager, but internal staff people or outsiders could, and sometimes do, take on that role. Leading by setting expectations and modeling is usually the role of the manager, but occasionally these tasks are carried out by a staff specialist or outside consultant. While collecting data, diagnosing, and implementing the changes are often the responsibility of a staff specialist or consultant, they are sometimes carried out by the manager leading the organization.

Three different terms—*manager, change agent,* and *consultant*—will be used in this book to refer to individuals who might be involved in carrying out the various roles associated with change. Because of the many different ways in which the roles are mixed between individuals, the terms will be used somewhat interchangeably. The book's intention is to convey what is known about the total process of organization change and development. Who carries out various parts of the process, while of significance, is less important than a full appreciation of what has to happen for an organization to move successfully through major transitions. Nevertheless, to help clarify who typically carries out various change roles, the book will be consistent in the terms applied to different roles. The term *manager* will be used to refer to the person heading an organization. The term *change agent* is the most general term and will be used to refer to the individual, staff specialist, consultant, or manager, or a team of these individuals responsible for initiating and managing the organizational change effort. The term *consultant* will be used to refer to an internal or external organization development specialist, usually an applied behavioral scientist or a personnel specialist, who brings knowledge in organizational diagnosis, alternative organizational approaches, change strategy, and intervention methods. **9**

OD Defined

This description of organization development leads to a formal definition of OD that will guide us in the remainder of the book.

OD is a system-wide process of data collection, diagnosis, action planning, intervention, and evaluation aimed at: (1) enhancing congruence between organizational structure, process, strategy, people, and culture; (2) developing new and creative organizational solutions; and (3) developing the organization's self-renewing capacity. It occurs through collaboration of organizational members working with a change agent using behavorial science theory, research, and technology.

The material in this chapter has tried to convey something about the uniqueness of organization development compared with other approaches to organization improvement. Because what distinguishes OD from other approaches helps to define it more clearly, a list of its basic tenets follows:

1. *Organization development seeks to create self-directed change to which people are committed.* Obtaining collaboration of people in the change is the means for obtaining commitment. Less participative approaches to change aimed at improving congruence are also used in organization development in situations which require rapid change or in which employees do not have the capacity to participate.

2. *Organization development is a system-wide change effort.* It starts with the assumption that organizations are complex systems and that its subunits, levels of management, and components (process, people, structures, etc.) are all interdependent. Changing one means that change in the others is inevitable.

3. *Organization development typically places equal emphasis on solving immediate problems and long-term development of an adaptive organization.* The latter objective is met by developing an organization in which individuals are encouraged and have competence to confront problems. However, change efforts which are aimed at only one of these objectives are also considered organization development so long as the goals are based on a valid diagnosis of the organization's needs.

4. *Organization development places more emphasis than other approaches on a collaborative process of data collection, diagnosis and action for arriving at problem solutions.* The assumption is that unless the process is "right," there will not only be low commitment to planned change but managers will not learn to use the OD process.

5. *Organization development often leads to new organizational arrangements and relationships that break with traditional bureaucratic patterns.*

6. *In organization development efforts, the change agent brings two types of competencies to the organization.* He brings *knowledge* about organization design, management practice, and interpersonal dynamics. He also brings *skills* in working with individuals and groups.

Plan for the Book

Now that the forces leading to organization development and an overview of what is meant by OD have been discussed, we will move to an examination of its theory, process, social technology, and strategy. The book has been divided into five parts.

Part I deals with the conceptual foundation of OD. Ideas relevant to understanding the dynamics of organizations and how they change are discussed in Chapters 2 and 3, respectively.

Part II is concerned with the process change agents employ when they intervene in organizations. Chapter 4 develops some of the assumptions which underly OD strategy. The next three chapters present the successive steps of selecting and entering the target organization (Chapter 5), collecting data and diagnosing problems (Chapter 6), and planning and managing change (Chapter 7).

Part III provides a description and evaluation of the intervention methods currently practiced in OD. These are the tools change agents use to diagnose problems and catalyze change. The methods described are those which have been found to be effective in various situations in the last two decades. Chapter 8 presents diagnostic methods for developing an awareness and understanding of problems. Chapters 9, 10, and 11 are concerned with three types of methods, each suited for intervention in a different aspect of the social system.

Part IV deals with strategic issues associated with systems-wide change. Chapter 12 deals with the problem of sequencing and orchestrating interventions so that they have the desired cumulative effect. The remaining chapters deal with the questions of where OD should start, how it might be spread throughout a larger organization, how it should be evaluated, and how it might be institutionalized.

Part V presents three sets of cases which describe organizational problems and the intervention strategies used to deal with them. These are teaching cases which allow an analysis of organizational problems and an evaluation of the OD strategy and methods applied. No effort to improve organizational effectiveness is without its problems and unexpected consequences. These cases provide an opportunity to learn about them.

NOTES

1. The terms "he" and "him" refer to both women and men. They have been adopted as a convention to simplify sentence structure and improve readability.
2. "T" groups will be discussed in more detail in Chapter 11.
3. Parts of this section have been taken with only slight modification from Beer and Driscoll (1977).

UNDERSTANDING ORGANIZATIONS AND HOW THEY CHANGE I

OVERVIEW

This part of the book will explore the conceptual and theoretical foundations of organization development. In order to improve organizational effectiveness a manager must have a conceptual framework for diagnosing organizational problems and coming to an understanding of their causes. For this purpose, open systems thinking and theory will be introduced in Chapter 2. It is then applied to the development of a systems model of organizations. In Chapter 3, basic concepts needed to understand how organizations change will be introduced. At the core of these concepts is the idea that organizational change is a complex process of social learning subject to principles of learning.

UNDERSTANDING ORGANIZATIONS AS SYSTEMS 2

In order to improve the effectiveness of organizations one must fully understand their complexity. Some of the most frequent causes of failure in organizational change efforts come from an incomplete understanding of the multiple causes of a problem. A superficial and incomplete diagnosis of the problem then leads to an incomplete action plan in which only a few of the critical organizational dimensions which influence behavior and results are targeted for change. Just as often, an inadequate diagnosis leads to organizational arrangements or management practice that cause unanticipated secondary problems (see Cases 2–1 and 2–2).

Organizational improvement efforts which do not identify the root causes of the problem or which do not anticipate the consequences of planned organizational change, fail to develop credibility among organizational members. Apathy or resistance develop, the momentum of change is lost, and the organization may ultimately regress back to earlier states. Unanticipated consequences, failure to achieve the desired momentum of change, and repeated attempts to change followed by regressions are indications that the change agent has not fully understood and acted upon the organization as a system.

But what is meant when organizations are referred to as systems and how does understanding that help in planning a change effort? This chapter will deal with the nature of organizations, present a systems model of organizations and its conceptual underpinnings, and discuss how such a model might help, indeed how it is essential, in planned organizational improvements.

A SYSTEMS VIEW OF ORGANIZATIONS

In Chapter 1 a strong argument was made for viewing organizations as dynamic entities continually interacting with their environment, changing and adapting to develop congruence between people, process, structures, and external environment. This dynamic view helped explain why bureaucratic organizations, the dominant form of organization when the environment was stable, are under stress and new organizational forms are evolving. It **15**

CASE 2-1

A small electronics firm experienced a high rate of turnover in its engineering department, a key to the company's success. The turnover occurred immediately after the Vice-President of Engineering had departed and was attributed by the president to the strong personal relationships this vice-president had established with the engineers.

However, a closer analysis of the problem indicated that there were many more fundamental problems causing the turnover. The company's business had evolved over a number of years from small R&D contracts, which one or two engineers could complete, to larger-scale production-run contracts in which many engineers, purchasing, and production peple were involved. The turnover of engineers was a function of their frustration in getting things done in this new environment. They could no longer design the system alone. A manufacturing function had now created rules and procedures which engineers needed to take into account. A manufacturing manager who was autocratic enforced these procedures arbitrarily, making life difficult for the engineers who had been hired to be creative.

Thus the changes in business and subsequent changes in tasks had violated the engineers' needs and expectations. Furthermore, no structural mechanism or procedure existed to facilitate the new coordination required within and between engineering and other functions.

The Vice-President of Engineering had held the effort together through his relationships with engineers and other functions. When he left, no other organizational forces were in place to facilitate the complex coordination required. The president of the company was busy on new acquisitions and had not actively provided leadership for the functions. The new engineering manager lacked the unique leadership and management skills held by the old vice-president. So-called engineering project leaders did not understand their roles, nor did other engineers or manufacturing people accept their influence. The measurement systems encouraged manufacturing to emphasize efficiency, making them less receptive to the many ongoing design changes that were required.

A plan to find a new Vice-President of Engineering would have been totally inadequate in dealing with the problems. A clarification of roles and a reorganization of engineering along project lines was needed. Project leaders needed clarification of their roles and new skills to act as coordinators. A control system that allowed for tradeoffs between the efficiency orientation of manufacturing and the design interests of engineering was needed. Similarly, the president needed to become more involved in the day-to-day affairs of the company, while the Manufacturing Vice-President needed to modify his arbitrary style.

CASE 2-2

Elimination of assembly lines on a production floor of an electronic plant resulted in each worker assembling a whole product. These changes were aimed at increasing the involvement, motivation, and satisfaction of these employees. While the changes had the desired effects on motivation and satisfaction, a new set of unanticipated problems arose.

Supervisors, who had been used to traditional assembly line jobs, found that the new way of organizing work gave far more initiative to workers than before and diminished their previous authority. Supervisors were now required to facilitate more than direct. Some supervisors had difficulty adjusting. While some might adjust with the help of education, others would probably have to be replaced. Workers who now had new responsibilities wanted to be paid more but the job evaluation system of the company prevented this. The elements of decision making and initiative now required in the jobs were not weighed sufficiently. Finally, when inventory was too high, company policy called for layoffs based on seniority.

Uness these problems could be solved, organizational improvements would be jeopardized by workers who felt underpaid for new responsibilities, by supervisors who might undermine the changes, or by worker insecurity.

also provides a historical and developmental perspective for any one organization and aids in diagnosing the current state and problems within that organization.

Healthy organizations sense changes in the environment and make adaptations in the way they function to accommodate new environmental demands. They may also elect to interact with only parts of a larger environment based on assessment of their capacity to respond. Finally they can try to influence their environment to be consistent with organizational arrangements and dominant managerial practices (Starbuck, 1976).

Systems Theory Applied to Organizations

Systems theory, the ideas that help explain the dynamic interrelationships of several parts of a larger whole as it interacts with its environment, has in the last several decades been applied to organizational theory (Kast & Rosenzweig, 1970; Katz & Kahn, 1978; Lawrence & Lorsch, 1967; Rothlisberger & Dickson, 1939; Stogdill, 1959). Even more recently systems theory has found its way into organization development where it has helped in organizational diagnosis and intervention strategies (Beer, 1976; Beer & Huse, 1972; French & Bell, 1978; Huse, 1975; Kotter, 1978). Applying systems theory to organizations leads to the following list of general characteristics.

1. Organizations are composed of several components or parts which are in interaction with one another while at the same time part of an identifiable whole. These components may be subunits or they may be dimensions such as people, process, structure, and culture.
2. Organizations, having more or less permeable boundaries, interact with an external environment from which they obtain energy/matter or information as inputs and to which they export a product or service as outputs. (Energy/matter means people, electricity, money, materials, etc.)
3. Organizations are a network of people, structures, and technical operations that transform the raw materials, such as energy or people, into a product or service desired by users in the environment.
4. Organizations have feedback mechanisms that allow various parts or components to adjust to other parts and components. Similarly, there is information flow between the **17**

organization and its environment that allows it to adapt and influence. Market research departments are examples of external sensing functions, while various interdepartmental meetings are examples of internal feedback mechanisms.

5. Entropy, or a running down of the system, will occur if energy is not continuously imported and converted into valued outputs that allow reinvestment and further development. For social systems, the most important maintenance source is human effort and motivation. Thus the motivation of people in the organization becomes just as important a source of energy as financial and other energy/matter resources.

A Social Systems Model of Organizations

The idea that organizations convert inputs such as energy/matter and information from their environment into outputs that are useable by the environment can be translated into a social systems model of organizations. This model is presented in Figure 2–1. It synthesizes a diverse body of research, theory, and OD practice in a large multinational corporation over an eleven-year period.[1]

The model specifies the relationships between the major organizational components which have to fit or be congruent in order for an organization to be effective. These are:

1. Environment
2. Organizational Outcomes
3. Human Outputs
4. Organizational Behavior and Process
5. Organizational Structures
6. People
7. Culture
8. Dominant Coalition

The model specifies a flow of events beginning with the qualities that people bring with them (*people*) and ending with the attitudes and psychological states of organizational members (*human outputs*) after they have lived and worked in the organization for some period of time. The organization's *structures* (reward systems, policies, control and evaluation systems, etc.) signal organizational members what behavior is desired and reinforce (reward or punish) actual behavior. Thus, structures shape *organizational behavior and process.* Structures and process together mediate the relationship between people's needs, expectations, and capacities when they enter the organization, and the attitudes and capacities developed as a result of living and working in the organization. Organization *culture,* commonly held beliefs about how the organization is and should be operating, is formed by all four of the components just described but also influences and shapes them. Similarly the *dominant coalition,* a small number of key decision makers, impact all of the aforementioned organizational components through their position of power and influence in the organization but are also influenced by their experience in the organization with all of the components listed. Economic indicators such as profit, and quality of work life indicators such as turnover, reflect the organization's performance (*organizational outcomes*) in its market, and social and technological *environment.* Organizational outcomes are a function of all the components of the social system working in concert but are particularly well predicted by the organization's human outputs.

It should be clear, however, that while this way of describing an organization is a convenient way of thinking about the flow of a social system, any part of the system can

FIGURE 2-1 A Social Systems Model of Organization

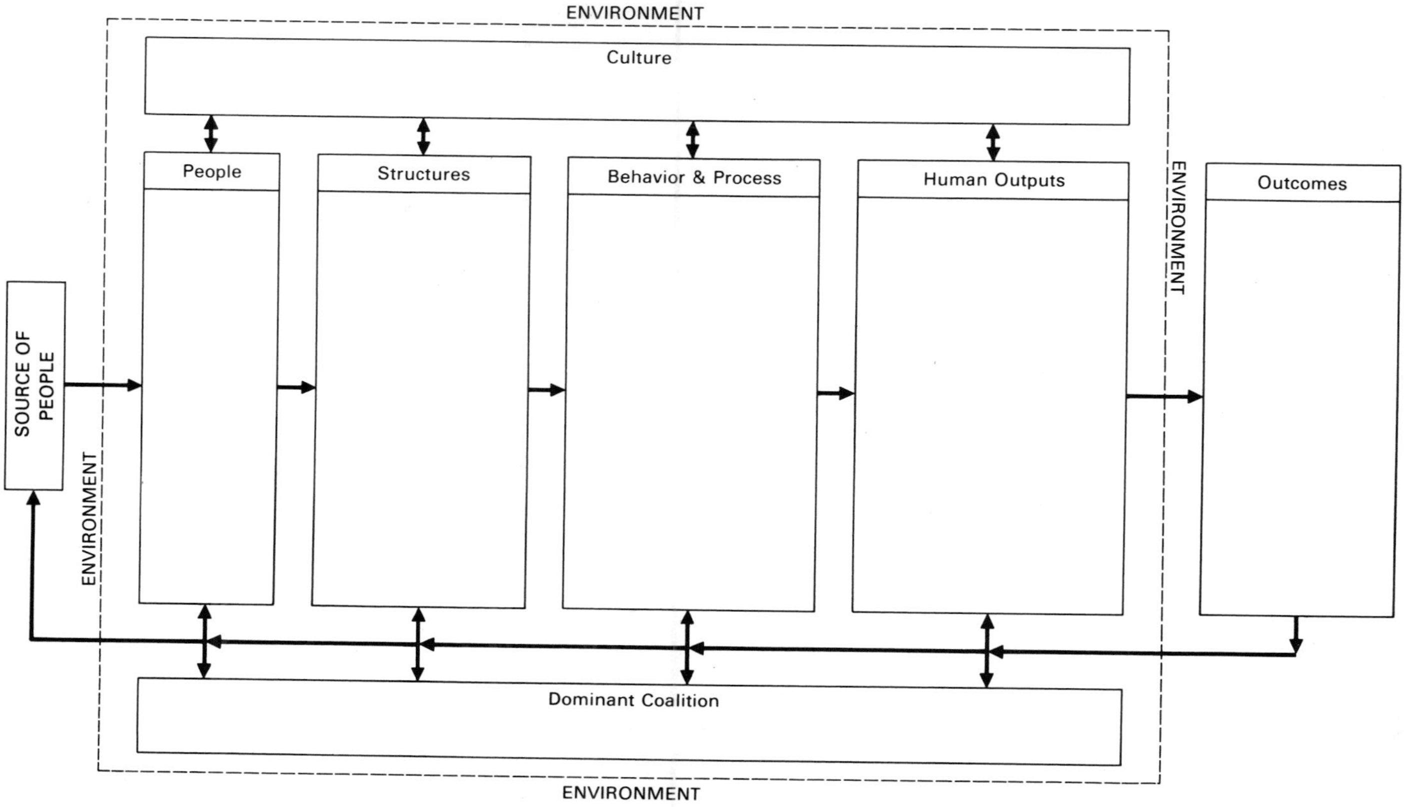

affect any other part. The feedback loops in the model (Figure 2–1) illustrate these and other interdependencies.

The social systems model does not explicitly recognize tangible assets such as buildings, inventory, money, and materials as organizational inputs. The reason for this is not that they are unimportant but rather that the model provides a framework for understanding organizations as social systems in which these other inputs, though equally important, are not center stage.

Indeed, an organization with financial resources or technology superior to its competitors can probably operate successfully for long periods of time with relatively low human output and quality of work life outcomes. Sooner or later, however, inability to attract, keep, motivate, and influence talented people will lead to reduced effectiveness of the social system in transforming human energy into profit. This in turn will lead to reduced financial and technological resources. Organizational specialists and managers must keep this in mind when estimating the return on investment in organization development. They must also remember that investment in organization development can itself lead to an increase in tangible assets of the corporation over the long term.

Practical Value of a Social Systems Model

As the two cases presented at the beginning of this chapter show (see Cases 2–1 and 2–2) the planning and implementation of organizational improvements require an understanding of the complexity inherent in social systems. Managers or organizational specialists can adopt the model presented in this book or develop their own, but if they are to be successful in managing organizational effectiveness they *must* internalize a social systems perspective for the following reasons:

1. A model provides a taxonomy of key organizational dimensions that guide data collection and diagnosis, without which the latter becomes confusing and difficult.
2. Some sense of the complex relationship between key organizational dimensions is useful in diagnosing the causes of a given problem and appreciating the circularity of causes and effects.
3. A model can be useful, as we shall see later, in categorizing intervention methods by the component or dimensions of the organization to which they apply. This allows a more systematic, efficient use of change methods.
4. A model forces managers to be quite specific about the outcomes (economic, attitudinal, and behavioral) they desire and how the intended organizational changes will affect these outcomes. Without a model, organization changes are often based on what other managers are doing, what is in vogue, or the manager's own values.

The case examples in the beginning of this chapter illustrate the model's applicability quite clearly. Turnover among engineers and its potential effects on profits (organizational outcome) was related to changes in the business (environment), which caused organizational structure, personnel policy, roles, measurement systems (structures), and expectations by engineers (people) to become outdated. These structures and inappropriate leadership practices by the president (dominant coalition) prevented the organization from developing required coordination between functions (organizational behavior and process).

As the social systems model is discussed in more depth, its capacity to provide a convenient shorthand way for diagnosing organizational problems and planning improvements will become evident. Someone else, perhaps the reader, might draw such an

organizational model quite differently. Kotter (1978) has developed a somewhat different model, but one that contains many of the same components and relationships. The similarity of his model, developed quite independently of the present model, suggests that the components and relationships presented in Figure 2–1 would also appear, though perhaps in somewhat different form, in models developed by other organizational specialists.

THE COMPONENTS OF THE SOCIAL SYSTEMS MODEL

This section will deal with each component of the model presented in Figure 2–1, describing more fully what kinds of organizational phenomena are subsumed under it and how it relates to other components. The components will be discussed in the order in which a typical diagnostic process might proceed. The first component discussed is organization environment. This is followed in turn by discussions of organization outcomes and human outputs; organizational behavior and processes which produce these outcomes; and structures, people, and culture, the major driving forces of behavior.

The sequence of this discussion demonstrates certain biases in approaching organizational diagnosis. Perhaps the most obvious is the concern for understanding the environment. The functionality of organizational attitudes and behavior can only be evaluated in relation to the organization's environment and the task which the organization faces if it is to succeed in its environment. Finally, organizational structures, people, and culture can only be evaluated in light of behaviors observed or desired. The reader is cautioned to remember, however, that in systems thinking everything is connected to everything else and another sequence of diagnosis may work just as well as long as it encompasses *all* the relevant components.

A Social System Interacts with Its Environment

Organizations interact with their environment by importing people, and using their energy to make products or provide services that are exported into the environment. The relationship between a social system and its environment is much more complex than it is for a technical system. For one thing it is difficult to define what the boundaries of an organization are. Where does the organization leave off and the environment start? For example, employees are hired by the organization and are physically and mentally inside the organization much of their lives. But they are also members of a society, are influenced continually by society, and continually transmit social concerns and changing values to the organization.

Similarly, management practices, corporate strategy, policies, structure, and other means the organization uses to convert people's energy into performance outcomes, are directly and continually influenced by the environment through legislation, market forces, new knowledge, and so on. This interaction had led to the conception of social organization as open systems as opposed to more closed technical systems (Katz & Kahn, 1978).

What aspects of the environment are relevant for an organization? Is it society as a whole, the political and governmental system, other companies in the same market, the financial community, the technology of the organization, or the local community in which the organization finds itself? Clearly all comprise an organization's environment to the extent that they place demands on the organization and there is an interaction, but several aspects of an organization's environment are particularly relevant to its structures and management practice.

1. *Market environment.* This is defined by the type of product or service which an organization provides, the type of customers it serves, and/or the industry of which it **21**

is a part. Some markets are complex and competitive while others are less so, thus, placing differing demands on the organization for market sensing, decision making, and responsiveness to customers and competitors. In general, successful organizations can be separated from unsuccessful ones by the appropriateness of their structural form and management process to their environment (Burnes & Stalker, 1961; Lawrence & Lorsch, 1967).

2. *Technological environment.* Each organization operates within a different product technology and uses different technologies to make a product or deliver a service. The rate of technological change and innovation will define the task of the organization. For example, how much the organization must stay in touch with the basic sciences that support its technology defines how extensive its R&D operations need to be, and how closely these must be linked with other parts of the organization that use the technology. Second, the technology for making the product and delivering the service also affects the nature of jobs at the working level and the opportunities for providing people with motivating tasks. The importance of technology in influencing the structure of organizations (Woodward, 1967) and the behavior and attitudes of people (Davis, 1966; Hackman, 1977) has been widely documented. Indeed, it has led to the concept of an organization as a sociotechnical system in which behavior and attitudes are influenced by technology and these in turn affect decisions about the way technology is applied to jobs (Trist et al., 1963).

3. *Social environment.* The social environment in which an organization operates may be defined by the values and culture of the society. These affect organizations directly through legislation and government regulations and indirectly through the expectations and values of its employees. An organization must be sensitive to the values of society to avoid being sanctioned for management practices which violate these values. Recent revelations about illegal corporate political contributions and payoff practices in foreign countries illustrate this point. The changing values of Swedish workers fostered by higher levels of education and social legislation influenced Volvo's decision to experiment with more attractive and interesting alternatives to assembly line jobs (Gyllenhammar, 1977).

An organization's environmental complexity and degree of uncertainty are particularly important dimensions to assess (Galbraith, 1973; Lawrence & Lorsch, 1967; Thompson, 1967). By these is meant the extent to which there are numerous forces acting on the organization and the extent to which the environment is changing unpredictably. Uncertain and complex environments place very difficult information processing and decision-making demands on organizations. They must be able to sense change rapidly, bring people together who have the latest information for problem solving, and make decisions responsive to the most recent environmental trends. Such organizations require new and different managerial processes, structures, and information handling systems (Galbraith, 1973). Some of these organizational forms and the problems associated with adopting them will be dealt with in Chapter 10. For the moment, the reader should note that examining the environment is important in understanding the task of the organization and its required structures and management process. This organization/environment perspective is a central part of what is meant by a systems view of organizations. Below is a list of the important environmental dimensions to be considered.

ORGANIZATION ENVIRONMENT

Markets

Competitive Position

Technology
National and Local Government Legislation
Social Culture
Uncertainty
Complexity

A Social System Has Multiple Purposes and Performance Outcomes

On a very long-term basis an organization's survival is dependent on how well it has been exchanging with its environment. If a business organization delivers a valued service or product at lower cost than its selling price, it survives. The effectiveness of this exchange can be measured by the *amount of profit* the organization returns since this determines how much can be reinvested to maintain current operations or develop new business opportunities. Thus profit, return on investment, and other financial indicators are the most frequently stated purposes and criteria of organizational performance.

There are other criteria and purposes, however. An organization must fulfill the needs of its members for a secure job, equitable monetary compensation, meaningful work, and a compatible social environment at work. The organization must provide for a satisfactory quality of work life, or it will ultimately be unable to attract, keep, motivate, and influence employees.

These criteria of performance create conflicting demands. Managers are often forced to tradeoff one objective against another. They may reduce profits to pay workers more or they may pay a dividend while firing people to reduce costs. How they tradeoff between these organizational outcomes will be determined by the costs to the organization of low quality of work life. Unfortunately these costs cannot always be assessed with the same precision, ease, and frequency as more tangible costs. Perceptions of quality of work life are quite subjective and their behavioral and economic consequences quite variable. Moreover, objective measures like absenteeism and employee turnover are difficult to attribute to specific events or actions by managers, and their exact costs to the organization are not always immediately apparent. Despite these difficulties in measurement, experience and research suggest that the impact of quality of work life outcomes do have an intermediate to long-term impact on economic performance of the organization.

In many countries (particularly western Europe), legislation which makes firing employees difficult is increasing the cost to organizations of low quality of work life, by preventing these costs from being passed on to the individual and society. Making it more difficult to fire employees whose performance has deteriorated forces management to search for conditions which may be demotivating employees. Thus, despite difficulties in assessing the economic value of quality of work life outcomes, managers must weigh the impact of their decisions on both sets of outcomes and balance them appropriately.

In summary, the ultimate outcomes by which an organization may judge how favorably it is exchanging with its environment are listed below:

OUTCOMES

Economic Measures
    Profit
    Return on Investment
    Rate of Growth

Quality of Work Life
    Turnover

23

Absenteeism

Ability to Attract Good People

The economic and quality of work life outcomes listed above are a result, among other things, of the attitudes people have about themselves, their jobs, their management, and the organization. The next section deals with these attitudes.

Attitudes and Psychological States Are System Outputs

One of the characteristics of systems, particularly social ones, is that there is a considerable time lag between the ultimate achievement of goals and indicators within the system that provide early warnings that goals will not be achieved. The research of Rensis Likert and his associates, has shown that employee attitudes and psychological states, such as satisfaction, commitment and motivation, will predict quite well declines in profits several years hence (Likert, 1967). Recently, employee attitude measures have been directly linked to costs in a bank (Mirvis & Lawler, 1977), a bank's service image (Schneider, et al., undated), and unionization activity (Hamner & Smith, 1978). These and other studies demonstrate the link between the condition of an organization's human assets and performance. Thus, the way an organization is managed (the functioning of its social systems) affects employee attitudes and competence and these can help predict the *ultimate* capacity of the organization to perform in its environment. Some of the human outputs that research and OD practice have shown to be important are in the following list:

HUMAN OUTPUTS

Clarity of Goals

Clarity of Roles

Feelings that the Organization Is Effective

Motivation and Energy Level

Commitment

Feelings of Personal Growth and Competence

Competence of Employees

Extrinsic Satisfaction

Intrinsic Satisfaction

Willingness to Collaborate

Willingness to Risk New Ideas

Trust and Supportiveness

Awareness of Personal and Organizational Realities

Saying that human outputs are predictors of organizational performance is not an attempt to imply that all of them are equally important to all organizations nor that they are independent of each other. One organization may require extremely high levels of commitment and risk taking while another may require only a moderate or even a low amount. The amount required will depend on the benefit that a given human output provides in comparison to the cost and difficulty of obtaining it. For example, an organization that manufactures complex electronic equipment may require a substantial amount of collaboration or risk taking with new ideas while a company that makes bottles in a relatively simple and stable environment will not.[2] Similarly, the types of people employed by the organization, their needs and expectations, will determine the kinds and amounts of satisfactions the organization must provide to attract, keep, and motivate them.

By analyzing the task or environment a manager can rank the relative importance of various human outputs. This rank ordering can be compared with a diagnosis of actual attitudes in the organization. Discrepancies and a diagnosis of their causes can lead to a clearer understanding of which managerial and structuring approaches are most appropriate and which types of people might be hired. Much of organization development practice involves collecting attitudinal data that reflect human outputs and helping managers diagnose their implications for organizational change. Many of the diagnostic interventions described in Chapter 8 are methods for assessing the state of an organization's human outputs.

We now turn to an examination of those parts of the organization that affect human outputs.

Organizational Behavior and Process

The behavior of people and the process by which they interact is the means by which goods are sold, products manufactured, work coordinated, and budgets and plans developed. Behaviors and interactions are the means by which potential energy and motivation are converted into results. The more congruent the behaviors and interactions are with the organization's purpose and task, the more effective the organization will be in achieving its performance goals. From this perspective, the job of managing an organization is the job of managing and guiding behavior.

The human processes in an organization are dynamic and transitory. Thus they are often difficult to observe and measure. Managers are usually so immersed in the content of their transactions—the technical problems, the financial decisions, the marketing strategy—that they miss the process by which the content is dealt with. Research and experience point to the fact that when process is consciously examined and managed by organizational members, they perceive improvement in the quality of decisions, coordination and effectiveness, clarity of goals and strategy, involvement and motivation, and satisfaction, among other processes and outcomes (Dyer, 1977; Friedlander, 1967; Hackman, 1976). A good deal of organization development work involves helping individuals and groups examine, and thus control, their process and behavior. These methods and techniques are called *process interventions* and will be examined in Chapter 9.

Many behaviors and interactions are required to manage and run an organization. Below are listed those processes that research and practices have found important in understanding and improving organizations. The list is not exhaustive nor are these categories independent of each other.

ORGANIZATIONAL BEHAVIOR AND PROCESS

Leadership and Supervision
Communication—Quantity and Quality
Intergroup Relation and Integration
Conflict Management
Decision-making Process
Problem Solving
Planning and Goal Setting
Group and Meeting Process

25

Interpersonal Relations

Evaluation and Control Processes

Critique and Renewal Processes

There is no prescription implied by these categories about what is the "right" process for managing an organization. Research about what behavior constitutes effective management has shown that it depends on a variety of situational factors such as the needs and expectations of the people involved, their loyalty and commitment to the organization, the task, the information available, and who has the information (Fiedler, 1967; Galbraith, 1973; Morse & Lorsch, 1970; Vroom & Yetton, 1973).

There has been considerable controversy in the field of organizational behavior between advocates of *contingency theories* on one hand and *normative theories* on the other. Contingency theories of management suggest that the kind and amount of behavior desired (leadership, integration, conflict management) depend on the organization's environment and/or the characteristics of its members. Normative theories suggest that all organizations need to approach certain ideals like openness, participation, or confrontation of conflict.

This controversy is still largely unresolved due to the fact that advocates of these different viewpoints implicitly assign different values to various organizational outcomes and measure these outcomes on different time horizons. For this reason, the question of whether organizations should strive for high levels of participation, or open communication and planning, to mention only a few processes, is best answered by looking at what the costs are compared to the benefits.

All processes and behaviors take time and money to develop and perform (i.e., whether planning or good interpersonal relations) and must compete with other investments of time and energy. The systems view of organizations suggests that the degree to which each process should be developed must depend on environmental and task demands on the one hand and employee needs and desires on the other. For each process dimension at least some knowledge exists that can help managers make decisions about the behaviors appropriate for their organization, though space limitations do not allow a discussion of this body of knowledge.

Perhaps even more important than this knowledge, however, is the capacity of managers and workers to examine how they are working together so that inappropriate processes can be corrected based on firsthand knowledge of the task and people's needs. This, of course, is the essence of organization development.

Historically, OD has been almost exclusively concerned with improving organizations through intervention methods aimed at changing process or behavior directly (Leavitt, 1965). But laboratory training methods and other interventions aimed at helping people and groups examine their behavior have been found to have only short-lived effects. Thus, attention has increasingly shifted to the examination of structures within organizations which guide and shape behavior. We now turn to a discussion of these structures.

The Influence of Structures

Structures are the formal aspects of an organization. They signal to people that certain behavior is desirable and that rewards are likely to result if they practice it. In designing an organization to obtain desired behavior and results, managers typically use the following structures or design tools.

STRUCTURAL DIMENSIONS AND DESIGN TOOLS

Organization Structures

Job Design or Structure

Types and Frequency of Formal Meetings

Personnel Policies and Systems

   Rewards and Compensation System

   Management Development and Promotion System

   Labor Relations Policy

   Performance Evaluation and Development System

   Recruitment, Selection, and Transfer Policies

Control and Measurement Systems

   Management Information Systems

   Accounting Systems

   Budgeting Systems

Geographic Location and Physical Layout

There are many examples of how structures are used by management to obtain desired behavior. For example, pay systems, particularly bonus systems, are designed to obtain high levels of motivation and goal accomplishments from senior executives. Piece rate incentive systems are designed to obtain high levels of effort from production employees. The specialized jobs of the assembly line are designed to closely control the behavior of workers and reduce undesired deviations in work practices. Financial budgets and control systems are aimed at getting functional managers to emphasize certain goals deemed important for the organizations. The structure of the organization which has functional managers reporting to a common general manager is aimed at ensuring that inevitable conflicts between functional goals will be resolved in the best interests of the organization.

Unfortunately, research and experience indicate that these structures do not always induce desired behaviors and sometimes cause undesired or dysfunctional behaviors. For example, managers may budget sales or profits at lower levels than they expect to achieve for fear of negative consequences if they miss their targets (Lawler & Rhode, 1976). Functional goals without proper balancing of integrative goals can cause undesired competition and conflict between groups (Walton & Dutton, 1969), or incentive systems may reduce worker receptivity to technological changes (Whyte, 1955). Still other structures like pay systems, job design, or office layout can cause frustration and dissatisfaction if they are not consistent with employee expectations, or if they block task accomplishment.

Because structures that stimulate and reinforce desired behavior and reduce as much as possible undesired behavior are so important, the long-range decisions managers make concerning the design of the organization's structures are very important. Organization development must therefore include a diagnosis of the impact of structures on behavior attitudes and task accomplishment and help in the design of alternative structures. We will deal with specific examples of these *structural innovations and interventions* in Chapter 10.

If structures influence organizational behavior and behaviors must be consistent with the organization's environment, then the structures appropriate for any given organization must be consistent with its particular environment. In recent years, so-called contingency **27** theories of organization have articulated this viewpoint (Burns & Stalker, 1961; Galbraith, 1973; Lawrence & Lorsch, 1967; Miles & Snow, 1978). Research supporting these theories has shown that successful organizations in uncertain and dynamic environments use structures and control systems quite different from unsuccessful organizations in the same environment and successful organizations in less dynamic environments. Thus, structures and environment or strategy (the organization's selected environment) must fit in order for an organization to be successful. The electronics firm described in Case 2–1 is an excellent example of a firm whose performance suffered as a result of not adapting its structures to a new business environment.

Unfortunately, not all organizations approximate the adaptive capacity of the theoretical social system. The structures of organizations are often determined by long-held values, personal experience of success, and beliefs of managers about the "right" way to organize rather than more flexible and contingent viewpoints. An example of this can be seen in new managers who restructure an organization they have just taken over to resemble the organization they have left. The blockade of Cuba ordered by John F. Kennedy in 1961 is cited by Weick (1973), to illustrate that organizations are not naturally adaptive systems. A blockade of Cuba was ordered as a fifty-mile perimeter for specific strategic reasons; but naval regulations and tradition specified a 500-mile perimeter and that's where the Navy placed the blockade. Apparently the Navy could not change its regulations (structure) when confronted with a new environment and task.

In summary, organizations approximate social systems to the extent that structures do seem to differ with different environments and different types of people. Generally more rigid and "mechanistic" structures are found in stable environments, loose and "organic" structures in dynamic environments (Burnes & Stalker, 1961). But organizations are far from perfect social systems and there are many examples of maladaptive structures that shape inappropriate behavior.

People Are the Raw Material of Social Systems

Organizations recruit and select people on the basis of their estimated potential to achieve certain desired levels of performance. Industrial psychologists have for years attempted to predict the performance of individuals by identifying and then assessing those individual characteristics which best predict performance on the job. While these attempts have been somewhat successful, the correlation between individual characteristics and performance criteria have at best been moderate, while the relationship between individual characteristics and more ultimate organizational performance criteria is often nonexistent (Schneider, 1976).

One reason for this is that individual characteristics comprise a potential only. There is some evidence that low correlations between individual characteristics and performance criteria are a function of inappropriate organizational arrangements, such as job design, organization structure, and management process. Thus organization design and process play an important role in unleashing people's potential.

The steel mill described in Chapter 1 is an example of this phenomenon. The individual needs, abilities, and skills to increase productivity by 32 percent were present all along, but organizational arrangements to allow this potential to be unleashed were not. To the extent that management style and job structure, for example, fit the needs, expectations, and abilities of organizational members, more of their potential competence will be realized (Hackman & Lawler, 1971; Morse & Lorsch, 1970; Turner & Lawrence, 1965; Vroom, 1960). The importance of organizational arrangements in eliciting full human potential probably increases with the complexity of the task and required coordination.

A mismatch between the organization and the characteristics of people in it, as our discussion of bureaucratic organizations implied, often occurs because the structures and managerial processes are based on certain invalid assumptions about people. Douglas McGregor (1960), Robert Blake and Jane Mouton (1964) and Chris Argyris (1962) have pointed out that a manager's implicit assumptions about people's needs, values, abilities, and expectations will be revealed in the way he manages. They have argued persuasively that the behavior of many managers and the assumptions underlying the design of many organizations are inconsistent with what is known about people. Changes in education, society, and public policy within the more industrialized countries of the world are probably increasing this gap between people and organizations.

But for this notion of individual/organization fit to be operationally useful, a social system model of organizations must at least specify which individual characteristics are important for a manager to examine and take into account in attempts to improve organizations.

It is often useful to distinguish between the "can do" or ability components of performance and the "will do" or motivational components of performance. Some managers tend to emphasize one component to the exclusion of the other, thus missing the fact that performance is a function of an interaction between abilities and motivation. The relationship has been conceptualized (McGregor, 1967) as follows:

$$P = M \times A$$

$$\text{Where} \quad P = \text{Performance}$$
$$M = \text{Motivation}$$
$$A = \text{Abilities}$$

We now turn to a discussion of ability and motivation as important components in total performance. To this list must be added, however, expectations, or what people perceive will happen when they behave or perform in certain ways.

Individual's skills and abilities. Historically, the field of organization development has been heavily influenced by the values and belief systems of the human potential movement which developed in the '50s and '60s. People in this movement, and many OD people, adopted the view that almost anyone had the potential to grow and develop into what they wanted to become. If there were problems in performance, they were a function of the organizational climate and supervision.

Thus, ability was perceived to be less of a constraint on human performance in organizations than was motivation. This relative inattention to ability, as we shall see in Chapter 11, came from the inability of OD specialists to deal with the problems of intervening in the competence question. If a manager is trying to develop trust and collaboration, how can he fire people without destroying trust? Or, how can a consultant discuss the competence of an organizational member with management without destroying his relationship of trust with organizational members?

It seems rather clear that individuals do differ in abilities and skills and that these differences limit their capacity to respond to various situations. Differences in ability seem to fall into three primary categories; physical abilities, mental abilities, and interpersonal skills. Obviously, the required mix of these three dimensions and their various subcomponents, together with experience and education, will differ for each job.

Engineers may require more technical knowledge, a mental ability, than interpersonal skills; managers may require a high mental ability and interpersonal skills;   **29** production workers may require primarily physical and mental skills. However, as the organization's arrangements change, the skills required of individuals are constantly changing.

A gap between an organization's current and desired skill and ability mix can only be understood in the context of the organization's recruitment selection, promotion, and development systems and policies. The relative importance of replacement versus development as strategies for human resource development will depend, of course, on a diagnosis of weaknesses among people in the organization, a realistic assessment of whether they can be developed, and the relative costs and benefits of a replacement strategy.

Individual needs. Need is commonly acknowledged to be the springboard of motivation. Needs are an internal state in a person that causes objects or outcomes to become attractive. They range from basic psychological needs, such as hunger, to so-called higher order needs, such as esteem or achievement. Unless a person has needs he will not behave. The needs he has will determine the rewards he desires as well as the rewards the organization must provide to stimulate motivation. Thus, in efforts to improve social systems effectiveness it becomes extremely important to have a framework for analyzing the need structure of organizational members.

Many frameworks and lists of needs have been forwarded (Maslow, 1954; Murray, 1938) but research and OD practice have shown that a relatively short list, based on Abraham Maslow's work is sufficient (Lawler & Rhode, 1976).

1. Existence needs, such as hunger, thirst, and oxygen
2. Security needs
3. Social needs for belonging, companionship, support, love, etc.
4. Needs for esteem, status, and reputation
5. Needs for self-control, influence, and independence
6. Needs for competence, achievement and self-realization

It is generally agreed that these needs are arranged in a two-level hierarchy with existence and security needs at a lower level and esteem, autonomy, and self-realization at a higher level. A person is likely to experience all needs simultaneously. There is evidence that higher level needs will increase in strength as lower level needs are reasonably well satisfied. They are reduced in strength when lower level needs satisfaction is threatened.

Only lower level needs are likely to become less important as they are satisfied. Higher order needs are likely to stay high and even increase in strength as they are satisfied. Thus, the only continuous source of energy for a social system is in higher order needs. For example, the more that money is used to satisfy needs for security and well-being, the less powerful it becomes as a motivator. This is not the case with a reward such as completing a meaningful task which is likely to arouse even a higher need to achieve.

A process of organization development should lead to a social system designed to attract, keep, and motivate people with a variety of needs, as well as accommodate the general societal shifts in individual needs whereby people move from lower to higher order ones.

Individual expectations. People in organizations do not just react to organizational forces. They develop, at the very least, some general plans aimed at meeting their needs. For example, they purposely choose to work more or less or take certain career routes. These plans are often not detailed nor are the various options always fully investigated. Indeed these plans are often not conscious. People do, however, develop generalized ideas about what they want and how they would like to be treated by the organization. The organization in turn sends many signals that indicate what is reasonable for people to expect.

For example, individuals may expect pay promotions and job security if they act in certain ways, exert a certain amount of effort, or perform well. These expectations are a function of their need structure, the larger society of which they are a part, what the organization signals is reasonable to expect, and what other organizations offer.

Expectations are part of the individual's *psychological contract* with the organization (Schein, 1970). That is, the individual expects certain rewards in return for meeting the organization's expectations. When the psychological contract is violated by the organization, the person becomes dissatisfied and frustrated which leads to new behaviors—perhaps less effort or perhaps a decision to leave the organization (Kotter, 1973).

As with needs, expectations are developed and later met or frustrated through an interaction between the individual and the organization. A manager who desires to maintain a viable psychological contract between the organization and its employees, must understand what expectations are created or met by personnel policies, management practices, and organizational arrangements, and how changes in these may affect the fulfillment of these expectations (Thomas, 1974). The OD process often generates data about people's expectations and the extent to which they are being met or frustrated.

The individual and the organization: a motivational framework. The idea that employee motivation is a function of their needs and expectations in interaction with the organization has been formalized by some psychologists in what has come to be known as expectancy theory (Lawler, 1973; Porter & Lawler, 1968; Vroom, 1964). The theory states that the motivation to behave in a given way is a function of (a) people's expectancies or beliefs about what outcome or rewards are likely to result from their behavior and (b) the valence or attractiveness individuals attach to the outcomes or rewards as they estimate the outcomes' ability to satisfy their needs (Lawler & Rhode, 1976).
In symbols:

$$M = (E \times V)$$
$$\text{Where} \quad M = \text{Motivation}$$
$$E = \text{Expectance}$$
$$V = \text{Valence of an Outcome}$$

A manager's effort to achieve certain budgeted performance goals in his unit will be related to his expectations about what positive or negative outcomes, for instance a bonus or a promotion, are likely to occur as a result of achieving these goals. Of course, how much he values these outcomes will also determine the choice he makes about the amount of effort to exert. If a bonus is highly probable, but he doesn't need the additional compensation or recognition, the bonus will have little effect on his behavior. On the other hand, if the probability of saving his marriage by doing less at work is low, but saving it is very important, he may still reduce his effort.

The expectancy model suggests that individuals are highly rational decision makers in making choices about their behavior. This is, of course, not true. People do not fully understand their needs or their expectations. Furthermore, they are not capable of pro- **31** cessing all the information required to weigh outcomes, their probability of occurring, or their desirability. To do this would take too much time and energy. It is also known that people are content to satisfy their needs at some acceptable level rather than exert additional effort to optimize outcomes (March & Simon, 1958). Finally, people perceive the same situation differently and therefore may see the rewards available to them quite differently in terms of value or the probability that they will be obtained.

Despite arguments about specific elements, the expectancy model provides a useful framework for conceptualizing how social systems and people's needs and expectations interact to create certain behaviors and processes. There is evidence that organizational processes like leadership (House, 1971), structures such as jobs and pay (Hackman, 1977; Lawler, 1971, 1977) and culture (Frost, Wakeley, & Ruh, 1974) affect motivation. They do this to the extent that they provide valued outcomes (those that people want) and to the extent to which they shape expectations about the relationship between effort, successful performance, and rewards (James et al., 1977).

Managers who want to understand the behavior of people in the organization, must learn as much as possible about people's needs and how organizational policies and managerial practices shape their expectations. Only then can managers take positive action to reshape expectations as appropriate.

People are adaptive.   We would not want the reader to conclude that changes in organizational arrangements should always follow an assessment of member needs and abilities. Quite the opposite sequence is possible. Organization develpment can begin with changes in organization design and process or with educational methods aimed at individual growth in needs, expectations, and abilities. If people are given more freedom of action and influence over their goals and/or if they are taught to set goals appropriately, could it be that their need for achievement might increase?

There is evidence that such changes can and do occur (McClelland, 1965, 1969). Apparently, people's needs and expectations are learned and are subject to influence by their environment (Porter, Lawler, & Hackman, 1975). The adaptive nature of people can provide significant adaptive opportunities for organizations when a dynamic rather than static view of people is taken.

Such optimism, while well founded, must be balanced with the realistic view that not all individuals are equally adaptive nor are they unlimited in their capacity to grow. Even when organizational changes are made with the understanding that individuals who can't adapt or grow will leave, this strategy is limited by the rate at which the organization can manage an orderly turnover from less capable to more capable people.

Social Systems Have Cultures

So far a number of organizational components crucial to the understanding of organizations as social systems have been specified. But our description of organizations as social systems would fall far short of its mark if we did not introduce the concept of *organization culture.* In recent years researchers (e.g., Halpin & Croft, 1962; Letwin & Stringer, 1968; Schneider & Bartlett, 1968; Tagiuri & Litwin, 1968) and OD practitioners (Steele & Jenks, 1977) have been devoting increasing attention to this concept because much of individual and group behavior can be accounted for by the culture of the organization. Yet despite its importance, culture or climate, as it is sometimes called, is a dangerously elusive organizational phenomenon difficult to define and measure. Nonetheless, this section will attempt to do so.

32

What is culture? One of the reasons culture is difficult to define is its phenomenological nature. That is, it is a characteristic of the day-to-day environment as seen and felt by those who work in it. It is to organization as personality or self-concept is to the individual. It is determined by all of the components of the organization (structures, people, process, and environment) described in previous sections, yet, it is more than their sum.

As individuals in organizations work with others, are supervised, and are affected by policies and procedures, they develop a composite perception of their environment, which is often expressed by adjectives or short phrases such as "open," "risk taking," "warm," "tough," "soft," "impersonal," "informal," "rigid," etc. A shorthand view of what the organization is like and, therefore, what behaviors and individual values are acceptable within the organization, is developed. These shared beliefs and feelings which form an informal set of ground rules about what is expected and what will be rewarded (formally or socially), is the culture of the organization (Margulies & Raia, 1978).

Harrison (1972) has referred to culture as an organizational ideology which provides an important organizing theme for behavior. The more beliefs and values are shared about how to do things, the "stronger" the culture of the organization and the more influence and control it exerts on individual and group behavior (Ouchi & Price, 1978). According to Harrison, culture performs the following functions:

1. "Specifies the goals and values toward which an organization should be directed and by which success and worth should be measured."
2. "Prescribes the appropriate relationships between individuals and the organization (i.e., 'the psychological contract' that legislates what the organization should be able to expect from its people and vice versa)."
3. "Indicates how behavior should be controlled in the organization and what kinds of controls are legitimate and illegitimate."
4. "Depicts which qualities and characteristics of organization members should be valued or vilified; as well as how these should be rewarded or punished."
5. "Shows members how they should treat one another—competitively or collaboratively, honestly or dishonestly, closely or distantly."
6. "Establishes appropriate methods of dealing with the external environment— aggressive exploitation, responsible negotiation, proactive exploration."

While this list of behaviors and activities influenced by culture is not exhaustive, it is suggestive of the pervasive impact of culture (see Case 2–3). Thus culture represents the organization's cumulative learning, as reflected in many promotion, reward, and structural decisions. This tends to perpetuate beliefs and behavior, sometimes long after there are clear signals from the environment that change is needed. It is this phenomenon that caused Black & Mouton (1969) to coin the term "culture drag."

It is important to note that large and complex organizations do not typically exhibit single homogeneous belief systems or patterns of behavior. That is, there may be more than one culture in an organization. For one thing, there are the differences between the formal culture, which consists of idealized statements of what beliefs and behavior *should be,* and the informal culture, which consists of *actual* beliefs and behavior (Margulies & Raia, 1978). There are also likely to be different cultures in various functional groups in the organization, such as R&D or Manufacturing, as there are likely to be differences between blue collar, white collar, and management levels. That is, whenever the task requirements **33**

CASE 2–3

In one large corporation a widely held belief system existed that customer relations and a strong selling orientation were the key to business success. This belief system translated itself into a variety of practices, including the promotion to senior executive positions of salespeople who spent much of their time in customer relations activity. It resulted in values which emphasized smooth relations (common to sales functions) and eschewed disagreement, supported loyalty, and discouraged firing people. It resulted in an emphasis on growth in volume to the exclusion of sufficient concern for manufacturing efficiency. Thus, top management created policies and made decisions which favored new product development projects over cost reduction and the development of manufacturing technology. Predictably, manufacturing people were not valued and did not generally rise to the top. Not surprisingly, most key executives portrayed the same image. They dressed extremely well and had excellent interpersonal and verbal skills. They spent most of their time outside the company and little in managing it internally.

This pattern of values and beliefs prevailed over a period of fifteen to twenty years while the corporation grew significantly in size. But market shares declined by 20 percent, and profitability dropped significantly, because the business environment, which was becoming more cost-competitive, rewarded low cost and efficient producers.

have resulted in a unique combination of people, structures, and behavior, the confluence of these forces will create a unique culture.

In addition, the larger organization, of which these subgroups are a part, may also have a culture that is distinguishable from other large systems. Sometimes, as in Case 2–3, the culture of the larger systems is influenced by one group which has gained power and influence. In any case, even large and relatively heterogeneous corporations, such as IBM and ITT, are known to have unique cultures. The functionality of a strong culture for a large corporation will depend on the heterogeneity of its market environment and people.

Culture as a mechanism for socialization.   The discussion above points to the desirability of thinking about organizations as *social learning systems* where certain beliefs and behaviors are acquired, maintained, eliminated, or avoided (Margulies & Raia, 1978). it is commonly recognized that the shared values and beliefs that constitute culture are transmitted to new members through a process of *socialization*. That is, individuals change and modify their behavior as a consequence of membership in an organization (Schein, 1965). There are several mechanisms by which organizational culture is transmitted over time. Margulies & Raia (1978) list the following:

1. *Reinforcement*—Learning theorists (Hilgard & Bower, 1966) have long pointed to the importance of rewards in shaping behavior. Behavior that is so reinforced is likely to be continued. Organizations provide many desired outcomes which can reinforce behavior. Among these are money, promotion, intrinsic satisfaction, recognition, and peer approval. Indeed, the structures, people, and organizational process and behavior in the organization are the mechanisms of reinforcement that, as stated earlier, determine culture.

2. *Social modeling*—Much learning in organizations occurs from imitating the behavior of high status individuals. As in other forms of social learning, organizational members can be expected to adopt behaviors and values of others when they see these leading to valued outcomes (Bandura & Walters, 1963). Thus, key managers may be expected to have an important influence on beliefs and behaviors.

3. *Social interaction and influence*—The direct interaction of high status social models (managers, experienced hands) with organizational members through mechanisms such as performance appraisal, coaching, and meetings of various kinds, is an important socializing process. The interaction provides the means for social reinforcement of behaviors consistent with the culture.

4. *Selection and training*—While selection systems and training are examples of structures which provide reinforcements for culturally consistent behavior, these mechanisms are sufficiently important to receive separate mention. Selection of new people and replacement of employees who do not conform to cultural values is an obvious means by which culture is maintained. To this must be added self-selection in and out of an organization, as people learn that they can and cannot receive desired outcomes. Training programs also act to transmit cultural values. They often signal what is expected and what will be reinforced. They also teach desired behavior.

Culture and organizational change.   If organizational culture has such a profound effect on behavior, then the management of change requires an understanding of organizations as social learning systems. Indeed, OD is unique as a change strategy in that it explicitly recognizes change as a "normative reeducative" process (Bennis, Benne, & Chin, 1961). That is, behavioral change cannot occur without an explicit effort to reeducate people to adopt new values and norms. In most organizational changes, such explicit account of culture is not taken. Changes may be announced with little planning for changing the socialization mechanisms described in the previous section. If these mechanisms do work to support the change, it is often by accident.

To avoid culture drag, change agents must explicitly plan reinforcements, (incentive systems, performance appraisal systems and measurements, and control systems) social modeling (leadership by example), social interactions (communication about change, coaching, performance appraisal interviews, the development of group norms), and selection and training interventions (replacement of key people and educational programs) to support new behaviors.

Unfortunately the adoption of supportive mechanisms depends on a proper diagnosis of present ones, which does not always occur. To confront the culture explicitly can be threatening to managers as they recognize their own values in the process. Also managers may shy away from planned changes in these mechanisms on the false assumption that to plan change is somehow unethical or wrong. There is no question that such planned changes in socialization mechanisms constitute planned manipulations. However, these mechanisms are a fact of organizational life and affect behavior anyway, often guided by the unconscious motives of managers toward behavioral ends about which they are not clear and to which they would be opposed if they were. Thus cultures sometimes evolve that demand conformity, dishonesty, distortion of communication, and other behaviors that have negative effects on organizational effectiveness and quality of work life. Recent revelations about corporate political contributions and payoff practices in foreign countries indicate how culture that is not explicitly examined and shaped can reinforce unethical behavior.   **35**

The natural evolution of organizations is accompanied by changes in culture. Thus planned organization development requires planned changes in culture and periodic assessments of progress in shifting value and belief systems of the organization. This writer (1971a) has argued that a major indicator that an organizational change has "taken" and indeed may have some permanence is what he calls "climate emergence." This is the point at which people inside the organization begin to characterize the organization in new terms and become aware that a change has occurred. It is the point at which people with traditional values (those from other parts of the larger system) coming into the organization feel upset and lost in their first few months in the new culture or the point at which those with long tenure who cannot adapt leave the organization (see Case 2–4).

The importance of viewing organizations from a cultural perspective cannot be over-emphasized. It is not sufficient to see only structures, process, behavior, and environment. While each of these are important in their own right, complete understanding of an organization cannot occur without the holistic perspective that the concept of culture provides. For this reason organizational diagnosis and change requires that managers and change agents find ways to visualize culture and verbalize it. It is important that events during the process of change, such as the ones described in Case 2–4, be used to gain an understanding of how culture is changing and where it is evolving.

To date there are few good measures of culture and so its assessment must be primarily clinical in nature. In forming these judgments important sources of data are the reaction of people coming into an organization and of those leaving as well as who is promoted and what is rewarded. Perhaps the skills required to assess culture were best summarized by an applied behavioral scientist who has studied organizational climate and has attempted to measure it by questionnaires, when he said: "The best way I know to assess culture is to put up my antenna."

The Influence of the Dominant Coalition

The dominant coalition is *a group of key decision makers whose influence on the system is greatest* (Kotter, 1978; Miles & Snow, 1978). As we saw in the example of the sales-dominated company described in Case 2–3, this group has an enormous influence on all components of the social system and therefore on its culture. Thus, the fit between their values and beliefs and the culture required by the organization to be effective becomes an important question in any organizational diagnosis.

The job experiences, skills, cognitive orientation, personality, and values of these key people predispose them to perceive certain aspects of their environment and not others. Thus they define the environment and the organization's strategy in a way that is consistent with who they are as individuals, with their own self-concepts. Similarly, they are likely to model and reinforce behavior consistent with their own self-concept just as they are likely to select and promote people like themselves. The tendency for people to selectively perceive the environment based on their motives and to reinforce behavior and values consistent with their own has been amply documented in social psychological literature.

All of this suggests that one cannot understand a social system without knowing who the dominant coalition is (they may not always be the obvious people on the organization chart), what their background and experience has been, and what their personality and values are. The importance of the dominant coalition also suggests that any major attempt to help organizations adapt to changes in people and environment must include helping the dominant coalition understand how their own predispositions and behaviors have shaped the social system in functional or dysfunctional ways.

A plant in a large company changed the structure of jobs and the way decisions were made. Workers were given more responsibility for the total job, supervisors' roles changed, and the plant's management adopted a more participative management style. The change effort spanned a period of several years. At the end of three years, new people coming from more traditional plants reported feeling lost and uncertain about how to manage. They exhibited hostility towards the plant's management, who they characterized as weak and indecisive. They viewed the plant as out of control. They felt, at least until they were in the plant for several months, at odds with the "management philosophy" of the plant. Similarly, a number of individuals sought to leave the plant, feeling that it was not well managed.

Major organizational transitions invariably involve some fairly profound self-examination and change by the dominant coalition or they involve replacement of the dominant coalition. One of the more important roles for external organizational development consultants is to help the dominant coalition through this process. The board of directors can also play an important role by stimulating this process or by becoming directly involved in it. If they fulfill their intended role they should be able to be objective in their assessment of the organization's needs and the dominant coalition's characteristics.

Overview of the Social Systems Model

Each component of the social systems model presented in Figure 2–1 has now been discussed. In Figure 2–2 the social systems model has been reproduced with all the dimensions listed in the previous sections included. The model does not specify explicit linkages between various dimensions, partly because of the large number and partly because of the circular cause and effect relationships between them. Also we simply do not fully understand the relationship between all these dimensions and are unable to specify all the circumstances that moderate these relationships.

Nevertheless, this social systems model and others like it, can provide managers and organizational consultants with a useful framework for collecting data systematically and diagnosing the causes of specific organizational outcomes (turnover, profits, etc.), attitudes, and behavior. The usefulness of a social systems model as a framework for planning organizational improvements will be discussed in Chapter 8. That chapter will deal with diagnostic methods and will show how the model presented in this chapter and others like it have been used by managers to diagnose and improve organizations.

ASSESSING SYSTEM LEVEL FUNCTIONING

Inherent in a systems view of organizations is a contingent view of management. The right organizational design, person, or management style *depends* on the desired outcomes for the social system and the characteristics of the various interdependent parts of the sys-

FIGURE 2-2   A Social Systems Model of Organizations

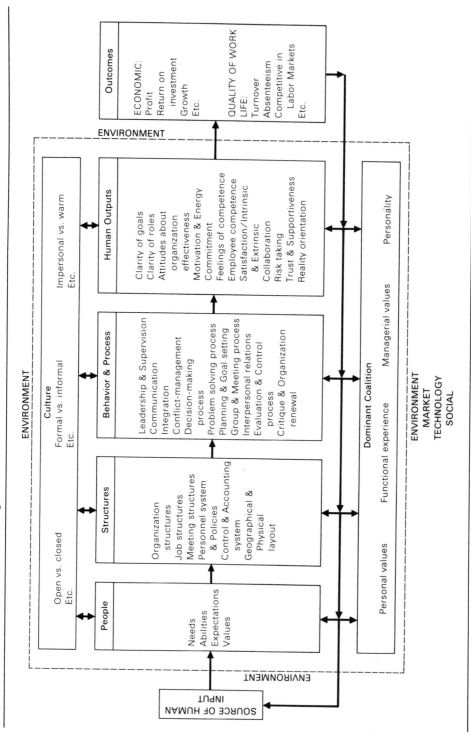

tem. This means that managers must decide (with influence from other stakeholders) what outcomes they want from the organization and only then, together with the assessment of the current situation, will the appropriate way to organize and manage emerge.

This contingent view of organizations makes it difficult to assess the effectiveness of a given managerial approach or social system. Any number of fit combinations between the various components of the social system may be equally good, depending on the desired outcomes. Leaving the question of the manager's own values and inclinations aside for the moment, a systems approach means that the manager is put in the unhappy situation of having to make frequent assessments about how to manage. The fit or systems perspective takes away the easier route of looking to management principles as guides for whether the organization is being managed right. It makes earlier sound choices about organizational design and management style obsolete as organization strategy, people, or environment change.

Nevertheless, the concept of fit does allow the use of broader *meta criteria* which can be useful in determining whether a social system is functioning well over a longer period of time (5–25 years). These criteria are (1) *efficiency*,[3] (2) *effectiveness,* and (3) *health.* No specific organizational outcomes such as profitability or satisfaction are implied by these criteria. Rather, these are systems level criteria which allow an assessment of the extent to which the organization has adapted to internal and external changes, and the extent to which it has the capacity to adapt and cope with future internal and external changes.

Efficiency

This criterion may be defined as *the extent of fit between the internal components of the social system.* The more congruity exists between these components the more the organization will function smoothly, with relatively little dissatisfaction on the part of organization members. That is, there is likely to be relatively little interpersonal or intergroup conflict between various constituencies, such as supervisors and subordinates or union and management. Furthermore, individuals are likely to view the organization as meeting their expectations and are likely to be motivated and committed to the organization. To the extent that there are no overriding environmental influences, individual and organizational performance will also be high.

Thus, in an efficient organization, relatively little energy would have to be spent in social maintenance activities to keep people happy and keep them from leaving or unionizing. Quality of work life outcomes—such as turnover, grievances, or absenteeism—would be positive (low).[4]

Effectiveness

Effectiveness may be defined as *the extent of fit between the organization's environment and all the internal components of the social system.* The more congruity that exists between the internal social system components and the environment, the more the organization is likely to exchange favorably with its environment. That is, organizational performance indicators such as customer or client satisfaction, profitability, market share, or growth in volume, are likely to be positive (high). Furthermore, people in the organization are likely to feel a greater sense of competence as they experience task accomplishment and success from their efforts.[5]

Recent research by Miles & Snow (1978) indicates that the most rapid and effective organizational adjustments, ones that result in the least losses in organizational effectiveness, were ones that were preceded by appropriate changes in structure and process That is, it was not sufficient for an organization to change its strategy by developing a new product/market thrust and/or by developing new technology to produce the new product or service. Unless it translated this thrust into a new conceptualization of organizational structures and management process and implemented these new structures and processes early, financial losses and ultimate failure in the new strategy (ineffectiveness) were likely to result.

Organizational Health

As stated in Chapter 1, an adaptive organization is one which can sense problems resulting from a lack of congruence between various social systems components, respond to this information with changes, yet continue to test reality for changes that might be required in the future. Thus, organizational health may be defined as *the capacity of an organization to engage in ongoing self-examination aimed at identifying incongruities between social systems components and developing plans for needed change in strategy (environment), structure, process, people, culture, and the dominant coalition.* Such a healthy organization is likely to maintain organizational efficiency and effectiveness in the long term.

In recent research, Miles & Snow (1978) studied the adaptive process of a large number of companies in four industries and concluded that organizational adaptation is a function of some more or less active process of examination and change. They call this process the *strategic choice* approach. They argue that neither *natural selection*, a more or less chance process by which social components develop or do not develop congruity, nor *rational selection*, a completely conscious process of developing congruity, is at work.

Rather, the strategic choice view of organizational adaptation argues that organizational structure is partly determined by environmental conditions beyond the control of managers, and partly by top level decision makers (the dominant coalition) who know what is going on in the environment and make choices about structure and process when necessary. In addition, the dominant coalition attempts to manipulate the environment itself in order to bring it into alignment with the organization. Recently, for example, companies in the electronics industry successfully influenced legislation and public policy on Japanese imports which were cutting into their business.

The cumulation of many decisions about strategy, structure, process, people, and culture results in a strategic choice about how the organization will adapt. However conscious this process may be, it is often imperfect. The factors that prevent an organization from adapting to its environment and their implications for organizational health are:

1. *Delegation by top management.* Top management may become too involved in day-to-day operations to appreciate or understand the longer-range needs of their organization (Chandler, 1962). This suggests that a healthy organization is one in which decisions are delegated to the lowest level consistent with knowledge, information, and competence (Beckhard, 1969), thus freeing the top level to take a longer-range view.

2. *Valid data and diagnosis.* There may be limited valid data available about the environment or internal organizational problems. Limited data about the environment may be a function of environmental uncertainty and complexity, but it may also be a function of the ambitions of those who prepare data and recommendations for key decision makers. Similarly, the backgrounds and experience of the dominant coalition may cause them to diagnose data to fit their own predispositions. In both cases, personal motivation may distort the data gathering and interpreting processes. Fi-

nally, top management may not have valid data about internal organizational problems. Information about these problems is often distorted on the way up or never gets there at all.

This suggests that a healthy organization has a competent environmental sensing function (market research, technological assessment) and an ongoing process for collecting data about internal functioning such as efficiency of operations and people's attitudes. Not only must these processes be ongoing but they must provide valid data. Thus, the organization must value diversity, openness, and the resolution of differences through problem solving (Beckhard, 1969).

3. *Top managers' adaptability.* Chandler (1962) has argued that needed organizational changes may not occur if they threaten management's personal position, power, or psychological security. A culture that stresses collaboration rather than competition will probably reduce these threats. Similarly, managers who have a broad range of competence and see career options outside their organization or current career track, are less likely to feel threatened by new strategic choices.

This suggests that healthy organizations will have an ongoing process of performance evaluation and career development in which managers are given valid data about themselves, and are helped to increase the range of their managerial skills and values. Cross-functional and divisional transfers as well as management education are used by healthy organizations to accomplish this. Such organizations also actively assess performance and potential, promoting the most adaptive managers and replacing those who cannot adapt.

4. *The management of change.* One of the factors that frequently prevents adaptation is the ineffective management of change. Resistance develops because people are inadequately involved or committed. This occurs because the implications of the change for people hasn't been fully understood by management.

This suggests that managers in a healthy organization have a good conceptual understanding of how to manage change, the personal skills required to do so, and know or have available to them up-to-date methods for managing change.

The characteristics of a healthy organization listed above have not yet been fully documented by research but the known barriers to adaptation clearly point to them. In addition, OD practitioners entering inefficient or ineffective organizations often find that inadequate information systems about operations and people, barriers to open exchange of valid information, insufficient delegation, and/or limits in the adaptiveness of key managers, prevent adaptation. Indeed, the emergence of the field of OD itself is evidence that the process of collecting valid data and acting on the social systems in accordance with a diagnosis is needed by organizations to maintain efficiency and effectiveness in a rapidly changing environment.

Relationships between Criteria

An organization may or may not be high on all of these system level performance criteria at any one time. For example, an organization can be very efficient if it has people with low needs for responsibility managed with a highly directive management style. There would be little frustration or dissatisfaction, but the organization would not necessarily be effective. This would depend on the demands of its environment. In a rapidly changing market environment the organization would be ineffective, but in a more stable environment it would be quite effective. **41**

On the other hand, an organization that has introduced a matrix structure to deal with a dynamic environment would be quite effective, but until behavior and other practices become consistent with the structure, it would be inefficient.[6] Either of these organizations could be unhealthy if an ongoing process of self-examination is not institutionalized.

An organization could be efficient, effective, but not necessarily healthy if it has historically operated in a stable environment. Such an organization could be subject to a major upset situation if society, employees, or its business should change rapidly and unexpectedly. Its hierarchical structures, directive management practices, dependent people, and closed culture needed to operate in a stable environment, do not foster, indeed discourage, the processes we have said are needed for a healthy organization.

In such an environment, managers will find that they have sufficient information and knowledge to make most of the decisions and thus, unlike managers in more uncertain environment, will not be forced to learn how to delegate decisions to lower levels. Similarly, such organizations are not likely to be hiring young "knowledge workers" (Drucker, 1969) who are likely to demand more responsibility for decisions and more open communication. There are simply no pressures on such organizations to develop the dimensions of a healthy organization.

Perhaps the best example of this dilemma is the steel industry. Recent foreign competition has shown steel companies to be both ineffective and unhealthy. It is clear that in recent years they have not examined their situation and acted to improve their capacity to compete. Thus while they have been efficient (in an organizational, not economic sense) and, until recently, more or less effective, they have not been capable of self-renewal.

The apparent contradiction between organizational arrangements that seem to exist and work in stable environments, and the managerial processes needed for adaptation, present a dilemma for organizations in such environments. Can they or should they develop the characteristics of a healthy organization while still retaining the more hierarchical and tops-down approach that seems to work in stable environments? Indeed, can they develop such characteristics without undermining the efficiency of their routine operations? New organizational forms such as collateral or parallel organizations in which overlay structures are developed for sensing, planning, and renewal activities may provide the solution to this dilemma (Carlson, undated; Zand, 1974). We may also find that more participative approaches to management typically found in organizations which operate in dynamic environments may be applicable, in somewhat different form, to organizations in more stable environments (Miles & Snow, 1978; Blake & Mounton, 1978).

It is highly unlikely that the reverse condition, a healthy but inefficient and ineffective organization, is likely to exist for very long. The renewal processes in a healthy organization would stimulate efforts by management to make changes needed to align the various social systems components with each other and with the environment, thus achieving efficiency and effectiveness fairly rapidly.

THE SYSTEMS PERSPECTIVE AND OD VALUES

The field of organization development has historically been associated with a number of humanistic, optimistic, and developmental assumptions and values (French & Bell, 1978). For example:

1. Organizations should provide personal growth and development for people.
2. Organizations should encourage openness and collaboration.

3. Organizations should encourage the expression of feelings.

Inherent in these and other normative positions about what organizations should be like are implicit assumptions and values about what organizational outcomes are desirable. The social system perspective, on the other hand, holds that congruity is the only criterion by which organizations can be judged and that there are many organizational arrangements that can result in congruity.

Which structures, processes, and culture an organization develops will depend on which people and strategy the organization chooses and vice versa. Of course, implicit in these strategic choices about the way an organization ought to adapt are values. The social systems perspective of organization development assumes that managers and other stakeholders, not OD practitioners or OD theory, need to decide about personal and organizational outcomes (value judgments). Thus, organization development is a process of clarifying these choices based on a diagnosis of the current state of fit between social system components and the outcomes to be expected with alternative strategic choices.

Organization development theory need not and should not take a normative position about how organizations ought to function. This suggests that a development effort may take an organization in a direction opposite to traditionally stated OD values as long as the outcomes of such an effort have been clarified. Whether a change agent wants to help an organization move in such a direction, is a matter of personal values and choice.

The reader will recognize a certain similarity between some of the OD values (openness, collaboration, etc.) and what were described earlier in this chapter as the probable characteristics of healthy or adaptive organizations. This is not surprising, since many OD practitioners implicitly assume that an organization should be adaptive and that this is a desirable outcome for all organizations.

While it is likely that as the rate of change in the environment accelerates organizations will need and want to become more adaptive, it can be argued that this too is a strategic choice for which costs and benefits can be assessed. For example, should a management that expects to operate in a stable environment for the foreseeable future invest in developing an adaptive organization? This would depend, of course, on the costs of doing so, the importance management attaches to survival, the resources the organization has to invest in this process, and management's values.

Organization development cannot specify what management should do; it can help clarify the choices. If this is done, it is much more likely that decisions to invest in organization development will be made with more commitment and will result in longer-term organization development efforts.

Given this social system perspective, the only values that need to be associated with organization development are those of informed choice. That is:

1. Organization development must help organizations generate valid data about the state of the organization in relation to its environment.
2. Organization development must help organizational stakeholders clarify desired outcomes.
3. Organization development must help organizations make strategic choices based on a diagnosis of the current state and desired outcomes.

This is not to say of course that change agents do not or should not have values. They clearly do. It does say that change agents or consultants should be clear and open about their values. Only then can they be helpful to organizations in making informed choices. **43**

NOTES

1. The author is indebted to the management of Corning Glass Works for providing an environment which allowed the development of OD and this conceptual framework. Thanks are also due to numerous members of Corning's OD department. In particular, I would like to acknowledge the contribution of Dr. Alan Hundert.

2. The differential impact of organization environment on required human outputs is nicely illustrated by two cases—Higgins Equipment Co. (C), and Empire Glass (B)—Harvard Business School. These cases are available through the International Collegiate Case Clearing House, Harvard Business School, Boston, Mass. 02163.

3. The concepts of efficiency and effectiveness were first formulated by Chester Barnard (1938).

4. There is substantial research evidence to support this general proposition. Specifically, research suggests that satisfaction, motivation, individual performance, and/or organizational performance are highest when reward systems are consistent with the needs and expectations of employees (Porter & Lawler, 1968), job design is consistent with the needs of employees (Hackman & Lawler, 1971; Hackman, 1977), organization structure is consistent with the needs of employees (Morse & Lorsch, 1970), performance evaluation procedures are consistent with organizational values (Miner, 1968), supervisor style fits subordinate needs (Vroom, 1960) and there is fit between the individual and the climate of the organization (Schneider, 1972).

5. Evidence for this proposition comes from research which suggests that when organizational structure, culture, and/or process are consistent with the environment and task, organizational performance is higher than when they are not (Burns & Stalker, 1961; Lawrence & Lorsch, 1967; Miles & Snow, 1978; Schneider, Parkington, & Buxton, undated; Woodward, 1967). The research of Morse & Lorsch (1970) suggests that when organization structure and management process fit the task, unit performance and people's feelings of personal competence are higher than when there is a poor fit between these components. For example, a low performing R&D laboratory was structured and managed quite similarly to a high performing plant, but quite differently from a high performing R&D laboratory.

6. Matrix structures (to be discussed in Chapter 10) are structures in which people within different functions are joined by horizontal structures such as program teams or business teams. They work for two bosses, a functional manager, and program or business manager.

HOW ORGANIZATIONS CHANGE 3

The view of organizations as systems presented in the previous chapter, clearly assumes that organizations continually change as their environments and their members change. Unfortunately, there is also substantial evidence that organizations do not make major changes in a smooth and constant manner. This unevenness has become particularly evident in recent years as rapid changes in the external environment have demanded rapid changes within the organization.

Change seems to occur in fits and starts. Organizations remain stable for long periods, then go through periods of massive and revolutionary change, which often leave them in a state of confusion and disarray. Sometimes, attempts to innovate in one part of an organization are resisted successfully by other parts, resulting in maintenance of the status quo.

Thus, because people and groups do not seem to be infinitely adaptive, organizations fall far short of being idealized as adaptive and coping systems (Schein, 1970). Attitudes and beliefs seem to lag behind those the organization needs if it is to change. One company president described this phenomenon in the following way.

> "I've got to get this organization moving, and soon. Many of our managers act as if we were still selling the products that used to be our bread and butter. We're in a different business now, and I'm not sure that they realize it. Somehow we've got to start recognizing our problems, and then become more competent in solving them. This applies to everyone here, including me and the janitor. I am starting with a massive reorganization which I hope will get us pulling together instead of in fifty separate directions (Greiner, 1967).

One reason that there is an attitude lag is that it is difficult to develop and maintain the process of communication and mutual influence that has to go on between those who see the need for change and those who do not. In Chapter 2 we referred to this phenomenon as "cultural drag"—the inability of organizations to change the norms which guide and

45

shape behavior rapidly enough (Blake & Mouton, 1969). The existence of this phenomenon suggests that an organization can maintain "thrust" only if a planned and systematic change overcomes its members' traditional values and attitudes.

The difficulty of creating readiness for change and the motivation to implement and sustain change, may be thought of in terms of the cost of changing to organizational members. Change will occur only when these costs are outweighed by a number of factors which can create positive motivation to change. This relationship between positive forces which support change, and the cost of change, may be expressed in the following change formula.[1]

$$Ch = (D \times M \times P) > C$$

Where   Ch   =   Change

D   =   Dissatisfaction with the status quo

M   =   A new model for managing or organizing

P   =   A planned process for managing change

C   =   Cost of change to individuals and groups

From this formula we can see that change will occur only when sufficient (relative to the cost of change) dissatisfaction exists with the status quo by those who must change (D); when there is a new and clearly defined approach to managing the organization (M), which is believed will solve the problems; and when the process for managing the change is sufficiently well planned, incorporates appropriate assumptions about change, and includes effective intervention methods (P). Many organizational changes falter when one or more of these elements is not present in sufficient quantity, or when one of them is totally absent.

In the vignette above, the president of the company has a clear idea of how the company should be organized to achieve desired changes in attitudes and behavior (M). However, this reorganization will not be accepted and will not achieve stated goals unless the managers who must change their approach to the business become as dissatisfied (D) with the current state of affairs as the president, and a process of change is planned (P) which develops commitment and competence to change throughout the organization. The president is at a crucial point in the change process. Rapid implementation of reorganization without sufficient development of motivation to change, and without a planned process for change, could cause the change to falter. As we shall see, perhaps the most frequent cause of failures in organizational change comes from an overreliance on new models, insufficient attention to the development of dissatisfaction, or readiness to change and a flawed process of change. Often an assessment of the situation, using the change formula, can help clarify weaknesses in a change strategy.

This chapter will examine each of the major elements in the change formula in more detail. What causes sufficient dissatisfaction to create momentum for change and what can be done when dissatisfaction does not exist? How are new models for managing brought into an organization? What do we know about different processes for change and their relative effectiveness? What conditions must exist for change to be sustained over time? Finally, we will examine the role of leadership in managing the change process. These ideas are important to an understanding of specific intervention strategies to be discussed in Part II.

PRESSURE LEADS TO DISSATISFACTION AND CHANGE

If there is one thing of which researchers are very certain, it is that organizations do change when they are under pressure and rarely when they are not (Beckhard, 1970; Greiner, 1967). High rates of turnover or absenteeism, high grievance rates, complaints and hostility, sabotage, and threats of unionization or strikes are among the many *internal* pressures that have lead to organizational changes. For example, after a fifty-seven-day strike that shut down its manufacturing lines, a major engine manufacturer began to experiment with new methods of communication and job design in its manufacturing facilities. This strike had a disastrous impact on profits, and pointed up how vulnerable the company's market share was to labor strife. Also, the top management of Volvo launched a major modification of its traditional automobile assembly line in several of its plants in response to extremely high absenteeism and turnover rates, as well as severe quality problems (Gyllenhammar, 1977).

External pressures that trigger change include the inability to remain competitive in price or respond with new products to innovations by competitors. Pressure to change can also come from community or consumer interest groups as well as from government regulations. For example, a major consumer goods manufacturer was losing market share on a major new product because it was unable to transfer technology from R&D to manufacturing. It hired outside consultants to help launch organizational changes aimed at improving coordination between these functions. In another example, when FIGHT, a Rochester, New York, community action group organized by Saul Alinsky (Beer & Driscoll, 1977) threatened Eastman Kodak with a "long hot summer" if its demands were not met, the company responded with a program for hiring 600 hard-core unemployed. Finally, in response to the surgeon general's report on smoking and subsequent government pressures on the industry, the big six tobacco companies created major changes in their product lines and advertising practices while at the same time reducing their dependence on the cigarette market through diversification (Miles & Cameron, 1977).

Crisis, more than the well-intentioned warnings of people at lower levels of the organization about problems, gets the attention of top management. Similarly, crisis can get the attention of lower levels if they have been unaware of pressures on the organization. The case of the steel plant described in Chapter 1 is a good example. The threat of the plant closing and loss of jobs energized people to act.

Crisis provides the motivation to change. It sufficiently raises dissatisfaction with the status quo to overcome resistance caused by the costs of change to organizational members. These costs are the pain of change itself which may threaten individual or group identity, sense of competence, power, status, pay, and even job security. These costs can be felt at all levels of the organization. A chief executive officer (CEO) of a major Fortune 500 company described the role that crisis played in motivating him to create change:

> Why weren't the cuts made earlier? Why had the company been allowed to get so overweight? In his own defense, the CEO said: "It was tough making these cuts, particularly when you lived in a small town where you knew a lot of these people." He admits that a generation of prosperity had made the company complacent, and reminds listeners that it's easier to make hard decisions when the pressure is on than when it isn't. He didn't act soon enough, but it's not difficult to understand why he held off, hoping that the economy would pull him through. Where is the businessman who hasn't from time to time put off making these tough choices when things were going relatively well?[2]

47

It is clear from this description that the reason change occurred is that the CEO's dissatisfaction with the status quo exceeded the pain or costs associated with the change. The fundamental reason some crisis or pressure seems to be so important in setting the stage for change is that it creates a state of readiness and motivation to change. Kurt Lewin called this the "unfreezing stage" in the change process (Schein, 1961). It is the stage at which old beliefs, values, and behavior lose strength in the face of data that disconfirm the manager's view of his or the organization's effectiveness. The unfreezing itself is the source of the energy for change. Energy is expended by organizational members to restore performance to acceptable levels. They do this to satisfy their own needs for competence and to satisfy those who are monitoring the performance of the organization (top management, the board of directors, the financial community, etc.). Too much pressure, however, is known to cause rigidity and is likely to result in resistance and other nonadaptive responses. This suggests that moderate amounts of pressure are likely to be most effective in motivating change (Broadhurst, 1957).

Just as major changes in organizations usually occur in response to internal and/or external pressures, so many changes flounder and fail because the top managers who want to create a given change have ignored the importance of readiness and motivation to change. A top manager may be dissatisfied with the state of affairs in the organization, but others who must respond to change neither see a crisis nor feel the same dissatisfaction. They are not as motivated to change as is top management. For them, the cost of changing their managerial pattern is higher than their level of dissatisfaction.

There are many familiar examples of organizations attempting to create changes that do not take hold. Top managements have created planning departments and procedures in the hope of improving planning only to find one or more years later that this idea is widely resented and that it has been ineffective. The planning department is ultimately disbanded. Clearly, the dissatisfaction with planning was felt at the top level but not at lower levels. The unilateral pressure to change created resistance and hostility directed at the source of the pressure, the planning department. Similarly, the recommendations of external management consultants often fail to stimulate change because neither they nor top management have developed readiness to change among managers.

Data Feedback as a Source of Pressure

Does change occur only as a result of crisis? Fortunately, the answer seems to be no. There is substantial evidence that people in organizations are motivated to act on problems before they become a crisis if they are provided information about these problems (Cammann, 1974; Lawler & Rhode, 1976). The most pervasive example of this is how rapidly managers in organizations will respond to a measurement and control system that indicates there are certain financial problems in their unit. Similarly, a corporate president may respond with an affirmative action program to data from a governmental agency, such as EEOC, which indicates that the number of minorities hired fell short of certain goals.

While information about markets and financial performance is regularly available in organizations, information about the state of the organization's social system is not. This is particularly true about attitude data which, as the discussion in Chapter 2 indicated, can provide early warnings of financial problems. Therefore, attitude data must often be specially gathered and provided to the appropriate managers. Feedback of consultants' interviews and attitude surveys of employees can motivate managers to act on organizational problems that may be at the root of financial problems. Direct discussion between top management and lower levels can also provide an awareness of problems that will

FIGURE 3–1   A Model of the Effects of Data Collection on Behavior

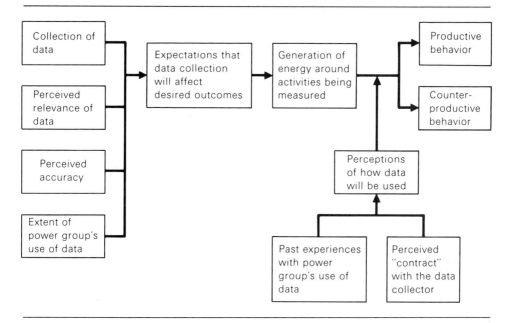

Adapted from David A. Nadler, *Feedback and Organization Development: Using Data-Based Methods,* © 1977, Addison-Wesley, Reading, Mass. Fig. 4.2. Reprinted with permission.

stimulate change. Finally, individual performances evaluations can motivate people to change.

A number of conditions shown in Figure 3–1 must exist for data to energize (motivate) managerial action on problems measured by the data (Beer, 1977; Nadler, 1977).

First, data must be collected and publicly available. The simple act of measuring an activity can stir some interest in examining it. But, the data must also be seen as relevant to currently important problems. Data, particularly data about the social system, will not receive much attention unless managers are somewhat dissatisfied with certain aspects of their organization and see the data as helping them deal with their concerns.

Second, the data must be perceived as accurate or else it will be rejected, particularly if the motivation to work on certain problems is low.

Third, managers who will use the data must perceive that powerful groups inside and outside the organization ascribe importance to the data. Data (attitude, financial, or other) that is not seen as important to one's supervisor, top management, or outside groups (such as government of shareholders) is simply not going to generate a lot of motivation to act. The greater the relevance of the data to felt problems and the greater its ascribed importance to powerful groups, the more managers will perceive that the data collection and analysis process will result in desired outcomes. Relevance will cause managers to see data as helping them personally while ascribed importance to powerful groups will cause them to perceive probable rewards and sanctions based on the data. Naturally, the more internal motivation exists, the less potential rewards and sanctions are important as motivators. In most situations, a mix of both sources of motivation exists and is necessary to generate energy around data.

49

However, to the extent that the source of motivation for the data collection and analysis process is its ascribed importance to powerful groups, there is a potential at least for counterproductive behavior (see Figure 3–1). If managers expect that the data will be used to sanction them, based on past experience or on contact with those collecting the data (consultants, staff groups, or other representatives of the power groups), much of the energy will be directed to preventing negative sanctions rather than solving problems. Employees may decline to fill out a questionnaire or be interviewed; they may provide false information that makes them and their managers look good; they may direct their energy to making the numbers look better rather than solving the basic problems; or they may defend themselves by finding fault with the data itself and discrediting its accuracy (Argyris, 1952).

There are two ways to avoid these problems. First, the power group can send clear signals that it will use the data to develop solutions for the future rather than as a means of punishing past behavior. Such a nonevaluative stance toward problems reduces defensiveness of managers. Second, the data collection process should not start until managers who must act on the data can define, however vaguely, some problems they have. If they can do this or can be helped to do this prior to the beginning of data collection, they will see the data as relevant and will be internally motivated to act on it. This will be particularly true if they participate in planning the data collection process. This will be defined later as the shared approach to organizational change.

This discussion suggests that an organization will be more self-correcting (behave more like a system) to the extent that people are motivated to continuously identify problems, feel secure to dialogue about problems, and act on them because they are committed. In such healthy organizations (see Chapter 2 for a definition of organization health) people will seek data and respond to it in a productive way before a crisis develops. The organization will be more self-correcting as it relies more on multiple individuals and groups to improve efficiency and effectiveness, and less on power groups and external crisis.

CHANGE REQUIRES NEW DIRECTIONS AND MODELS

Crisis and dissatisfaction are not sufficient for major organizational change to occur. It is often quite easy for management to rationalize its problems by blaming forces beyond its control such as the marketplace, government policy, or a union. Externalizing the blame is a common symptom when people are under pressure and there is no clear direction for resolving the problem. Traditional wisdom in organizations often prevents people from analyzing the problems in new ways and coming up with a new vision for how the organization might operate to eliminate the root causes of the problem. Successful change efforts require new models for looking at organizational problems and/or new ideas for structuring or managing the organization (Buchanan, 1967; Greiner, 1967). An illustration of the role of new models can be seen in the case of union–management relations, presented in Case 3–1.

New models may come in the form of a new organizational design, accounting system, planning systems, or personnel policy. In these instances, a written report by a consultant may outline the new approach or a staff group may develop a new procedure. But new systems and procedures imply a new way of thinking, feeling, and behaving. Indeed, alternative models for improving organizational effectiveness invariably mean new behavior and attitudes. Thus, effective change requires that people understand these

50   and adopt them. A simple announcement of a reorganization is not sufficient to specify

CASE 3–1

A plant of a large manufacturing company had been having severe difficulties with union-management relations. Threats of strikes, continual strife, and a wildcat strike were part of the plant's history. Yet, the strategy of the division of which this plant was a part required that this plant expand its product base. Industrial relations personnel, along with the plant's management, were asked to resolve the problem. Despite continuous discussions with the union, which included a warning that the plant would not be expanded unless things improved, no progress was made.

At this point, an organization development consultant from the corporate staff, who had been working with the management group to improve trust and communication, suggested that management approach the union about the possibility of applying methods for improving trust and communication to union-management relations. After union leaders met the consultant and satisfied themselves of his objectivity and neutrality, both parties agreed to meet for two days to explore their relationship and work on improving it. In the meeting, the consultant set down ground rules for communication between the union and management group which they had not used before. These rules enforced listening and constructive dialogue. Immediate and long-term improvements in labor management relations were obtained.

Through the work he did with them as a team, the OD consultant helped management see that trust can be improved through changes in communication and behavior patterns. This led them to see the low level of trust between them and the union as a function of a circular process in which one party acted to confirm the other's negative perception. The new model helped them diagnose the problem differently, helped them surface different data (feelings, perceptions, past history that led to poor relations), and provided the basis for seeing cooperation as a workable alternative to strife and hostility. The new approach did not eliminate the reality that union and management have an adversary relationship. But it did provide alternative ways of dealing with many other problems and of removing anger and hostility from the traditional bargaining situation.

---

new behaviors and attitudes. Ideally, such changes ought to be communicated by the change agent in terms of the required new way of thinking, feeling and behaving. The change agent may add to an understanding of these new ways by modeling them himself or pointing to examples of new behavior by others in the organization.

In recent years, innovations in training programs aimed at developing more effective supervisory practices have incorporated video snapshots (on film or videotape) of effective supervisory practices in different situations. The objective is for trainees to emulate these models in later role playing exercises and on the job. Behavior modeling programs, as these supervisory training programs are called, are merely one example of how modeling new behaviors can be used to induce new ways of doing things. If organizational members are then carefully guided by the change agent in experimenting with new behavior and in experiencing new ways of thinking and feeling, they will be successful in applying the new model. As will be seen later in the chapter, such successes are the rewards organizational members need before the new behavior can be adopted permanently.

The case in improving management-labor relations described in Case 3–1, illustrates the importance of recognizing that solutions to organizational problems often mean new behaviors and attitudes which must be carefully nurtured by the change agent. The intergroup problem-solving meeting between union and management (see Chapter 9) suggested and led by the consultant, provided union and management with a new model for relating and working together. The behavior required in this meeting and the assumptions about communication and trust underlying it, were distinctly different from the traditional labor relations bargaining model which assumed an adversary relationship.

By modeling open and constructive communications and setting ground rules which were enforced, the change agent induced new behaviors which were successful. These early success experiences served as models for many subsequent union-management meetings in the plant over a two-year period. They resulted in the addition of a trust/problem-solving model of conflict resolution to the already existing bargaining and negotiating model. In addition, the experiences of this plant served as a model for union-management relationships in other plants which also adopted these approaches.

The Role of Outsiders in Change

New directions for organizational change often require outside influence. Without an outsider (or an insider with new ideas and immunity from sanctions by the power structure), those in power may not be able to reorient their perceptions of problems and possible solutions. A newcomer respected for his competence and supported by those in power (1) can be more objective in his appraisal; (2) will bring in new ideas from a different set of experiences; (3) can challenge established patterns of behavior by top people; and (4) can influence the people who make important decisions affecting the entire organization. In Case 3–1, only the plant manager and the union president had the power to initiate change, but their experiences with each other blocked them from seeing and adopting alternatives. The fact that the consultant was not part of the conflict and the fact that he had a different background and experiences made it possible for him to offer an alternative. Its adoption, however, depended on support by the union president and plant manager.

Outside influence required to reorient the organization to new directions can come from one of many sources:

1. Outside consultants
2. New staff groups manned with new people
3. A new manager transferred into an organization as its head
4. An internal group of consultants freed from traditional organizational constraints with a mandate to challenge accepted ways of doing things

The outsiders not only bring in new ideas and help reorient people, but also serve as cues to lower level people that management is interested in change. When those at lower levels feel that the problem is at the top, the outsider serves to reassure those at lower levels that change will occur. He can also transmit the views of those at lower levels to those at the top, thus providing them with data that may modify their views of problems and potential

solutions.

THE CHANGE PROCESS

If change involved only one person or a small group, dissatisfaction and new models might be sufficient to effect change. The source of the energy for change and the target would be one and the same. Unfortunately, change in large complex organizations involves many people, groups, and political constituencies. Thus, the agent of change must find ways to motivate a large number of people to change their behavior. This problem exists for all change agents regardless of whether they are outside or inside the organization, or whether they are at the top or bottom. In addition to dissatisfaction and new directions and models, the *process* by which people are moved to change their behavior becomes a third major factor in how organizations change. In fact, which approach to use presents the single most important problem in organizational change.

This section will examine three common approaches to large system change (Greiner, 1967), and the problem of motivating others, primarily from the perspective of top management. The assumption underlying this perspective is that no change can occur in hierarchical organizations, which most contemporary organizations are, unless dissatisfactions and a new vision exists at the top. Even if the initial source of dissatisfaction resides elsewhere in the organization, top managers must ultimately be committed to the change and exercise influence on others in the organization.

Top-Down Change

Many organizational changes are implemented through the authority of the top manager's position. The manager defines the problem based on information that is gathered by others and develops the solution by himself or with the help of a limited number of people. The information may be gathered by his immediate subordinates, members of a staff group, and/or a consultant. The solution may be recommended by them but the top person makes the final decision.

Once a decision is made, change is communicated and activated in a number of different ways:

1. *By decree.* Management informs people in the organization about changes by a memorandum, speech, policy statement, or verbal command. The communication is often impersonal and formal, and rarely specifies the required attitude and behavior change or the reasons. The assumption is that people will comply by changing their outward behavior even if they disagree with the change.

2. *By technology.* Many major organizational changes are technological ones. Sometimes these changes do not have the intent of changing behavior and sometimes they do, but they almost always have an impact on behavior. Henry Ford's assembly line had a major impact on the behavior and attitude of workers. More recently, the introduction of work processing into offices is changing the roles of secretaries and managers and is causing much dissatisfaction and uncertainty. People are told about technological changes but it is usually thought that they have little to contribute to the shape of the solution. It is assumed that people will accept new technology for the same reasons top management decided to introduce it.

3. *By replacement.* When top management is impatient with the slow pace of change following a decree, they often resort to replacing key individuals. A new plant or division manager is brought in. The assumption is that this new individual will bring **53**

with him new ways of looking at the same problems, that he has managerial skills or technical skills his predecessor didn't have, and/or that he will be able to make tough decisions about people and problems because he is less tied to previous ones. The reasons for replacements are rarely explained to people in the organization, although they attribute meaning to them.

4. *By structure.* As we saw in the previous chapter, changes in organization structure, formal roles and jobs, control systems, and many other aspects of the internal environments, are all means by which people's behavior can be influenced. While changes in structures are less directive and authoritarian on the surface, they are quickly felt by those in the organization. Structural change usually provides signals about desired behavior or specifies new relationships. It is assumed that people will respond to these signals and new relationships in a way intended by the structural changes. It is rare that the intentions underlying these types of changes are announced, though people clearly speculate about them and derive meaning from them.

Most top-down changes are unilateral. That is, only a few people, usually at the top, are involved in deliberations and make the decisions. For this reason, the changes are usually introduced very rapidly. For example, the operations division of a large bank introduced a whole new technology for processing transactions. As the managers themselves said, a bank was being transformed into a factory. Plans were made by a staff group with limited consultation from line managers. Between Friday and Monday morning, new machines, creating new jobs for almost everyone, were installed. A major cultural change, triggered by technological change, had occurred almost overnight.[3]

Bottom-Up Change

At the opposite extreme from top-down unilateral approaches to change, are bottom-up changes where almost complete responsibility for defining the problem and developing a solution is assumed by people at lower levels in the organization. This responsibility may be delegated by top management, or the initiative may be taken by an individual or group who sees the need for change. The form of the change process and its results are often quite similar, regardless of whether lower levels take the initiative or top management delegates complete authority. The key in these approaches is that management is not involved and knows little about the changes. There are several examples of bottom-up change:

1. *By training.* Attempts to influence the attitudes and behavior of large numbers of people sometimes take the form of massive training and development efforts, undertaken by the personnel or training department, often at the request of top management and sometimes at their own initiative. In recent years, organizations have used T-groups and managerial grid training in this way. These programs are aimed at improving individual self-awareness, sensitivity to group process, and leadership skills. Similar approaches have been applied in attempts to improve problem solving skills (Kepner & Trego, 1963), financial management, and other managerial skills. The assumption is that a change in knowledge and attitudes will lead to a desired change in behavior. The objective of the training may or may not be explicitly discussed and related to corporate strategy. Top management often does not attend the training, or if they do, they see an abbreviated version. They do provide the budget.

As the president of one company said to the Vice-President of Personnel, "You have $300,000 for training this year; go out and spend it."

2. *By staff group.* In recent years, management has attempted to introduce management disciplines such as operations research, organization development, and planning by setting up staff groups charged with the responsibility of getting line managers to adopt more sophisticated approaches to management. Sometimes staff groups have taken it upon themselves to be agents of change. The assumption is that the staff group will prod and teach new approaches to other managers through various procedures and requirements, usually endorsed by top management. Planning departments often require the submission of a yearly plan. In a sense, the staff group acts as the agent of top management in pushing for the desired changes, with management relatively uninvolved.

3. *By experimental unit.* Change in organization is sometimes brought about by designating one organizational unit (plant or division) as the site for trying a new technology, a new approach to management, or a new structure. Sometimes this is a conscious decision by management. Sometimes subunit managers adopt the role of innovators on their own with only limited involvement by top management. At other times, changes in one unit may occur as a result of pressures from workers or unions. Few reports or discussions about progress take place. The assumption is that the new approach can be adopted by other subunits and ultimately by the whole organization without significant top management involvement.

When management delegates the responsibility for change to individuals and groups at lower levels, they give up much of their power and influence over the definition of problems and their solutions. The effect is the same as when a lower level unit initiates change without consulting top management. Change is unleashed at lower levels without adequate integration with the beliefs and policies of the dominant coalition. There is a high risk of a clash between the assumptions underlying the change and the beliefs of the dominant coalition.

Shared Responsibility for Change

The top-down and bottom-up approaches represent extremes on a power distribution and involvement continuum. In the middle lies an approach to change, less frequently used (except in Japan), in which those at the top and those at lower levels are jointly involved in identifying problems and/or developing solutions. Top management does not decide everything nor do they abdicate authority and responsibility for the change to lower levels. There is almost continual interaction between top and bottom levels and a process of mutual influence occurs. There are several forms this can take:

1. *Through iterative communication.* With this approach, top management defines the problem and uses staff groups or consultants to gather information and develop solutions. These are then communicated to various lower level groups personally to obtain reactions. These reactions are used to modify the solution, and the communication process starts again. The assumption underlying this approach is that there is no way of involving others in the definition of the problem or its solutions, but that the solution can be improved and commitment obtained through involving lower levels after the fact. This is a procedure for overcoming the problems which result from planning for others when, for a variety of reasons, they cannot be fully involved. (Bass, 1970)

2. *Through decision-making task forces.* Top management defines the problem and solution parameters but seeks lower-level involvement by appointing task forces to develop solutions. Top management is then provided recommended solutions and they make the final decision. Task forces are composed of lower-level people who will be affected by the changes and have expertise in the changes contemplated. The assumption is that lower level people have the expertise to solve problems more effectively than the top or staff groups because they are closer to the situation. It is also assumed that their commitment to the change will be higher as a result of this involvement.

3. *Through diagnostic and problem-solving task forces.* This approach involves all levels of the organization equally and fully. Task forces composed of top, middle, and lower level people are formed to collect information about problems in the organization. These or similar task forces are also involved in developing solutions. The underlying assumptions in this approach are that all levels are needed to develop a high-quality solution, and that commitment on the part of lower and upper levels must build at about the same pace.

The shared responsibility approach usually takes longer to implement but results in more commitment. Perhaps the best example of its widespread use is in Japan where consultation prior to changes takes enormous amounts of time, much to the frustration of western observers, but generally results in high commitment and rapid implementation (Drucker, 1971). Indeed it could be argued that the shared approach is more efficient as a strategy for change because the time taken in deciding and getting commitment is more than made up for in efficient and rapid implementation.

Criteria for Judging Effectiveness of Change Approaches

All of the approaches described are used in varying degrees in creating organizational change. Often an organizational change mixes these approaches. The top-down and bottom-up approaches have been the most frequently used because they are consistent with many of the assumptions about management associated with mechanistic and bureaucratic organizations. The shared responsibility approaches are less frequently used and have only recently found their way into implementing organizational change in the United States and Europe. But which of these approaches is most likely to be effective? Judging their effectiveness is not easy. Different criteria might be applied depending on the position of the person in the organization (top or bottom), the interest group of which he is a part (union, management, customer, and so forth), the time horizon used in making the judgment, and the values of the person making the judgment. The following are some of the criteria which can be legitimately used to judge the success of a change effort:

1. The change comes closer than any other choice to *satisfying* the *needs* of various interest groups in the organization.
2. The change is *faster* than any other competing option.
3. The change results in the *immediate performance improvements* expected.
4. The change results in the *long-term performance improvements* expected.
5. The change results in the least possible *psychological and organizational strain.* Keleman & Warwick (1973) have defined strain as the anxiety resulting from the change and/or the frustration which results when change falls short of expectations.

6. The change *"takes"* and is internalized by people throughout the organization, thus requiring no controls to sustain new behaviors.

7. The change results in the fewest possible unanticipated and *dysfunctional effects*.

8. *People feel more responsible* for future organizational improvements after the change than they did before it. The organization has enhanced its potential for renewal in the future.

It should be clear from reading this list why individuals viewing the same change may disagree about its relative effectiveness. First, they may not be applying the same criteria to the evaluation. Some managers may measure the effectiveness of a change by the reaction of various interest groups and by short-term results. Others may judge its effectiveness by long-term results and the human costs associated with the change. Different individuals will simply attend to different outcomes depending on their experience, situation, and values.

Second, even if they are applying the same criteria, they may place different values on attaining them. Implicit in each criterion are dollar costs and benefits to the organization, and human costs and benefits to its members. Even if dollar value could be measured and agreed to, no two people or groups looking at the same change are likely to evaluate its human impact in the same way. For example, is it better for people to feel responsible for future change or improvement? Depending on the situation and the values of managers, the valence ascribed to this criterion may be quite different. An authoritarian and participative manager would value different outcomes. Similarly, the undesirability of unanticipated and dysfunctional effects or the short-term/long-term tradeoffs may be judged quite differently by a manager planning to be promoted soon, than by a manager who will be heading the organization for some time to come.

Third, even if the same criteria are applied and there is agreement about their relative valence, they are extremely difficult to measure with any degree of accuracy. Organizational performance measures are the easiest to obtain, but even here many traditional financial measures of profitability may be poor indicators of success for specific organizational changes. Attitude and behavioral measures can be obtained but are often not taken, thus leaving the assessment of change on many of the criteria to the subjective judgment of managers. In the end, a manager's values and comfort with a particular approach dictates his preference.

Effectiveness of Change Approaches

However, some tentative statements about how each change approach measures up on each criterion can be made. If one assumes the criteria as given and does not ascribe a value to each of them, one can draw on past research and experience in change to project the most likely outcomes of each approach.[4]

Table 3–1 summarizes the overall ratings of these approaches on each of the previously stated criteria. A rating of High (H), Moderate (M), or Low (L) is used to estimate the extent to which each criterion is likely to be achieved by each change approach. Be cautioned that these are overall estimates and that any given situation might contain unique circumstances that would modify these estimates. Most importantly, the culture of the organization, and the needs and expectations of its members, will affect the outcome of the change on each of the criteria. A top-down approach may satisfy more criteria in an autocratic culture than it will in a participative culture. Nevertheless, the pattern of rating is instructive about the likely effects of each change approach.

TABLE 3-1   Evaluation of Change Strategies

Evaluation Criteria

Approach to Change	(1) Multiple Constituencies Satisfied	(2) Speed	(3) Immediate Results	(4) Long-Term Results	(5) Strain	(6) "Take"	(7) Dysfunctional Effects	(8) Renewal Potential
Top-Down or Unilateral	L–M	H	Potentially	L–M	H	M	M–H	L
Bottom-Up or Delegated	L–M	L–M	H (for unit or people directly involved)	L	M–H	L–M	H	L–M
Shared	H	L	M	H	L–M	H	L	H

Letter designations mean the following:
   L= Low
   M= Medium
   H= High

Top-down change. Top-down approaches are likely to be very rapid (criterion 2). New structure and procedures will be in place almost immediately after the change has been initiated, and new behavior is likely to be seen quickly as people respond to top management's new expectations. For these reasons, if the solution is appropriate to the problems that triggered the need for change in the first place, the changes will probably obtain immediate results (criterion 3). One of the problems with top-down changes is that solutions are not always appropriate because people who know about the problems are not consulted. Nevertheless, with good staff work this can be overcome. It is the speed of top-down changes that make them very attractive to managers under pressure to obtain immediate results.

It is evident that the problems of top-down change occur because of its effects on the other criteria. Top-down changes do not usually reflect the needs of individuals (criterion 1) unless top management is well attuned to their needs. But if management were so attuned, it would not likely use a top-down approach. Furthermore, lower levels in the organization cannot adjust their needs and roles to be more consistent with the solution until after the change has been activated. By then, their motivation is likely to be too low. This is why, of course, substantial evidence exists that participative changes result in more commitment (Beer & Davis, 1976; Coch & French, 1948; Fleishman, 1965).

Because the change is rapid and people are not involved, top-down change is likely to result in a lot of psychological and organizational strain (criterion 5) (Keleman & Warwick, 1973; Trist & Bamforth, 1951). Or, the top-down initiative is likely to raise expectations about change beyond management's or the organization's capacity to meet these expectations (Reddin, 1976). Depending on the prevailing culture, a top-down change is also likely to result in moderate-to-slow commitment and low "take" (criterion 6); thus it runs the risk of regression or reversal as resistance develops (Coch & French, 1948; Fleishman, Harris & Burtt, 1955; Lawrence, 1969). But with controls, management can often make it stick. However, in an authoritarian organization where people are compliant, the "take" might be high, even without management controls.

Because the change has usually been planned in isolation from groups in the organization who manage related systems, top-down change also runs the risk of incurring dysfunctional effects. For example, changes in technology that affect job roles may not fit existing job evaluation systems, causing employee dissatisfaction with pay. Similarly, because top-down change can reduce trust significantly and tends to increase dependency, people in the organization are not likely to have learned to take responsibility for future organization renewal (criterion 8). In fact, they have learned the opposite.

For all these reasons, long-term results (criterion 4) of top-down change are questionable. They could be high, if the success of the change depends heavily on technology and not on people. But if the commitment of people is needed to make the change work, long-term results are likely to suffer. In particular, top-down approaches negatively affect those criteria that are related to quality of work life. Cases 3–2 and 3–3 are illustrative of the problems of top-down change.

Bottom-up change. Bottom-up approaches, whether delegated by top management or initiated at lower levels without management's approval, are likely to have different advantages and run into different problems. These changes are likely to be much slower (criterion 2) in affecting the total organization. Even if one unit adopts a change, or attitudes are changed by training, there is still a long way to go before the whole organization is affected (Walton, 1975). Indeed, one of the potential outcomes of bottom-up approaches are dysfunctional effects (criterion 7). These are possible if changes in experimental units or in people are not supported by changes in management's style, and in **59**

CASE 3-2

A large bank created rapid technological change within its operations with low involvement of people in the division and with equally low involvement of other divisions. This resulted in immediate and long-term performance improvements, but there were also many problems: morale dropped, anxiety rose, there were attempts at unionization, and the relations between the operating and the marketing people of the bank, who felt that service declined as a result of the change, were impaired. Long-term results were threatened by massive backlogs in check processing as people struggled to learn new jobs and adapt. These effects probably caused long-term problems with the bank's customers.

First National City Bank, A & B, 1975. Reprinted by permission.

CASE 3-3

The top man of a government department decided to introduce Management by Objectives (MBO) by participative means. At my suggestion we had a launch meeting to discuss it. At this point, several errors had been committed. MBO, certainly in the traditional format, is not suitable for most government departments, as power is so diffuse. The top man's autocratic decision was hardly the way to introduce a participative approach and the launch would raise expectations above delivery point. There was great excitement at the meeting about the new management style. Everyone thought things would change completely and immediately. However, over the next few months, budgets were done the old way and some key decisions were imposed autocratically. A program that might have been a success if introduced slowly got a bad name in the opening months because of the raised expectations.

From W. J. Reddin, *Group & Organization Studies*, March 1977, 2(1), 33-41. Copyright © 1977 by International Authors, B. V. Reprinted by permission.

the larger organization's internal environment (Beer & Huse, 1972; Fleishman, Harris, & Burtt, 1955; Reddin, 1976; Sykes, 1962). For example, work redesign experiments in the plant of a large company may become isolated and ultimately fail because either corporate personnel do not support the change with pay systems, or top management doesn't reward the plant's management for innovation.

Bottom-up approaches have dysfunctional effects because the changes usually result in the satisfaction of only some constituencies or interest groups (criterion 1). Many groups and people that need to support the change are usually not involved, nor does the uninvolved top management ask these groups to support the changes. This often results in political resistance from parts of the organization opposing the change (Marris & Rein, 1973; Pettigrew, 1976). In top-down change, the resistance is likely to be from employees who feel no sense of control over their destiny, while in bottom-up change the resistance may come from uninvolved interest groups. Even top management may resist when changes in their own behavior are required to support changes they may have authorized

people at lower levels to make.

Bottom-up change is likely to show immediate results in the part of the organization in which it is initiated, assuming it is executed competently (criterion 3). Perhaps it is because of the visibility of immediate results that resistance develops in groups not involved in these early changes. People in these groups become threatened and concerned about implications for their power and role in the larger organization, and refuse to support innovative managers in their attempts to sustain and spread change. These pressures result in moderate-to-high psychological strain for innovators in staff groups, experimental units, or training programs (criterion 5). Anxiety about careers, insecurity, and dashed expectations are likely outcomes of bottom-up changes.

These pressures are, however, counterbalanced by high levels of commitment and "take" in the units directly involved in the change. Managers often develop an enthusiasm for their innovations which comes close to religious zeal, sustaining innovative practice in the experimental unit. Nevertheless, the "take" (criterion 6) in the organization as a whole, is only low to moderate. This is because of resistance and because top management does not actively encourage others to change, lowering the chance that change will spread and be adopted by the whole organization.

Thus, in the long term, bottom-up approaches must be rated as having a low probability of affecting the organization as a whole (criterion 4), even when there is initial success in an experimental unit or through training (Walton, 1975).

Finally, bottom-up changes are likely to generate only low-to-moderate amounts of renewal potential in the organization (criterion 8). Staff groups, experimental units, or trainees may feel responsible for continued efforts at improvement without prodding from the top. But this self-motivation will be reduced as they run into barriers or as some of the leaders of the change leave (Beer, 1979; Pettigrew, 1975b, Walton, 1974). Furthermore, no one else in the organization has been involved or has learned to take responsibility for the change.

The effects of bottom-up change just described come about because this approach does not include top management. Even if management early on delegates authority to a staff group to initiate change, their subsequent distance from the change means that they are not ready to change their own behavior (Argyris, 1974). Nor are they ready to influence others to change their behavior, or make changes in the organization's internal environment when this is required to support the very change they authorized. As Reddin (1976) points out, the penalty of mutiny (even mutiny initially approved by the top) is death (see Case 3–4).

Shared responsibility.　Approaches to change that involve various levels of the organization in some of the ways described earlier, have the very distinct disadvantage of being slow (criterion 2). The many meetings to develop mutual influence over problem definition and/or solutions take an enormous amount of time.[5]

It is understandable that these approaches might not be used very frequently, given the demands of time on the busiest people in the organization. It takes less time to delegate authority for change or to make decisions on structural changes, than it does to sit in endless meetings attempting to develop a consensus. Furthermore, the shared approach may be inconsistent with values of key managers and the culture of the organization. Those who have dealt with Japanese companies realize that decisions take a long time and involve many; for impatient Americans this process is frustratingly slow (Drucker, 1971).

Because the shared approach takes time, immediate turnaround of the problem situation is not likely, particularly if the organization is large. On the other hand, the evidence seems to suggest that the shared responsibility approach measures up on most of the other criteria. Because many groups are involved and can influence the final solution, **61** shared approaches usually end up satisfying more interest groups in the organization (criterion 1). This influence not only satisfies their needs but, one can argue, also leads to widespread commitment (Coch & French, 1948; Fleishman, 1965) and therefore "take" (criterion 6). People internalize the change and behave in new ways without as much control from top management.

Similarly, psychological and organizational strain (criterion 3) are probably lower than in top-down approaches. Since the process of mutual influence and communication allows adjustments of expectations to realistic levels as the change progresses, strain from dashed expectations would be lower than in other approaches. But a different kind of strain may exist in this approach, namely the anxiety associated with long periods of uncertainty as the change process unfolds.

The widespread involvement of groups also allows more parts of the organization to make adjustments in their operations consistent with the intended changes. Thus, fewer dysfunctional effects are likely to occur (criterion 7). Involvement also means that many people are likely to come away feeling responsible for future improvements (criterion 8). All of these factors are likely to lead to a successful change in the long term (criterion 4).

The picture that emerges is one of a relatively slow change process, moderate short-term results, but high levels of support in the organization, few unanticipated or dysfunctional effects, and good long-term results. The main reason for these effects seems to be that various parts of the organization are brought into a process of problem identification and solution before any final decisions are made. This allows reciprocal adjustments in various procedures, structures, roles, and attitudes as the final decision is formed.

The shared responsibility approach is more consistent with the systems nature of organizations than either of the other two approaches. Change emerges only after some internal consistency is assured between the design of the organization, the process of management in the organization, people's needs and expectations, and top management's attitudes. A culture that is consistent with the new direction develops before and during the change, thus eliminating culture drag.

Shared approaches to change are possible only in organizations where the culture encourages and management is skilled in a participative process of decision making. Because many organizations are not participative, these approaches are less frequently used than top-down and bottom-up approaches. But it is possible for an organization to learn how to use shared approaches in the process of applying them to a given change. Such a learning process requires substantial reeducation in basic values and behavior. For this reason, most OD efforts require a consultant who acts as a counselor and helper, at least at the beginning of the change effort. Case 3–5 illustrates a shared approach to managing organizational improvement.

Shared approaches adopted by managers who are not ready for them or do not know how to execute them, would not have the same outcomes described above. The benefits of fast change would be lost. At the same time the advantages of higher trust, and lower organizational strain, commitment, and satisfaction would be lost because of the lack of skill and resolve with which the approach would probably be applied.

CASE 3–5

A small (100 employees) unionized plant of a large multidivisional manufacturing company had been losing money for a period of two years. A new plant manager charged with turning the plant around was appointed. After consultation with union leaders, the plant manager shut the plant down for a day and organized a meeting of all employees (managers and hourly work force). At this meeting, he communicated to employees the severity of the situation by presenting data about the plant's financial performance and its declining efficiency. Following his presentations, mixed groups of managers and hourly employees were formed and asked to discuss the problems of the plant. Their task was to list the major problems which they felt blocked improved plant performance and to present these to the larger group.

Following a presentation of problems, the plant manager and his staff met to classify problems into homogeneous groupings. These homogeneous problems were then assigned to newly formed functional task forces whose responsibility was to work on solving the problems in order of priority. Recommendations for solutions were presented to the plant manager and his staff. Their decisions to accept or reject recommendations were then communicated back to the task forces and ultimately to the plant as a whole.

Within three months of the original meeting, several task forces had solved important problems and the plant reached a break-even performance level. Enthusiasm and commitment were high in the plant and it eventually became profitable. The plant manager with the help of an OD consultant had designed and implemented a shared approach to diagnosing problems and managing improvements in the operation of the plant. Not only did the process improve profitability, but it served to increase commitment of employees to the plant and to find ways to improve operations. (This case example is an application of the confrontation meeting to be discussed in Chapter 9.)

ORGANIZATIONAL CHANGE REQUIRES EARLY SUCCESS AND REINFORCEMENT

The conditions that appear necessary for organizational change to begin, develop a direction, and spread throughout a large complex organization have been described. Yet, for organizational change to be sustained or "take," reinforcement is required.

Early Success Is Intrinsically Rewarding

In order for change to spread throughout the organization and become a permanent fixture, it appears that early successes are needed (Beer & Driscoll, 1977; Greiner, 1967). A change in structure, a new way to organize work at the plant level, a new budgeting and planning system, a new compensation system, or other types of changes must work effectively by criteria valued in the organization. The criteria may be profitability, lower costs, a sense that things are running smoother, no strikes, fewer grievances, or whatever outcomes managers value.

It is desirable but not necessary for the results of a change to be quantifiable. In fact, experience with change suggests that a direct positive experience by managers with the change may be at least as powerful, if not more powerful, than quantitative measures of success seen at a distance. In one company, productivity improvements in a new plant experimenting with work restructuring and participative management, did not convince managers at headquarters that the innovations were good. The plant, according to one manager who had never visited it and did not know its people, "is still weird and the approach still communistic." Thus, direct *feelings* of success appear to be more important than quantitative *measures*. When individuals, groups, and whole organizations feel more competent than they did before the change, this increased sense of competence reinforces the new behavior and solidifies learning associated with change.

Because early success is especially important, the first change must be sufficiently small and within the competence of management so it can be executed successfully. Thus the selection of the first target and steps for change are critical to the successful completion of system-wide change.

Early Reinforcement through Extrinsic Rewards

The intrinsic feeling of success is not sufficient for patterns of organizational behavior to change permanently. Self-confidence is quickly eroded and new questions about competence arise, if the multitude of extrinsic rewards available within the organization do not immediately follow the early indicators of improved performance. Among others, such rewards include recognition by supervisors and peers, promotion, and monetary rewards.

For employees to experience these rewards immediately following major changes in behavior patterns, a number of complementary changes within an organization must typically occur. Kurt Lewin called this the "refreezing" phase of the change process (Schein, 1961); new behavior and attitudes unfrozen by pressures that stimulated change are solidified. This is the phase where social-system components (Chapter 2 provides a description) become congruent with, and thus support, intended change in one or more components. Many changes in organizations fail because the organization does not support, indeed often frustrates, new behavior. At least four sources of organizational support must exist for individual, group, and organizational changes to become permanent (Beer, 1971a; House, 1967).

1. *Formal systems.* Structures and formal systems of the organization such as personnel policies and practices, pay systems, performance appraisal systems, and the budgeting system must become consistent with new behaviors (see Chapter 2 for a list of other structures).

2. *Exercise of formal authority by superiors.* The manner in which managers administer or translate the formal systems to subordinates must be consistent with the direction of change. This is extremely important because people in the organization may not

perceive actual changes in formal systems unless managers transform their own behavior and attitudes. The influence of managers cannot be underestimated. Subordinates tend to respond to managers' expectations because they are the instrument of rewards and sanctions (House, 1971).

A most vivid example of this occurred after a human relations training program. First-line supervisors changed their attitudes, then six months later, reverted back to earlier ones. The shift backward was directly related to the attitude of *their* supervisors; those who worked for more autocratic supervisors regressed the most (Fleishman, Harris, & Burtt, 1955).

3. *The primary work group.* Individuals are strongly influenced by social pressures coming from group norms. That is, they tend to adopt attitudes and behaviors supported by their immediate peer group. Thus, any change must be supported by an individual's peer group if it is to be permanent. For instance, a survey of individuals who came forward to be "converted" during a Billy Graham crusade, indicated that only those individuals who were subsequently integrated into local churches maintained their faith (Schein, 1961). This suggests that efforts to change individual behavior will not be successful unless the person is moved into a group that will support those behaviors.

The implications for broad organizational changes involving large numbers of people is that the attitudes and relationships within a group must be changed to support new behavior patterns. This means that successful organizational change requires that groups throughout the organization examine the norms governing their behavior. The group development methods to be discussed in Chapter 9 can be useful tools for this.

4. *Cultural emergence.* Persistence of wider organizational change depends on members perceiving that the organization's identity and values have changed (Beer, 1971a; discussion provided in Chapter 2). Only when this has occurred is change more than skin deep. Moreover, such a shift in perception is necessary for new behavior to be reinforced. Naturally, this perceived shift will come as a result of all the changes described above. The more quickly cultural emergence occurs, the more quickly change will be "locked in."

The more an understanding of the "logic"[6] underlying these new values and managerial patterns is retained within the organization, the less likely the organization is to revert back to earlier, unadaptive states. The departure of just a few key managers associated with the change can significantly erode retention. This suggests that a manpower planning process which assures some continuity is important not only in sustaining a newly emerging culture but also in preventing the organization from revisiting earlier nonadaptive states. Alternatively, a historical record of the events and the logic which led to organizational change, may also prevent erosion of newly learned managerial patterns. Unfortunately, no practical methods for doing this have been developed to date.

ORGANIZATIONAL CHANGE REQUIRES LEADERSHIP

By now the reader will recognize that the process of organizational change is a process of organizational learning. For a collectivity of people in an organization to move through the phases of change outlined in this chapter, the top manager of the target organization must see his role as that of orchestrating a learning process. Roy Ash, the president of

Addressograph-Multigraph, has said, "The really important change in a company is a process of psychological transformation" (Peters, 1978). This "psychological transformation" is one in which people in the organization are guided through phases beginning with the building of problem awareness or dissatisfaction, followed by the setting of new expectations, the development of new models, experimentation with new behaviors, and finally, ending with the reinforcement of newly acquired attitudes and behavior.

Setting Expectations

The leader of the organization must find ways to present organizational members with data that helps them understand internal or external pressures which have led to his dissatisfaction with the status quo. The data he chooses, and the timing and manner of presentations and discussions, are all important in raising awareness of problems and building a consensus for change. The leader may call on staff groups or consultants to help him collect and present data, but he must articulate the meaning that this data has for change in the organization. The leader must go beyond the data in articulating an overriding theme, vision, or central new value which is to guide organizational behavior in the future. Through the articulation of a new direction, the leader sets expectations for what behaviors and attitudes are desired and worthy of reward.

CASE 3–6

The general manager of a one billion dollar manufacturing organization introduced his intentions to improve coordination between functions through an elaborate combination of formal and informal mechanisms. He asked an OD consultant to help in planning and running a two-day meeting of his staff aimed at improving mutual trust and teamwork (team building). This was followed by another meeting at which the consultant presented her findings about problems in the organization. A series of discussions led to a decision to introduce a matrix structure as a means of enhancing teamwork and integration.

Following consensus at the top, the consultant helped the general manager and his staff plan a series of full-day meetings aimed at communicating to all salaried employees the results of the diagnosis, the general manager's expectations for more collaboration, and the plan to introduce a matrix organization. All of the functional heads attended the presentations, symbolizing that the top team was together in setting this new direction. The presentation was carefully put together and all members of the top staff took time to reach consensus on a number of questions anticipated from people at lower levels. In this way, their answers to questions, which were to be solicited in small groups following presentation, would be consistent. Furthermore, thirteen days, over a period of two months, were taken to make presentations in geographically dispersed plants and sales offices. The time and effort this took, the presentation of change goals, the consistency of the response to questions, and the general manager and his staff's presence at all meetings, clearly communicated the direction and importance of the changes.

A skilled leader carefully times the articulation of new expectations to follow natural events such as poor profits, a strike, or the availability of compelling data about a problem. In this context, new expectations have more meaning and can therefore energize organizational members to action. Not only is timing important, but so is the selection of the forum for presenting data and articulating new directions. What meeting or conference is chosen, who attends, and who makes presentations are all important in getting attention and communicating intentions. (See Case 3-6 for an example of how a leader can set expectations for change.)

Thomas Peters (1978) has argued that a leader who wants to set new expectations and articulate new directions for an organization has a number of symbols at his disposal that communicate, often nonverbally, his expectations of organizational members. A leader sends messages by how he spends his time; reports he reviews; whom he invites to meetings; public statements he makes; agendas he sets for meetings; and how he uses and treats members of his personal staff. Peters argues that an effective leader sends more consistent messages by consciously managing these symbols. He cites Richard E. Neustadt's research on presidential leadership and power as an example:

> The professional reputation of a president in Washington is made or altered by the man himself. No one can guard it for him; no one saves him from himself . . . His general reputation will be shaped by the signs and patterns in the things he says and does. These are the words and actions he has chosen day to day. (Neustadt, 1960)

Inducing New Behaviors

Skillful leaders consciously and meticulously plan to bring subordinates together in settings (meetings. conferences. etc.) that will stimulate desired behavior and minimize the possibility of undesired behavior. Once again, Peters (1978) lists a number of examples of setting variables that can induce and support behavior consistent with the leader's expectations.

1. *Presence or absence of top managers.* Since top managers serve as important models, the leader's decision to be present at certain meetings, and display certain behaviors and attitudes, is important.
2. *Location of group meeting.* Moving the time or location of a key meeting, or creating a new type of meeting (place, membership, and/or purpose), can signal that new behaviors are desired. Moving a review meeting from headquarters to the field not only sends new messages, but provides for new interaction patterns.
3. *Agenda control.* The agenda specifies expectations and desired behavior by the order and time spent on certain subjects. It can also specify who will present, discuss, and interact on certain topics.
4. *Attendance.* By inviting certain people, levels, and groups, patterns of interactions and communication are stimulated. Signals are also sent about status, responsibility, and accountability.
5. *The leader's questioning approaches.* The questions leaders ask are important in shaping others' behavior. Asking about revenue or customers induces different behavior than asking about costs and efficiency.
6. *Goal setting.* The goal leaders set with their subordinates focuses attention on those areas they consider important, and specifies certain behavior.

67

As we shall see, many intervention strategies and techniques in OD are planned settings for interaction, aimed at inducing desired behavior and attitudes.

Reinforcing Desired Behavior

Leaders can have a personal impact on organizational behavior by the patterns of praise and recognition they provide. Privately telling people they are doing a good job when their behavior is in line with the change objectives, writing formal letters of thanks, pointing up desired behaviors as strengths in a performance appraisal interview, and praising certain elements of a group's performance are all examples of social reinforcement that a leader can use. Typically, positive reinforcement of desired behavior has been found to be more effective than an attempt to drive out undesired behavior through negative reinforcement. Once again, frequency and consistency are important for these relatively "mundane" events to have an impact.

Beyond the design of formal organizational mechanisms, the leader as a person is an important instrument in stimulating change in organizational behavior. Leaders who can articulate a new direction, consistently use symbols to communicate their vision, model desired behavior, create settings to induce desired behavior, and consistently reinforce behavior through praise and other means, are skilled change agents. They can manage and control a complex process of change.

Unfortunately, many managers do not naturally possess the needed knowledge about organizational learning to orchestrate the change process. Nor do many leaders possess the self-awareness or skill needed to maximize their effectiveness as instruments of change. Often they don't have these skills because they have not had the opportunity to acquire the knowledge or learn the skills. When this is the case, an OD consultant can be helpful as a member of the change team. His knowledge of organizations and organizational change can help plan the manipulation of formal organizational mechanisms. His knowledge about leadership can help him coach and counsel a manager in how to use symbols, settings, and reinforcements. His knowledge of intervention methods provides a pool of previously tested symbols and settings for inducing certain behaviors and attitudes. If the consultant is personally skillful as a leader, he may be able to model for the manager the leadership skills needed. At crucial points in the change process, or in specific settings, the consultant may even augment the leadership capacities of the manager. Thus, an OD consultant may be an essential partner in managing change.

Summary

This chapter has presented a model for understanding how successful change typically unfolds within organizations. Crisis triggered by external and internal pressures typically leads to the dissatisfaction needed for change to occur. But data about activities requiring examination and change may also be used to create dissatisfaction. A new model usually brought in by an outsider is required as an alternative to ineffective managerial patterns. The new approach becomes a means of converting increasing dissatisfaction into positive motivation for change.

There are three alternative processes for moving change along. Top-down change is rapid and may get immediate visible results, but usually does not gain long-term employee commitment. Bottom-up change can develop commitment in a part of the organization but runs the risk of being rejected by the rest of the organization just as it succeeds. On the other hand, shared change, while slower, develops more widespread commitment and long-term results. The effectiveness of a change, measured by a number of criteria such as its speed, the results obtained, dysfunctional effects, and its long-term stability, can be directly traced to the use of a change process or a mix of these processes.

To sustain change early, success is required so that new behaviors are reinforced. This typically occurs through feelings of competence generated by performance improvements and by social and formal rewards provided by the organization. These must support the emergence of group norms and organizational culture consistent with new directions.

Organizational change seems to resemble a learning process. Instead of one individual, however, *many people* in the organization must develop readiness and motivation; they must find a new approach; they must learn about the new approach, and become committed to it. This organizational learning process is extremely complex and requires careful orchestration by the change agent if it is to reach a successful conclusion. The next chapter will deal, in some detail, with intervention strategies a change agent might use to help an organization move through its learning cycle.

NOTES

1. A version of this formula originated with Dr. Alan Burnes, a former associate of mine at Corning Glass Works. I recently discovered a similar formula in Beckhard and Harris (1977), who attribute it to David Gleicher.
2. With the exception of the names, which have been eliminated, this quote comes from an interview with a CEO reported in "Corning Glass: On the Way Up," *Forbes,* 1977.
3. For a complete description of this example, see the First National City Bank cases (A) and (B), 1975. These may be obtained from the International Collegiate Case Clearing House, Harvard Business School, Boston, Mass. 02163.
4. There are numerous case studies of change efforts (for example, Guest, 1962; Jacques, 1951; Lawrence, 1958; Seashore & Bowers, 1963; Sykes, 1962). Some studies have examined many changes in an attempt to find some common patterns associated with "success" (Buchanan, 1967; Greiner, 1967). There are also numerous theories of change (Zaltman, 1973).
5. An excellent description of such a process and the enormous time and energy that it takes is to be found in "Patient Schemers," (*Fortune,* 1965) which describes the efforts of top management at Union Carbide to centralize a very decentralized organization.
6. The term "logic" has recently been used by Beddows, Lane, & Lawrence (undated) to connote the underlying assumptions governing the technical, social, and organizational patterns chosen by an organization in its efforts to adapt. The term was originally used by Rothlisberger and Dickson (1939).

INTERVENTION STRATEGIES
A Process for
Improving Effectiveness

OVERVIEW

How can organizations be helped to develop efficiency, effectiveness, and health? The managers of the steel plant described in Chapter 1 were unable to develop these qualities in their organization, leaving crisis as the only means by which change could occur. But what strategies might a manager or a consultant have taken to intervene in the organization so that its members (management, office employees, and plant labor) might have dealt with root problems earlier? What approaches might have increased not only efficiency and effectiveness, but also organizational health?

Part II will outline the processes for creating change that have become identified with organization development. To denote their purposeful and systematic nature, these change processes are called intervention strategies. Most organizational changes could be characterized by the fact that they are largely unplanned and do not reflect clear and accurate assumptions about organizations and how people in them change. Many of these assumptions were discussed in Chapters 2 and 3.

While there are some differences among organization development professionals about what constitutes effective intervention strategies, there are also many areas of agreement. Common agreement comes from a growing body of experience and documented cases (Argyris, 1970; Lippitt, Watson, and Westerley, 1958) as well as from studies that have compared successful and unsuccessful organization development efforts (Bowers & Hausser, 1977; Buchanan, 1967; Greiner, 1967).

ASSUMPTIONS UNDERLYING OD STRATEGY 4

Managers have been changing organizations through a variety of means for a long time. But as the discussion in Chapter 3 indicates, many top-down and bottom-up strategies do not achieve success on all criteria by which the effectiveness of a change might be judged, particularly long-term results, "take," organizational strain, satisfaction by multiple constituencies, and capacity for renewal (organizational health). Intervention strategies discussed in this part of the book are based primarily on the shared approach to change. Thus, these interventions take somewhat more time to implement but are aimed at achieving success on all the criteria discussed in Chapter 3. The following are some of the key assumptions underlying these interventions.

OD GOALS AND VALUES

As discussion in earlier chapters has indicated, OD has several goals and values. They are:

1. To help organizations solve problems of efficiency and effectiveness arising out of incongruities between the major social system components described in Chapter 2.
2. To help organizations, to an appropriate extent become healthier more adaptive systems. This usually means helping them increase diversity, openness, confrontation of differences through problem solving and delegation of decision making to the lowest possible level consistent with available information and competence (Beckhard, 1969).
3. To help managers diagnose the current state of the organization, clarify desired outcomes for the future and make strategic choices that will guide the adaptation process.

While these goals are relatively parsimonious, there are several potential inconsistencies among them and between them which lead to potential problems in the practice **73** of OD. It is a lack of clarity about these inevitable inconsistencies that has led to disillusionment, as practice does not live up to theory, or as theory applied without regard to the realities of practice results in failure.

First, as the discussion of organization health in Chapter 2 pointed out, the goals of greater efficiency and effectiveness may not always be consistent with the goals of organizational health. An organization whose primary strategy is to defend a market segment by cutting costs and improving production efficiencies, will need to be relatively hierarchical and directive in its management style (Miles & Snow, 1978). These characteristics are potentially in conflict with the characteristics of organizational health. Management faces a dilemma if it also wants to increase health to prepare for changes in people and environment. It must learn to apply what Miles has called a human resource approach to management (Miles, 1965), while not straying from the management practices and organization designs required for a defensive strategy of improving production efficiencies. Thus, OD in such an organization could not possibly be the same in process or goals as OD in an organization operating in a more dynamic environment and evolving to more organic structures.

Second, there are potential inconsistencies between a participative process of free and informed choice, needed to gain internal commitment, and the organization's short-term needs to be efficient and effective. For example, is it possible for a participative process that stresses internal commitment to result in decisions that make the organization more directive and hierarchical, if that is what the environment demands? In effect, is OD applicable to all situations, or only those situations in which the organization is moving to more organic and participative forms? This question is extremely controversial and a clear answer does not exist. In theory, at least, a process that stresses free and informed choice should make it possible for an organization to adopt any designs or any management style. In reality, however, few organization development programs result in moving the organization toward more functional and bureaucratic forms (for example, model II organizations in Fouraker & Stopford, 1968). The vast majority of OD efforts are associated with movement to more organic forms and participative styles.

It is more than likely that this trend is primarily a function of the general evolution of organizational forms from model II to model III (decentralization) and beyond to matrix (Davis & Lawrence, 1977). However, it is possible that OD outcomes are influenced by interventionists who value participation and more organic structures. They may find it difficult to help an organization move to more traditional bureaucratic forms.

Third, there are potential inconsistencies between both the process assumptions underlying OD and the goal of organizational health on the one hand, and prevailing managerial values and sophistication of managers on the other. It is the assumption of this book that the means of change must be reasonably consistent with the ends (Beer & Driscoll, 1977). Thus, when the goal of OD is organizational health, interventions must be as consistent as possible with the character of adapting and renewing organizations, or it is unlikely that these ends will be achieved. This means that the change process must adhere more closely than usual to the values of participation, informed choice, openness, and resolution of differences through problem solving. Yet, when short-term pressures for results are too severe or the management too unsophisticated or traditional, interventions which are *not* consistent with these values may be called for (i.e., more consistent with the organization's current values). They may be the only ones that can practically influence the system. Thus, in the short term (this could be two or three years in a five- to ten-year OD effort) inconsistency between the process of OD and its long-term goal of organization health may exist. In the short run, these should not be seen as failures by the change agent to live up to the goals and values of OD. But, in the long run, OD interventions must evolve to congruence with the characteristics of a healthy organization and the values of informed choice, if they are to help organizations approach health.

If there are inconsistencies between goals, values, and practice, why not modify the goals and values? Because of the long-term developmental nature of OD and the adaptive nature of organizational members, one can argue that modifying goals and values to fit current practice precludes ever reaching them. On the one hand, maintaining rigid adherence to OD goals and values precludes the possibility of providing practical and immediate help to an organization in trouble and thus gaining entry and credibility with members. On the other hand, gaining entry and credibility by disassociating with the goals and values of OD prevents the change agent from helping the organization achieve the desired goal of organizational health. As in most human affairs, the answer seems to lie in being prepared to live with inconsistency between long-term ideals and short-term reality. This means never losing sight of long-term goals but never failing to modify goals to suit the immediate situation. Only in this way is it possible in the long term (five to twenty-five years) for managers to learn the skills and values needed to manage an adaptation process guided by informed choice and aimed at efficiency, effectiveness, and health.

The implications for the change agent are that he must be continuously aware of how his change strategy is inconsistent with OD goals and values. He must also be aware of why this inconsistency exists and the time frame in which greater consistency is likely to be reached. He must also periodically examine the degree to which inconsistency between personal values and OD goals for a given organization makes him less useful to the organization, or the extent to which his values have been co-opted by the system. Total acceptance of inevitable inconsistencies may signal the latter while disillusionment and feelings of failure may signal the former. Neither of these well serves a change agent in pursuit of a long-term process of organizational learning and adaptation.

SCOPE OF CHANGE

All OD interventions, regardless of where they start, have the social system of the organization as their domain. The change agent must diagnose and plan for interventions necessary to create changes in desired outcomes in any part of the organization. For this reason, OD efforts are characterized by multiple and properly sequenced interventions (more on this in Chapter 12) aimed at changing as many facets of the social system as needed to unfreeze the organization. The change agent must help managers perceive organizational development as encompassing the whole system.

PROCESS OF CHANGE

An effective process of organization development tests for or develops the conditions for successful change described in Chapter 3: a state of dissatisfaction with the status quo so that motivation to change is present; a new model for diagnosing and/or solving the problems identified; a participative process which enhances internal commitment; and the management of events to assure early success experiences.

By developing the conditions necessary for effective change, OD interventions attempt to mobilize and motivate forces for change inside the target organization rather than appealing to higher authority. It is an inside-out strategy rather than an outside-in strategy. This is not to say that mobilization of motivation to change inside the organiza- **75** tion is not helped by outside pressures (Beer & Driscoll, 1977). OD interventionists simply attempt to get managers in touch with the reality of existing pressures rather than forcing changes using their own or other's authority. Commitment to change is developed through involvement in examining these pressures and developing alternative organizational solutions.

Thus OD is primarily a normative-reeducative strategy rather than a coercive one or a purely rational or logical one (Chin & Benne, 1976). That is, OD interventions assume that significant changes in management practice will occur only when the persons involved in the change are made to modify their old normative orientations (beliefs about how things ought to be done) and develop commitments to new ones. Such changes in normative orientation are thought to involve change in attitudes, values, skills, and significant relationships, not just changes in knowledge, information, or intellectual rationales for a given practice. Coercion is thought to be inadequate as a primary strategy because basic managerial attitudes and beliefs are not changed by this method, though compliance may be obtained.

This is not meant to imply that all OD changes are fully participative or entirely normative-reeducative. A mix of normative-reeducative, coercive, and rational strategies is typically employed. Indeed, major changes in norms in hierarchical and bureaucratic organizations often occur only when someone in authority gets the process started. Moreover, normative reeducation does not imply that only education is used to create changes in norms. As we shall see later, replacement of individuals or a process of natural selection brought about by a normative-reeducative approach, can materially aid the process of cultural change. Nevertheless, the primary approach in OD is to change attitudes, beliefs, and culture through participation and involvement.

THE CHANGE AGENT/INTERVENTIONIST

Organization development requires an outsider or someone with an outside perspective (Argyris, 1970; Greiner, 1967). An outside perspective may come from a consultant, a new manager, or an enlightened manager who is able to step outside the traditions of his organization. This outsider, as has already been discussed, brings in new ideas and viewpoints that help organizational members approach old problems in new ways. In a very real sense, the change agent is a major part of the intervention in the organization's affairs. It is his discrepant views of the organization's problems, of how to implement effective change, and what is ideal behavior and management practice (Argyris, 1970) that help mobilize the organization's resources for change. It is conflict between the change agent's perspective and the organization's traditional one that offers the opportunity for new and creative approaches.

While the differences in knowledge, values, and belief between the change agent and the organization creates difficult problems for the person in this role (to be discussed later in the book), it is an essential feature of all OD interventions. An effective interventionist manages this gap so that it is large enough to offer creative tension but not so large that a relationship between himself and the organization cannot be established and maintained. On the one hand, this means that the change agent is always ahead of the client organization in modeling new behavior but never so far ahead that a break in the relationship is inevitable. On the other hand, the discrepancy between the change agent and the organization can never be so small that the change agent presents no new alternative or creative tensions.

76

The change agent must modify his behavior in accordance with the state of client or target organizations.[1] At an early stage in the relationship, the change agent may compromise his outside perspective more than in later stages. However, if an OD program has gone on for a long time and the change agent still finds himself compromising a great deal, then it might be an important internal signal that the organization is not changing to incorporate new models and ideas.

Where change agents do not have this range of behavior, they must call in others who do at appropriate stages in the change process. Managers recognize the limitations of some individuals to adopt different roles when they replace one manager with another. Close examination of management succession in an organization undergoing transition might show that a manager's early attempts to stimulate changes through persuasion and education (a low-tension approach) really prepared the organization for more radical managers brought in later on. Unfortunately these patterns of succession are often unplanned and not seen as important tactics in a larger change strategy. Thus they violate good OD practice.

Research and theory is far from settling the issue of how much the change agent should confront the organization or be discrepant from it. Some OD theorists and practitioners insist that early confrontation of the client is essential lest the client perceive the change agent as inconsistent (Argyris, 1970). Others are more tolerant of inconsistencies in the interventionist's behavior and pose this as a problem to which there is no clear-cut answer (Miles, 1974). The position of this book is that there are things to be said for and against both sides. So with no "one right way," the change agent's skill lies in being appropriately confrontive or discrepant based on his assessment of the situation and the time horizons of the OD effort.

The discussion of the change agent's role in stimulating and sustaining organizational change has been purposely vague about who a change agent might be. The change agent might be a professional external OD consultant, a professional internal OD consultant, a staff manager interested in changing a single dimension of the organization, or the general manager of the target organization. Any of these people alone or in combination are practicing OD when they conform to the *general guidelines* for intervening in an organization outlined in this part of the book.

As the OD process is described it will become clear to the reader that a manager or staff specialist might have particular problems in conforming to all the steps in the intervention process, particularly entry and contracting. Managers are often placed in organizations by top management without involvement by the target organization, creating certain problems for them. Nevertheless, to the extent that they would like to achieve the goals and objectives of OD, these managers must find ways to overcome these problems in applying the OD intervention process. This can be done and has been done by creative and skillful managers (Guest, 1964).

However, to stress the outside perspective and the discrepancy that must exist for effective change and development to take place, intervention strategies in Part II are described from the perspective of the professional interventionist.

SOURCES OF POWER FOR THE CHANGE AGENT

The discussion so far clearly suggests that the change agent cannot rely very much or very long on the hierarchical authority of management. What, then, is the change agent's source of influence in his relationship with the organization?

The answer lies in a mixed model of power, one that probably relies on hierarchical authority in early stages of a change effort and on the intrinsic satisfaction and feelings of competence derived by organizational members later in the change effort. Thus, while the change agent may be brought in by a power figure early on in the change progresses, he must develop other sources of influence. These sources derive from the change agent's personality, values, role, and ascribed knowledge and expertise (French, 1956; Pettigrew, 1976). They are as follows:

1. *Power from high assessed status* by the client organization. The client sees the change.agent as speaking a similar language, sharing his concerns, or even dressing similarly. This provides the change agent "deviation credits" that allow him to challenge the established order.
2. *Power from developed trust.* Trust develops if the change agent is reasonably consistent in handling data and staying within the role boundaries he has explained to the client. Trust also develops if the consultant avoids relying on authority figures to act on his behalf.
3. *Power from expertise* in the content (theory and knowledge) and process of organization development.
4. *Power from established credibility.* If the change agent has demonstrated his effectiveness with previous clients, or there have been successful interventions with the current client, members of the organization will allow themselves to be influenced.
5. *Power from dissatisfied constituencies.* To at least some individuals and groups in the organization, the change agent represents an opportunity for them to influence the power structure of the organization. These dissatisfied constituencies see the OD effort as helping them meet their needs

The need to develop these sources of power does not mean change agents should not be supported by top management—they need to be. Indeed, it would be difficult to envisage a change agent entering a hierarchical organization and staying in it without the blessing of formal power figures. There are many compelling reasons for the change agent to develop and retain formal authority as a source of power. To be effective at all levels, however, the change agent needs to balance it with other sources of power and to avoid using formal authority. More about this later in the book.

NOTES

1. In this book we will refer to the organization undergoing change or development as the "client" or "target organization." These terms will be used interchangeably.

CHANGE TARGET SELECTION AND ENTRY 5

SELECTION OF CLIENT ORGANIZATION

The identification and selection of the target organization is perhaps the most important step in the intervention process. As discussed earlier, internal motivation is *the* crucial factor in an OD intervention because the energy for change must come primarily from inside the organization. There is relatively little reliance on authority figures outside the organization to push it towards change.

This central fact suggests that the change target (group or organization) must select itself rather than being targeted for change by the change agent or top manageent. This does not mean that the change agent cannot approach a management that has problems to explain how OD can be helpful (Harrison, undated). It does mean, however, that the dialogue that results from this contact leaves management in the position of making a "free informed choice" about whether or not to proceed (Argyris, 1970).

The change agent must clearly resist what Ray Miles (1972) has called the "Mafia Contract." In this approach to OD top management directs the change agent to "fix" a manager or organization. Such a request or directive undoubtedly means that management in the target organization is not ready or motivated and that a meaningful dialogue between the unit level manager and his boss has not taken place. Furthermore, a change agent responding to such a top-level request could not possibly establish the relationship of trust needed to launch a change effort.

Staff specialists in organizations have often found that a directive from top management to line managers can be more harmful than helpful to their efforts to have line organizations adopt the management practices for which they are functionally responsible. Such directives often lead to resistance to staff initiatives by line groups and ultimately to anger and hostility, directed not only at the staff group but at the change itself. If top management is so frustrated that it has to direct others to make change happen, it needs help in developing a dialogue with unit managers that will help them understand the pressures operating on top management. Only this understanding can lead to internal motivation.

FIGURE 5–1   A grid for analyzing the forces pushing for change and their potency

Potency of Forces	Forces Pushing Toward a Change	Nature of change demanded:				
		Owners	Legislation	Employees	Trade Unions	Social Values
HIGH						
MEDIUM						
LOW						

From Richard Beckhard and Reuben Harris, *Organizational Transitions: Managing Complex Change.* © 1977, Addison-Wesley, Reading, Mass. Figure 4.1. Reprinted with permission.

It is important, however, that change agents make their own assessment of an organization's potential motivation to change, before investing a great deal of time in the entry and contracting process. The pressures on the organization coming from outside forces such as legislation, technology change, and competition, or from internal pressures such as turnover, dissatisfaction, or labor strife need to be identified and their potency quantified.

One way to determine if an organization needs to change, should change, or might be ready to change is to list all potential forces for change coming from inside or outside the organization, and rate each one on the extent to which it supports change. Figure 5–1 is a grid for analyzing the sources and potency of forces for change. It illustrates some typical forces a manager might assess to determine readiness for a particular change. A change agent could list other forces he chooses along the top of the grid and proceed with an analysis based on available data. When the change agent is a manager, an analysis of his own organization will tell a lot about the readiness for change of people in the organization including the manager himself. A failure to do such an analysis can lead to abortive organization development efforts. Just as organization improvement efforts get started, the manager and/or the OD consultant discover that there is insufficient energy among organizational members to sustain improvement efforts.

If the change agent is a consultant or staff manager in a larger organization where there are several change targets, it is important that he distinguish between the importance or criticality of the problem and the probability that the change effort will be successful. There is an understandable tendency to select as a target the organizational unit with the most critical problem. However, if this unit's motivation to change is lower than another unit's with a somewhat less important problem, the long-term credibility of OD as a change strategy may be served by selecting the latter. In selecting OD targets, the trade-off between the importance of the problem and the probability of success must be continually assessed.

An assessment of an organization's readiness to change inevitably leads to the question of top-management support. It is difficult to conceive that a change effort could be successful unless the top manager of the target organization supports it. This is particularly true in hierarchical organizations where the top manager sets the tone through his personal style and management of control and reward systems.

A shared approach to change is not possible unless the top manager of the target unit is motivated and involved. However, this does not necessarily mean that the manager to whom he reports need be equally motivated. It is important, however, that this higher manager provide the manager of the target organization with sufficient freedom to take risks and experiment. If the higher manager feels he must control all change plans, the target unit's internal motivation to change will be reduced.

Even more than freedom, it is desirable that the target manager be supported by his boss in his OD work. This becomes particularly important as the inevitable problems in the change program develop or if performance of the organization drops. A supportive higher manager can help the key unit manager through these problems and protect him from short-term performance demands that can compromise the planned changes.

The discussion so far suggests there are a number of criteria which might be used in determining the probability of bringing a major organization development effort to a successful conclusion. At the very least, these criteria may be used to develop realistic expectations about success. In circumstances where choices of change targets are possible, these criteria can help in selecting the change target which offers the highest probability of impacting an important organizational problem. The following is a more complete list of factors to be considered.

1. The readiness of the key manager and his subordinates to create change in the organization and in themselves.
2. The importance of the problem to the target organization and to the larger system of which it is a part.
3. The capability (skills, knowledge, managerial competence) of people associated with the problem to make the changes needed.
4. The values of the key managers and their compatability with OD intervention strategies.
5. The probability that a "critical mass," a self-sustaining organization improvement effort motivated and powered from within the unit, will develop (Harrison, undated).
6. The degree of political support for organization development and the particular change objectives at levels above the change target.
7. The competence of the change agent (manager and/or consultant) to manage the change.

A change agent who is contemplating an OD effort should assess these factors before deciding to go ahead. Indeed, an accurate assessment of where and whether to go ahead with an OD effort heavily determines success or failure. It is so important that a fairly elaborate process for testing and/or developing motivation for change and laying the proper ground for an OD effort is required. This is the entry and contracting process to be discussed in the next section.

ENTRY AND CONTRACTING

The essence of the entry and contracting process is that it is a sequential series of steps with go/no-go choice points by which a change agent (consultant or manager) can determine whether the conditions for successful change exist or whether they have been **81** successfully developed in earlier steps. It is also the means by which the change agent is introduced to the organization, creating expectations about his role and relationship to the client system. Though the process applies most clearly to an OD consultant, many elements can be used by a new manager or even an existing manager to determine and/or develop readiness for organizational change.

The first few contacts between the change agent and the target organization are crucial because they set the tone for the relationship. On the one hand, if the change agent is directive and controlling, the managers in the organization will build expectations for this behavior in the future and will either resist or become dependent. On the other hand, if the change agent is confronting, supportive, and shares a willingness to influence and be influenced, the relationship is more likely to evolve along these lines. To the extent that the change agent can model this behavior, organizational members will be able to understand better what OD is and evaluate their readiness to engage in it. In a very real sense, the first few meetings are themselves a significant intervention and should adhere as closely as possible to the basic requirements of an effective intervention (Argyris, 1970).

1. *Valid information.* Any intervention must generate valid and useful information that describes the problems experienced by the organization and the factors contributing to these problems. To be classified as valid, the data cannot be distorted or overly biased by any one constituency in the organization, and particularly not by management or the change agent. The data must represent the total client system.

2. *Free informed choice.* Decisions about what action will be taken to deal with problems generated by the client are made by the client with a clear idea of their objectives and consequences. Free and informed choice places the locus of decision making in the client system and makes it possible for the client organization to remain responsible for its own destiny.[1]

3. *Internal commitment.* The course of action chosen by the client has been internalized and the individual or group feels responsible for its choice. Internal commitment means that the client (individual or group) is making a choice because it fulfills his needs, as well as those of the system, and gives him a sense of responsibility. At the same time, the client is fully cognizant of the negative consequences associated with the choice.

Adherence to these intervention principles means that an OD presentation or a sales pitch about its potential value to the organization is not the way to begin. Similarly, management training in behavioral science as a means of getting started in OD is not generally advisable. While these approaches are often used by change agents, they result in giving the organization members the wrong impression of OD. They do not clearly signal that OD is a process of *self-examination* and *problem solving* that applies to managing the organization's most important problems and that OD relies on a heavy investment of time and energy by members of the organization. The power of first experiences in developing expectations about OD also suggests that beginning with one type of intervention, such as team building or job enrichment, can lead the client organization to equate OD with that particular intervention. Case 5–1 provides an example of an inappropriate entry process which led to difficulties later.

First, an effective beginning for an OD effort engages the management of an organization in surfacing valid data about their current state (strengths and problems), what they would like it to be in the future, and how they intend to get there (Beckhard & Harris, 1977; Buchanan, 1967; Burns & Greenberg, 1974). Such a process not only helps members of

An OD group in a large multidivisional company had successfully helped in introducing innovations in work design and participative management in one plant. Upon hearing about the innovations, a plant manager of a much larger plant expressed interest in applying similar innovations at his plant. He expressed strong support for the values that these innovations represented.

In response to this interest, an OD specialist was assigned to consult with the plant. He began by holding a series of seminars in behavioral science concepts. Incuded were sessions on McGregor's Theory Y and Herzberg's theory of work motivation. The intent was to stimulate further interest in the application of these ideas among all managers in the plant. Shortly after the seminars, several managers in the plant began to experiment with the application of these ideas in their respective departments. As the OD consultants viewed it, another plant level OD effort was under way.

However, three years later, the efforts at changing the culture of the plant had made little progress. Only a few managers were applying the new ideas. The consultant could command the interest of management *only* when things were going well and slack time existed. Meanwhile, a number of major problems developed in introducing new technology into the plant. The consultant failed in his attempts to help management with these problems and to have them see the relationship of his work to these current problems. Managers simply did not see the OD consultant as a generalist who could help them diagnose organizational problems and plan for improvements. To them, organization development meant the application of participative management, an impression developed during the consultant's training seminars at the time of entry. Organization development did not mean problem solving for greater organizational effectiveness.

the client organization determine its readiness to change, but also gives the change agent an opportunity to learn about the organization's problems as well as the key manager's competence and readiness to engage in OD.

Second, an OD effort cannot begin until the client organization and the change agent have established ground rules for their relationship. This is the contract between the interventionist and the organization. Its purpose is to head off potential problems that might later reduce trust between the change agent and the organization and endanger the development effort.

The following are specific steps a management team might take (with or without the help of a consultant) to begin a major organization change and development effort.

Clarification of Deficiencies and Motivation to Change

Where are we? Assessment of their own motivation to change can best be accomplished through key managers diagnosing *the present state of their organization*. By answering the question "What are the strengths and weaknesses of our organization?" they can begin to define the change problem. The pooling of answers and a discussion of differences between individual managers can lead to important new insights. In fact, this may be the first time the managers have come together to talk about their perceptions of **83**

the organization's problems, and they may discover that they share common dissatisfactions. Not only can this discovery clarify the problems but it can also energize the group to action. However, difficulty in arriving at a consensus or suppression of negative or dissenting views will deenergize the group. The change agent can move managers through these difficulties by "pushing" them to explore their readiness to embark on an organization development effort. Such difficulties provide three important opportunities:

1. The change agent and management team can back away from a change that is not likely to succeed because of lack of motivation.
2. The managers can resolve their different views, alleviate their personal anxieties about careers, and/or deal with political considerations, thus molding a consensus and developing internal commitment.
3. The entry and contracting process also gives the top manager an opportunity to assess his managers' motivation and potential competence to provide leadership in the change. If consensus is not reached or if the change falters at later stages because of individual deficiencies, the manager is in a better position to make a decision about replacing those that may be blocking change.

Naturally, the issues of manager motivation and competence should be a matter of open discussion between the change agent and individual managers and should be dealt with at the earliest possible stages in the entry and contracting process. Only a process (such as the one proposed in this section) that surfaces resistance so that it can be seen and felt by the top manager, provides him the opportunity to make the difficult personnel evaluations and decisions often required to move change along. Experience with many change efforts leads to the conclusion that the issue of replacing key figures who are blocking change is often not dealt with soon enough or explicitly enough.

Finally, it is important that statements of problems go beyond symptom identification. Poor intergroup relations for example, may be a symptom of more fundamental problems in structure, culture, or measurement systems (Beer, 1971b). A question such as "What are the causes of this problem?" can help move a group to root causes, but perhaps a more important question is "Why is this a problem?" or "What would be different or better if relations improved?" Such questions help managers specify the economic and human outcomes that would change if the problem were eliminated, and clarify the stakes involved (Beckhard & Harris, 1977).

Where do we want to be in the future? Managers of an organization contemplating a change need to define the *state of the organization they desire in the future.* In effect, they must specify the outcomes they would like and how they think the organization should function to achieve them. If the change required is an increase in minorities hired, retained, and accepted by the organization, managers must specify not only numerical goals but also behavior and attitudes in various parts of the organization as well as the changes in rewards, controls, and policy needed to achieve them. The description of the desired organization should be detailed and specific. See the model presented in Chapter 2 for help.

Resources required to begin. Having identified the desired future organization, a management team can assess the magnitude of the change required and the needed resources (time, energy, money). How many meetings and task forces will be set up? What additional diagnostic activities are required? How many people will have to be placed on special assignments? What money will be needed for travel, for consulting help, and so forth? What performance decrements will be suffered during the change? This type of discussion brings managers face to face with what they will have to do to create and support change.

The importance of anticipating and planning for the resource and time demands of a major change effort cannot be underestimated. Managers are not always willing to assign people to tasks associated with the change effort because they see these activities as taking time away from more immediate and pressing problems. OD efforts often slow down because the organization cannot unhinge itself from its present pattern of activities. Indeed, as the situation gets worse people seem to put even more time into the same patterns and are prevented from engaging in the change tasks.

During this process the change agent must clarify for himself the amount of energy and time that will be required on his part and whether he can afford them. Many OD efforts have had their momentum slowed and failed because the change agent could not respond to the organization's increasing need. Many change agents (particularly managers) underestimate the time required to follow-up change with numerous supporting interventions, such as visits to all parts of the organization and meetings with various groups.

Evaluation of Change Effort

One of the most difficult and neglected aspects of organizational change is evaluation. In the early stages of a change effort, as managers become enthusiastically involved in taking action and fixing problems, doubt about the success of the changes recedes into the background. Yet, it is inevitable that organization development will run into barriers, new and unanticipated problems will emerge, there will be personal pain and adjustment for managers, and doubts will develop about the competence and effectiveness of the change agent. Managers will ask:

1. Is the change we have been working on happening?
2. How do we know OD is really working?
3. What are the contributions to profits?
4. Is the time in meetings and extra activities worth it?
5. Is John X, our change agent, effective?

The subject of evaluation will be dealt with later in this book. For the moment, it is important to stress that agreement should be reached at the entry and contracting stage about who will conduct evaluations, what will be evaluated, how it will be evaluated, when it will be evaluated, and what will be done with evaluation results. The joint discussions and ultimate agreement on evaluation help to "lock in" this process early. They prevent the target organization or the change agent from reducing time and energy committed for evaluation. They prevent managers from changing the focus of evaluation to serve personal and political agendas that may emerge as the change effort progresses.

This is likely to happen most often in connection with evaluation of the change agent himself. For instance, it is inevitable that negative feelings about the interventionist (manager or consultant) will occur due to the discrepancy between him and the client. So, at the time the interventionist will need and want as much feedback as he can get to adjust behavior and strategy, the client will be reluctant to give it. When this situation develops, it is too late to expect a valid evaluation because a request for one is inevitably seen as an attempt by the interventionist to obtain support and acceptance. Only prior agreement to periodic evaluations (with dates specified), their content, and the importance of negative feedback when it is warranted, can avoid this dilemma.

Managers who have a hierarchical relationship to people in the organization, find that valid feedback is even more difficult to obtain than for professional consultants. However, such feedback is even more important, given the leader's actual and potential influence on the organization change and development effort. With the use of new methods such as team building, in which subordinates provide managers with feedback about their behavior (Chapter 9 provides description), "rate your boss" techniques, and if needed, the help of a third party consultant, such an evaluation process is possible.

Establishing an Effective Relationship with the Client Organization

Perhaps the most important thing that happens during the entry and contracting process is a clarification of mutual expectations that can prevent later disappointments. Trust, communication, and mutual confidence are all vital to maintain a shared approach to change. Listed below are several areas where, experience shows, clarification is particularly important. Many of these apply to consultants only but others apply to change managers as well.

1. How much is the consultant to be paid?
2. How are sensitive data to be handled? (This is particularly important for internal consultants, who can be easily suspected of being conduits to top management.)
3. How much responsibility for the change is the change agent going to take and how much are managers expected to take? Establishing shared responsibility is critical.
4. Who is the client? For internal consultants this is an important question to clarify. Is the client the manager who called in the consultant, the total system he manages, or the larger corporation of which the unit is a part? There are no clear answers to this question but clarity is needed about how to handle situations in which multiple loyalties are involved.
5. What is the role of the change agent? Is he to be an expert, a facilitator, or both? Managers are so used to having consultants tell them what to do that they become uncomfortable with process consultants who push the client to make decisions.
6. Is the consultant expecting to conduct research in connection with the intervention, and if so, will it be published?

The discussion of mutual expectations inevitably leads to the question of the fit between the change agent and the client. It is possible that the change agent's and client's expectations are not mutually compatible. Moreover, the "chemistry" between the change agent and manager may not be right. It is the responsibility of the interventionist to raise the question of fit and to discuss it openly with managers. Not only will this clarify those instances where someone else is needed, but it will also further improve the relationship between manager and change agent.

Overview of the Entry and Contraction

If the top management team of an organization is not involved in reaching a consensus about the root causes of problems in their own organization and in defining future directions, the change will probably eventually falter. Each manager will have different reasons for supporting organizational improvement efforts, making it more difficult to resolve problems as they arise. Furthermore, without an explicit entry and contracting process as a *hurdle* prior to the start of an OD effort, the change agent and the management team cannot gauge whether their dissatisfaction with current conditions sufficiently exceeds anticipated difficulties (personal and political costs) to provide the energy required to move change along. Moreover, the process provides the best opportunity for the change agent and client to establish whether or not they can meet each others' expectations, thus preventing later surprises which may cause deterioration in trust and mutual confidence.

Yet, in most organization development efforts, the entry and contracting process is implicit rather than explicit. The change agent and/or management rush into major efforts to change the organization, only to find down the road that they do not agree about what they are doing and why they are doing it. Why does this occur?

In some instances, the change agent's own needs to establish his credibility or authority lead him to articulate a solution early, thus forcing him into a selling mode. A consultant may feel he needs to do this to be retained or a manager may feel he needs to do this to establish the control he perceives is consistent with his position. Starting by getting the top group to agree on problems and their causes seems weak and indecisive. In other instances the change agent (manager or consultant) may wish to avoid the discomfort of surfacing differences in views and readiness to change, and the management team colludes in this avoidance. There is an implicit assumption that somehow, once the change effort is under way, those who are early dissenters will be persuaded to come along. Unfortunately, this rarely happens.

Avoiding an explicit entry and contracting process is simply an example of the common human tendency to short-circuit steps which may lead to conflict and discomfort. The need for speedy action is also used to rationalize this avoidance. Experience and research suggests (see Chapter 3) that later problems in implementation may cost more in time and inefficiency than "front end" investments in developing understanding and commitment. Change agents must simply face up to the reality that time so invested in an explicit contracting process, and the risks associated with it, are more desirable than the problems of proceeding without commitment.

The process outlined in this section is equally applicable to a change effort managed by the key manager without consulting help as it is to one involving a professional interventionist. There is no reason why a manager could not follow, with some modifications, the essential elements of entry and contracting to test for or develop readiness for change in subordinates and to clarify mutual expectations about his role in leading the change.

Figure 5–2 presents one model for an entry and contracting process that has been found useful by some internal OD consultants (Burns & Greenberg, 1974). It presents a series of steps starting with the first contact and ending with an action plan. The first contracting meeting is the one in which the change agent and management team come together to work through many of the issues discussed in this section. This meeting must take place with the top team of the organization and may be repeated with lower level management teams as they become involved in OD plans developed at the top.

The contracting meeting is designed to develop broad strategic plans for change based on data known at the top of the organization. However, these data may not always be complete. Inevitably, the action plan developed by the top team calls for further diagnosis, a step in the organization development process discussed in the next chapter.

NOTES

1. It is impossible for an individual or group to reach the ideal implied by the term *free and informed choice*. No individual or group is fully capable of knowing itself so well that an objective assessment of all alternatives and consequences can be made. Furthermore, no individual or group is free from hidden or irrelevant (to the task) forces which influence the choice at hand. Nevertheless, an imperfect process which attempts to reach this deal will still develop more internal commitment than other approaches.

FIGURE 5–2   The entry and contracting process

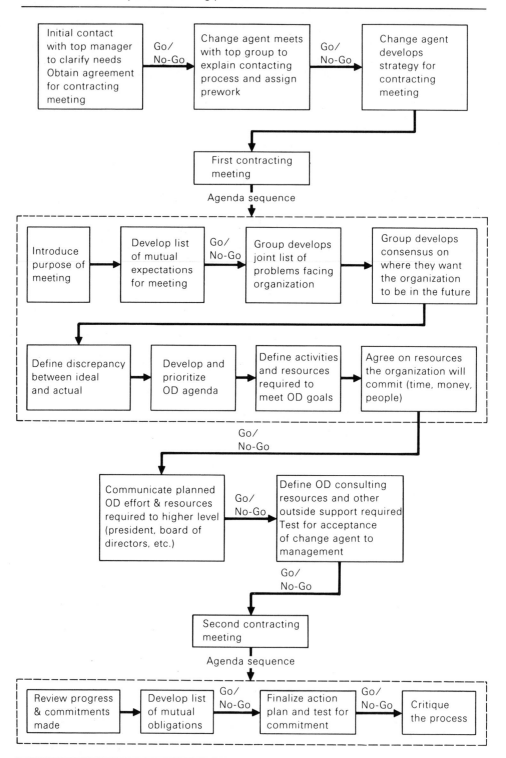

DATA COLLECTION AND DIAGNOSIS

6

The entry and contracting process usually involves only the leaders of the organization. If a decision is reached to undertake an organization change and development effort, there are often many remaining questions about the nature of the problems and their location in the organization. The contracting process is likely, therefore, to be followed by a diagnosis of the total organization or of some subparts.

Management commissions a professional OD consultant and/or an employee task force to collect data from a wide variety of people and parts of the organization. Such a process can lead to a more representative and therefore more valid diagnosis, and can also involve more people. With the diagnosis, management is for the first time making a public admission of problems and its willingness to do something about them. This stimulates people, orients them to change, and increases their willingness to provide valid data about the organization.

Thus "organizational diagnosis is the process of publicly entering a human system, collecting valid data about human experiences with that system, and feeding that information back to the system to provide understanding of the system by its members." (Alderfer, 1976).

Systematic collection of data is not a typical event nor is it a passive process of studying, researching, and learning about the organization. Diagnostic activities can themselves change the behavior and attitudes of people. As previously pointed out, optimism about management's commitment to change will increase as a result of a diagnosis. Some interventionists have found that problems and patterns of interaction can change simply as a result of the questions organizational members expect to be asked or are asked (Alderfer & Brown, 1975). Thus a diagnosis is itself an intervention. For example, as a result of interviews by an OD consultant prior to a management team-building meeting, individual managers began to exchange the answers they gave. By the time the team-building meeting was held, they had acted on one of the problems surfaced by the interviews. To do so, they had to change their patterns of communication, another problem surfaced by the interviews.

Interviews with employees also act to release feelings of frustration. Therefore,

89

morale may improve temporarily (Dickson & Rothlisberger, 1966; Rogers, 1951). However, a diagnosis is mainly a precursor to action. Sometimes it serves to uncover new problems or perspectives, but it often serves to sharpen understanding of problems vaguely felt and first articulated in the contracting process.

The major task in organizational diagnosis is collecting valid information about organizational problems, while at the same time developing motivation to act on the problems. Employees who have developed distrust of management and have given up hope that things can be better, cannot easily be candid in an interview or on a questionnaire. They either distrust the change agent and fear repercussions, or they lack the energy to provide useful data about the organization.

The diagnostic process must deal with these problems if valid and useful data is to be obtained. For this reason, how the diagnosis is announced, how people are involved in it, and what methods are used to collect information become important questions. The next several sections consider these critical issues.

APPROACHING THE ORGANIZATION

Diagnosis involves getting information from people about the organization. It involves outsiders who will move through the organization to talk with people, sit in meetings, or administer questionnaires. Unless the consultant and the diagnosis are properly introduced, distrust and lack of cooperation will prevent the interventionist from obtaining valid data. This will almost certainly be the case with managers below the top group who are not involved in the contracting process.

For these reasons, top management must introduce the consultant and the diagnosis to organizational members. If the organization is small, management can bring all employees together to explain the purpose of the diagnosis, to introduce the consultant, and to state the ground rules for handling data (issues of confidentiality). If the organization is large, top management can meet with managers at the next lower level to discuss issues surrounding the diagnosis. These managers can meet with the next level and so on down through the organization.

Regardless of how the diagnosis is introduced, management must promote a discussion with lower levels which will clarify the following questions and issues (Argyris, 1970).

1. How did the research or diagnosis begin?
2. Who invited whom?
3. How were the consultants selected?
4. To whom will feedback be given or a report sent?
5. What kind of data is to be included in the feedback?
6. How is the project to be financed?
7. How can people in the organization be helped to participate or not participate?
8. The probable fears that employees may have about trusting the consultant.
9. The fears the consultant and/or management may have about whether to trust the responses of people in the organization to interviews or questionnaires.
10. The invitation to confront the consultant on any concerns or issues.
11. What may happen if anyone prefers not to become involved or provide information for the diagnosis.

12. The consultant's and management's awareness of how much they depend on people in the organization for a successful and valid diagnosis. They should communicate their recognition that if trust is not present, the entire diagnosis is questionable. The consultants should invite people to tell them if they feel there are valid reasons why the project may fail.

There are likely to be differences among various types of organizations in the ease with which a diagnosis can be introduced. In business and government organizations where authority is centered at the top, a decision by top management to proceed with a diagnosis is likely to be sufficient to gain the cooperation of lower level managers in setting up meetings to discuss the issues previously listed. In looser organizations, such as universities, certain community agencies, volunteer organizations, community action groups, and professional organizations, where authority is more diffuse, the process of launching a diagnosis is likely to be more difficult and therefore different (Alderfer, 1976). Following agreement on a diagnosis with the head of the organization, the change agent may have to contract for the diagnosis with each subunit before proceeding with a meeting to clarify the issues. Often the most practical way of doing this is to bring the heads of each major subunit together in a committee to explain the diagnosis and obtain agreement on the procedure for carrying it out.

Agreement to proceed in the system-wide diagnosis and the process used to obtain this agreement is crucial. Organizational members' willingness to respond positively to the diagnosis is largely determined at this point.

A CONCEPTUAL FRAMEWORK FOR DIAGNOSIS

The problem in many organizations is that people are not able to step away from their immediate experiences or frustrations and see them as a pattern indicative of systemic problems. An important contribution of the change agent is providing a framework for collecting and analyzing data that will allow an analysis of the organization as a system (Buchanan, 1967). For this, the organization will often need a professional interventionist.

Chapter 2 provided a very broad systems framework for diagnosis. Interviews, questionnaires, and observations could focus on getting data in all or some of these categories. However, there are many other broad frameworks which might be used (Blake & Mouton, 1968b; Kotter, 1978; Likert, 1967). Levinson (1972) provides a framework for organizational diagnosis organized much like a psychiatric examination. It includes the following major categories of information.

1. Genetic Data
   A. Identifying information
   B. Historical data
2. Description and Analysis of Current Organization as a Whole
   A. Structural data (equipment, policy, personnel systems)
   B. Process data (communication, decision making, etc.)
3. Interpretive Data
   A. Current organizational functioning (entire atmosphere, use of knowledge, awareness, reality, etc.)
   B. Attitudes and relationships (relations to peers, customers, and between groups, etc.)

91

4. Analysis and Conclusion
   A. Organizational integrative patterns (post, current, and future effects of environ-
      ment on organization and vice versa)
   B. Summary and recommendations

Typically, a broad systems framework is most useful during the entry and contracting process when a diagnosis of the total social system is required to pinpoint major problem areas. Once these problem areas have been identified, narrower theories and frameworks can be useful in diagnosing a single dimension or a particular problem of interest in the social system (Beer, 1976). For example, if a social system diagnosis indicates that one of several problems facing the organization is that clerical employees lack challenging work, then a more detailed diagnosis of clerical jobs and the attitudes of employees in these jobs might be performed. Such a diagnosis could use the job design theory and associated measurement tools developed by Hackman and Oldham, which will be dis-cussed in Chapter 10 (Hackman, 1977; Hackman & Oldham, 1975). For problems in coordination between functions, such as marketing and manufacturing, the organization/ environment theory of Lawrence & Lorsch (1967, 1969) could be used for a diagnosis (see Corning Glass Works cases in Appendix for an example). There are numerous other theories which could be useful in diagnosing specific organizational dimensions.[1] The important thing is that the theory be conceptually useful and thought to be valid.

WHO SHOULD GATHER THE DATA?

One of the key issues in diagnosis has to do with the degree of involvement by members of the organization. Traditional social science research approaches (influenced by the physical sciences) have emphasized the importance of distance between the researcher and the subjects of the research. The social scientist is advised to tell as little as possible to research subjects about the purpose of the research, and to interact with them as little as possible for fear that the data collected will become contaminated. Similarly, following the medical model of diagnosis, social scientists engaged in helping the organizations improve their effectiveness often perform the diagnosis, make their own interpretation, and tell management what should be done.

In organizational diagnosis, this is not sufficient. One of the purposes of the diagnosis is to clarify and raise employee levels of consciousness about problems so they will act on them. It is not likely, nor does experience suggest, that the readiness to act will be high when the diagnosis is conducted by the interventionist in isolation from organizational members. Such a diagnostic approach places the members of the organization in a relationship with the interventionist that is quite similar to the relationship between an authoritarian manager and dependent subordinate (Argyris, 1968, 1970). Organizational members in this situation comply with the interventionist by filling out questionnaires or being interviewed, but they display little interest in the problems being diagnosed and are not likely to be energized to action.

For many of the same reasons, the validity of the data collected by this process is suspect. This is particularly true in the diagnosis of organizations, where members can answer accurately, but not necessarily "honestly." Data are valid to the extent that people are in touch with their deepest feelings and frustrations about their work experience. A diagnostic process that keeps employees at a distance is *not* likely to create conditions for surfacing these kinds of data. There are many methods for involving employees in diagnosis (Alderfer, 1976; Argyris, 1970). These will be examined in the next section and in more detail in Chapter 8.

Organization development practice has tended to emphasize the involvement of organizational members in diagnosis for many of the reasons cited. Perhaps the strongest reason is that historically, much of OD practice has been aimed at changing the behavior and attitudes of individuals and groups. Its approach to organizational change has thus been patterned after psychotherapy practices, where the client must come to understand himself before change is possible.

But in organizational development, as we have already seen, changes in behavior can also be brought about by changes in organization structure, rewards, and measurement systems. These changes are within the control of a small group of managers at the top of the organization. Because changes in organization design are intended to have an impact on the behavior of others, they do not always require high levels of self-understanding. Thus, they can be based on analysis done by consultants rather than emotional understanding developed through involvement in the diagnosis.

There are still other reasons for viewing the question of client involvement as contingent on a number of situational factors. In organization development, as compared with group development, large numbers of people are involved—sometimes more than can be brought into a participative process of data collection. Sometimes, an emergency requires a rapid diagnosis which makes it practically impossible to involve many people. There are also situations where the client's motivation is already high and further involvement is not necessary. All of this suggests that there may be times when less, rather than more client involvement is called for.

The interventionist is faced with a choice between *client-centered* diagnosis with high involvement by members of the organization, and a *consultant-centered* diagnosis with relatively less involvement (except of course, for answering questions). There are many considerations that go into this choice and some of these have been listed in Table 6–1. Indeed, the question is not whether employees should be completely involved or not involved at all. It is to what *extent the client should be involved* in the diagnosis.

The considerations listed in Table 6–1 can be helpful in answering the question of how much client involvement in the diagnosis is needed. It can be seen that a *client-centered* diagnosis is more appropriate when the organizational problem involves core issues—the behavior and attitudes of the client, when the client's involvement is needed to increase motivation to change, and when the people in the client organization are relatively sophisticated and can carry out the diagnosis themselves. On the other hand, a *consultant-centered* diagnosis is more appropriate when the organizational problems involve systems and structures, when the motivation to change is high and involvement is not needed to increase it, and when the problem is subtle and requires consultant expertise.

METHODS OF DATA COLLECTION

While the process by which data are collected is of crucial importance in influencing data validity and usefulness, the methods chosen to collect data also influence these outcomes. This section will briefly outline the methods available and the strategic considerations in choosing one or the other method, many of which have their roots in the social sciences. Other sources provide a more detailed or technical discussion of these methods (Nadler, 1977; Bouchard, 1976).

TABLE 6–1 When to use consultant vs. client-centered diagnosis

Considerations	Client-Centered	Consultant-Centered
Intended effect on behavior and attitude	Direct—data are intended to affect attitudes and behavior	Indirect—data are intended to change policies and structure which in turn affect behavior
Primary data recipient or client	The people who receive the data are the change targets	The people reviewing the data are not the change targets. They must make decisions affecting others.
Content of the problem diagnosed	Behavior, interaction, and attitudes in the organization	Structures, systems and policies which affect behavior
Basis of acceptance and commitment	Change in values or norms coming from involvement	Rational analysis and logic
Specificity of request for diagnosis	Vague and ambiguous about problems	Specific and clear statement of problem and information needed
Extent of client comfort and skill in examining process	High levels of process awareness	Low levels of process awareness
Client-consultant relationship	Low levels of trust	High levels of trust
Subtlety and complexity of problem and its causes	Relatively clear and simple	Complex and very subtle
Extent to which data threaten client directly	Low threat. Data do not deal with issues of competence nor will they affect issues of power	High threat. Data reflects on competence and will affect issues of power
Motivation to change	Low	High
Breadth of diagnosis	System-wide	Narrow—focus is one dimension of the organization

There are four basic methods for collecting data on how organizations function and how people in them feel and behave.

1. *The interview.* The simplest and most direct way to find out what is going on in an organization is to ask people. Their experiences of satisfaction or frustration, their description of how things work, and their analysis of problems can paint a rather quick and rich picture of the organization.

   There are several types of interviews. On the one extreme is the *unstructured* interview, in which the interviewer asks very general questions and provides little guidance. On the other extreme is the *structured* interview, in which the interviewer asks very specific questions and guides answers into predetermined response categories (yes or no; or, very satisfied, partially satisfied, etc.) There are many degrees of structure in between.

2. *The questionnaire.* Because a questionnaire is self-administered, it can be given to many people at once. In many questionnaires the questions are standardized and the responses fixed; the data are quantifiable. There are many methods for asking questions and obtaining responses. These methods have been widely researched for their reliability (degree to which the same response will be obtained at another time). Many different questionnaires have been developed and are available for measuring dimensions of organizational behavior (Shaw & Wright, 1967). A change agent can

utilize these or develop his own to ask questions relevant to a given situation and in a language familiar to people in the organization.

3. *Observations.* A change agent can gather an enormous amount of useful data through observing what people do in an organization. All of the interactions and behaviors of the client during entry and contracting provide information about the client system. Furthermore, a change agent may choose to sit in on meetings or roam through an organization during the diagnostic phase to learn through observation. Observation allows the data collector to be directly in touch with behavior in the organization, thus eliminating the bias of the employee's perceptions. However, the bias of the observer is substituted. Observations can be recorded informally or formally through the use of guidelines, check lists, specific questions, and response categories.

4. *Secondary data.* Organizations collect enormous amounts of data as part of their routine operations. Financial data on costs and profits as well as data on absenteeism, turnover, and grievances are often available. Similarly, there are memos, and internal and external reports. All of these sources of data can be tapped by the change agent without interfering with people's work and at a relatively low investment in time and effort.

Each of these methods has distinct advantages and disadvantages which must be understood. In general, no one method is ideal and, as we shall see, each is best complemented by another. The following criteria can be used to evaluate the four major methods of data collection:

Richness— The extent to which the method elicits information about people's feelings, the complexity of events, and underlying rationale and motivation for behavior.

Conveys empathy—The extent to which the method conveys to people the concern and interest of the change agent, thus encouraging them to reveal deeper-held attitudes.

Efficiency—The cost (time and money) of administering and analyzing the data obtained by a given method.

Flexibility—The extent to which questions can be revised or new ones asked as a result of information obtained from an earlier question.

Validity—The extent of bias stemming from the predisposition of the person providing the data and from the person collecting the data.

Ease of analysis   The ease with which the data can be categorized, quantified, and
and presentation— summarized, as well as ease with which they can be represented.

Table 6–2 summarizes some of the advantages and disadvantages of each method, using these criteria.

In general, to obtain the best possible results on all criteria, these methods ought to be mixed. Recent research has demonstrated that proper sequencing of methods not only offers the most efficient but also the most valid data (Alderfer, 1968; Alderfer & Brown, 1975, Argyris, 1970; Keleman, 1968). Sitting in on meetings to observe and get to know the business of the organization, helps build the rapport needed to obtain valid information. This prepares organizational members to talk comfortably and openly in interviews and helps consultants get a better understanding of the organization. With this understanding, they can ask better questions in unstructured and semistructured interviews. These interviews are useful in further developing a comprehensive and in-depth under- **95**

TABLE 6–2   A comparison of different methods of data collection

Method	Major Advantages	Major Potential Problems
Interviews	1. Source of rich data 2. Convey empathy 3. Flexible—can revise as interview proceeds 4. Increases validity by building rapport	1. Efficiency—consumes time and is costly 2. Validity—interviewer can bias responses and bias can influence analysis 3. Ease of analysis—difficult to code and quantify
Questionnaire	1. Efficiency—can use with large samples at relatively low cost 2. Validity—responses can be quantified and are not subject to bias of analyst 3. Ease of analysis and presentation—large volume of data can be analyzed and presented	1. Conveys little empathy and thus reduces depth of data 2. Provides little richness and thus makes interpretation of data difficult 3. Flexibility—may miss important issues 4. Validity—various response biases such as leniency may reduce validity 5. Ease of presentation—numbers may not energize people
Observation	1. Validity—data on actual behavior rather than reports of behavior 2. Validity—real time, not retrospective 3. Flexibility—can easily shift focus	1. Ease of analysis—difficult to code and quantify 2. Efficiency—costly and time-consuming 3. Validity—limited sample and potential observer bias 4. Empathy—can potentially create feelings of being manipulated, unless unobtrusive
Secondary Data	1. Validity—high credibility and no response bias 2. Ease of analysis—good for financial data 3. Efficiency—not costly to obtain and usually not costly to analyze	1. Flexibility—can only analyze phenomena on which data exist 2. Validity—data largely self-report 3. Ease of analysis—coding and interpretation problems except for financial data 4. Empathy—no relationship developed with people 5. Richness—generally low

Adapted from David A. Nadler, *Feedback and Organization Development: Using Data-Based Methods,* © 1977, Addison-Wesley, Reading, Mass., Table 7.1. Reprinted with permission.

standing of the organization's problems and their interrelationships. In effect, observations and interviews allow a diagnosis of the total social system. When this has occurred, questionnaires can be constructed to measure specific dimensions of the organization with reasonable efficiency and with better motivation by respondents to provide valid data, than if questionnaires were used immediately.

Such a data collection process was used in a diagnosis of a business unit experiencing problems of coordination and intergroup conflict (Beer, 1971d). Data collection started with observations in meetings, was followed by interviews, and then by more focused questionnaires which quantified the perceptions of intergroup relations across the whole organization. A comprehensive organizational diagnosis is likely to require such a "system of measurement." It has the distinct advantage of allowing one method to confirm results obtained by another (Campbell & Fisk, 1959).

The discussion so far has not explicitly mentioned an often overlooked method of measurement. The consultant or diagnostician is himself a measure of what is going on in an organization. He should not ignore his own reactions to people and organizational activities as the intervention process unfolds. If a consultant feels uncomfortable, insecure, overcontrolled, or that people are withholding information, to mention only a few potential reactions, it is an important piece of data about the organization (Alderfer, 1968; Levinson, 1972). The consultant should periodically ask, "How am I feeling about my interactions with people in the organization." "What's my reaction to what I see?" Being in touch with one's own feelings can surface important insights about the organization.

FEEDBACK OF DATA

Collecting data about problems, even when that process has appropriately involved organizational members, is not enough. There are many examples of elaborate data collection efforts which resulted in little or no change. For example, a major data collection effort came to an unsuccessful end when, in the final feedback meeting, the managers questioned the validity of data, strayed frequently from discussing them, and generally displayed defensiveness and a lack of motivation to work on problems raised by the data.

Many of the problems that occur during feedback are a result of failures in the entry and contracting phase to detect lack of motivation or to try and create it. They may also be due to a lack of involvement during the data collection phase. However, some of the problems are due to factors in the feedback process itself (Klein, Kraut, Wolfson, 1971; Nadler, 1976).

Feedback does not automatically lead to change. As seen in Figure 6–1, feedback of data must first motivate the recipients to act. Perhaps the most important factor in energizing action is that the feedback occur in some sort of group meeting in which the key people who can act on the data are present. A written report is not sufficient. The group setting not only ensures that discussions needed to resolve issues occur, but it can stimulate greater interest and group pressures for action. Several other factors inherent in the feedback meeting—*content* and *process*—are also related to the energy released by the feedback and the extent to which this energy is channeled into problem solving, rather than defensiveness.

Feedback Content

To motivate action (see Figure 6–1), data itself must be seen as meaningful and relevant to the recipients. That is, it must be about those aspects of organizational functioning that directly relate to the day-to-day lives of the people receiving the feedback. The feedback report must avoid jargon and should be expressed in the words of people in the organization. The validity of the data in the eyes of the recipients can be enhanced by reviewing the procedure used to collect it and the sample from which it was drawn. Furthermore, the amount of data needs to be limited so that it can be properly digested. Too often, data overload causes attention to stray and energy to decline. Finally, the data must be about problems the group can do something about. This suggests that data about the organization as a whole should be fed back to top management while each lower level group receives data only about its own operations.

97

FIGURE 6-1   Possible effects of feedback

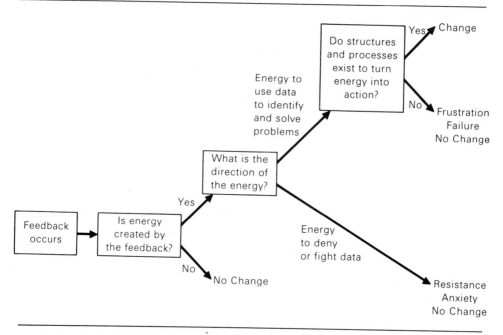

From David A. Nadler, *Feedback and Organization Development: Using Data-Based Methods,* © 1977, Addison-Wesley, Reading, Mass. Figure 8.1. Reprinted with permission.

Feedback Process

Even if the data energize the recipients, this energy, as Figure 6-1 shows, can be mobilized to deny, resist, and repudiate as was the case in the earlier example. This defensive behavior protects the group from the anxiety associated with discussing negative information about the group as a whole. Not only may a group want to protect its perception of itself as effective, it may also want to protect individuals' perceptions of themselves as competent. the greatest fear is that the boss may be hurt sufficiently that he becomes an ineffectual leader or that he will react negatively and punish others in the organization.

These fears are often well out of proportion to what typically happens in feedback meetings and can be reduced if the change agent is nonevaluative, matter-of-fact, and descriptive about findings. A simple presentation of how people perceive problems and their consequences avoids accusation, faultfinding, and attribution of motives to recipients of the feedback (Anderson, undated). Avoiding these reduces anxiety and defensiveness and enhances the likelihood that the group will engage in an open discussion of the data. Avoiding defensiveness on the part of the boss is particularly important since this reaction would immediately raise anxiety and resistance in the group. The change agent can do much to prevent any of these reactions and to promote problem solving by preparing the boss for feedback with a preview of diagnostic results, and by coaching him in how to respond constructively. Finally, a discussion with the group about these dynamics prior to the meeting and some simple ground rules for discussing difficult issues (to be discussed further in Chapter 9) can promote the risk taking which will be required to deal with difficult issues. People come into feedback meetings with hopes as well as anxieties—hopes that things can improve. Avoidance of negative reactions early in the meeting reinforces these hopes and promotes risk taking. In short, the feedback meeting process must be stage-managed by the manager and/or consultant to avoid defensiveness and promote open discussion and problem solving (Schein, 1969).

Below is a summary of the major elements which must be present for a feedback meeting to be successful:

1. *Agreement about* the *data* to be collected and *method* of feedback should be developed prior to data collection.
2. The *feedback* should be *consistent with expectations* of managers developed in number 1 above.
3. Feedback should be provided in a *group setting* where open discussion can be promoted. An *off-site* meeting which provides a relaxed setting often helps.
4. Data must be *relevant* to important concerns of the group, must be *understandable,* and must not overload recipients with information.
5. The group must be *able to do something* about the data themselves.
6. The *process* of the meeting must be *managed* to avoid defensiveness and promote risk taking and problem solving.
7. The *change agent* must be trained to *manage* the *meeting* process so that the objectives in 6 above are achieved.

NOTES

1. There are several other examples of such theories. For a diagnosis of pay systems and their impact on motivation and satisfaction, Lawler's psychological theory of pay might be used (Lawler, 1971, 1977). For a diagnosis of leadership and supervisory style, Fiedler's theory of leadership might be used (Fiedler, 1967).

7 PLANNING AND MANAGING CHANGE

A successful feedback meeting, where management is stimulated to change, can often lead to a state of euphoria so high that people neglect to ask the pragmatic questions, "What should we become?" or "Who should do what when, where, and how?" The management team leaves the feedback meeting with strong motivation to change but only the vaguest idea about the form of the change or the specific activities that will lead up to it. Part of the reason for this often lies in inadequate time allotted in the feedback meeting to planning and managing change. To avoid frustration and failure (see Figure 6–1) after a successful feedback meeting, substantial attention to these issues must be given during and after the meeting.

DEVELOPING AND TESTING POSSIBLE SOLUTIONS

A management team must translate diagnostic insights into specific and concrete ideas about how a problem may be solved. For example, managers in an organization experiencing intergroup conflict may not know how to alleviate these problems short of removing people. Yet there are other possibilities, such as improving communication and relations or creating structures which will promote coordination.

While organizational members know a lot about their own organization, it is sometimes difficult for them to envision new options. Change agents play a critical role in this process, bringing new ideas and potential solutions that, as managers or consultants, they have found useful in other organizations (see Chapter 3). Sometimes, reading about new ideas and approaches can stimulate the development of options, or specialists in certain innovations can be brought in to present their ideas. Together with the expertise managers have about their own organization, new ways of doing things or new structural solutions can often be jointly developed. This "increases" managers' understanding of new options and helps them make an informed choice, thereby increasing commitment.

Unanticipated outcomes of change can cause disillusionment, feelings of manipulation, resentment, frustration, or disappointment. These feelings create loss of motivation and reduce momentum just when momentum is crucial. There are two typical reasons for these unanticipated outcomes. First, managers rush into change without spending sufficient time understanding all the ramifications. Second, even if all the ramifications are understood, key people in the organization are not informed about them and contingency plans are not developed to deal with them. For example, a new plant start-up, in which major innovations in job design were incorporated (all work was done in autonomous production teams), fell well below scheduled production goals in the first year. This in turn resulted in pressures on the plant from higher management, and for a time jeopardized the change momentum in the plant.

To avoid these problems, it is important that the change agent lead organizational members through a process of *anticipatory testing*. This process involves projecting the consequences for people and profits of each change alternative. A change agent, who is experienced in planned innovations, can help managers understand potential consequences by asking questions which cause them to anticipate, or by projecting consequences to clarify what might happen. Sometimes this is not enough, and the only way for managers to get a real appreciation of what the change will mean is to experience it vicariously. They can visit organizations that have adopted the contemplated change, allowing firsthand discussions with people who have been through similar organizational improvement efforts. Such visits seem to be required when major innovations are being contemplated (Myerseth, 1977).

Another approach change agents often take is to create small-scale changes in one part of the organization to provide managers firsthand experience with positive and negative outcomes. A small, successful experiment in moving away from assembly line operations in one department of a plant, despite problems associated with it, provided a clearer idea of counterbalancing benefits. It helped management gather motivation and competence in planning larger-scale changes (Beer & Huse, 1972).

ACTION PLANNING

During the option development and testing phase, the general outline of an organizational solution is developed. For example, it is determined if an affirmative action program will be needed, or if a matrix structure is appropriate. However, to implement a major organizational change and development effort effectively, a specific plan for action is required. Such a plan specifies what, who, when, and even *how* change is to be carried out. An action plan may include:

1. communication meetings about the changes planned;
2. individual attendance at training programs;
3. timing for specific structural changes and the steps that will be taken to clarify roles;
4. new meetings or meeting formats;
5. creating a new evaluation system;
6. designating task forces to work on problems;
7. transferring and promoting individuals to support change;
8. collecting further data about specific problems;
9. changing accounting or control systems;
10. intervention, such as team building or intergroup meetings; and
11. developing support for change from key individuals whose commitment is needed. **101**

The action plan is a plan for the "process" (Beckhard & Harris, 1977) by which change is to be brought about, not the content of each step. The plan is flexible and reviewed periodically to make changes based on the experience with prior steps. The fact that the action plan specifies goals, a path to these goals and allows measurement of results, enhances motivation (Lock, Cartledge, & Keppel, 1968).

It is important that (1) an action be formally recorded in a memo and a copy provided to each individual; (2) individual responsibilities and dates are specified; (3) there is advanced agreement about review dates; (4) individuals are given the time to accomplish goals; and (5) they are rewarded for accomplishing their part of the action plans. Too often managers are expected to accomplish their change goals in addition to their routine goals. This creates a situation in which one set of goals, usually the change goals, tends to suffer. Change goals are more risky, typically less well rewarded, and require new competence. For this reason, an effective action plan must be accompanied by transition structures that differentiate change activities from routine activities, and reward their achievement (Beckhard & Harris, 1977).

MANAGING ORGANIZATIONAL TRANSITIONS

If an action plan for change is to succeed, an enormous amount of activity must follow. Observers of change have noted that because organizational changes often follow a crisis, they demand a lot of time and energy from managers at a time when they are at least able to invest the energy required to achieve change momentum. The demands are particularly heavy on top managers and leaders in the system, who travel to all parts of the organization communicating about changes, clarifying new goals and roles, resolving conflicts, and encouraging change. Furthermore, change managers must often go through the emotional trauma of replacing people in key positions throughout the organization. For these reasons, many change agents become overloaded during the transition phase and they and the organization pay a price. They may lose energy and simply become worn-out by the job of managing change. The organization may lose effectiveness as important routine problems get less attention than they require and new and secondary problems develop.

Any change program involves a fairly lengthy period of implementation. For major changes in large complex organizations, such a period may be years. During the transition, the greatest danger is a loss of momentum. What are the causes of this and how might change be managed to ensure continued momentum?

Sustaining Motivation to Carry out Plans

As people begin to engage in the change activities and the magnitude of the emotional and material investment required are first realized, motivation and enthusiasm for the change will be significantly reduced. For the first time, people in the organization may realize that certain present satisfactions, such as the pleasure of pursuing old goals or behaving in accustomed ways, will have to be given up if new performance levels are to be accomplished.

There are typically four areas in which organizational members may experience losses due to change:

1. *Loss of competence.* Most changes place demands on organizational members for new attitudes, skills, and behavior as former ways of doing things must be discarded.

The sense of competence which comes from successful performance of old roles is diminished before insecurity and threat associated with new role demands can be overcome.

2. *Loss of relationships.* Organizational changes typically mean new interaction patterns as people are reassigned or new settings for decision making are created. The loss of familiar and valued relationships and the energy required to work out new ones is experienced as a cost of change by those affected. At the plant level, the introduction of autonomous work teams typically results in the creation of new relationships, as does the introduction of project or business teams when an organization moves to matrix. (Matrix is a form of organization to be discussed in Chapter 10.)

3. *Loss of power.* There are few organizational changes that do not result in a shift in power and influence. Some parts of the organization and some role incumbents gain power while others lose it. For example, creating more challenging jobs on the shop floor reduces the traditional power of the first line supervisor and usually results in resistance to change.

4. *Loss of extrinsic rewards.* Organizational changes result in increased compensation and perquisites (offices, cars, parking spaces, etc.) for some. Others may lose rewards or see fewer opportunities for a significant increase in them in the future.

As organizational members come face to face with these changes in their psychological contract they begin to lose motivation to change, motivation which may have been high in the planning stages. Organization inertia is intensified. Lippitt, Watson, and Westerley (1958) give the following example of this phenomenon.

A case in point is a hospital experiencing acute morale problems in its regular nursing staff. A survey showed that the problems were caused, at least in part, by certain types of authoritarian procedures practiced by the head nurses—and the head nurses themselves became fully aware of what they were doing. In a series of discussion groups they explored ways in which these procedures might be changed. But these discussions produced very little change. The discussions had given the head nurses a clear intellectual understanding of what was wrong but had failed to commit them wholly to the necessary change effort. In other words, the intentions of the head nurses were still indeterminate and they needed to explore more deeply the question of precisely what would have to be given up in order to accomplish their ultimate aims.

Loss of motivation can also occur after a change has actually been made. In one instance, two years after an organization moved from a functional structure to a matrix which demands more delegation, competence, and collaboration, management decided to abandon the new structure. The problems of making the structure work outweighed their previous perceptions of the benefits. The managers found that they lacked the skills and attitudes required for the change. A further cause of the regression was their feeling of being overburdened with meetings when their time was extremely limited.

The change agent cannot create motivation where it does not exist, but he can listen, encourage, support, coach, educate, and counsel. These actions will reduce frustration and anxiety and thereby prevent loss of motivation. Sometimes the most effective strategy is to help the client regress to an earlier state and evaluate the effectiveness of this previous state. In the case described above, the regression back to a functional structure was short-lived because the managers began to relive problems which had caused the need for change in the first place. The comparison of the solutions' relative effectiveness **103** was easier because both had now been experienced. The consultant's role in motivating the managers was to help them accurately assess the costs and benefits of a change despite their emotional upset at the time.

Finally, continued enthusiasm by the change agent, particularly when he is the manager, can support sagging motivation. Extensively communicating his expectations for change to all parts of the organization will be seen as support for the change and will motivate people to adopt it.

Linking

Because organizations are systems, a planned change in one part often must be accompanied by changes in other parts of the organization. For example, a change in organization structure may require changes in people, compensation systems, job descriptions, control systems, and corporate policy. To obtain these complementary changes, the change agent will have to communicate with staff groups and corporate management who have responsibility for these interdependent dimensions and parts of the organization. He must help them understand how their policies and practices impinge on the planned change and get their cooperation in modifying them. Similarly, change in one functional department may require complementary changes in other functional units because these units are interdependent in accomplishing their tasks.

Change efforts have frequently failed because the necessary linkages were not established. When organization structures and jobs change, the old job evaluation and compensation systems often retard the change because they don't fit. One organization was unable to implement job enrichment because the Industrial Relations division would not reevaluate the newly enriched jobs.

Perhaps the most frequent reason for the regression of change is a failure by people in the change target to keep top management informed and obtain their support. Top management not only can influence the attitudes of staff groups, but they control the movement of key managers in and out of a subunit. Nothing can slow the progress of change more than the replacement of key managers with individuals who are not supportive of the implemented changes.

Developing a Support System

Change is not only difficult for people at lower levels in the organization but also for the change agent. The change agent should maintain a discrepancy between himself and the organization. He cannot do this, however, if he is dependent on people in the organization for emotional support. Thus he is forced to maintain "psychological distance" from others. The tensions created by this relationship, while useful to the organization, can significantly reduce the change agent's confidence and the thrust he needs to move change along.

For this reason, change agents often need to create support systems for themselves. A support system is a network of people with whom one has close relationships. These people can provide emotional support while also helping the change agent confront his own assumptions. Top managers creating major organizational changes often develop a support system by replacing key people who report to them with managers who they know and on whose loyalty they can count. While a loyal staff may provide emotional support, they may not always provide the clash of ideas needed to keep improvement efforts on track. Internal OD specialists often find support from peers within their own staff group, or

from professionals outside the corporation who offer an environment of congruent values.

It is important that change agents recognize the need for a support system and plan to build one in advance of the difficult periods that are an inevitable part of major organizational transitions. Not to do so is to plant the seeds of one's own destruction and perhaps those of the improvement effort. It is important however, that the support system not become so supportive that the change agent is sealed from confrontation of his basic assumptions (Argyris & Schon, 1976).

Developing Competence of Those Involved in Taking Action

Change requires new skills and competence on the part of organizational members. Sometimes new technical skills are required, but most often, the biggest demand is for interpersonal skills. A change may require stronger leadership, more delegation, more openness, less controlling behavior, more listening, more collaboration, and so on. That is, change requires reorientation of a person's values, attitudes, beliefs, and behavior. It is the lack of personal competence or adaptability which often prevents change from occurring. Someone may know how to be directive, but has never learned to be participative, and therefore is tied to old behavior by necessity, not choice.

The change agent must help those involved in the change to adopt new behavior. Where knowledge is required, traditional training programs can be used. But in the area of personal competence, on-the-job counseling and coaching is required. Small group discussions that explore behavior changes, workshops in which new behaviors are practiced through role playing, or other experience-based training methods can be used. These methods must be integrated into the overall change plan. There are numerous methods for helping people change and these will be discussed in Chapter 11.

FOLLOW-UP STRUCTURES

The discussion above clearly suggests that *the most* important problem facing organizations (groups or large systems) in the transition phase is follow-up. Follow-up is the key to sustaining motivation, developing emotional support for managers and change agents, linking, and developing competence. The importance of follow-up is supported by research which demonstrates that consultant involvement before and after team-building interventions was associated with greater effectiveness when compared to team-building interventions in which there was little consultant involvement (Friedlander, 1968). Similarly, Frohman (1970) reports that consultant help and guidance increased the effectiveness of survey feedback interventions.

While it's not clear from these reports what the consultants did, it is likely that they helped people develop competence needed to move change along, brought people and groups together, helped the client to review progress, provided emotional support, and in general served as a symbol and prod for change. There is no one way to follow-up. By definition, follow-up activities are organic and can only be planned in response to events as they develop. What can be specified are the managerial structures and processes that have been found useful in planning and ensuring follow-up (Beckhard & Harris, 1977).

First and foremost, there is a need for one person to be the project leader for the implementation phase. While this may be the general manager or chief executive officer, in many change efforts it can also be an internal consultant, a manager, or a personnel specialist assigned to the organization.

For example, in a major change at a railroad, the new chief executive took responsibility for the initial phases of change but later brought in an outsider he was close to who, **105** as executive vice-president, was given the responsibility to manage the change in its implementation phase. When a large aerospace company decided to move to a matrix organization, the Vice-President of Industrial Relations and personnel specialists reporting to him were given the responsibility for managing the change.

If the person with the project management responsibility is an organizational member, dependence on external consulting resources is reduced and the organization has a better chance of developing a capacity for renewal.

It is equally important that the person managing the change have certain qualifications (Beckhard & Harris, 1977; Beer, 1976).

1. The person should have clout and be able to mobilize the resources needed to keep change moving.
2. The person should have credibility with key executives and all the other major constituencies in the organization.
3. The person should have access to all levels and parts of the organization to make good communications possible (linking).
4. The person should have the interpersonal skills and the OD consulting skills needed to counsel, coach, support, encourage, help, train, and educate the people affected by the change.
5. The person should understand the innovations or changes being attempted so that he can act as an expert in helping managers understand the changes being implemented.
6. The persons should be skillful in some OD interventions needed to move change along—particularly process interventions. Specialists can be called in for other interventions (examined in the next four chapters).

The assignment of a person to the role of change manager is not sufficient. Structures and processes must be developed that involve others in the planning, implementation, and review of change. The more people formally designated and assigned roles in the change plan, the better. Such structures and processes sometimes create commitment to change by those involved where none existed before; they provide support mechanisms for managers who must act as change agents; they provide clarity about the dual tasks before the organization—running the business and managing change; they provide a critical mass of people who become concerned about the progress of change.

Many alternative structures are possible (Beckhard & Harris, 1977). Their main feature is the assignment of change responsibilities, in addition to normal job responsibilities, to a group or groups of people (see Case 7–1 for example).

1. *The hierarchy.* Responsibility for managing parts of the transition are given as additional work to managers in the hierarchy. For example, while introducing matrix, functional managers were given responsibilities as coaches and counselors to business teams. Their job was to help these teams become effective.
2. *Representatives of constituencies.* A group made up of representatives from different constituencies is given the responsibility for managing the change. In many quality-of-work projects aimed at democratizing the organization, improving productivity and making work more satisfying, union-management committees plan and manage the change. In an example of a nonunion plant, a task force of production, clerical, and managerial employees was assigned the responsibility for managing a change.

CASE 7–1

A large manufacturing company embarked on an organizational improvement effort aimed at increasing integration between marketing, manufacturing, and R&D. A structural change to a matrix organization (see Chapter 10) was decided on by the top management team and a series of changes in roles and decision-making processes were to accompany this change. An OD steering committee was formed to help the top manager and the OD consultant monitor the change and provide additional consulting help to managers. The committee was composed of ten people representing a multifunctional diagonal slice of the organization. The internal OD consultant became the working chairman for the committee. But, the top manager was the formal chairman.

The committee received training from outside consultants in the problem of transitioning to a matrix. They met periodically to pool information about how the change was going and to report to the top manager about their findings. The OD consultant periodically asked members to assist in diagnosis and interventions. Once a year, steering committee mmbers became involved in a formal diagnosis of progress in organizational change, and made recommendations about further steps which might be taken to assure that change progressed satisfactorily.

The committee served several useful purposes. It broadened the constituency for change by deeply involving ten key people who played important roles in the marix at various levels. The OD steering committee served as an important sensing mechanism for ongoing diagnosis of problems. For example, when problems on one business team developed, one of the OD steering committee members became an important source of data to the OD consultants about the problems and a source of ideas about their solution. The steering committee provided additional change resources to help with diagnosis and interventions. Finally, the OD steering committee became a formal mechanism for reminding managers throughout the organization about what they had to do to keep change moving along successfully. The committee particularly served as a reminder to top managers about expectations for improvement which they had created themselves in announcing the matrix organization.

3. *Task force of change agents.* When many consultants and change managers are involved in an organizational improvement effort, they can be brought together as a task force to manage change. In a large company, planning to change work structures in several plants, a group of corporate and plant personnel people together with outside consultants formed such a team.

4. *Natural leaders.* When there are informal leaders in the organization, their involvement as a task force to manage change can add support and credibility to the change. They automatically carry the trust and confidence of organizational members. For example, in a professional association, these might be high status professionals who have high visibility and serve as role models to others.

5. *A diagonal slice of the organization.* Particularly when a change cuts across many different levels and functions, a task force composed of representatives from these **107**

levels and functions can be used to manage change. This representative can help in "sensing" how the change is going in different subparts of the organization, implementing change activities, and recommending modifications in change strategy.

These and other structures can be set up to ensure that the work needed to support change continues. Whatever their composition, groups can be involved in planning, monitoring, evaluating, rediagnosing, and reviewing change. In hierarchical organizations, these groups must be linked, through a review process, to the top management team who carry the power to help move change along or stop it. Such a link is critical to preventing later surprises.

MAKING INTERVENTIONS

"The term OD interventions refers to the range of planned programmatic activities organizational members and change agents participate in during the course of an organization development program" (French & Bell, 1978, p. 47). Interventions are the methods or techniques of OD which help create changes in individuals, groups, and organizations as a whole. There are a large and growing number of these interventions. They constitute the social technology of organization development. An action plan for change should specify the type and sequence of interventions required to move change along. The interventions must be selected for their relevance to the organizational problems, not for their current popularity. Unfortunately, many organization development efforts start with an intervention like team-building or MBO (Management by Objectives) because executives in the organization undergoing change are convinced by other executives that these methods are the answer to all their problems. The intervention is not chosen for its relevance to the problems of the organization or the stage in the change effort in which the organization finds itself.

The reader has probably noted that much of our discussion of organization development so far as not touched on the techniques so often associated with OD. This has been intentional. OD is a general change process very much like the process described in this chapter, *not* a particular technique or set of techniques. The techniques are useful tools brought in at the right time for the appropriate job. For this reason, it is often best if decisions about which intervention methods to use come later rather than sooner in the change effort. These intervention methods and the date when they are to be applied become part of the action plan managed by the mechanism described earlier. Furthermore, it's best if interventions are tailored or at least modified to fit the situation and the problem. An organization development effort should not be thought of as a series of formal prestructured "off-the-shelf" events, though off-the-shelf interventions can often be helpful. The most effective interventions are often those in which the change agent is available to discuss problems, to help diagnose, to challenge and ask questions, to consel, to coach, and to provide support.

Nevertheless, there are many known interventions to choose from. Part III will provide a description of these methods, a discussion of the theory and assumptions underlying them, and an evaluation of the situations in which they might be most effective.

INTERVENTION METHODS
Activities, Settings, and Structures for Inducing and Reinforcing New Behavior*

OVERVIEW

Change agents have many intervention methods to choose from to improve organizational effectiveness. While it is best to tailor interventions to specific situations, a number of planned activities and structural forms have emerged as the most commonly used intervention methods. These represent the tried tools available to managers and consultants for changing and reinforcing behavior. A discussion of these interventions conveys what in fact happens in many OD efforts. It also defines the knowledge and skill a change agent must possess to use these interventions effectively. Though they have been reasonably well defined through successive applications in the last decade, effective change agents often tailor interventions to suit the situation in which they are to be used. Thus, their description in the next four chapters is in no way intended to convey that there is one way to apply them—there are many ways. When a specific procedure is described, it is for the purpose of giving the reader a "feel" for the intervention. Furthermore, for each intervention an attempt has been made to describe the assumptions and rationale underlying it.

The many intervention methods available can be classified into four major categories. The first of these categories includes diagnostic methods, which apply to the social system as a whole. Each of the remaining three categories includes interventions which primarily impact one component of the organizational model presented in Chapter 2. The four chapters in this part of the book will describe some of the most commonly used interventions.

---

*Several chapters in this part of the book are based on a more technical and research-based discussion of this same subject in Beer, M., "The Technology of Organization Development," in Dunnette, M. (ed.), *Handbook of Industrial and Organizational Psychology*, Chicago: Rand McNally, 1976. For a more detailed cookbook description of how to apply diagnostic intervention to be discussed in the next four chapters, see Fordyce, J. K. and Weil, R., *Managing with People*, Addison-Wesley, Reading, Mass., 1971.

Chapter 8—*Diagnostic Interventions* are mainly intended to gather data about the total system or its parts and to create a setting for feedback and diagnosis.

Chapter 9—*Process Interventions* are activities intended to have an impact on organizational behavior and process. Through these interventions, organizational members are helped to examine and change their behaviors.

Chapter 10—*Structural Innovations and Interventions* are intended to have an impact on the structures of the organization. Structural innovations are new designs which an increasing number of organizations are adopting, as they attempt to cope with changes in people and environment. Structural interventions are the methods available for diagnosing existing structures, and implementing changes.

Chapter 11—*Individual Interventions* are intended to change people in an organization. They are strategies and methods for selecting, training, and developing individuals so that fit between people and other social system components might be improved.

The chapters in this part of the book have been ordered to reflect my bias about the most likely and effective sequence of interventions in a system-wide OD program. As we shall see in Chapter 12, there are several considerations in sequencing interventions, but more often than not, an OD effort will start with a diagnostic intervention. It will then be followed by process and/or structural interventions (the order will depend on the situation). Individual interventions (particularly training), though frequently used first to change organizations, are most often (but not always) useful to support changes induced by process and structural interventions. Competence problems often do not become apparent until an organizational change is well underway.

DIAGNOSTIC INTERVENTIONS 8

No planned organization change and development effort can proceed without a diagnosis of the organization and its environment. This means that managers must gain an understanding of their organization as a total system. The social systems model presented in Chapter 2, and recreated in Figure 8–1, is provided as a conceptual framework that might help managers diagnose their social system.

Data for a diagnosis should be collected about and from the organization's environment. Such data clarifies the relationship of the organization to its environment and therefore its effectiveness. It can also provide the external pressures needed to develop dissatisfaction and readiness to change (see Chapter 3). For a business unit, data about the environment may include information about market share, competitive pressures, and customer attitudes. In the case of a staff group in a larger corporation, data may include attitudes toward the staff group's services by clients and top management.

A diagnosis must also include information about how people in the organization see its functioning internally. This should include data about all social system components of the organization. Such data not only provide a perspective of how the organization is coping with its environment, but also the extent of fit between its internal components and, therefore, its efficiency. At the same time, data about people's attitudes toward the organization and its problems can provide the internal pressures needed to create readiness for change.

Historically, however, diagnostic methods have often been more limited in scope. For example, survey feedback methods, to be described later, typically obtain data about dimensions such as employee satisfaction, supervision, communication, and commitment (the human outputs and organizational behavior components of the social system). These types of data may then be used to infer potential problems about the fit between structures and people, and the organization's strategy. Often, an interpretation of attitude data by organization members during feedback meetings is needed to understand the structural, cultural, and environmental causes of the problems (Heller, 1969).

More recently, diagnostic methods have focused on systematic collection of data from the environment and about the environment as a first step in diagnosis. For example, **111**

FIGURE 8-1 A Social Systems Model of Organizations

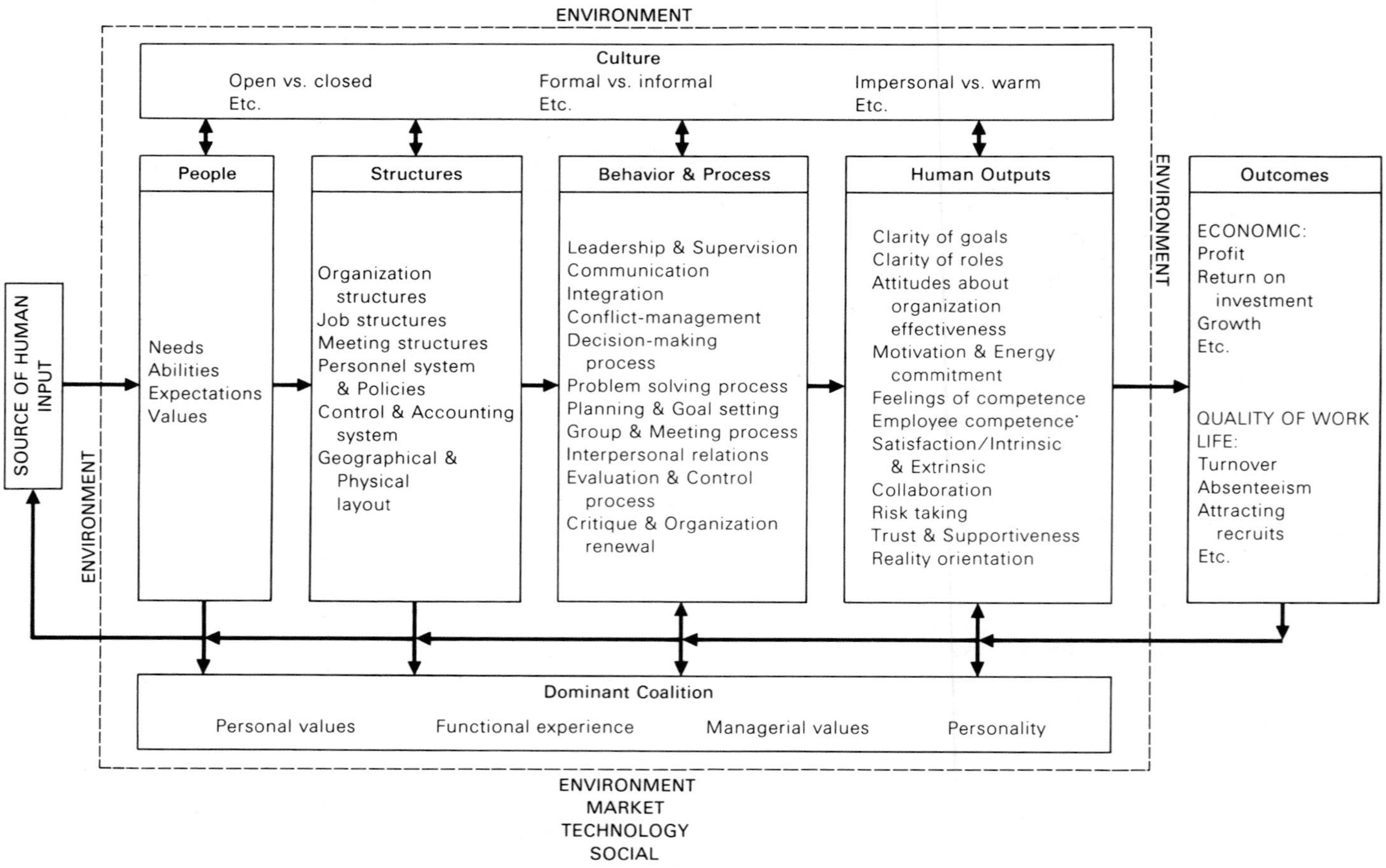

ENVIRONMENT

Culture
Open vs. closed
Formal vs. informal
Impersonal vs. warm
Etc.

People	Structures	Behavior & Process	Human Outputs	Outcomes
Needs	Organization	Leadership & Supervision	Clarity of goals	ECONOMIC:
Abilities	structures	Communication	Clarity of roles	Profit
Expectations	Job structures	Integration	Attitudes about	Return on
Values	Meeting structures	Conflict-management	organization	investment
	Personnel system	Decision-making	effectiveness	Growth
	& Policies	process	Motivation & Energy	Etc.
	Control & Accounting	Problem solving process	commitment	
	system	Planning & Goal setting	Feelings of competence	QUALITY OF WORK
	Geographical &	Group & Meeting process	Employee competence	LIFE:
	Physical	Interpersonal relations	Satisfaction/Intrinsic	Turnover
	layout	Evaluation & Control	& Extrinsic	Absenteeism
		process	Collaboration	Attracting
		Critique & Organization	Risk taking	recruits
		renewal	Trust & Supportiveness	Etc.
			Reality orientation	

Dominant Coalition
Personal values   Functional experience   Managerial values   Personality

ENVIRONMENT
MARKET
TECHNOLOGY
SOCIAL

SOURCE OF HUMAN INPUT

ENVIRONMENT

the organizational mirror, to be described in this chapter, is a method for giving a management group an understanding of how people in their environment (customers, clients, other managers in the system, etc.) see their organizational unit. Structured questionnaires and procedures to facilitate this process have also been developed (McManus & Burnes, 1975). Even more recently, diagnostic methods have been developed which help managers plan organization development (as opposed to reacting to pathologies) by helping them go through a systematic analysis of their environment or strategy followed by an analysis of internal organizational arrangements and attitudes. These approaches have been called open systems planning. They capture the essence of the systems view taken in this book and will also be described in this chapter.

Thus, choosing a diagnostic method involves understanding whether the diagnosis is part of a planning process for organization development or whether it is a reaction to organizational pathology. A choice of diagnostic interventions also involves a decision about the scope of the diagnosis, particularly the extent to which the diagnosis is to focus on organization-environment relations versus internal problems.

Furthermore, choosing a diagnostic intervention involves a tradeoff between scientific rigor on the one hand, and ownership and commitment to the data on the other (see Chapter 6 for a discussion of this issue). When the primary purpose for gathering data is change in attitudes and behavior, organizational members, more than the consultant or researcher, must understand the data and develop an awareness of problems facing the organization. In this instance, diagnosis is an awareness and consensus-building process in which problems members have known about right along become public and the organization develops a public statement about needed solutions. To accomplish these objectives, diagnostic methods are needed that involve organizational members in identifying and diagnosing problems. Traditional scientific concerns for reliability of measurement become less important than gaining awareness and commitment.

However, when the purpose of the diagnosis also includes contribution to knowledge, an objective evaluation of an OD program, or the evaluation of an intervention method, the choice of field research methods probably becomes more important (Bouchard, 1976). In these instances, the diagnostic intervention chosen may be more methodologically rigorous. Indeed, choices of a diagnostic intervention should be based on a prioritization of the following potential goals:

1. Creating awareness among organizational members
2. Collecting data for analysis and diagnosis
3. Using data to provide expert opinion about the design or redesign of management practices and organizational structures
4. Changing attitudes and behaviors
5. Monitoring and evaluating the effectiveness of the change program
6. Assessing the effectiveness of an intervention method
7. Contributing to knowledge about organizations

Because one diagnosis may have several of the above objectives, tradeoffs and compromises in diagnostic methodology must often be made.

The diagnostic interventions described in this chapter do not comprise all interventions available today. They have been chosen for discussion because they represent the variety available in both scope and method.

OPEN SYSTEMS PLANNING

The environment surrounding most organizations is increasingly turbulent. Markets are changing, the life cycle of new technology is becoming shorter, and competition is becoming fiercer. These realities are forcing organizations to change their strategy and reassess their organizational arrangements more frequently. Similarly, organizations are being forced to respond to a number of environmental demands simultaneously. This in turn places a strain on the organization's resources and requires more conscious decisions about the priorities of these various demands. Without a clear statement of strategy or mission, choices about priorities, resource allocation, and organizational arrangement become very difficult.

These environmental demands have resulted in experiments with open systems planning methods designed to help key executives clarify their strategic objectives and implement system-wide planning (Emery & Trist, 1965; Krone, 1974).

Open systems planning is a process by which managers distance themselves from their organization and systematically examine the relationship between their organization and its environment. Following a definition of the environment and their strategy in it, managers can specify the demands of the environment and its implications for the kind of human outputs, people, structures, culture, organizational process, and behavior required. By comparing the actual state of the social system with the required state, a plan for organizational improvement can be developed. Several alternative approaches to open systems planning will be described.

Open Systems Planning Using a Social Systems Model

An assumption underlying this book is that organization models are at the core of all organizational change efforts (Tichy, Hornstein, & Nisberg, 1977). A model may be explicit or implicit in the mind of a change agent, but it influences how the diagnosis of an organization and the planning of change is approached. A model provides the guidelines for choosing what to attend to in collecting diagnostic information about an organization and for arranging the collection of information into meaningful patterns. It forms the basis for deciding about the root causes of problems reported by managers in the organization. As Tichy, Hornstein, and Nisberg (1977) point out, "the organization model functions much like a physician's model of the human system. The physician conducts tests, collects certain vital information on the human system, and evaluates and interprets this information based on his model. Once the diagnosis is made, the model guides the selection of the appropriate medical intervention. An organization model is used in a similar fashion to guide the collection of information, its analysis, and the selection of interventions."[1]

For these reasons, a social systems model for understanding organizational dynamics was presented in Chapter 2. Such a model (see Figure 8–1) can be used by consultants and managers to understand what is happening in their organization and to plan organizational improvements, given certain strategic goals or desired outcomes. For example, in a highly turbulent market environment, where the highest priority is new product development, willingness to take risks with new ideas and collaboration between functional groups is very important. If these human outputs are assessed (through data collection and diagnosis) to be lower than desired, a strategy will have to be developed for changing the organizations social system.

114   Because of the interdependence of the many components and dimensions of a social

system, managers contemplating permanent improvements in the human outputs of collaboration and risk taking will have to plan multiple changes in the system (people, structures, and process). To identify the dimensions in a social system component needing change, an assessment of each dimension and its potential effect on risk taking and collaboration will have to be performed. Then action plans for making changes in certain components and dimensions must be developed.

The social system model shown in Figure 8–1 may be used to help managers diagnose and plan improvements in their organization. This can be done by presenting the model to managers as a way of helping them understand organizational diagnosis. The model may then be used to guide an identification of problems in their organization and an analysis of their causes. The managers generate data from their own experience or through a more formal process of data collection to support their contentions about outcomes and their causes. Case 8–1 provides an example of such a process.

CASE 8–1

A plant manager and his staff met with a consultant in an off-site meeting. They were presented the model in Figure 8–1. With the model posted on the wall, a lecture and discussion about social systems and the model followed. The model then guided a diagnosis of the plant's organization. The group started by discussing organizational outcomes. It is at this point that turnover among salaried employees (quality of work life outcome) was identified as a problem while satisfaction was expressed with the plant's gross margin (economic outcome). With the help of the consultant, the plant's top management group began to push back into the causal variables that might explain the turnover problem. They agreed that concern about job security (human output) was causing the turnover.

Following a discussion of several process and structural variables which might account for insecurity, they discovered to their surprise that there were several causes for feelings of insecurity which they had not previously considered. The plant manager (dominant coalition) had strong beliefs about the need for a systematic objectives setting and review process. Thus, he had introduced a management by objectives system (MBO) and training program (structures) into the plant. In fact he served as the instructor himself to demonstrate the importance of MBO. In the year that followed, clearer and much better-documented goals emerged.

When the diagnosis, guided by the social systems model, turned to the environment, the group realized that they were introducing MBO at a time when the plant's orders were dropping. Therefore, goals set at the time of MBO's introduction were less valid. Not only were goals previously set less valid but the better and more explicit measurement system, associated with MBO and the tough tone that the program and plant manager conveyed, was causing the insecurity and turnover.

This analysis allowed the group to plan specific steps aimed at reassuring people and making the MBO system less threatening. The plant manager in particular, gained significant insights into how his assumptions about the need for MBO had to be modified in light of current business conditions and the climate in the plant.

115

Another way of utilizing the model in Figure 8–1 is to use it as the basis for constructing an interview protocol and/or a questionnaire. With this approach, management learns about the model as part of planning for a diagnosis. A consultant and/or task force may develop the data collection instruments, collect the data, and analyze them in accordance with the model. The model is again used with managers in feedback of the diagnosis and in planning actions for improving organizational effectiveness (see Case 8–2).

Defining a Core Mission and Mapping the Environment

Beckhard and Harris (1977) have recently provided a detailed description of a process which might help a top management group distance itself from the organization and define some fundamental strategies and organizational responses. This approach to open systems planning is different from the social systems approach in that it does not provide managers with a model. Rather, a management group is guided through a series of activities which in effect clarify the organization's core mission and therefore its agenda for improving organizational effectiveness. It is best that a group plan one or more meetings to go through the following seven steps:

1. *Determining the "core mission" or strategy of the organization*—The mission of the organization is not its objectives. Rather, it is its fundamental reason for being. Obviously, there are several reasons for being. A business can define its mission as maximizing return on investment for shareholders, providing a useful service or product to society, providing employment, or developing new technology. The first step in open systems planning is for top management to come to a consensus about which is the most important mission (this is the "core mission" according to Beckhard & Harris, 1977) and to check its conclusion against actual day-to-day decisions which reflect the implicit core mission up to that point.

2. *Mapping the demand system*—A technique called "environmental mapping" has been developed to facilitate this next step, a visual listing of institutions, groups, and conditions which require something of the organization. These could include unions, customers, government agencies, or the board of directors. A smaller list of the most important demanding institutions is developed and their specific demands listed.

3. *Current response pattern*—The organization's current response patterns to these demands are discussed and posted. More importantly, the group must agree on what they would like their response pattern to be. Should the organization "do as little as it can," "just enough to satisfy requirements," or "actually pursue satisfying the demand to the maximum?" For example, an organization can try to go all out in meeting the demands concerning pollution of environmentalists or government, and allocate a lot of people and capital to the problem, or it can do just enough to get by.

4. *Projected demand system*—Top management must next make a five-year projection of the likely demands if the organization does nothing. A comparison of the current response pattern against the projected demands can clarify the consequences of the current response pattern and set the stage for planning changes. For example, are union demands for improved quality of work life going to increase? If so, how do these demands compare with the capacities of managerial and professional personnel to respond now and in the future?

5. *Defining the desired state*—Top management must next agree on the desired response pattern of the organization. What should be emphasized or deemphasized? Does management want to be the employer with the best quality of work life, or have

the best record on environmental concerns? These discussions are helped by the earlier definition of the "core mission." A periodic return to this can help clarify choices.

6. *Goal setting and activity planning*—Goals for meeting certain demands are set and prioritized. Activities, resources, projects, and reorganizations are set in motion to support the goals indentified. These may be focused on responding to demands or on a plan to modify environmental demands (for example, lobbying for legislation).

7. *Anticipatory testing of cost effectiveness*—The reality of the work done can be tested by analysis and discussion of the economic, personal, and social costs associated with each major goal. The goals become part of the strategic planning process.

The steps just outlined are just one process by which a management group can try to distance itself to develop a picture of the organization in relation to its environment. Such a process can help management reach a consensus about the organization's basic mission and strategy and, accordingly, how it should function. The important thing is not the specific procedure but the clarification and consensus about environment, mission, and strategy.

Fitting Organizational Structure and Process to Strategy

Miles and Snow (1978) have developed a different diagnostic framework for open systems planning, that can also guide management's inquiry into the fit between its strategy and the organization's structures and processes. Based on research in some eighty firms, they identified four strategic archetypes which seem to be generalizable across industries. These are:

1. *Defender*—A firm whose primary mission is to protect a relatively narrow market niche by continuously increasing efficiency through cost reduction.

2. *Prospector*—A corporation that seeks to enter a variety of new markets through technological and other innovations. These firms are typically effective in the markets they serve but somewhat less efficient.

3. *Analyzer*—A firm whose objective is to combine the defender and prospector   **117**

strategies. It seeks to emphasize efficiency in some businesses and effectiveness in others.

4. *Reactor*—A firm whose strategy changes continuously in response to internal and external events, thus preventing a clear definition of its strategy.

Miles and Snow found that the first three strategic typologies were consistently linked to certain organizational structures and processes, a confirmation of the congruity or fit ideas discussed in Chapters 1 and 2. Defenders were typically organized functionally and managed in a directive manner from the top. Prospectors were typically decentralized and each product division was given substantial freedom to organize and manage in accordance with its environmental demands. Analyzers tended to have matrix structures and a more collaborative and participative culture than defenders (see Chapter 10 for a further discussion of these organization design options). Furthermore, strategy (domain choice as they call it) and structures and process (administrative arrangements as they call them) had to be congruent with product and manufacturing competence (engineering arrangements as they call them) for the firm to be successful. Even more importantly, for purposes of open systems planning, they developed a decision-tree approach to organizational diagnosis and planning. A management group at a series of off-site meetings can try to diagnose the current fit between its organizational strategy and its structure and management process by following the checklist shown in Figure 8–2.

First, the top management group must decide which of the four strategic archetypes best describes their organization (What am I?). Having done so, they must decide if they want to continue following their current strategy (Is what I am what I want to be?). Depending on whether the answer is yes or no, management must answer different questions.

If the answer is *yes* (the strategy being pursued is what management wants to continue doing), the next question becomes whether the current strategy is viable given forseeable environmental conditions (see left side of Figure 8–2). If the answer is *yes*, a series of questions which follow are aimed at clarifying whether structures and management processes are congruent with the strategy (Am I consistent in all areas—domain, engineering, administration?). Further questions in this sequence guide management toward planning training and development efforts to maintain consistency or toward the redesign of organizational structures, control systems, and reward systems, or the recruitment of different types of people if present employees are not consistent with current strategy.

If management decides that the strategy they are pursuing is not what they want to do—they answer *no* to the question: Is what I am what I want to be?—a different series of questions listed on the right side of Figure 8–2 guides the discussion. These questions involve identifying a new strategic thrust (for example, moving from a defender to a prospector) and the organizational arrangements and training and development activities (interventions) that will be needed to develop a new state of congruity among organizational strategy, structure, and process.

Each pattern of alignment among strategy, structure, and process has risks associated with it. If management chooses a defender strategy, it must consider the risks associated with a competitor's introduction of a totally new product or technology which makes obsolete the organization's current basis of competition. Therefore, the last step in Miles and Snow's open systems planning process is a discussion of how the organization might ensure against the maximum risk incurred by their choice of strategy and organizational arrangements. For example, should they acquire a company or keep some R&D going? Should they have a market planning group sensing the environment for early signs of major upheaval?

FIGURE 8–2   A Diagnostic Checklist for Open Systems Planning

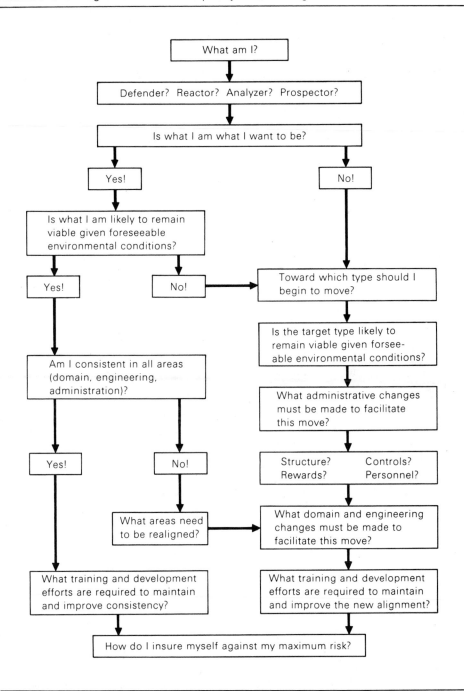

From Raymond Miles and Charles Snow, *Organizational Strategy, Structure, and Process* (New York: McGraw-Hill, 1978) p. 109. Reprinted by permission.

Open Systems Planning in Perspective

In all the approaches to open systems planning described in this chapter, the model simply guides the analysis through which a management group must move. The model or checklist cannot ensure that management will have the open dialogue which surfaces feelings and problems needed to complete the diagnosis. Nor can a model or checklist assure that following each phase of the discussion a consensus will be reached about problems, strategy, or the actions needed.

However, to successfully complete an open systems diagnosis, consensus will be needed. To help management achieve consensus, an OD consultant may be needed. This person should act as (1) a process consultant (Schein, 1969) helping the group examine and manage its deliberations constructively and effectively and (2) an expert consultant who can prepare analyses or help the group think through analyses needed to answer successive questions such as: "What is our strategy?" "Is our strategy likely to stay viable given foreseeable environmental conditions?" "If a change is needed, what administrative changes are also needed?" If one consultant does not have both these skills and no one in the management group has expert resources at his disposal to do the needed analyses, more than one consultant will be required.

Miles and Snow report a number of cases in which their diagnostic framework was used in open systems planning. Not all of these applications were successful. Failure was associated with personal agendas of one or more top people (see discussion of "Barriers to Organizational Health" in Chapter 2) that were in conflict with organizational changes called for by the diagnosis. These experiences suggest that density of facts and sophistication of analysis are no more important than a process that leads to new awareness, change in attitudes, and commitment to change.

Despite some of the potential difficulties a management group might encounter in successfully completing an open systems diagnosis, there are a number of important effects such a process can have on the dominant coalition.

1. They become aware of the complexity and dynamics of social systems and the multiplicity of design variables and interventions to be activated in order to create change.
2. They gain an appreciation of the time and energy that will have to be invested to create needed changes. This will be particularly evident as they target dimensions of the organization for change and develop action plans to support change goals.
3. They will be clearer on the outcomes to be achieved by an organizational improvement effort and the tradeoffs between alternative strategies. For example, if changes needed to increase collaboration and risk taking require more upheaval than is acceptable to them, they will be forced to confront the alternative of changing their strategy to compete in less dynamic markets. A system framework helps force informed choices about what the organization should be.
4. They may become more aware of how their own predispositions have affected strategy and the social system. This awareness will be sharpened if they openly acknowledge that they are an important influence and accept data about the effects of their influence.

Because of these effects, open systems diagnosis and planning can be an extremely important and powerful intervention at the very beginning of an organizational improvement process. It helps top management to see their organization as a system interacting with its environment. It stimulates reexamination of this interaction and the organizational arrangements needed to achieve the desired organization/environment relationship. Once the broad parameters of this relationship have been defined, an intervention to obtain more data about the internal functioning of the organization may be needed. The next section will deal with such an intervention, a systems-wide diagnostic approach called *survey feedback*, designed to catalyze improvement efforts throughout an organization. Again, the technique of questionnaire and analysis is less important than the process of discussion and consensus-building.

SURVEY FEEDBACK

Survey feedback is a process by which a change agent, working collaboratively with organizational members, obtains data about the organization and its problems. He uses interviews, questionnaires, and/or observation to collect data about the organization. The data are then analyzed, summarized, and fed back to the people who generated the data, usually in a meeting of natural work groups, although larger groups are sometimes assembled. Following the feedback, the group, with its manager present, tries to reach consensus on the major problems the data indicate. Having done this, the group develops action plans aimed at solving the problems. An action plan might include a change in a given management practice and the activities required to bring it about. In all cases, the people assigned to carry out each activity and the dates by which they are to be completed and reported are indicated.

The most frequently used survey feedback model is one in which a consultant interviews people in the organization, interprets the data, and feeds back the conclusions to a meeting of key managers. As the discussion in Chapter 6 indicated, this approach has advantages and disadvantages, depending on the situation and goals of the diagnosis. The biggest advantage is that interviews provide very rich information about many organizational problems and their interrelationships. The biggest disadvantage of this approach is that it is far too costly if information is to be collected from and fed back to many groups at several levels of the organization. Thus, interviews are most useful when a diagnosis of major organizational issues is needed for feedback to a small number of top managers. However, questionnaires are more practical when feedback to a large number of people and groups is desired so they can become involved in improvement efforts at their level.

The original survey feedback model developed at the Institute for Social Research at the University of Michigan (Mann, 1957; Mann & Likert, 1952) calls for gathering data by means of a questionnaire. This is followed by a series of interlocking feedback conferences with family groups starting at the top of the organization and cascading sequentially down to lower levels. According to this model, it is best that the manager of the group lead the meeting, rather than the external change agent, so that ownership of the data is transferred to the group. To accomplish this, the consultant briefs supervisors prior to the feedback meeting about the content of the findings. He then trains them in how to conduct the meeting so that it has a participative atmosphere designed to lead to innovation and commitment. The result is organization-wide involvement in the survey and feedback process at a reasonable cost and within a relatively short time period. A consultant can be present at the meeting as a *resource* in interpreting the data, as an *expert* who can help solve organizational and management problems, and as a *process consultant* who helps the group examine and critique how they are working in the meeting.

The Michigan survey feedback model reflects two concerns that grew out of the work of Floyd Mann and his colleagues. First, they wanted to make questionnaires more useful to organizational members by getting them involved in discussing the data and develop- **121** ing plans for change. Second, they saw the survey feedback process as much better than training programs for helping supervisors learn about leadership. What better way to learn than to be confronted with feedback from your subordinates in an atmosphere where discussion and problem solving can go on? There are three main components of survey feedback: data, group feedback meetings, and process analysis.

Data

The first question to answer when designing a survey, is what kind of data should be gathered and fed back. If the questions asked in a survey or interview touch on salient organizational problems, the survey feedback process will be seen as highly relevant and important. Under these conditions, people in the organization will invest a lot of energy in providing valid data and in discussing them following feedback. If the data requested are seen as abstract, theoretical, and not relevant to the target organization, this will not happen.

To tailor a survey to the target organization, change agents must have some idea of what the problems are, so that questions which tap areas of concern can be included. They can obtain an overview of the areas that ought to be surveyed by conducting preliminary interviews with employees, or by involving them in designing the survey itself. For example, in some organizations task forces composed of people from various levels and parts of the organization have been used to develop a survey instrument so that it solicits data about problems felt in all parts of the organization. Once the relevant areas have been identified, questions from existing questionnaires can be used or questions can be specifically written for the survey. Both the process of development and the resultant content enhance the survey's relevance.

Too often, change agents using surveys rely on standardized and psychometrically sound questionnaires, designed to measure theoretical constructs of interest to the developer but not to the organization. Important problem areas that might be identified through preliminary interviews and observations are missed, preventing change agents and organizational members from developing a full understanding of what is going on in their organization. Of course, standardized survey instruments have advantages: no development time is required; they have been thoroughly pretested; the instruments are psychometrically sound; the questions on the survey tap a wide range of areas important in diagnosing organizations; and comparison data from other organizations or subunits is often available from its developers.

The best known such instrument is the Survey of Organizations developed at the University of Michigan (Taylor & Bowers, 1972). It assesses areas such as communications, goals emphasis, extent of participative management, decision making, coordination between departments, and employee attitudes. A quite different survey instrument is the Corporate Excellence Diagnostic (1968) developed by Blake and Mouton. It is operationally oriented and obtains data about six major business activities such as financial management, human resources, and marketing.

The problem with standardized survey instruments is not only their perceived, but also their real relevancy to a given situation. When a railroad recently underwent decentralization, the Survey of Organizations was administered to diagnose reactions to the reorganization and to track progress. The problems that people were experiencing in making the new organization work were fairly well known and documented in a series of interviews conducted earlier by a consultant. These problems included ambiguity associated with new roles, managerial competence of new division managers, and the relationship between newly decentralized divisions and staff groups at headquarters.

Unfortunately, the Survey of Organizations does not obtain data directly relevant to these problems. At best, some inferences can be made. Thus, the feedback from the questionnaire data proved to be of little help in facilitating the change and tracking it. Why the consultant's interviews, which did clarify the problems in terms relevant to the organization, were not used for this purpose, is not clear. (Baxley Railroad (A) & (B), 1977).

Of course, there are compromises that can obtain the advantages of standardization while meeting the requirements for relevancy. A core survey instrument that measures generally relevant dimensions can be used in combination with a tailor-made instrument that gets at situation-specific problems. In a large corporation, the core instrument would be standardized across all units while a tailor-made survey (questionnaires or interviews) could be used in each subunit.

Group Feedback Meetings

Even if the appropriate decisions have been made about the contents of the survey, a survey-feedback intervention can easily be undermined by an ineffective feedback process. Of central importance is that feedback take place in a family group meeting with a summary of findings for that group. Such feedback meetings are far superior to written reports about survey findings. They are also better than large meetings composed of people from diverse groups in which overall findings are presented (Klein, Kraut, & Wolfson, 1971). Group meetings to discuss the unit's data are important because they situationally induce people to talk to each other and their boss about problems in the group—problems they may not have been able to talk about before.

The meeting provides the opportunity for the group to develop a consensus about how it functions, what needs to be changed, and how it should be changed. The meeting, if it follows the guidelines discussed in Chapter 6, captures the potential energy available in the group for change and directs it toward problem solving. Moreover, the feedback process can help the group become more skillful in self-examination and problem solving and can foster norms that will encourage similar self-examination in the future.

Indeed, the open discussion and sharing of feelings in front of the boss can create an immediate change in the capacity of the group to deal with future problems. Of course, such an open discussion may be difficult to achieve. But it can occur to the extent that the manager models the process and encourages a climate of openness. Managers can be helped to run effective feedback meetings through prior training and/or through the presence of a skillful consultant who intervenes when necessary. "Word of mouth" that the first few meetings went well also creates hope and encouragement for lower level groups who have not yet been through the process. There is more probability that subsequent feedback meetings will be successful.

A survey can, of course, be taken and fed back to top management only. This approach may be appropriate when the survey is intended to result in top level organization design decisions in which management does not feel lower levels can be involved. This approach does not, however, provide the potential for unleashing energy for change at all levels of the organization and probably limits change to structural and policy issues.

Process Analysis

A group feedback meeting provides the unique opportunity for a group to learn about itself not only from data, but also from its own behavior. In the process of discussing the data, usually with the help of a process consultant, a group can examine its decision-making process, the climate for open discussion, provide feedback to individuals, and **123** develop its skills in self-examination. Through this process, both the manager's supervisory skills as well as the group's capacity to function effectively can be enhanced.

Unfortunately, many survey-feedback interventions do not take advantage of the experiential learning potential inherent in them. Survey-feedback is much more than questionnaires, statistical analysis, and reports of results. Without follow-up conferences throughout the organization, a sophisticated survey's data will not be accepted and used. Interlocking conferences held without supervisors who are committed and skillful will not be sufficient. Effective supervisors and group meetings without effective support, involvement and follow-up by the change agent will also fall short of producing significant change (Frohman, 1970). When these conditions are met, however, survey-feedback has been reported to be an effective intervention (Baumgartel, 1959; Bowers, 1970). When the survey-feedback process is not seen as relevant, when the commitment of managers to change and improve is not effectively tested through an appropriate contracting process, or when it is imposed from the top without gaining commitment first, survey-feedback often fails. Too often, change agents respond to requests for a survey only to find management walking away from the survey without fulfilling commitments to feedback and action planning. Not only is an opportunity for real impact lost, but also the organization has wasted its time and people become more disillusioned than ever. A change agent planning a survey-feedback intervention can prevent these negative outcomes by assuring that the conditions of relevancy, commitment, and effective feedback are fulfilled. Often, so much time and energy is spent on questionnaire construction and data analysis that the change agent loses sight of the importance of these conditions for an effective survey-feedback intervention (see Case 8–3).

THE CONFRONTATION MEETING

The confrontation meeting (Beckhard, 1967) is a diagnostic technique designed to quickly identify major problems faced by an organization and to mobilize the organization's resources toward solving them. There is no survey instrument or sophisticated measurement process. A large group of people from several levels in an organization are brought together for a day—it may be an afternoon of one day and a morning of the next day. Although a consultant is present, the general manager of the organization opens the meeting. He describes the purpose of the meeting and attempts to create a supportive climate so that individuals will take the personal risks needed to surface problems. Assurances are made about the anonymity of the data.

Participants are divided into small groups of five to eight people representing different organization units and levels. Bosses and subordinates are not placed in the same group. The top management group meets as a group, but (according to Beckhard) without the general manager. The assignment is, "Think of yourself as a person with needs and goals in this organization. What behavior, procedures, ways of work, attitudes, etc., should be different so that life would be better around here?" This same question can be asked many different ways. The point is to focus on problems in the organization that prevent members and the organization from being more effective. After an hour, each group reports its problem list to the larger group. This usually takes a half-day. With help from the consultants, leaders then combine the categories during the midday break.

In the afternoon, new groups are formed along functional and expert lines which fit the problem categories identified. The senior person in the organization for that function or problem area heads the group. They go through the list and select three or four items **124** which affect them most, discuss these, find solutions, and determine the action needed

A team of consultants was asked by the management of a small company to help them with organization development. The company had previously been involved in some OD activities. A senior consultant to management suggested the consultant team would be able to surface problems and stimulate organizational improvement. The following case provides an example of the difficulties the consultant team ran into in obtaining the involvement and commitment so necessary in an effective survey-feedback intervention.

The consultants interviewed people at the upper levels of the organization to develop a preliminary diagnosis. This led them to feel that "communication" was the central problem. In a meeting with management they presented their preliminary diagnosis and suggested that a survey be conducted. An academic colleague was brought in to present a questionnaire thought to be suited to this purpose. The questionnaire was complex and reflected the academic's interests in communication, not necessarily the key issues of interest to management. Despite management's criticism of this first meeting and the questionnaire, a decision was made to go ahead. In effect the consultants did not pay sufficient attention to early signs that commitment of management to the questionnaire was low and its relevance was in question.

Nine months after the survey was administered, the results had been analyzed and computer printouts were ready. Unfortunately, many personnel changes had taken place in the meantime and these created a climate of insecurity. Furthermore, the time lag between administration of the questionnaire and feedback further reduced the already low level of commitment to the survey-feedback process. Despite this, management continued to support the OD project and the feedback process began.

The consultants worked hard to transfer ownership for the data to supervisors and their groups throughout the organization. They organized data, briefed supervisors, trained them to run the feedback meetings, and provided ground rules for communicating about the data aimed at encouraging candor. Despite these efforts, the consultants ran into a number of problems in the feedback phase:

1. Supervisors were uncomfortable assuming leadership in feedback meetings. Many did little more than introduce the consultants and explain the project. With that, they turned the meeting over to the consultants. When asked why they were there, individuals said "because we were told to be here."

2. Not surprisingly, the consultants found themselves doing the talking as they discussed objectives, norms for the meeting, and the data. The more they talked, the less others participated.

3. In a period of fifteen minutes, the consultants tried to familiarize groups with eleven different questionnaire variables. This led to confusion.

4. Individuals became preoccupied with each item in the questionnaire. Frequently, someone would choose to discount certain data because he felt the specific items relating to a variable were invalid, misinterpreted, or ambiguous.

5. Many groups concluded they were problem-free, refusing to acknowledge problems suggested by the data. Even where survey results dif-

fered from their expectations, they found ways to rationalize the results. The absence of comparison data from other groups did not help.

6. As the consultants tried to turn the meeting back to the groups, members became frustrated with what they perceived as excessive nondirectiveness.

7. Time invariably ran out before justice could be done to the data or, more importantly, before action planning could go into effect.

In a post-mortem of this project, the consultants arrived at a number of conclusions. First and foremost, management saw the survey-feedback interventions as little more than an exercise to "improve communication." There was no attempt to link survey-feedback to key managerial problems. The use of a complex academically oriented questionnaire did not help increase the relevance of the intervention. Thus, the project was the consultants', not management's, from the beginning. They also concluded that a more directive approach on their part would have helped, given the lack of ownership of the data in the feedback meetings by group members. Finally, the consultants concluded that the time lag between administration of the questionnaire and feedback was far too long and that they had disregarded important changes in the climate of the organization caused by key personnel changes. They never tried to relate the survey-feedback process to these events. In short, survey-feedback was a project rather than part of a program of organization development.

and plan timetables to begin work on the problems. They also select additional items to which top management should give highest priority and develop a partial plan to communicate to the rest of the organization about the meeting. Each group reports to the total group the results of their work, and the meeting ends. Figure 8–3 provides a flow diagram detailing a procedure for a confrontation meeting recommended by Fordyce and Weil (1971).

Beckhard recommends a follow-up meeting to review progress toward goals developed during the confrontation meeting. Both follow-up and positive action on the results of the meeting are critical; otherwise, a loss in trust and credibility results.

The confrontation meeting can mobilize an organization toward an action plan in a shorter period of time (one day) than survey-feedback. Therefore, it is probably best used when an organization faces some sort of crisis or stress, such as the loss of a key customer, a new top manager, a new product introduction, or a new threat from a competitor. In these situations there is often a wide gap between the perceptions of top management and those closer to the problem at lower levels. Like the survey-feedback process, the confrontation meeting is an attempt to close these gaps and build organizational consensus about problems and needed action. Without consensus about the problems, the organization is unable to mobilize energy and resources to act.

Beckhard feels that the qualities which make the confrontation meeting useful are that it provides rapid diagnosis, catharsis, and involvement in problem identification and problem solving; it increases influence of lower levels, thereby increasing commitment; it short-cuts normal bureaucratic barriers to decision making; and it enhances the quality of decisions by placing problems where the information is.

The chief difference between survey-feedback (questionnaire or interview) and the confrontation meeting is the direct involvement of organization members in the diagnosis.

FIGURE 8–3 Procedure for Confrontation Goal-Setting Meeting

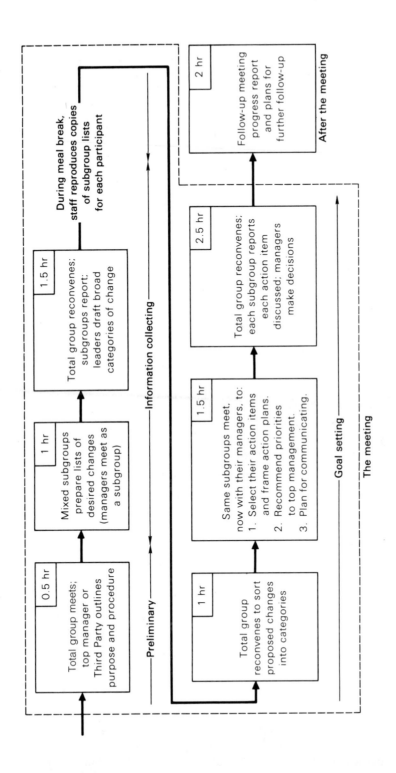

0.5 hr	1 hr	1.5 hr
Total group meets; top manager or Third Party outlines purpose and procedure	Mixed subgroups prepare lists of desired changes (managers meet as a subgroup)	Total group reconvenes: subgroups report; leaders draft broad categories of change

——Preliminary——

——Information collecting——

During meal break, staff reproduces copies of subgroup lists for each participant

1 hr	1.5 hr	2.5 hr
Total group reconvenes to sort proposed changes into categories	Same subgroups meet, now with their managers, to: 1. Select their action items and frame action plans. 2. Recommend priorities to top management. 3. Plan for communicating.	Total group reconvenes: each subgroup reports each action item discussed; managers make decisions

——Goal setting——

——The meeting——

2 hr
Follow-up meeting progress report and plans for further follow-up

After the meeting

From J. K. Fordyce and R. Weil, Managing with People, (Reading, Mass., Addison-Wesley, 1971), p. 94. Reprinted by permission.

With the former, the questionnaire and/or the consultant's interview generate the data, which are then presented to the group. With the latter, there is no intermediary step, which is its greatest advantage and at the same time its greatest pitfall. There is no question that data generated by organizational members themselves are "hotter," more relevant, and, therefore, are seen as more important than data generated by a survey or consultant. However, this very quality may be threatening to people in the meeting. Thus, problems that require risk taking may not surface. Not surprisingly then, crisis situations, which generate moderate pressures and can stimulate a willingness to take personal risks, are regarded as the best environment for a confrontation meeting. In short, by creating a special situation where openness can occur, the meeting attempts to stimulate the kind of communication that should have been occurring in the organization all along.

There is no one way to run a confrontation meeting. The procedure described above has been applied in a variety of ways and levels with some success. Bennis (1969) describes such a meeting in a small R&D firm where problems of competitiveness between project teams, lack of decisions about future direction, and questions about the manager's leadership were identified. As a result of the meeting, several changes occurred including the appointment of an administrative manager to take over some of the leadership.

In another instance, a confrontation meeting with all salaried and hourly employees in a small plant was effective in preventing a shut-down because of unprofitable operations. Within twelve months of the confrontation meeting, the plant was able to reduce its loss rate from $1,000,000 a year to $200,000 a year (Huse & Barebo, 1970; see Case 3–5). A variation of the confrontation meeting design was used in one large multinational company by bringing together 300 of the corporation's key managers from across the world and dividing them into small groups to identify major corporate problems. A number of task forces were put together to pursue identified problems, including one on energy, well before energy problems had reached crisis proportions.

It is mainly through these reported outcomes of confrontation meetings that one can evaluate their effectiveness and the conditions when they seem to work best. Reports of failures would help speed up our learning, but there have been no such reports.

OTHER DIAGNOSTIC TECHNIQUES

The differences between survey-feedback and the confrontation meeting highlight the extremes in diagnostic interventions: one usually relies on the consultant to generate the data and on more rigorous measurement methods such as the questionnaire; the other relies on the people in the organization to generate the data and the softer measurement method of lists. The trend in the field of OD seems to be going in the direction of less rigorous, more organic, and more involving techniques where organizational members engage directly in diagnosis, problem solving, and goal setting. The assumption underlying this trend, an appropriate one in my view, is that organizational members engaged in this type of diagnostic process will feel ownership of the findings and thus develop a commitment to correcting the problem. They will also learn how to diagnose organizational problems. They will become more aware of process and be able to recognize organizational problems on their own. Some other organic and involving diagnostic interventions are described very briefly below.

Sensing Meetings

This is essentially an unstructured group interview through which a manager can be informed directly about the feelings, attitudes, and problems at lower levels of the organi-

FIGURE 8–4   Procedure for Manager's Diagnostic Team Meeting Series

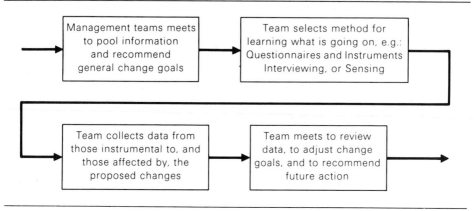

From Jack Fordyce and Raymond Weil, *Managing with People* (Reading, Mass.: Addison-Wesley, 1971), p. 91. Reprinted by permission.

zation that are not normally accessible. People from several parts of the organization may be chosen depending on the problems or needs of the manager. This meeting technique was developed and has been used widely at TRW, a large diversified corporation serving the automotive and aerospace markets. It can be used at both the salaried level and with nonexempt employees. Sensing meetings can also be tape-recorded for wider use later.

The Manager's Diagnostic Meeting

The top manager, assistants who have broad contacts within the organization, representatives from various levels of the organization, and a consultant meet as a team to assess the effectiveness of the organization and to determine where and if change is needed. The team may gather information by the sensing meeting method, questionnaires, or interviews. The point of this tool is to pool information and diagnose periodically, although recommendations for change in goals and strategies can result. See Figure 8–4 for a flow diagram which details the procedure for this meeting.

The Family Group Diagnostic Meeting

This meeting is a vehicle through which a work group gathers data about its own performance, critiques them, and decides on further steps for change, if necessary. The manager may suggest categories in which information is to be gathered, such as planning, achieving goals, what is done best, what is done worst, and how the group works together and with other groups. These categories are provided before the meeting. Data gathered are discussed and recategorized by major themes and actions planned (for example, a team-building meeting or intergroup meeting discussed in Chapter 9). The meeting is a simple way for a group to generate its own data, rather than relying on a consultant to do it. This method has all the advantages of direct involvement although there may be limited openness if the group has had no previous development experiences and a supportive climate does not exist.

The Organization Mirror

The organization mirror allows managers in an organizational unit to obtain feedback from other groups with whom they deal (users of a service, customers, suppliers, and so forth).   **129**

FIGURE 8–5 Procedure for the Organization Mirror

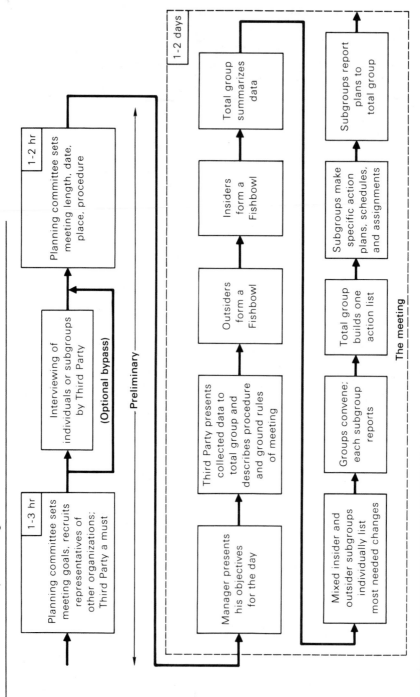

From Jack Fordyce and Raymond Weil, *Managing with People* (Reading, Mass.: Addison-Wesley, 1971), p. 102. Reprinted by permission.

A consultant gathers data ahead of time from people who deal with the unit and presents the information to the organizational unit with these people (outsiders) present. With members of the organizational unit listening, the outsiders are then asked to sit in a circle facing each other to discuss their perceptions of the group and their interpretations of the data (this is often called "fishbowling"). Members of the organizational unit are then asked to sit in a circle to discuss what they heard the outsiders say and identify issues needing clarification. The outsiders respond to questions of clarification. The meeting then goes on to a joint identification of major problems, problem solving, and action planning for improvement. Figure 8–5 provides a flow diagram of a procedure for running an organizational mirror.

The Diagnostic Task Force

A diagonal slice of the organization is commissioned as a task force to assess its health and effectiveness. This group may interview people and/or develop and administer a questionnaire with the help of a consultant as a resource. They take responsibility for feeding back the data to each work group and to top management of the unit. Such an approach has been used successfully at all levels of an organization. In one situation, a representative group of managers, nonexempt employees, and hourly employees were joined together in a task force. They identified barriers to more effective functioning of their plant and areas where quality of life in the organization could be improved.

DIAGNOSTIC INTERVENTIONS IN PERSPECTIVE

The array of diagnostic tools described in this chapter offer the change agent a wide range of choices. The important point is that the choice *not* be based on comfort or experience with a diagnostic method, but rather on the situation and the diagnostic goals of the intervention. No firm ground rules exist for making these choices. But the scope of the diagnosis, the extent to which standardized measurement is important, and the extent to which client involvement is important in creating attitude and behavior change are all considerations. These issues were discussed in Chapter 6 and at the beginning of this chapter. The reader may find the considerations in choosing a client versus consultant-centered diagnosis discussed in Chapter 6 the most useful in making a decision on a diagnostic approach. It is important to recognize, however, that in large scale OD efforts several different methods may be used in combination. By using each method for purposes to which it is best suited, the strengths of the various diagnostic methods can be maximized and their weaknesses minimized.

One thing seems clear—the frequency, relative sophistication, and commitment with which diagnostic methods are utilized by managers in an organization is perhaps the best indication of the organization's health and self-renewing capacity. It is generally accepted that it can be several years before a decline in human outputs such as motivation, satisfaction, or innovation is followed by a decline in profits or an increase in employee turnover (Likert, 1967). The larger, more complex, and financially or technically endowed the organization is, the longer this time lag is likely to be. For this reason, healthy organizations are ones in which managers diagnose the social system to identify and solve management problems as routinely and with as much confidence as they turn to the financial information system to identify and solve business problems. Indeed, the day may come when organizations will require managers to assess the efficiency, effectiveness, and health of their organizations on a regular basis as opposed to waiting for problems to   **131** arise. The use of sensing meetings and questionnaire surveys in a very few companies is approaching this degree of institutionalization. For example, IBM surveys 250,000 employees a year to routinely assess the health of the social system (Dunnington, 1978).

Diagnostic interventions obviously do more than "unfreeze" the organization by providing data and identifying problems. The application of these techniques also changes attitudes and behavior, particularly the more they involve people. But they are not likely to be sufficient to do so. Problems at the individual, group, intergroup, and systems level will undoubtedly require further attention and more powerful techniques for changing behavior and attitudes. The next chapter will deal with a set of methods aimed at intervening directly in organizational behavior and process.

NOTES

1. Tichy, N., Hornstein, H., and Nisberg, J., "Organization Diagnosis and Intervention Strategies: Developing Emergent Pragmatic Theories of Change," in Burke, W. W., *Current Issues and Strategies in Organization Development*, (New York: Human Science, 1977), p. 363.

PROCESS INTERVENTIONS 9

Very few tasks in complex organizations can be completed without the interaction of interdependent people and groups. These interactions are the *process* by which things get done. Unfortunately, this process is not always efficient and effective. For example, two scientists may not be able to complete an R&D project because of interpersonal difficulties; a management team may be unable to reach effective decisions because of the manager's style; redundancy and conflict may develop in a group because of unclear goals and roles, or distrust and hostility may develop between groups that have to coordinate their work. Because managers understand that these problems can affect morale and organizational effectiveness, they spend an enormous amount of time dealing with them.

The importance of these problems was acknowledged in Chapter 2, by the inclusion of organizational behavior and process as one of the components in the social systems model. Indeed, the job of managing an organization can be said to be that of obtaining behaviors that fit the task demands and strategy of the organization. The types of behaviors and processes listed in Figure 9–1 are offered as dimensions of behavior and process that are important in most organizations.

As Figure 9–1 shows, these behaviors directly affect human outputs and organizational outcomes and are and can be influenced by all the other components of the social system. A manager who wants to influence behavior can do so by changing selection and training practices, redesigning organization structures, and changing his own behavior. But often, direct intervention is required in the relationships that are blocking effectiveness. Effective working relationships between people and groups depend on their capacity to communicate feelings and perceptions and on the development of a relationship of mutual influence. This can only be achieved by getting people together to listen to each other, negotiate, problem solve, and work through feelings. In the past twenty years a number of techniques have been developed for helping groups do this effectively, constructively, and without undue risks to the "psychological safety" of individuals.[1] These *process interventions* are an important part of any system-wide change where people must learn new behaviors and develop new relationships.

A process intervention is a set of activities, usually led or facilitated by a consultant, **133**

FIGURE 9-1   A Social Systems Model of Organizations

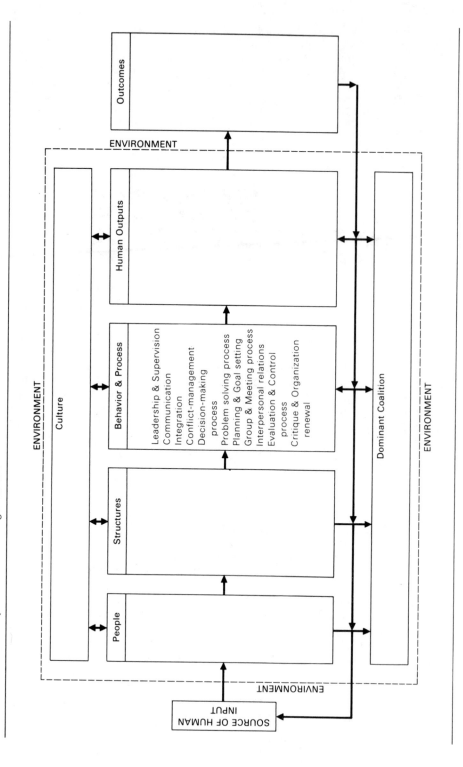

which is aimed at helping individuals and groups examine and act upon their behavior and relationships (Schein, 1969). Work or organization related behavior and interactions are examined as they occur in the organizational setting (for example, in meetings). Often special meetings may be created in which interactions and relationships in the past are diagnosed and plans are made for improvement. The objective is to create changes in the behavior and interactions that block task accomplishment and/or the satisfaction of organizational members. The conditions usually necessary to accomplish these objectives are:

1. the presence of a third party to collect information from organizational members about how they view each other and the process by which they work together;
2. an open face-to-face discussion of the data by the people who are part of the process being examined;
3. a segment of time in meetings or a special meeting away from the work setting that allows uninterrupted discussion, reflection, and action planning for improvement; and
4. the creation and enforcement by the third party of norms and ground rules to control the discussion and thereby ensure psychological safety and a problem-solving approach to conflict.

A "*setting*" in which these conditions are present can be a powerful tool for managers who want to stimulate and reinforce open dialogue about problems. Such a dialogue, if followed by action planning, leads to solution of immediate problems, and the learning of new process skills such as communicating, resolving conflict, and managing group decisions. These new skills then become part of the way things are done in the organization.

Process interventions are likely to create more permanent change than traditional training and educational methods. The biggest reason for this is that new attitudes, behaviors, and relationships are learned within the work setting and primary group. Unlike individual changes induced by training, learning which develops in a process intervention is more likely to be reinforced by the supervisor, peers, group practices, and group norms. This is because all components of the group are examined and dealt with at once and commitments to change are made .simultaneously. Furthermore, since process interventions deal with problems which affect the immediate task, process changes, if successful, are likely to be reinforced more quickly with improvements in performance (see Chapter 3 for a more detailed discussion of these change issues). In this way, new behavior is rewarded and regression is prevented.

Process interventions have their origin in group therapy, laboratory or sensitivity training (see Chapter 11), and clinical psychology. Though these techniques could be called therapeutic in the sense that they are aimed at attitude and behavior change, they do not generally have the same objectives of personality change or reorientation associated with psychotherapy. Aimed at an examination of work related attitudes and behavior, process interventions are more limited. Of course, because organizational behavior is a function not only of organizational learning but also of long-held values and beliefs rooted in early experience, process interventions sometimes deeply affect individuals and relationships.

By depth of intervention is meant the extent to which data fed back to individuals affects their sense of self. This is likely to happen when the person gets feedback that contradicts his beliefs, values, and assumptions about himself and the world around him (his self-concept). But this feedback may be directly given to a person or it may be **135** implied by a discussion of management and organizational practices. When feedback leads to a public discussion of a person's belief and values, the intervention is deeper than when it does not. Thus, the *focus* of the feedback and the *openness* with which data is discussed both influence the depth of the intervention (Harrison, 1965).

For example, sensitivity training is likely to stimulate direct reexamination and discussion of core values and interpersonal style—a deep intervention. For this reason, it is not recommended as a process intervention and will be discussed in Chapter 11 as a *personal* development experience rather than an organizational intervention. Team building, on the other hand, will cause reexamination of a group's work practices and relationships. While these may reflect core values and assumptions, particularly those of the manager, they are not generally discussed directly in the team-building meeting. Because they are not, team building reaches only moderate depth. Finally, critique of meeting effectiveness is the least threatening to self-concept since only meeting behavior is examined. Feedback about this behavior is less likely to focus on core values and any implication of this feedback for these values is not generally discussed.

How deep an intervention should go has to be carefully planned and controlled by the change agent. It should be consistent with what is required to obtain enduring solutions, the readiness of the individual or group, and the change agent's intervention skills (Harrison, 1965). It is possible, of course, that the readiness of individuals will be lower than the depth required to obtain an enduring solution. In this instance, the change agent must decide how far to push. In general, some leadership of the group into territory that reveals new information or provides new insights is needed for the intervention to be effective. Experience suggests, however, that organizational improvements can generally be accomplished with relatively "shallow" *process* interventions. Though the change agent can influence the depth of almost any process intervention, most of the interventions to be discussed in this chapter are of only moderate depth. Table 9–1 evaluates process intervention depth and focus.

PROCESSING MEETINGS

At higher levels of management in large organizations, managers may spend well over fifty percent of their time in meetings. Such meetings are used to share information, coordinate the activities of diverse functions, and diagnose and solve problems. Virtually every part of an organization's life is touched on in one kind of meeting or another: the current performance of the organization; analysis of new business opportunities; new product strategies; review of key personnel in the organization; organizational and morale problems; and labor relations and management topics. Meetings are, therefore, important both as a source of information for understanding and diagnosing the organization and as a forum for intervening directly in critical aspects of organizational life.

Meetings can have several effects. They can help build and maintain relationships between people and groups that must coordinate their activities or, if they come off poorly, can reduce trust and collaboration; they can provide a forum for surfacing undistorted important information or they can create an atmosphere where information is withheld and manipulated; they can be crisp and efficient or they can be long, tedious, and demotivating; they can lead to high quality problem identification and decision making or to inaction, procrastination, or compromise solutions that do not solve problems.

A basic assumption underlying OD practice is that a meeting's outcome is a function of the process of the meeting itself. That is, meetings are effective to the extent: the goals and objectives of the meeting are clear and shared; the chairman of the group has

TABLE 9-1 Depth and Focus of Process Intervention

Intervention Depth	Intervention Focus	Intervention Content	Intervention Methods					
			Meeting Processing	Group Development			Intergroup Meetings	Interpersonal Peacemaking
				Goal Model	Role Model	Interpersonal Model		
LOW	Task Issues	goals & strategy planning policy procedures types & frequency of meetings time management	X	X	X		X	
	Process Issues	role expectations delegation decision making communication conflict management integration	X		X	X	X	X
	Personal & Interpersonal Issues	leadership style personal work style interpersonal relation trust & mutual confidence mutual influence				X		X
HIGH	Competence Issues	knowledge & experience credibility personal effectiveness group's effectiveness openness to feedback				X		X

Intervention Depth: LOW ◄─────────────► HIGH

appropriate control of the interaction process; problem-solving stages, from information sharing through choosing an alternative solution, are separate and occur in the proper order; the problem-solving climate is confrontive; and the individuals who have the most knowledge about a problem influence its solution. Another assumption is that process problems occur in a meeting because the participants are not skilled in managing and critiquing either their meeting process or the underlying organizational processes and problems.

An OD consultant can help a group develop more effectiveness in meetings by helping to examine the meeting's dynamics and the underlying interpersonal or organizational issues that may be affecting its process. By doing this, the change agent improves the effectiveness of the meeting itself as well as the group's skills to examine meeting processes in the future. He may also contribute to greater awareness of fundamental organizational problems, thereby energizing the organization to act. By being there when problems surface, the change agent is in a position to help the appropriate individuals or groups work on them after the meeting. Finally, by being candid and open in looking at behavior, the change agent acts as a model and helps shape norms toward greater tolerance for self-examination and critique.

The means by which change agents can intervene in meetings vary widely. A consultant can observe and gain impressions, and when he feels that progress in the meeting might be helped by examination of the process, he can stop the meeting to feed these back. Or he can request that formal critique periods be set aside. The consultant can also catalyze examination of the meeting process by asking questions at critical points.

The purpose of these interventions is to stimulate people in the meeting to think about how they are conducting themselves (as individuals and as a group) and how this is affecting the quality of the meeting. The patterns of interaction, openness of communication, efficiency, atmosphere, and many other aspects of the meeting process come under scrutiny. The consultant can also provide feedback to individual participants after the meeting about their own behavior and its broader impact on the organization. Finally, some change agents (Argyris, 1971) have used tape recordings or video tapes of meetings to stimulate an in-depth analysis of individual and group behavior after the fact.

The effects of examining a meeting process can be quite powerful and pervasive. For example, Schein (1969) reports about one such instance where process consultation with a top management group resulted in substantial changes in the structure and agendas of its meetings. Upon examination, the group discovered that day-to-day operational problems were being discussed in the same meeting with policy questions, yet the nature of these problems and the processes they require are quite different. The first calls primarily for communication and a tightly run meeting, the second for exploration of ideas and a loosely run meeting. Two quite different climates and leadership styles were required for the two meetings, but because the agenda was mixed, neither was getting accomplished.

In another example, a major change to a project/matrix organization was aided by consultants sitting in on all twelve project team meetings (Pieters, 1971) for the first six months of the new organization's life. This was an enormous investment in consulting resources but significant benefits were obtained as groups learned how to function as project teams. Issues of project team leadership, intergroup conflict, meeting skills, and conflict management were among the issues that surfaced. The consultants estimated that process discussion at meetings was a significant factor in helping project teams learn how to function effectively. They also surfaced larger organizational problems that were blocking the effectiveness of project teams. Thus, discussing a meeting's process also served as a continual source of data about how the organization change effort was progressing.

FIGURE 9–2   An Organization as a Series of Linking Groups

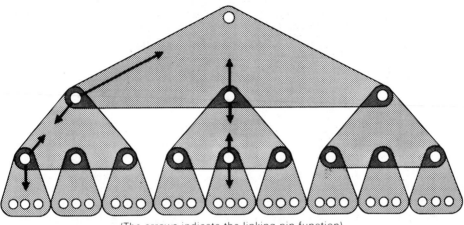

(The arrows indicate the linking pin function)

From Rensis Likert, *New Patterns of Management* (New York: McGraw-Hill, 1961), p. 113. Reprinted by permission.

Process consultation at meetings is an extremely important intervention and much more powerful than might be assumed at first. Perhaps its most important contribution to a broader change effort is that it allows the change agent to become tied into the organization's daily life. By helping others become more effective in meetings, he establishes relationships with people in the organization and a legitimacy for a process consultation role. This provides him with a source of power which if used properly, is an important ingredient in his effectiveness.

GROUP DEVELOPMENT[2]

The primary work group is probably the most important subsystem within an organization. Its importance in shaping organizational life prompted Rensis Likert's (1961) view of an organization as a series of small groups linked by individuals (linking pins) who are members of one group and managers of another (Figure 9–2). If all groups up and down an organization are effective in interpersonal relations, communication, problem solving, goal setting, and decision making, effectiveness of the organization as a whole would be high. Such effectiveness across the whole organization is an important prerequisite, not only for day-to-day task accomplishment and employee satisfaction, but also for organizational health and renewal.

Furthermore, the increasing use of temporary and permanent horizontal groups linking several functions engaged in a common task (project teams, task forces, business teams, etc.) has made group effectiveness even more important. Such groups are composed of members who are not bound by the traditional glue of formal authority and therefore require highly effective working relationships. Developing these is a difficult task and demands substantial new learning by group members. It is, therefore, not surprising that group development, also called team development or team building, is perhaps one of the more advanced and frequently used of all the OD interventions.   **139**

Deciding on Group Development

Group development is a process by which members of a group diagnose how they work together and plan changes which will improve their effectiveness. It begins with a contracting process in which the consultant attempts to determine what has triggered an interest in group development, how it fits with broader OD plans, and, most importantly, the manager's and group's readiness for it.

It is critically important that managers understand that group development is an activity in a broader plan for organization development. This is done through a meeting between the consultant and manager and later a meeting between the consultant and the group as a whole.

In these meetings, the consultant must be very clear about what group development is, how it fits into organization development, and the demands it will place on the manager and the members of the group. For example, it is essential that the manager understand that he must be willing to accept and even encourage criticism of himself and the group. Group members must come to understand that they will have to be willing to take personal risks in providing feedback to the manager and to others in the group and that they too will be receiving feedback about their effectiveness as group members. Both the manager and the group must be helped to understand that more open sharing of perceptions about each other and the group opens up important opportunities for personal and group development, opportunities that are not available through the more routine managerial processes of the organization. But they must also be helped to see that open sharing of information will change their perceptions of each other and the group, exposing them to the risks associated with any redefinition of reality. They must be informed that the greatest opportunity and risk is that associated with change in each person's perceptions of his own effectiveness and in the manager's changing perceptions of his subordinates. Finally, they must come to understand that group development may change the relationship of their group to the rest of the system.

At the same time, group members must be told about the confidentiality of group development proceedings and, in some detail, about the ground rules for interpersonal communication the consultant plans to enforce to facilitate a *constructive* and psychologically safe exchange. Without this information, the manager and the group cannot make a balanced determination about how the opportunities for personal and group development compare with the risks. Indeed, until groups are told by the consultant what ground rules he intends to provide and enforce, they are typically quite apprehensive and are not in a position to make an informed decision.

Even after being fully informed, each individual is likely to see different personal risks and opportunities and will therefore make different determinations about the potential value of group development. This is particularly true of very ineffective groups where members have doubts about each other's competence or where power struggles exist. Thus, those groups that may need group development most, may reject it if left to a consensual decision. While consultants may differ in their approach to this problem, experience suggests that in these situations it is best that the manager make the ultimate decision to go ahead. The only exception to this would be in cases where a group has a strong tradition of participative group decision making. The manager's decision is in effect a policy decision about the process by which the group will be managed. Individuals can make decisions about the extent of their participation and the personal risks they want to take, but the manager makes the decision about the process by which he plans to run the group.

140   A manager's decision to go into group development strongly influences group norms in the direction of open self-examination. A willingness to engage in this process ultimately becomes a requirement for group membership, a requirement that may not match each member's needs and expectations but which does ensure a more efficient, effective, and healthy group in the long run.

Collecting Data

Because of the difficulty a group might have surfacing issues in the meeting, the consultant often interviews group members in advance of the meeting. In this way, the barriers to open communication which prompt the need for a group development meeting are minimized. The interviews provide a vehicle by which group members can experiment with openness without risk. They can see the consultant's reaction and ask his advice about the potential difficulties in dealing with certain issues. They can formulate their feelings and thoughts and hear themselves say difficult things. This prepares them to be more open after the data is presented by the consultant. Participants are, of course, told that information they provide will be fed back in the meeting and are urged to specify what parts of the interview they would prefer to keep out of the meeting. For the consultant, these discussions are an important opportunity to enrich his understanding of the issues and the difficulties which might arise in the meeting.

Data collected and discussed in a group development meeting include: individuals' perceptions of the manager's approach to leading the group; their perceptions of each other and their relationships, and group problems associated with goals, roles, meetings, decision making and planning. For the top management group of a unit, data about the effectiveness of their organization, particularly as it relates to their management of it, may also be collected.

The Meeting

Shortly after the data has been collected, the work group meets away from the work place (off-site) in order to avoid day-to-day interruptions and pressures. Depending on the size of the group, the meeting can take from two to three days. During the meeting, the consultant feeds back the data to the group. Then the consultant categorizes the problems and presents them, usually with charts, for group discussion. With the help of the consultant, the group then sets the agenda for the remainder of the meeting by deciding the sequence in which major categories of data (interpersonal, group, and organizational) are to be tackled. The consultant can suggest those problems which, when tackled first, make subsequent discussion and problem solving easier. The discussion of each area is followed by action planning, which occurs either as the meeting progresses or at the end of the meeting. It is crucial that sufficient time be left for action planning. It is the action plan that allows review and follow-up.

The meeting itself consists of a systematic discussion of each category of problems and the data associated with it. For example, each individual may have a chart which describes how people see him just as there may be a chart on how people perceive meetings, if they are a problem. For many groups this may be the first time they have openly confronted certain difficult problems and conflicts. The consultant plays several roles in ensuring that this occurs successfully.

1. He helps the group develop or himself presents ground rules (norms) for conducting the meeting in such a way that barriers to group effectiveness are surfaced and problem solved. (These norms can be posted on the wall for continual reference throughout the meeting. An example is provided in Table 9–2.) **141**

TABLE 9–2 Meeting Norms

Hindering Behavior	Helping Behavior
Practice gamesmanship	Be open
Play it safe	Take personal risks
Don't tell others	Provide feedback—share
Conform	Respect individuality
Avoid conflict	Use conflict
Distrust others	Trust others
"Win-Lose"	Problem solve
Tear down	Support others

2. He helps the group examine and critique its own process in the meeting.

3. He offers expert knowledge about interpersonal, group, and organizational problems.

4. He acts as a neutral third party who can approach conflicts without bias or personal involvement.

5. He teaches subjects such as leadership, group process, and conflict resolution.

6. He models effective interpersonal behavior and interactions.

7. Finally, the consultant may act as a counselor to individuals during or following the team meeting.

The demands on the group development consultant are many, and not any one person can fulfill all of them, though the most effective can function in most of the roles. The ability to fulfill these roles depends more on personal effectiveness than an advanced degree in the behavioral sciences. In fact, in many organizations, properly trained personnel specialists and managers can act as group development consultants. This in-house resource is highly desirable if group development is to grow and spread throughout a large organization.

Follow-Up

If problems have been successfully confronted and discussed, the removal of some barriers to group effectiveness is underway by the end of the first meeting. During this first meeting, the group is dependent on the consultant to develop a climate conducive to risk taking. The group, however, must learn to maintain that climate without the consultant. Follow-up interventions such as additional group development experiences or laboratory training experiences (T-group or Grid, which will be discussed later) are often needed to ensure an open climate without the consultant's presence. Frequently, an effective group will finally be able to resolve many issues during day-to-day interaction, thus eliminating the need for further formal group development meetings. This elimination is a positive sign that the group is more effective and should not necessarily be construed as a deterioration in group effectiveness. However, because most groups find it difficult to discuss all process issues in the context of the daily routine, periodic group development meetings are probably useful in maintaining effectiveness.

Results

When sucessful, the result of this process is to remove the immediate barriers to effectiveness and to develop the group's self-sufficiency in managing its process and problems. It is *not* necessarily the development of more participative decision making, greater team cohesiveness, or any other normative state. This is why the term "group development" rather than "team building" was chosen. The surfacing of data about members' dissatisfaction with group functioning and their involvement in shaping remedies, usually leads to solutions which fit the group members and the task. Some groups may decide on more teamwork, others will limit the amount of teamwork. However, in a world where the environment is increasingly turbulent, teamwork is required more frequently and group development often becomes team development.

Just as group development may lead to more congruence among group members, leader, procedures, and task, so it sometimes leads to new strains with other parts of the organization. As a group identifies changes it must make to increase effectiveness, it is not uncommon for it to find that changes are required in its relationship with other groups. Thus, the outcome of the many group development activities is a need for more work at the interfaces between the group and the larger system. Just as this need arises, the group may also begin to turn inward, particularly when the result of group development has been an increase in group cohesion. This can lead to reduced interaction and trust between the group and others in the organization. The change agent must help the group anticipate these problems and deal with them constructively.

Three Models of Group Development

There are three distinct applications of the group development process described above (Beer, 1976). In designing a group development meeting, each of these models may be used in pure form, but most often they are mixed and integrated on the basis of the problem faced by the group, the depth of the intervention desired (see Table 9–1) and the skills of the consultant and manager.

The goal-setting model. Group members are involved in the process of developing individual and group goals with the help of a consultant (Beckhard, 1966; French & Hollman, 1977; Likert & Fisher, 1977). Such meetings have been used to obtain agreement on the strategic direction of the organization as well as more specific goals such as sales, return on investment and profit. They may also be used to set goals for change in the organization's structures and processes so that these are congruent with strategic goals (see Chapter 8 discussion of open system planning). However, the goal-setting model is also applied to lower levels where more specific task goals are the focus.

Goal-setting meetings can have several possible purposes. They may be used to energize a group to become more goal oriented and see themselves as interacting with an environment. They may be used to work through conflicts about which goals should be set, conflicts that may be decreasing coordination and cohesion. Finally, they may be used as a means of increasing individual motivation to achieve goals.

A number of studies have shown that group participation in goal setting not only forces the resolution of differences about what the goals should be, but it also raises individuals' level of motivation and commitment to achieve the goals. These occur because team goal setting makes the goals more explicit and creates group norms supporting the goals and their accomplishment (Bennett, 1955; Lewin, 1947; Pelz, 1958).

The interpersonal model. Group members meet to exchange their perception of each other and their relationships. The assumption underlying this model is that an interpersonally competent group is more effective than one that is not (Argyris, 1962). In such a group, people share feelings and differences nonevaluatively and without attribu- **143**

tion of motives, thus creating a climate of mutual trust, supportiveness, and confidence. Therefore, such groups stimulate more risk taking, better problem solving, and more effective decisions.

The problem with group effectiveness is that the conditions leading to it are highly interdependent and mutually reinforcing. Trust leads to risk taking which leads to more open communication. But open communication and risk taking are necessary to develop trust. Ineffective groups find it difficult to break a negative cycle of low trust, low risk taking, and poor communication which locks them into a state of low interpersonal competence. Members of the group find it too risky to break such a cycle for fear of being hurt or distrusted for their effort. An outsider is often needed to help create the conditions which will prevent the type of evaluative communication which has decreased trust in the first place. If such communication can go on long enough for trust to build, the cycle is reversed and the group is on its way to greater interpersonal competence and effectiveness. There are a number of techniques for doing this.

One approach involves collecting from each group member his perception of others' behavior (including that of the boss) (Beer, 1976). In an interview he is asked to provide several behaviors for each person that help group effectiveness and several that hinder it. During the meeting, each person's *helping* and *hindering chart* is posted on the wall and discussed by the group. The lists provide a structure for the discussion and a measure of control for the consultant who has put the lists together. They also speed up involvement as members are faced with owning up to items they provided. The manager should usually receive feedback first, thus modeling a willingness to work cooperatively. The consultant prepares him for this role to ensure that this first critical step goes well. The consultant can also provide ground rules for giving and receiving feedback (Anderson, undated), often posted on charts which guide participants in how to communicate competently. Table 9–3 provides an example of such ground rules. Rules which the giver of feedback should follow are listed along the left side of the table. Along the right side of the table are rules which the receiver of feedback should follow if he wants to hear and understand more.

The consultant, the structure of charts, and the ground rules for communication reduce the risks of this meeting well below that of more unstructured T-groups. Unanticipated and difficult issues are not likely to arise without the consultants knowledge and, with the enforcement of norms for communication, are likely to be handled constructively. Experience has repeatedly demonstrated that this model is a reliable, safe, and usually effective way of increasing trust, communication, and risk taking. Naturally, much follow-up is required to maintain these positive results.

The role model. Group development can involve a discussion by group members of their roles and a negotiation process in which roles are adjusted to satisfy both individual needs and task requirements. A "role" represents a set of behaviors which a person in one organizational position feels obligated to perform and which persons in other organizational positions expect that person to perform (Katz and Kahn, 1978). The assumption underlying the role model is that a person's behavior is not only influenced by interpersonal relations but also by what he thinks others (boss, peers, the organization) expect. Some of these expectations are formalized in job descriptions and in goals with which a person agrees, but many expectations are developed over time and are much less formal.

Some problems in organizations exist as a result of conflict between what is expected from the individual and what he is able or willing to deliver (role conflict). When individuals do not fulfill others' expectations, the result is often disappointment and loss of

144

TABLE 9–3   Ground Rules for Giving and Receiving Feedback

Giving Feedback	Receiving Feedback
Helps	**Turns On**
—providing specific behaviors—what was said or done	—paraphrasing what you have heard
—providing recent examples	—requesting clarification of feedback
—conveying feelings of concern—intend to be helpful	—checking other's perception of the feedback
—conveying equal power in relationship—you control the exchange as much as I	—summarizing what several people have said
—being descriptive; not evaluating other person	—speculating about examples of your own behavior that might have led to feedback
—describing own feelings as consequence of other's behavior	—exploring the feelings created by the feedback
—revealing your underlying assumption	
Hinders	**Shuts Off**
—giving general or vague feedback	—justifying your actions
—providing old examples	—building a case for why you do what you do
—using power to drive feedback home	—apologizing
—evaluating and judging other person	—promising not to do it again
—attributing negative motives	—overinternalizing feedback (assuming it is all true)
—fault finding, accusations, blaming	
—bringing up behaviors that the others can't change	

credibility and trust. These reactions in turn result in reduced coordination, cohesion, and teamwork. When the environment or task changes rapidly it is easy to see how new expectations can develop faster than they can be clarified and agreed to.

Many more problems in organizations develop because individuals are often uncertain about what is expected of them (role ambiguity). Research suggests that role ambiguity results in anxiety and job dissatisfaction, which in turn causes a loss in organizational effectiveness and an increase in employee turnover (House & Rizzo, 1972). It is likely that ambiguity tends to increase the amount of energy devoted to protecting oneself and decrease the amount of energy put into the task. If this happens an intervention aimed at clarifying and getting agreement on roles should release energy and reduce the negative consequences of role conflict (Bennis, 1966).

There are many variations of role perception and clarification meetings. All of the techniques involve individuals presenting their view of their role, generating a discussion of it, and modifying it based on group member expectations. For example, the Role Analysis Technique (RAT) is a method by which each individual presents his perception of his role (Doyal & Thomas, 1968). He then solicits others' expectations of him and states his expectations of them. After a discussion of all roles, group members revise their roles and present them for final acceptance.

Responsibility charting has also been found useful in helping groups sort out who has primary responsibility for initiating a decision and who must be consulted for review or approval. Figure 9–3 provides an example of a responsibility chart in which decisions and actions are listed along the left side of the chart and individual actors or groups along the top. Individuals in a group come together to discuss and agree on who will initiate a decision, who has the right to veto, who must be informed, and so on. For each decision individuals are assigned a code after consensus is reached (see code in Figure 9–3). Responsibility charting has been found to be particularly useful in clarifying the often ambiguous and overlapping responsibilites in matrix organizations. Chapter 10 has a **145**

FIGURE 9–3

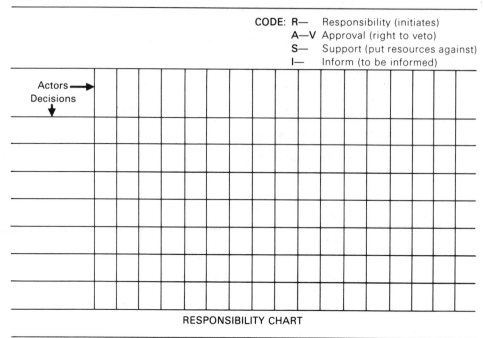

CODE: R— Responsibility (initiates)
A—V Approval (right to veto)
S— Support (put resources against)
I— Inform (to be informed)

Actors → Decisions ↓																	

RESPONSIBILITY CHART

From Richard Beckhard and Reuben T. Harris, *Organizational Transitions: Managing Complex Change* (Reading, Mass.: Addison-Wesley 1977), p. 79, Figure 6.1 Reprinted by permission.

discussion of matrix. Case 9–1 provides an example of how responsibility charting can be used.

On the assumption that interpersonal probelms can be dealt with through negotiating expectations of behavior, Harrison (1973) has developed a "Role Negotiations" approach to group development. Such an approach, he claims, is more suited to the reality of many organizational settings in which power, coercion, and competitiveness prevent the resolution of differences through open dialogue. Members of the group bargain and negotiate changes in each other's behavior. Each person is asked to list for each other person in the group those things which the other person should *do more* or *do better*, those things which the other should *do less,* and those things which *should not be changed.* Agreement on changes are negotiated and contracted for in writing. With this method, major conflicts and ambiguities can be averted or handled without having to work through interpersonal issues, an emotionally charged and difficult process. However, unlike the interpersonal model, this method cannot increase the interpersonal competence, and therefore the health, of the group.

Application on Group Development

One model of group development is rarely used by itself. Goals, roles, and interpersonal behavior are interdependent and cannot usually be treated separately. Thus, many group development meetings use more than one model, or the use of one model leads to the need for another meeting using one of the other models. The consultant, together with the group, must decide on the appropriate model or combination and sequence of models.

But what happens when a consultant is not available? How are these decisions to be made by an untrained manager? Indeed, can group development proceed without a consultant? Experience suggests that it can if the leader is sufficiently competent interpersonally and understands the dynamics of team building. Once a group, with the help of a consultant, has begun to reverse the mutually reinforcing conditions of low trust, low risk taking, and poor communication they should be able to continue on their own in meetings, particularly after they have learned the basic ground rules and skills for conduct. Unfortunately, this does not always happen because the leader is not sufficiently competent and therefore dependence on the consultant has developed. It is the consultant's responsibility to wean the leader and the group from this dependence as quickly as possible.

One solution is not to develop dependence in the first place. There are several highly instrumented methods of team development which a group may use (Plovnick, Fry & Rubin, 1975; Blake & Mouton, 1968a). Grid Team Development, designed by Blake and

---

CASE 9–1

A multinational firm that had several domestic product divisions, decided to increase integration between its international operations and its domestic operations by adopting a matrix organization. In this organization, foreign subsidiary managers would not only work for their current bosses, vice-presidents in charge of geographic regions (Europe, South America, etc.), but also for vice-presidents in charge of domestic product divisions that made products sold by the subsidiary. The adoption of a world-wide matrix created tremendous ambiguity about who was responsible for what. For example, who was to be responsible for developing product strategy, the subsidiary manager selling that product in his country or the product division manager who now had world-wide responsibility for this product line? If it was to be the subsidiary manager's responsibility, who had approval responsibility, the vice-president in charge of the region or the domestic division manager? If both had approval responsibility, whose approval was more important? Responsibility for many other decisions such as pricing, allocation of manufacturing capacity, labor relations, local government relations, and

research and development also needed to be clarified. The ambiguity the new structure created caused much apprehension and anxiety.

A management consulting firm helped guide the process of responsibility charting by developing charts like the one in Figure 9–3. They developed a list of major decisions normally taken in running the business from interviews with relevant managers in domestic and international operations. With this list filled in on the left side of the responsibility chart, managers in domestic and international operations, associated with a given product line, met to discuss who would have primary responsibility, who would be consulted on decisions, and who would approve decisions. Managers reported that the process of agreeing on how the responsibility chart was to be filled out served to clarify expectations, increase mutual trust and confidence, build relations, and decrease anxiety. Even though the charts were rarely referred to once the role clarification meetings were over, the process of working through them was thought to have contributed to the effectiveness of the organization.

FIGURE 9–4   Procedure for the Family

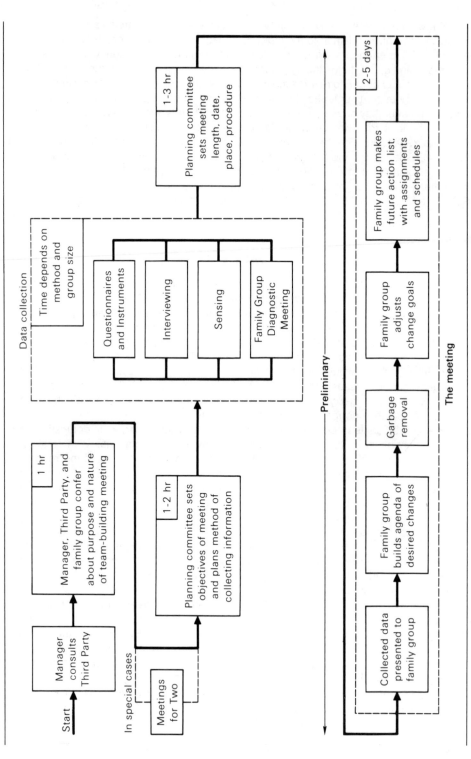

From Jack K. Fordyce and Raymond Weil, *Managing with People: A Manager's Handbook of Organization Development Methods* (Reading, Mass.: Addison-Wesley, pp. 120–121). Reprinted by permission.

Mouton, relies on standardized questionnaires to collect data in advance, and detailed procedures to guide the group through several of the models already described. But group members are expected to attend a one-week seminar which prepares them personally and conceptually for team development. Furthermore, Grid Team Development is part of a larger Grid OD program which starts at the top (see Chapter 12). Therefore, each manager (linking pin) has been through the process once with his own boss and peers. The greatest advantage of instrumented group development is that it does not create dependence on the consultant and therefore the process is not likely to stop when he leaves. On the other hand, it does require patience with a standardized procedure, unresponsive to the problems of any given group. The result can be loss of motivation before the group actually gets to the important issues.

Regardless of the group development method chosen, do groups become more effective? The answer to this must be based primarily on the experiences reported by managers and consultants. There is no question that group development has become one of the most frequently applied process interventions. It has been used with task forces, family groups, project teams, functional teams, old teams, and new teams. Many organizations have used the approach, notably TRW in the introduction of matrix management in the systems group (Davis & Lawrence, 1977). Experience suggests that group development is a powerful intervention and that it has the potential of dealing with many process problems in an organization. Research evidence supports this view (Friedlander, 1967, 1968; Golembiewski & Kiepper, 1976). Problem-solving effectiveness, approachability of the leader, mutual influence, personal influence, intergroup trust, and meeting effectiveness have all been found to increase as a result of group development. This is particularly true when there is consultant involvement with the group before the meeting and follow-up after. Consultant follow-up can be expected to serve as a reminder to complete action plans and to help individuals who are having difficulty. Of course, this reinforces an important point. Group development cannot be seen as one meeting. It is a process of self-examination and improvement which effective groups have and ineffective ones don't. The formal group development intervention is only a catalytic event which is intended to develop an ongoing process where one does not already exist as part of the group's life. This process can not only increase efficiency and effectiveness, but also health.

Figure 9–4 presents a flow chart which outlines a team-building process for which a group takes major responsibility. Though a third party (consultant or personnel specialist) may be involved, a committee plans the meeting and collects the data. A group which has been through a team-building process with a consultant should be able to follow such a process without help. Indeed, in organizations which have been involved with OD for a long time, team-building meetings without consultants are routinely used by managers to maintain group effectiveness.

But does an organization have the right to sponsor interventions which, as stated earlier, can on occasion have an impact on deeply held values and beliefs? The answer to this would be clearly no, if it were not for the fact that the alternatives to such interventions are potentially as powerful and probably more devastating to individuals. In the adaptation process, groups and organizations inevitably seek greater congruence. Thus, when markets or leadership change, individuals who do not fit are often transferred, demoted, and more than occasionally, fired. When group development has a deeply felt impact it is more than likely that problems of fit between the individual and the group have been clarified for the first time and the individual is confronted with his own reality. Group development has hastened a personal crisis (facing up to the need to change or to leave) but it has not created one that would not appear later in a much less constructive manner. **149**

Consistent with the values of OD, the individual is provided with information which clarifies the choice of changing or leaving. In this way the individual is given opportunities to control his own destiny and the organization's adaptiveness is enhanced.

INTERGROUP INTERVENTIONS

In most organizations, conflict between groups is quite common. Organizations usually develop differences between functional groups, such as sales and manufacturing, as a means of responding to diversity and uncertainty in their environment (Lawrence & Lorsch, 1967a). Manufacturing must organize for stability and efficiency while sales must organize to relate to and service customers. To accomplish these diverse tasks, sales must hire different people than manufacturing, and each must manage its people in accordance with their unique expectations and the function's task requirements. If such differences did not exist, neither group could get its job done effectively. Imagine a sales organization managed in the highly structured and closely controlled way typical of a plant. Salespeople would be unhappy, demotivated, and, indeed, unable to get their job done—a job that requires responsiveness to the customer, not a schedule. But these natural differences between groups create some understandable barriers to mutual understanding and collaboration. When the groups are interdependent, these barriers can create some serious problems in meeting their common goals.

For example, when sales' success depends on delivery, service, and quality from manufacturing, and manufacturing's efficiency is dependent on sales' capacity to generate volume and project sales volume and mix accurately, there is ample opportunity for each group to disappoint the other. If the functions also compete for scarce resources (money, power, people, attention from top management) and are physically separated, a mild conflict can generate into intense competition and animosity. Though the nature of the relationship is different, similar conflicts often develop in large organizations between line and staff, headquarters and divisions, parent and subsidiary, and union and management.

The increasingly uncertain and complex environment in which organizations operate, often requires close coordination between interdependent groups on tasks. The cost of intergroup conflict under such conditions becomes high, and means must be found for eliminating hostility and destructive conflict while maintaining needed differences. There are structural solutions to these problems, which will be discussed in the next chapter. But often these solutions are not workable unless sufficient trust and mutual confidence exist between groups, allowing them to work through their differences constructively. Some techniques that behavioral scientists have developed to deal with intergroup conflict will be described, but first the dynamics of intergroup conflict must be understood.

The Dynamics of Intergroup Conflict

The differences between groups cause members to tighten their loyalty and identification with their respective group. As this occurs, group members see each other as more and more similar and others as quite different. Greater cohesion within each group occurs and competitiveness between them is heightened. As competition increases, the groups' perceptions of each other become more negative. Distortions in perception of the other group creep into the relationship to justify behavior and attitudes with regard to the other group. Each group sees only the best parts of itself and the worst parts of the other group. A self-fulfilling intergroup conflict develops which continues to reinforce itself unless bro-

150

ken by an external force or intervention (Alderfer, 1976; Blake et al., 1964; Walton & Dutton, 1969).

The Intergroup Laboratory

A method for resolving such intergroup conflict was developed by Blake, Shepard, and Mouton (1964). The process begins with a consultant establishing a trusted third party relationship with the two groups prior to bringing them together. This relationship-building phase includes interviews which allow the consultant to do a preliminary diagnosis and ends with a contract with both groups for a meeting between them at an off-site location.

There are numerous variations on the procedures used during the meeting. Following are those found to be useful:

1. Ground rules (norms) such as those in Tables 9–2 and 9–3 must be presented and discussed at the start of the meeting. These are aimed at enhancing a constructive interchange.

2. Each group is asked to meet privately to answer the following questions:
   How do we see ourselves?
   How do we see the other group?
   How do we think they see us?
   They discuss the answers to these questions and then one-word phrases or adjectives are posted on charts. Table 9–4 provides an example of answers to these questions from an intergroup meeting between engineering and manufacturing groups (Alderfer, 1976; Burke, 1972).

TABLE 9–4   Intergroup Perceptions

Engineering	Manufacturing
We see ourselves:	
stable	competent
cooperative	error prone
creative	hard working
•	•
• *We see them:*	•
•	•
unstable	error prone
not creative	no sense of urgency
industrious	unified as a group
•	•
• *They see us:*	•
•	•
in ivory towers	constantly changing
error prone	error prone
intrusive	inflexible
•	•
•	•

From J. R. Hackman and J. L. Suttle, *Improving Life at Work: Behavioral Science Approaches to Organizational Change* (Santa Monica, Calif.: Goodyear, © 1977), pp. 285. Reprinted by permission.

3. The groups are brought together for an exchange of images. This can be an emotional meeting with real dangers that the conflict will escalate as one side accuses the other. To prevent this, each side is allowed only questions for clarification.

4. The groups are again separated and asked to identify the problems that exist between them which are causing the perceptions they have just heard. They present their diagnosis in a joint meeting. Again, only questions for clarification are allowed.

5. The two lists of problems are then consolidated by two individuals representing each group.

6. A consolidated list is then prioritized and subgroups composed of members from each group go to work on solving these problems. For those problems that cannot be solved in the meeting, an action plan that will lead to a solution is developed, and responsibilities for carrying it out are assigned.

The intergroup laboratory has been applied with some modifications to the relationship between functional groups in industrial settings, labor and management, headquarters and field organizations, contractor and subcontractor, foreign service officers and the administrative staff of the State Department, and mergers. Most of these interventions have been reported to be successful indicating that the technology does work in a wide variety of settings (Alderfer, 1976; Beer, 1976). Their effectiveness seems to lie in the intervention's capacity to break the negative cycle of perceptions and behavior. (See Case 9–2 for an example.)

Under tightly controlled procedures for communicating and listening, better mutual understanding and trust are developed long enough to get joint agreement to steps that will deescalate the conflict, and hopefully get a positive cycle of trust and cooperation going. If these positive attitudes can be translated into the solution of task problems which have been created by poor integration, an increase in organizational effectiveness will occur. However, the intervention's success is based on one overriding assumption—that the groups brought together have a common superordinate goal or can come to recognize such a goal. Indeed, the intervention is aimed at helping groups develop common goals, the main ingredient in cooperative relationships. Unless the possibility for such superordinate goals exists, an intergroup laboratory is not likely to be successful. Experience with successful applications of this intervention to union-management relations does indicate, however, that groups which have a *mix* of conflicting and common goals can benefit from this intervention (Driscoll, 1978).

INTERPERSONAL PEACEMAKING

The dynamics of intergroup conflict can also be seen in the relationships between individuals. Role differences and competition for power, resources, and recognition are frequently the cause of such conflict. When the individuals in conflict are important members of the organization, not only the normal personal costs created by such conflicts arise, but also organizational costs. The individuals place enormous energy into maneuvering around each other, and the energy they put into the task is reduced. Similarly, their capacity to coordinate and their adaptability is reduced.

In one example of such a conflict, two very key scientists, who needed to coordinate their work and share findings and plans for research, were in such severe conflict that they were withholding information, avoiding each other, and even attempting to make the other look bad in the eyes of their colleagues. When the task requires collaboration between

CASE 9-2

A manufacturing plant and regional sales district were locked in an intergroup conflict which not only resulted in stormy interchanges but also caused problems in customer relations. The plant perceived sales as concerned only about volume and pleasing the customer, not about the plant's costs. The district sales manager and his salespeople saw the plant as unresponsive to customers, conservative, and overly concerned about costs and long manufacturing runs.

One particular phone conversation on a Friday afternoon was often cited as an example of the conflict. The district sales manager was calling to find out why the sales service department had been turned down by the plant on a special request to send products to a large and important customer. The plant manager explained that three days was too short a time for turning around a large order and that it would disrupt operations in the plant, other customer orders, and the whole month's production schedule. Besides, the plant manager told the district manager, "You guys are just not willing to tell the customer that he can't have what he wants. It's your job to manage the customer, not respond to every wish." At this, the district manager lost his temper and accused the plant manager of caring only about his "gross margin" (plant profit). The shouting match that ensued resulted in the plant manager hanging up.

As part of a larger OD program aimed at improving cooperation and coordination between functional groups, a corporate OD consultant met with the plant manager and district sales manager to determine their interest in working to improve relations and coordination. They both agreed to an intergroup labo-

ratory as a means of improving integration. The plant manager and his staff, and the district sales manager and his salespeople came together at a motel for two days to work on the problems in their relationship. The manager of the sales service organization, which often found itself in the middle of this conflict because of its responsibility to represent sales to manufacturing, was also present as a neutral observer.

The intergroup meeting closely followed the procedure outlined on page 151. Each group met separately to develop a list of what bothered them about the other group and what they thought the other group was writing about them. When the plant manager presented the plant's list to the sales district, the matter of the phone call and its indication about sales' lack of concern for profitability was cited. One of the salespeople immediately jumped up to explain why that particular customer was so important. The plant manager's face tightened and they could all see that he was about to become defensive. At this point, the consultant called attention to the ground rules for communication (see Table 9-3) which stressed active listening and nondefensive behavior on the part of the group receiving feedback. Another potential shouting match was averted and the groups began to listen to each other.

As a result of a successful perception exchange, a number of factors which were triggering poor relations and coordination were surfaced. The role sales service could be playing in managing the relationship between sales and the plant was clarified. The groups also realized that demands from the major customer which triggered the phone call had been the basis of many other conflicts. During the second day, sub-groups composed of plant and sales people developed action plans for solving these and other problems. For example, the plant manager and district sales manager agreed to visit the customer to determine why erratic demands were being made and what to do about them. The sales service manager committed himself to developing a set of ground rules, agreed to by both parties, by which he would handle unusual customer demands. Over the next year, relationships and coordination improved and there were more frequent meetings between the two groups to solve problems.

such individuals, resolution of the underlying issues in the conflict has to be achieved. Often a separate intervention which focuses on just the two individuals is required.

A consultant, who is seen by both parties as neutral in the conflict, can help bring two individuals together to develop a constructive dialogue about their differences and help them plan for modification in their interactions. The objective may be to increase trust and mutual confidence through resolution of the conflict, or to merely control the conflict so that minimum required coordination is obtained. The consultant must choose between these objectives based on his diagnosis of the causes of the conflict and the situation. If resolution of the conflict is the objective, the process for doing so is quite similar to that described for intergroup conflict. The consultant sets up a situation for a controlled problem solving dialogue and uses himself as a process consultant during the meeting. While the meeting between the two has a planned structure, much of what the consultant does is on an ad hoc basis—responding and initiating as the situation demands. Walton (1969) has provided the following list of specific consultant interventions found useful in resolving an interpersonal conflict. They are listed in roughly the order in which they might occur.

- Initiating agendas for the meetings of the two parties
- Structuring the setting of meetings to be maximally facilitative of constructive exchange
- Helping the parties provide each other with honest and constructive feedback about their reactions to each other
- Suggesting specific ways in which discussions between the parties might proceed
- Restating views of the parties, making sure they are heard and heard accurately
- "Refereeing" the interaction between the parties, and sometimes even providing mild rewards (and punishments) for productive (and counterproductive) behavior by the participants
- Helping parties to diagnose the reasons for their conflict
- Diagnosing (and sometimes attempting to change) the conditions that have caused poor dialogue between the parties
- Obtaining agreement for changes in behavior and periodic review and follow-up

One can see in Walton's listing of the interventions that the consultant is a key element in the success of the interpersonal peacemaking intervention. The following are attributes required of an effective consultant:

1. High professional expertise regarding social process
2. Low power over fate of principles

3. High control over process when confrontation takes place
4. Moderate knowledge about the principles, issues, and background factors
5. Neutrality or balance with respect to substantive outcomes, personal relationships, and conflict resolution methodology (Walton, 1969)

These attributes have been listed here because they are particularly important in dealing with an emotionally laden interpersonal conflict. But except for degree, these attributes for a consultant are also a requirement in all of the process interventions and some of the diagnostic interventions described so far. This point will be taken up again when the attributes of an effective consultant or change agent are discussed later.

PROCESS INTERVENTIONS IN PERSPECTIVE

In almost all organizations there are numerous problems in communication, trust, and relationships which block organizational efficiency, effectiveness, and health. A process intervention can be used as an entry point for dealing with these problems directly. If this approach is taken, the change agent has to expect that the intervention will surface a lot of data about the organization and thus will constitute the first step in an organizational diagnosis. This occurs most frequently when group development with a top management team leads to a diagnosis of the whole organization, utilizing the methods discussed in Chapter 8. However, the reverse sequence is more likely in systems-wide organization development efforts. A diagnosis is commissioned, and this diagnosis leads to an action plan which calls for both structural and process changes. In these instances, the structural changes are usually implemented first and process interventions are used to help people adapt their behavior and attitudes to the relationships and roles required by the new structures (see Case 9–1).

The advantages and disadvantages of these sequences will be discussed in Chapter 12. For now, it is important to note that organization change means behavior change and that simply announcing structural changes or calling for new behaviors is not sufficient. Process interventions can be used to initiate change or as a follow-up to other changes. But they *must* be used to reduce organizational and psychological strain, to prevent dysfunctional effects, to obtain satisfaction with the change from as many constituencies as possible, and to prevent regression to earlier states. (See Chapter 3 for a discussion of these change outcomes.) In other words, process interventions, which involve organizational members in the change process, can help individuals adapt to change.

Unfortunately, process interventions are underutilized in many organizational changes though effective managers will recognize that they have been applying these methods in less formal and systematic ways. An understanding of these methods can therefore help managers improve their own competence as change agents or increase their sophistication as consumers of consulting services.

It should be clear that process interventions rely heavily on the personal competence of the change agent. While the emphasis may differ, they all require some of the following behavior and skills:

- Observing and diagnosing process at the interpersonal, group, and intergroup levels
- Helping to set conditions for effective communication (agendas, norms, physical space, meeting membership, information presentation, leadership)
- Facilitating communication through asking questions, restating, refereeing, summarizing, suggesting new procedures, helping others to provide feedback and **155**

critique, providing feedback and critique
- Modeling interpersonal competence and effective communication
- Reinforcing individual and group behavior that facilitates good process or mildly punishing behavior that does not
- Helping to develop action plans that will "lock" new processes in place at all levels

One can see from this list that process interventions are a complex learning process: First, individuals and groups are helped to see old behavior as inadequate (developing dissatisfaction); then through specially designed meeting structures and change agent interventions, old behavior is examined and new behavior stimulated and reinforced (change); and finally, action plans that support behavior change are developed (refreezing). The reader will of course recognize that this sequence follows the general change model outlined in Chapter 3. The change agent (particularly the manager) must be skilled in orchestrating this process and thus must understand the basic learning paradigm underlying all process interventions. He must also support it through his own personal behavior and skills—he is the catalytic agent.

NOTES

1. Psychological safety refers to the conditions needed to preclude feedback which can seriously damage a person's sense of self-worth, and thereby his mental health.
2. For a comprehensive discussion of group development see Dyer (1977).

STRUCTURAL INNOVATIONS AND INTERVENTIONS 10

The previous chapter presented a variety of intervention methods managers might use to effect changes in the way people (individuals and groups) perceive themselves and others, and interact. While these are potentially very powerful methods for changing organizational behavior and process, the systems view of organizations, which is the viewpoint of this book, suggests that any changes which occur through process interventions will be short-lived unless they are supported by structural changes. For example, greater trust, mutual understanding, and teamwork resulting from a team-building intervention are not likely to be sustained unless changes in the reward system or control system follow. In fact, an alternative to beginning organizational improvement with process interventions is to start with structural change. The social systems model presented in Chapter 2 and shown again in Figure 10–1, acknowledges the importance of various formal structures and systems in shaping organizational behavior.

That organizational improvement can start with structural change is, of course, not a new idea. Managers routinely use such changes to deal with problems of ineffectiveness. Unfortunately, assumptions about how alternative structures shape behavior are not always clear to them nor are they always correct. There is a tendency to cling to known and tried structural solutions even when considerable evidence exists that they have many dysfunctional effects which outweigh their benefits. There is also the opposite tendency of adopting new structural solutions because everyone else is doing so. When this is done, it is without fully understanding the conditions under which these solutions are appropriate and the implementation steps needed. These problems are caused by managers' lack of knowledge about innovations developed in other organizations, the problems that led to their adoption, the consequences of their adoption, and the problems of implementing them.

The change agent's role as social architect (Havelock & Havelock, 1973) requires that he be sophisticated regarding management practice in other organizations. He must also be aware of developing research and theory regarding alternative structures. In other words, if the change agent is to make structural interventions he must help managers to translate broader knowledge about organizational structures into specific solutions rele- **157**

FIGURE 10–1 A Social Systems Model of Organizations

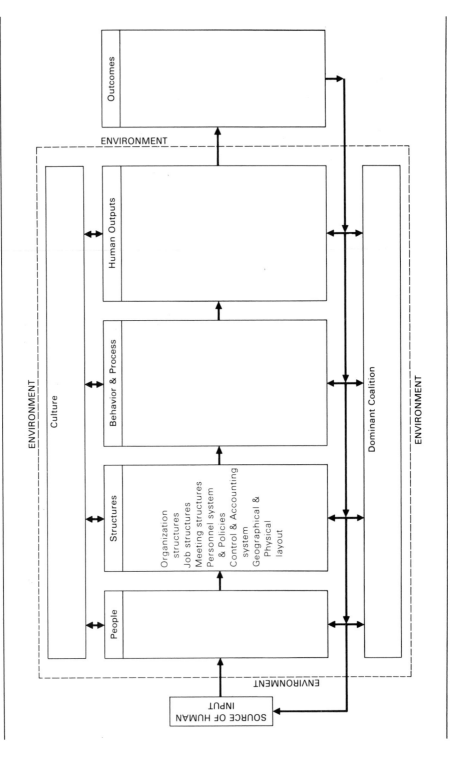

vant to their problems. Therefore, added to the role as a process consultant, helper and facilitator, and his role as a diagnostician, the change agent must be a knowledge translator, solution builder, evaluator, systems monitor, and innovation manager (Havelock & Havelock, 1973). He must advocate a new solution that seems to fit a particular problem, help managers evaluate it objectively, and implement it effectively.

This chapter will review the major innovations and interventions available to change agents in five structural dimensions:

1. Organization design
2. Job design
3. Reward systems
4. Performance management systems
5. Control and accounting systems

One chapter cannot do justice to the innovations and interventions about to be discussed, but it can describe briefly the major structural forms which are emerging from managers' efforts to respond to changing conditions. In each case, the intervention's conceptual underpinnings and a brief summary of considerations in its application will be offered.

Traditionally, OD has been almost exclusively concerned with diagnostic, process, and individual interventions—what Leavitt (1965) has called the "people approaches" to change. But if OD is to live up to its definition as system oriented, structural interventions must be included in the OD territory. The challenge will be to understand how to integrate structural interventions with other more "people" oriented interventions. A question which remains unanswered is how much participation by organizational members is possible when sophisticated system analysis, concepts, and models are the basis of change.

ORGANIZATION DESIGN—MOVING TOWARD MATRIX

We are going through an era where a new structural form is emerging. As Alfred Chandler (1962) documented in his historical survey of business organizations, new organizational forms have emerged as older structures no longer effectively served changing market environments. Just as the *functional organization* emerged out of the industrial revolution and the *federally decentralized* form of organization pioneered at General Motors by Alfred E. Sloan emerged in the twenties, so *matrix* is emerging as the organizational invention of the postindustrial era (Bennis & Slater, 1968; Toffler, 1970; Davis & Lawrence, 1977). It is imperative that change agents understand this revolution in organizational form for several reasons. First, an increasing number of organizations are experiencing problems for which matrix is the appropriate organization. Second, the emergence of the matrix alternative makes it even more important that the criteria be understood for deciding which of the three major organizational forms is appropriate. Finally, problems associated with the adoption of matrix seem to be a major reason for the emergence of OD programs.

There are basically three types of organizational forms from which to choose. These have been documented by studying the evolution of organizational forms since the beginning of the industrial revolution (Chandler, 1962). They have also been identified through a number of cross sectional studies. Successful and unsuccessful organizations operating in different market environments or with different strategies have been compared to find if differences in organizational form exist (Burns & Stalker, 1961; Galbraith, 1973; **159**

Lawrence & Lorsch, 1967; Miles & Snow, 1978). Research findings have clarified the conditions for which each of the three organizational forms are best suited.

Functional Organization

The functional organization is the oldest of the three organizational forms. It emerged from the industrial revolution as owner-managers hired professional managers to rationalize and gain control over new and growing enterprises. To increase the efficiency of the organization, they chose to organize people by task specialization or function and to control these functions centrally through an operating plan and budget. In a business enterprise, these functional divisions might be sales, production, research, and finance. In a medical school, they are likely to be discipline-based such as medicine, surgery, biochemistry, etc. (Beckhard & Harris, 1977).

This type of organization usually produces a limited line of related products or services with a common core technology (means of providing the services or making the product). It tends to be a cost efficient and profitable means of providing standardized products or services on a high volume basis to relatively stable markets. As long as products or services do not have to change rapidly, specialized functions operating in a manner best suited to their task need only be coordinated at the top. Thus R&D might operate with little formality, with few schedules and with people who are relatively independent. On the other hand, production operates on a tight schedule, within a hierarchical structure, and with people who are willing to take direction. Similarly, discipline based specialization will produce ways of thinking and working which are suited to their discipline but which are different from other disciplines. Yearly plans and routine procedures are sufficient to coordinate or integrate these *differentiated* functions because the environment is stable and/or the strategy calls for continuing to do more of the same thing.

Decentralized Organization

The decentralized organization is one which emerged as firms began to diversify products or services. This diversification caused top management to become overloaded by an increasingly large and quite different set of marketing, finance, production, and technical problems. Top management ceased to be able to process the volume and diversity of information needed to run the business (Galbraith, 1973). To deal with this problem, management formed separate and self-contained divisions to handle each major product or service. These divisions had their own general manager and were measured on profit. At General Motors, this led to the emergence of the different car divisions (Chevrolet, Pontiac, etc.). In a consumer products company, it might lead to separate divisions for major categories of consumer products. Each division now faces all of the business problems faced earlier by top management but the diversity of the problems and the information processing load is reduced by serving a more limited product/market domain. Top management of the organization now devotes its time to monitoring the financial performance of these divisions, allocating capital resources and helping these product divisions achieve their goals. Often some corporate staff groups are formed to help top management monitor the division and to give the divisions the help they need.

The decentralized product organization seems to be found where the strategy of the firm is to move into new market areas (Miles & Snow, 1978). It is a way the firm can be responsive to each of the markets (be effective) by setting up product divisions whose form fits each different market. But duplication of resources in each division makes it a more expensive organization to operate.

FIGURE 10–2   A Matrix Organization Structure

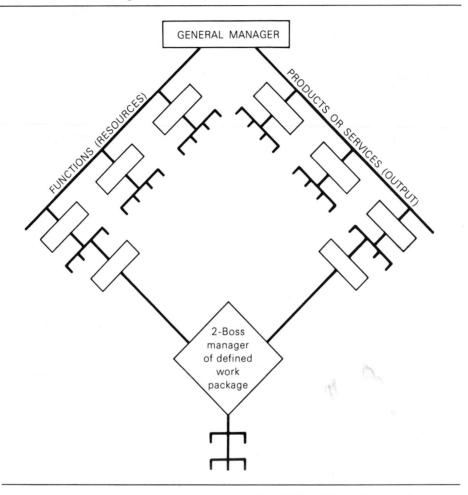

From S. H. Davis and P. R. Lawrence, *Matrix* (Reading, Mass.: Addison-Wesley,© 1977), p. 22. Reprinted by permission.

Matrix Organization

The matrix (Davis & Lawrence, 1977) is an attempt by managers to obtain the benefits of efficiency (lower cost) inherent in the functional organization and the benefits of effectiveness (responsiveness to markets) inherent in the decentralized firm. Faced with the dilemma of centralization versus decentralization, managers invented an organization which retains functional specialization but develops a coordinated response to different product/market domains or programs.

In a matrix, as Figure 10–2 shows, individuals within each function are assigned to a mission or product oriented organization while retaining their membership in the functional organization. Thus, some number of individuals work for two bosses (the two-boss manager), a functional manager and a product or program manager. The diamond-shaped organization is intended to convey that functional managers and product or pro-   **161** gram managers should have equal power, though the focus of their concerns is different. A product or program manager is responsible for managing functional resources to achieve program and profit goals. A functional manager is concerned with developing a professional function and supplying its resources to the programs or businesses in the quantity and quality they require.

The term matrix has come to mean different things because there are so many variations on the basic theme of dual focus and assignments. There are project organizations, usually the first step toward a matrix, in which individuals within functions are assigned to a *temporary* task force for the duration of a program. In this instance, they may work with a project manager and are responsive to the project's demands while continuing to report only to functional managers. There are *permanent* overlays in which key functional representatives are permanently joined in a team responsible for running a business or managing an ongoing program. They may work with the business managers, but continue to report to the functional manager, or they may work for both managers (a full matrix). Whatever the formal organization structure, matrix management is characterized by joint planning and decision making between functional groups at levels below the top. Unlike the functional organization where all decisions are made at the top, people in a matrix are assigned to tasks, programs, and businesses based on their access to needed information and resources. Thus, delegation of decisions to lower levels and a culture in which people can disagree and collaborate simultaneously are an absolute requirement. Usually these behaviors have to be supported by formal mechanisms such as dual appraisal (by both bosses) and career planning.

The important difference between matrix and the other organizational forms is the diffusion of formal power and the emergence of power based on knowledge and competence. Thus, this organizational form represents a significant departure from the basic hierarchical or bureaucratic model of organization which has existed up to now. Its greater flexibility and ambiguities with respect to roles, power, and responsibilities make it an extremely difficult organizational form in which to live and manage.

Choosing an Organizational Form

The previous discussion and the one in Chapter 2 have identified a number of critical variables which must be considered in diagnosing the adequacy of a current form and deciding on a new one. These variables are discussed below and a summary of organizational strengths and weaknesses is shown in Table 10–1.

1. *The uncertainty of the environment: Functional* structures are more effective in stable environments, *matrix* structures in uncertain ones. *Decentralized* structures can deal with uncertainty and complexity for the total corporation but each product division must still face a choice of functional or matrix (Lawrence & Lorsch, 1967).

2. *Strategy: Functional* organizations are more effective for defending a market position through efficient cost effective operations (defender). *Decentralized* organizations are more effective for a diversified product growth strategy (prospector). *Matrix* organizations are more effective when both strategies are being pursued in different product lines (analyzer). (Chapter 8 discusses these strategic types as developed by Miles & Snow, 1978).

3. *Information processing capacity: Functional* organizations have a low capacity to process nonroutine information and deal with diverse problems. *Decentralized* organizations eliminate this problem by assigning each division or department a limited mission. But depending on the complexity of these divisional missions, some

TABLE 10–1   Strengths and Weaknesses of Different Organizational Forms

| Organizational Form | Variables to Be Considered in Evaluating Alternative Forms | | | | | |
	Environment	Strategy	Information Processing Capacity	Capacity for Shared Resources	Capacity for Diversity in Mission Focus	Difficulties in Implementation
Functional	Effective in certain/stable routine	Defend through cost effective-ness	Low	Not applicable	Not applicable	Low
Decentralized product organization	Effective in uncertain/dynamic complex	Grow through diversifi-cation (prospector)	Moderate	Low	High	Moderate
Matrix	Effective in uncertain/dynamic complex	Mix of efficiency and growth strategies	High	High	High	High

divisions may still experience information overload. *Matrix* organizations have a high capacity to process nonroutine information (Galbraith, 1973).

4. *Capacity for sharing resources:* This does not apply to a *functional* organization since all resources are generally focused on one product or strategy. *Decentralized* organizations make it difficult to share resources across separate divisions, although corporate staff groups are one way. Indeed, decentralization causes duplication. *Matrix* organizations allow extensive resources sharing (Davis & Lawrence, 1977; Miles & Snow, 1978).

5. *Diversity in mission or product focus: Functional* organizations are poor in their capacity for handling product or service diversity. Both *decentralization* and *matrix* allow a multiple mission focus.

6. *Difficulties in implementing: Functional* structures are the most traditional and the easiest for people to work in. The *decentralized* structures duplicate functional organizations in each division. They are easy to implement in the divisions but present new difficulties in the relation between corporate staff and divisions. *Matrix* organizations are the most difficult to implement due to culture changes.

Designing an organization means choosing one of the three different forms or inventing a new one. This means that the change agent must collect information on the organization's environment and strategy and determine if problems are due to a misfit between them and the existing organizational form. A clear understanding of the strengths and weaknesses of alternative forms then helps choose a new organizational form.

As examination of Table 10–1 indicates very clearly why, as stated earlier, more and more organizations are likely to move toward matrix despite the difficulties of implementing this form. As the environment becomes more uncertain and complex, as organizations adopt mixed strategies, as the need for rapid processing of nonroutine problems increases, and as the need to share resources is imposed by limited or inseparable resources (people, technology, and facilities) the matrix alternative becomes the best fit. Davis and Lawrence (1977) have listed the following reasons for the emergence of matrix:

1. *Outside pressure for a dual focus:* There is a need to identify a person or group to coordinate and manage functional resources so that they are responsive to program, customer, or business demands. In the aerospace industry, matrix was adopted by corporations to satisfy the Air Force's need for a single point of contact and coordination in their organization for each program. Advertising agencies, banks, and other institutions often have the same pressure.

2. *Pressure for a high information processing capacity:* As already mentioned, decentralized product divisions emerge when top management becomes overwhelmed with problems associated with several highly diverse programs or businesses. Matrix organizations emerge for the same reason but are a different response to the same problem due to pressure for shared resources.

3. *Pressure for shared resources:* When two or more programs or businesses require the same facilities, people, or machines the sheer expense or impossibility of duplicating these in each of several decentralized product divisions leads to matrix. Sharing resources makes matrix more flexible and economical.

The difficulty of making matrix work has caused Davis and Lawrence to suggest that matrix should be adopted only when all three of these pressures exist. But what happens when matrix is the only alternative available?

Issues in Implementing Matrix

Experience with the introduction of matrix organizations clearly points to a lengthy period of adoption (two to five years depending on size) during which people learn to work in the new structure (Beer et al., 1971; Whitmore, 1975). It may take six months to a year to perform a diagnosis, educate managers in how it works, and assign people to new roles. It may take several years for the new management practices required in a matrix to become incorporated in the culture of the organization. The following are some of the key problems in implementing matrix.

1. *Finding and training business or program managers.* Program and business management roles require general management skills. Lawrence and Lorsch (1967a) suggest that this *integrator* role, as they call it, requires an individual who (1) can empathize with the views of all functions, (2) has sufficient competence in each function to ask hard questions, (3) is seen as credible and (4) has the interpersonal skills to lead a group with diverse and sometimes conflicting views.

The problem is that most functional organizations do not have many individuals with these general management skills. Since only one general management job exists in these organizations no managers have had the experience and testing which comes with such a job. For the same reason, functional organizations typically do not provide cross-functional experiences to develop general management skills. Yet, the effectiveness of the matrix rests in great part on the selection of effective program or business managers.

For this reason attention has to be given to selecting individuals who have the potential for developing the characteristics specified by Lawrence and Lorsch. The broadest possible business knowledge and experience is obviously an important criterion. But individuals selected for "integrator" roles must also be assessed for their interpersonal competence and leadership skills. These are particularly important because they cannot be acquired as easily as business knowledge. Selection must be followed by heavy doses of orientation about the role, business education, and leadership training. Typically, those with the greatest potential to succeed in integrator jobs must be sold on taking them because historically, the route to the top has been through the functions.

2. *Developing and implementing dual performance evaluations and business management systems.* If some managers are to report to two bosses (functional and business) and be influenced equally by both, they must be evaluated by both. The process of dual performance evaluation is new to managers in functional organizations and they must be helped to learn how to go about it. The proper forms and set of procedures must be developed. Once again, training and coaching may be required.

Similarly, if business or program managers are to be responsible for profitability and other key financial indicators, the accounting system must provide this information for each business or program. This often means an extensive effort to separate costs, overheads, and sales by business or program. An action plan must be developed to do this.

3. *Dealing with greater role ambiguities.* The dual focus of a matrix creates ambiguities about responsibility, authority, and accountability. For example, is the program manager responsible for developing a plan? If so, who is responsible for implementation of specific functional tasks? Who decides about the people to be assigned to a program, functional or program managers? If the program fails, who is accountable?

In general, it can be said that the business or program side of the matrix is primarily responsible and accountable for deciding *what* will be done and by *when* it must be completed. The functional side is primarily responsible and accountable for *how* it will be done and *who* will do it. But these general guidelines are insufficient, and extensive discussions must occur to clarify roles. The role model of team building, particularly **165** responsibility charting (see Chapter 9), has been found to be a useful tool. Implementing a matrix means using this and other methods in the early stages before ambiguities raise anxiety and hostility toward the matrix (see Case 9–1 in Chapter 9 for a case of responsibility charting in a matrix).

4. *Getting functional managers to delegate.* Prior to adoption of a matrix, functional managers were involved in most business decisions. In a matrix many of these decisions are delegated to the appropriate business or program manager and his team. Functional managers find themselves less involved in business decisions. This leads them to feel less influential and even less competent. Thus, functional managers may resist delegating decisions to lower level teams. They may ask for detail reports from lower level functional representatives or as a group they may choose to keep responsibility for certain decisions at the top. This can easily undermine the efforts of business teams to make decisions and accept accountability.

It is the general manager's responsibility to help functional managers see their changing role. In particular, it is helpful to functional managers to understand that matrix means they can spend more time in developing the effectiveness of their functional resources. Having them make plans for the development of their function can focus them on their new role, that of providing high quality and timely functional resources to businesses or programs.

5. *Balancing power between the functional and program side.* The matrix is an inherently unstable organization. Functional managers may try to retain too much power. Power struggles can develop which can damage the collaborative climate required in the matrix. Perhaps more damaging is the quiet acquisition of too much power by one side of the matrix. This can result in the distortion of what otherwise would be balanced business decisions. If the business side gets too much power, appropriate functional competence may not be brought to bear on business problems. If functions retain too much power, the program side will not be able to integrate them into a coordinated effort.

It is the general manager's responsibility to balance power. He can do so by stating clearly his expectations about relative power, by symbols such as office size, titles and compensation, and by inclusion and exclusion of program and functional managers in meetings and decisions. This may be the most difficult implementation task in a matrix and requires continual vigilance.

6. *Developing a climate of open communication and collaboration.* A matrix is a high tension system in which different perspectives and orientations are brought into conflict to improve quality of decisions. High levels of interpersonal competence are required to manage the inevitable conflict over priorities, resources, and responsibilities—so is a culture which rewards confrontation and collaboration. Developing such a culture is one of the major implementation tasks in moving to matrix.

A planned sequence of process interventions and training programs may be needed to accomplish this. Group development meetings for business and project teams have been used extensively to increase trust and interpersonal competence. So have intergroup laboratories for functional groups that are having problems (see Case 9–2 in Chapter 9 for example). Training programs that develop interpersonal communication skills have also been used in implementing matrix. These and other process and individual interventions take significant time of managers and require OD consulting resources to implement. But they solve immediate problems, develop skills, and most importantly, send clear signals about the changes in behavior that matrix requires.

7. *Dealing with individuals who do not fit matrix.* It is inevitable that some individuals will not be able to develop or grow into the new roles created by matrix. For reasons already discussed, failures are particularly likely in the new integrating roles and among

functional managers. Performance appraisal and development becomes an important tool for helping these managers identify where they are having problems. These discussions can lead to a plan for personal development. But when these development plans do not result in needed personal adaptation, replacement decisions must be made to keep the momentum of change moving. Leaving a business manager in a job who cannot fulfill his role competently, erodes confidence in the matrix and slows organizational change. Therefore, part of implementing matrix means confronting difficult competence issues early and dealing with them constructively (see Chapter 11).

Summary

These and many other problems usually mean that a shift to matrix requires substantial OD resources not required by a shift to the other organizational forms. These include the time of managers and consultants to manage the change, training, processing meetings, team building, counseling, outplacement, intergroup interventions, and so on. (See Case 10–1 for a description of one company's experience.)

CASE 10–1

A billion dollar manufacturing concern experienced problems staying cost competitive and in introducing new products rapidly. Market shares and return on investment declined over the period of a decade. External OD consultants were called in to diagnose these problems. Following interviews at several levels, a feedback meeting with the top management group was held. The business performance problems were diagnosed to be caused by poor fit between the functional organization and a changing, more competitive, business environment. A matrix organization, as well as changes in the organization's culture, were recommended.

A series of meetings between the consultants and management took place over a one-year period to discuss these recommendations and their implications for organization development. Management accepted the diagnosis as essentially accurate, but needed time to discuss matrix and test alternatives. During one meeting, three subgroups were asked to analyze the benefits and costs of three alternative organizational forms — functional, decentralized product divisions, and matrix. The general manager's leadership style and shared manufacturing facilities by all product lines, convinced management that matrix was the right choice.

Top management met many more times with and without the consultants to plan the transition to new structures. At these meetings, the specifics of the new organization took shape. A dual performance appraisal procedure was developed. A decision was made to pay bonuses to business team members on team performance. Business team managers and members were identified. The need for new financial information was identified, particularly cost and return on investment information by business.

During this time period, the top management team held a group development meeting. Each team member received personal feedback and the group grappled with its own ineffectiveness. One manager received a lot of negative feedback about his function and his style. All felt the team-building meeting contributed in increasing trust and increasing the capacity of the group to disagree openly.

About a year after the initial diagnosis, matrix management was announced to the top one hundred people. A one-day orientation training program was given. An internal OD consultant was hired to help in the transition. Similarly, an OD steering committee composed of managers was appointed to help in continual diagnosis of progress and in recommending improvement. Many meetings with individuals and groups were held to work through problems. Each business team held a special meeting to define roles and work on building a team.

By the end of a year-and-a-half, the matrix was in place. Two functional managers had been replaced and new managers, thought to fit the new direction taken with matrix, replaced them. Still, a number of issues—such as delegations of decisions to business teams and their responsibility for strategy versus implementation—were unresolved. Furthermore, new concerns emerged about the effectiveness of one business manager in managing his team.

JOB DESIGN

Historically, jobs in organizations have been designed on the basis of scientific management principles. These principles (Taylor, 1911) are based on the assumption that dividing work into simple and specialized jobs results in more efficiency and control over people and production, requires less skilled workers, and leads to greater profitability. However numerous studies (Beer, 1976) in the last thirty years have illustrated that job design, as currently conceived in most organizations, has some negative consequences. This seems to be particularly true of jobs at the shop-floor level where the assembly line has created work which requires little skill, is machine paced, repetitive, and provides little feedback of results. For some people, such work has been found to lead to dissatisfaction, surface attention to work, depersonalization, and feelings of alienation and frustration owing to lack of feelings of success. These psychological effects seem to lead to social and economic costs, such as poor mental health, shorter life span, higher incidence of coronary problems, high turnover and absenteeism, low product quality and labor-management problems (*Work in America*, 1973).

Experiment in Job Design

The growing awareness that routine and unchallenging jobs may have motivational costs greater than apparent economic benefits, led to a number of experiments in redesigning work (Beer, 1976). These experiments enriched jobs so that the worker performs a longer sequence and variety of operations, schedules his own work, inspects and tests the quality of his work, sets up and maintains his own equipment, and controls his own operations (Davis, 1957). These goals have been achieved by (1) rotating persons through jobs; (2) combining several jobs which together constitute a total or whole task; and (3) by forming autonomous work groups responsible for completing the total task (assembling a product or running a production line). More recently, whole factories and organizations have been designed according to these ideas (Huse & Beer, 1971; Lawler, 1978; Walton, 1971). One example of such a system-wide application is described in Case 10–2.

In general, these experiments in job design have been reported to improve job

satisfaction, motivation, labor-management relations, and quality and quantity of production. They have reduced indirect labor, absenteeism, and turnover (Beer, 1976). In the late 1960s and early 1970s, the national media turned the "blue collar blues" into a national issue. With its popularization, a number of nonprofit organizations concerned with promoting improvements in the quality of life at work have been formed, (for example, the American Center for the Quality of Work in Washington, D.C.). Despite the apparent success of many experiments, researchers are only beginning to understand why work redesign is effective when it is, what goes wrong when it is not, and how the strategy can be altered to improve its general usefulness as an approach to increasing quality of work life and productivity. But we do know quite a bit, and job design is quickly emerging as a major structural intervention for improving organizations.

Theoretical Foundations for Job Design Interventions

Herzberg's motivation-hygiene theory (Herzberg, Mansner, & Snyderman, 1959) has been a major impetus for the use of job design as a technique for increasing employee motivation and satisfaction. The theory suggests that if conditions leading to dissatisfaction with pay, working conditions, and other so-called hygiene factors are minimized, then motivation can be enhanced by providing employees with work that allows them to experience achievement, responsibility, advancement, recognition, and growth in competence (motivators). Herzberg strongly states that *only changes in work itself* can affect motivation. There has been much controversy over the validity of the motivation-hygiene theory, but the theory has stimulated programs in job design in many corporations.

CASE 10–2

A pet food manufacturer decided to expand facilities by building a new plant at another location. The existing plant had been suffering from various symptoms of employee discontent that led to indifferent and "inattentive" performance, which in turn was causing problems of waste, product recycling, and plant shutdown time. The new plant was planned by a small group of managers using behavioral science consultants and was constructed to take into account employee needs and expectations. The resulting design incorporated such features as:

"Autonomous work groups": Self-managed teams of seven to fourteen members, in which assignment of tasks to individuals are "subject to team consensus." Such teams also, for example, screen and select new employees to replace any members who leave the team, and in addition are given major responsibility for dealing with manufacturing problems that occur within or between teams.

"Integrated support functions": Such activities as quality control, normal equipment maintenance, and custodial duties are performed by the teams rather than being assigned to separate specialist groups.

"Challenging job assignments": All jobs consist of sets of tasks purposely designed to "include functions requiring higher-order human abilities and responsibilities such as planning, diagnosing mechanical or process problems, and liaison work.

From L. W. Porter, E. E. Lawler, and J. R. Hackman, *Behavior in Organizations* (New York: McGraw-Hill, 1975), pp. 451–452. Reprinted by permission.

169

At American Telephone and Telegraph, Robert Ford and his associates developed a two day Work-Itself workshop for supervisors and managers of client departments. The workshop included:

1. A review of Herzberg's theory
2. A free association "green light" session in which supervisors give their ideas about how a job could be redesigned
3. A "red light" session during which participants evaluate whether the changes suggested will, in fact, provide the worker a greater opportunity for motivator need satisfaction, or whether the changes reflect improvements in hygiene

The assumptions underlying this intervention are that only job design changes that affect motivators will increase motivation. Furthermore, workers who are to be affected by job design changes should not be involved in the process. If they are, the proponents of this approach claim, the participation in the change itself may cloud the impact of work design itself. While this may seem like a reasonable argument from a research perspective, it is highly likely some form of participation is desirable if workers are to be committed to change and if the design is to reflect worker needs.

The Herzberg theory and the job design interventions based on it have one other major deficiency. They do not specify the job characteristics that might be manipulated to increase motivator need satisfaction. By working backward from the need categories of the theory, it is up to participants in the "Work-Itself" seminar to identify these characteristics.

A Job Characteristic Model

More recently, some promising developments in theory and technology have occurred which speak to this deficiency and provide a more explicit framework for redesigning jobs. Based on his own research and that of others, Hackman (1977) has developed the job characteristic model shown in Figure 10–3. "As illustrated in the figure, five core job dimensions are seen as creating three critical psychological states that, in turn, lead to a number of beneficial personal and work outcomes. The links among the job dimensions, the psychological states, and the outcomes are shown to be moderated by individual growth need strength" (Hackman, 1977, p. 129).

According to Hackman, only people high in needs for self-esteem, autonomy, and self-actualization (Chapter 2 has discussion of individual needs as raw materials of a social system) are likely to be affected in the manner specified by the model. Thus, an important component of this theory which translates into strategic implications for job design is that not all individuals will want or need the same job experience or be affected by it in the same way. The model further specifies that not all job dimensions are equally weighted in their impact on the psychological states. Skill variety, task identity, and task significance together affect experienced meaningfulness of the work. Autonomy and feedback independently affect the other two psychological states. Thus, the core job dimensions may be combined into the following arithmetic expression which explains the relative impact of change in each job dimension (Hackman & Suttle, 1977, p. 131).

$$\begin{array}{l} \text{Motivation} \\ \text{Potential} \\ \text{Score (MPS)} \end{array} = \left[\dfrac{\text{Skill Variety} + \text{Task Identity} + \text{Task Significance}}{3} \right] \times \begin{array}{l}\text{Autonomy} \\ \times \text{Job Feedback}\end{array}$$

FIGURE 10–3   The Job Characteristics Model of Work Motivation

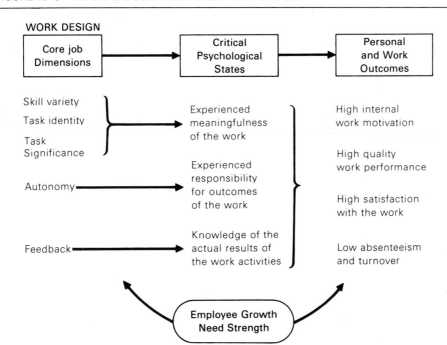

From J. R. Hackman and J. L. Suttle, *Improving Life at Work* (Santa Monica, Calif.: Goodyear, 1977), p. 129. Reprinted by permission.

The job characteristic model led Hackman and Oldham (1975) to develop a Job Diagnostic Survey (JDS). The great advantage of the JDS or similar surveys is that they allow a diagnosis of jobs using a conceptual framework prior to the intervention. While Herzberg's theory also provides a conceptual framework, it is far less operational, and lacks a tool like the JDS to translate need states into job characteristics. As Chapter 2 made clear, a diagnosis based on a conceptual framework, any valid and relevant framework, is an important ingredient in successful interventions. The job characteristics model and the JDS provide such a framework. *Prior to change, a diagnosis using the JDS can answer the following important questions (Hackman, 1977):*

1. Are motivation and satisfaction really problematic?
2. Is the job low in motivation potential?
3. What specific aspects of the job are causing difficulty?
4. How ready are the employees for a change?
5. What special problems and opportunities are present in the existing work system?

Principles for Designing Jobs

A number of principles for enriching work have emerged from efforts to improve quality of work life and productivity. These principles have been summarized by Hackman, et al., (1975) and their effect on the core job dimensions has been specified.

1. *Formulating natural work units.* This means grouping tasks so that, as much as possible, they constitute an identifiable and meaningful whole.

2. *Combining tasks.* This means combining what up to now may have been separate and distinct jobs into one, thus adding skill variety and task identity.

3. *Establishing client relationships.* This means giving the worker contact with a user of his product (another production department, a customer, a sales group, and so forth) and an understanding of the criteria by which the product will be judged.

4. *Vertical loading.* This means giving the worker as much responsibility as possible for planning, doing, and controlling. Thus, control management may have exercised is now given to workers. This often includes giving workers responsibility for quality control.

5. *Opening feedback channels.* This means giving the worker as much data as possible and as directly as possible about how he is doing and whether his performance is deteriorating, improving, or remaining constant.

Figure 10–4 illustrates how these principles affect the various core job dimensions, and thus provides a guide for how the job ought to be redesigned, given deficiencies in certain job dimensions identified by a diagnosis. For example, if the diagnosis shows that task significance is low, then formulating natural work units is the principle that needs to be activated.

These principles can lead to enriched or enlarged individual jobs or to the assignment of a total task to a team of workers. Which alternative is chosen will depend on the technology or physical work setting, individuals' needs for affiliation, and the motivational potential of each alternative. For example, in an electronic assembly operation, one person may be given the job of assembling the total product. Parts and tools can probably be provided at one station. In a process industry, like the dog food plant described in Case 10–2, this is impossible. It would be far too expensive if not technically impossible to design a dog food processing machine for every worker. In these cases, enrichment means designing a whole task for a team. The core job characteristics are being improved for the team's task and the individual experiences psychological effects through his membership in the team. But such team arrangement will only work if the people in the organization have reasonably high needs for affiliation.

Issues in Implementing Job Design Interventions

It seems quite clear that the theory and technology of job design has come a long way in the very recent past. Conceptual frameworks and design principles exist, diagnostic instruments have been developed, and workshops have been designed. By no means are these techniques exhaustive nor have they been fully tested in a wide variety of situations, but they do comprise a promising beginning. There are still many issues, however, for which we do not have clear answers and about which the change agent must use his judgment. These are as follows:

1. *How to handle individual differences.* The research and theory clearly indicate that individual differences in knowledge, skill, needs, and goals, interact with a job design strategy. Not all people equally desire or are equally capable of working on enriched jobs. The diagnostic methods discussed above are meant to identify the fit of individuals with a job design strategy. But what if the needs of people in an organization are not homogeneous? Organizations must find ways to design jobs of different complexities to accommodate individual differences. But whether the practical problems in doing this can be overcome is not clear.

FIGURE 10–4   The Effects of Design Strategies on Core Job Dimensions

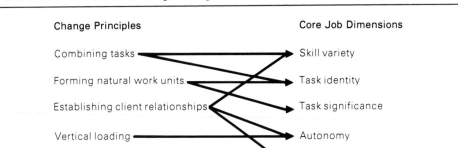

From J. R. Hackman and J. L. Suttle, *Improving Life at Work* (Santa Monica, Calif.: Goodyear, 1977), p. 136. Reprinted by permission.

An associated question has to do with individual adaptability. Would people's needs change to fit enriched jobs if they were put in them? There is some evidence to suggest that they would (Hackman, 1977). If this is so, job design interventions could be part of a system-wide initiative by management to obtain desired attitudinal, behavioral, and economic outcomes as opposed to a response to individual needs and motivational problems. Many of the widely reported job design experiments such as Cummins Engine's Jamestown plant, General Food's Topeka plant, and Corning's Medfield plant have been based on such a strategic perspective. Individuals do seem to adapt. The few that don't, leave.

2. *Effects on interpersonal relations.* There is evidence that job design changes significantly affect interpersonal relations. After job enrichment, strains seem to develop in the boss-subordinate relationship which can mitigate the benefits of the enriched jobs themselves (Walton & Schlesinger, 1979). Any change in job design must be accompanied by careful attention to these effects. Just as subordinates must adapt to their new tasks, supervisors must adapt to new roles and develop new skills in managing.

3. *Management-worker relations.* The amount of trust that exists between management and workers will affect the acceptance and viability of a job-design strategy. If trust does not exist even well-meaning efforts to redesign jobs will be met with suspicion. Thus, job design must fit into the context of the organization or the context must be changed to allow job design changes. Nowhere is this more true than in unionized plants where a long history of labor-management conflict sometimes exists. There is no better way to change the context than to include the union in the process of change. The American Center for the Quality of Work in Washington, D.C., has undertaken to sponsor just such projects on the assumption that only a joint effort can develop trust. The reader will recognize the potential value of third party interventions and intergroup interventions discussed in Chapter 9 as means for dealing with these problems.

4. *Fit with organization culture.* Job design changes require a reorientation of management's thinking about delegation and control. This reorientation is likely to be far easier in less hierarchical and more collaborative organizations (Porter, Lawler, & Hackman, 1975). Yet organizations differ on these cultural dimensions in part because of their market environment. Does this mean that job design interventions cannot be used to improve productivity and quality of work life in the large number of more hierarchical organizations operating in stable environments? They probably can be applied to these organizations but there is still much to be learned about how to implement them. **173**

5. *Fit with personnel systems.* New attitudes and expectations created by job design changes do not always mesh with old pay, job evaluation, performance appraisal, and other personnel systems. A change agent making job design interventions must resolve incompatabilities between these systems and the expectations aroused by job design changes. This often means dealing with staff groups who maintain personnel systems.

6. *Workers participation in planning change.* Most job design experiments do not involve the employees in the planning of change, or if they do, it is a superficial and halfhearted attempt. This is probably because in most organizations management makes these types of decisions themselves and because of managers' inherent distrust of workers and their motives. Yet their participation can significantly reduce resistance and increase commitment to job design changes. Moreover, workers know more about their jobs and their needs than anyone else and their knowledge can add substantially to the design solutions. Participation in job design decisions may be more practical than past practice may suggest. First, a relatively small number of workers are generally involved. Second, recent experience in several companies suggests that unions may be willing to collaborate, thus making it possible for those affected to participate in local changes. How much participation is practical and what form it should take remains an unresolved issue.

7. *Confronting difficult problems early.* It can be very tempting for a change agent to sell job design to management on the basis of its reported benefits without dealing with the difficult problems often created in union relations, pay, and so on. It is understandable, of course, that a change agent might not want to raise all the project's difficulties early on for fear that it will never get off the ground. Furthermore, it is easy for top management to let change agents do this because responsibility for such projects is normally delegated to lower levels in the organization. Thus, conditions are created for a less than optimal contracting process (see Chapter 5) and for a delegated change process (see Chapter 3) in which top management has no involvement and little understanding.

When the inevitable problems do arise, the credibility of the change and the agent of change are damaged. Even if the job design change is not killed outright when top management hears about the problems, it can be so compromised that it loses vitality. Thus, in the long run it would appear wiser to confront and resolve tough issues at the "front end." This, of course, reiterates the fundamental ideas about contracting and anticipatory testing discussed earlier in Chapter 5. These ideas seem even more important in job design interventions because of their visible and measurable effects on productivity, quality, and labor relations.

Summary

The revolution in job design is probably just beginning. We are likely to see continued interest in job redesign as a major approach to resolving problems of productivity and quality of work life. Indeed, TRW and General Motors are companies that have undertaken a corporate-wide program to improve quality of work life and productivity. Job design is a central intervention in this strategy (see TRW (A), 1978, for a case example). However, while we observe the undoing of scientific management on the shop floor, we may be seeing its reappearance in the office with the application of new office technology, such as word processing. Therefore, new job design models and interventions should increasingly be applied to this part of the organization as well.

TABLE 10–2 Overview of Reward System Requirements

Quality of Work Life

---

a. Reward Level	A reward level high enough to satisfy the basic needs of individuals
b. External Equity	Rewards equal to or greater than those in other organizations
c. Internal Equity	A distribution of rewards that is seen as fair by members
d. Individuality	Provision of rewards that fit the needs of individuals

---

Organizational Effectiveness

---

a. Membership	High overall satisfaction, external equity, and higher reward level for better performers
b. Absenteeism	Important rewards related to actually coming to work (high job satisfaction)
c. Performance Motivation	Important rewards perceived to be related to performance
d. Organization Structure	Reward distribution pattern that fits the management style and organization structure

---

From J. R. Hackman and J. L. Suttle, *Improving Life at Work* (Santa Monica, Calif.: Goodyear, 1977), p. 172. Reprinted by permission.

REWARD SYSTEMS[1]

Pay and promotions are among the most powerful means for influencing behavior in an organization because they are so important to people. Unfortunately, these reward systems do not always stimulate the desired level of motivation and performance required to achieve the organization's goals. Even worse, some systems that may stimulate improved performance may do so at the cost of widespread dissatisfaction with equity. On the other hand, reward systems that deal effectively with the issues of satisfaction and equity may not stimulate desired behavior and performance. Thus, a continual problem is to design reward systems that achieve an effective balance between these two objectives.

The more general goals of improving organizational effectiveness and employee satisfaction have been broken down by Lawler (1977) into specific requirements against which a reward system's overall usefulness can be measured (Table 10–2). To create employee satisfaction or quality of work life, a system must provide an adequate level of reward and equity, and it must fit the individual's needs. To contribute to organization effectiveness, a reward system can and should help attract people to the organization (membership), ensure regular attendance, motivate, and reinforce the management style and structure of the organization.

In recent years, there have been many innovations within organizations in the distri- **175** bution of money and promotions. While evidence about the effectiveness of these approaches is still sparse, these innovations have dealt with a variety of problems created by conventional approaches. A change agent concerned with improving organizational effectiveness and quality of work life in organizations should be aware of these innovations and sensitive to their possible application. A few of these innovations will be reviewed briefly below.

The Scanlon Plan

The Scanlon plan is an organization-wide incentive plan developed in the 1930s by Joe Scanlon, a union leader (Frost, Wakeley, & Ruh, 1974; Lesieur, 1958; McGregor, 1960). Simply stated, the plan jointly rewards management and labor on the basis of any labor savings that are achieved after the plan is installed. Savings are paid out in a monthly bonus based on a ratio of sales volume to total payroll expenses. This in effect is a measure of labor cost efficiency (assuming that wages and sales prices are corrected for inflation) over which employees are presumed to have control.

The Scanlon plan is much more than a pay incentive plan. As originally conceived by Joe Scanlon, it was supposed to create a climate that stressed common goals, participation, joint problem solving, and open communication. The plan involves extensive joint worker-management committees that are charged with finding opportunities for cost savings and reviewing the payment of the plan. The power of the plan lies in congruence between the pay system and the philosophy of participation it was designed to enhance. The philosophy is further reinforced by the committee structure and a consultative process.

The plan has been applied to both union and nonunion organizations and has generally been effective. Moore and Goodman (1973) list the following types of outcomes when the plan works.

1. The plan enhances coordination, teamwork, and sharing knowledge at lower levels.
2. Social needs are recognized via participation and mutually reinforcing group behavior.
3. Attention is focused on cost savings, not just quantity of productions.
4. Acceptance of change due to technology, market, and new methods is greater because higher efficiency leads to bonuses.
5. Attitudinal change occurs among workers and they demand more efficient management and better planning.
6. Workers try to reduce overtime; to work smarter, not harder or faster.
7. Workers produce ideas as well as effort.
8. More flexible administration of union-management relations occurs.
9. The union is strengthened because it is responsible for a better work situation and higher pay.

Central to the plan's success is the link between the management philosophy and the incentive system. In those companies where a process of management-worker participation has *not* developed along with the incentive system, the plan has not been successful (Frost, Wakeley, & Ruh, 1974). From a change point of view, it is not quite clear whether the participative climate or the incentive system should come first. Lawler (1977) has argued that the plan might be used to create such a climate where it does not exist. This may be so, but this will only work when an entry and contracting process has demonstrated that management is entering into the plan with a deep commitment to use participative management.

Open Job Posting

Promotions are perhaps the most important reward an organization can provide. Yet in most organizations they are planned in utmost secrecy. Complete control of the process is in the hands of top management. It can be argued that this process reduces organizational effectiveness. Decisions are made without benefit of firsthand information from people in the organization about their needs, goals, readiness, and competence. Thus, many decisions result in less than optimum fit between person and job.

Good centralized manpower planning systems can try to minimize these problems but they can't eliminate them. Furthermore, centralized and secret processes result in substantial dissatisfaction with advancement. Under them, people are not always sure they haven't been forgotten and do not have a sense of control over their destiny. These feelings can lead to lower commitment to the organization and to turnover. Indeed, the secretive nature of the process leads to a more closed climate in the organization.

In recent years, a number of organizations (Xerox, Polaroid, Texas Instruments) established the practice of openly posting available jobs and inviting individuals to nominate themselves. Such systems can have the following effects (Alfred, 1967): (1) employees gain authority previously held by management over their careers, thus equalizing power; (2) employees obtain open feedback from employers about their performance as they are accepted or rejected for jobs; and (3) because supervisors who provide a poor work climate will have trouble keeping and attracting employees, internal trouble spots can be pinpointed.

Of course, these positive outcomes depend on the extent to which employees are given open feedback about why they did not get a job. They also depend on the extent to which the organization forbids punitive measures by supervisors against those who leave their departments. As with the Scanlon plan, the climate and management practices in the organization have to fit the system. The system can be installed to support or extend an already existing climate, or it can be used as a lever for changing management practices. In the latter case, management must start open job posting with a clear idea that they are changing some fundamental aspects of their management culture, not just adopting a new technique.

There is no good research on open job posting systems. They do appear to have the potential for improving both organization effectiveness and employee satisfaction, but there are some unanswered questions. For example, is knowing one has been rejected for a job potentially more dissatisfying than the gains in satisfaction which come from control over one's career? Are the administrative costs of the system sufficiently offset by the gains?

Other Innovations

There are many other innovations in reward systems and practices to which this section cannot do justice. Some of these are (Lawler, 1977):

1. *Participation in promotion decisions.* Current and future peers and subordinates of the person considered, participate in the decision to promote.
2. *Cafeteria fringe benefits.* Individuals are given the opportunity to choose a package of benefits that suits their needs.

177

3. *Skill-based evaluation plants.* Pay grade is determined by the skills the person has regardless of the job he is currently performing.

4. *All salaried plans.* All employees, including nonexempt hourly employees, are paid a weekly or monthly salary.

5. *Lump sum salary increase plan.* When a person receives an increase, its total dollar value for the year is paid out in full.

6. *Performance pay plans.* Pay, usually in the form of a bonus, over and above a base salary, is paid out for previously specified performance achievements.

7. *Variable ratio plans.* Following B. F. Skinner's theories of reinforcement (1938, 1969) payment for certain behaviors (attendance for example) are paid out on an unpredictable (variable) schedule.

8. *Open pay. All* salaries and job classifications are public knowledge in the organization.

9. *Participation in decisions.* Employees participate in the process of designing the pay system, where individuals should fall in it, and/or what the salary of each individual should be.

A Diagnostic Framework for Choosing Reward Systems

These innovative systems and practices, plus the two discussed in more detail, have been rated by Lawler (1977) on the six reward system requirements listed earlier. They are presented in Table 10–3. The first three dimensions listed along the top of the table contribute to employee satisfaction and the next three to organizational effectiveness. Because these practices are presumed to be innovations, each one is rated on the extent to which it is an improvement over traditional practices. A rating of 0 means it is no improvement and a rating of 4 means it is a substantial improvement.

While these are Lawler's subjective judgments based on his scanning of the available research literature, these ratings do provide some idea of the kind of impact each given innovation is likely to have. The six dimensions are a potentially useful framework for diagnosing an organization and choosing a reward system innovation that meets its problems.

Implementing Changes in Reward Systems

Given Lawler's six criteria and his evaluation of the reward systems, who should decide which innovation might be applied to an organization? Traditionally, management, through the personnel function, would hire a consultant to advise them on a reward system and its design. If the consultant were up-to-date, he would have available to him Lawler's framework for diagnosing the organization, make a recommendation, and sell it to management. Once a choice was made, it would be announced by management and that would be the end of it. Employees are rarely asked to participate in these decisions. Management typically assumes that employees could not possibly be responsible enough to take the organization's interests into account in making decisions about pay.

Recent experimentation and research seem to disprove this widely held assumption and open up the possibility that even changes in pay systems may be amenable to a collaborative OD process. Indeed the data suggest (Cammann & Lawler, 1973; Lawler & Cammann, 1972; Lawler & Hackman, 1969; Scheflen, Lawler, & Hackman, 1971) that involving hourly employees to be affected by the pay system can make the difference in how effectively it stimulates performance or reduces absenteeism. Similarly, participation

TABLE 10–3 Evaluation of Reward Practices

Reward Practice	External Equity	Internal Equity	Individ- uality	Performance Motivation	Member- ship	Absen- teeism
Open Promotion and Job Posting	1	3	0	2	2	1
Participation in Promotion Decisions	1	4	0	2	2	1
Cafeteria Fringe Benefits	2	0	4	0	2	1
Skill Based Evaluation Plans	0	2	3	2	2	2
All-Salary Plans	2	0	1	0	1	0
Lump Sum Salary Increase Plans	0	0	3	1	2	1
Performance Pay Plans	2	2	3	3	1	1
Scanlon Plan	2	0	0	2	2	1
Variable Ratio Plans	0	0	0	0	0	0
Open Pay	1	2	0	2	0	1
Participation in Decisions	1	2	0	2	1	1

From J. R. Hackman and J. L. Suttle, *Improving Life at Work* (Santa Monica, Calif.: Goodyear, 1977), p. 226. Reprinted by permission.

of employees (through a task force) in designing a salaried pay system, resulted in increased satisfaction and reduced absenteeism and turnover (Lawler, 1977). Further- more, in all of these instances the resulting pay system did not saddle the organization with higher salary costs than management might have expected.

It appears that when employees are given the responsibility for making decisions about important issues like pay, they will behave responsibly. The results of higher per- formance and satisfaction suggest that system-wide structures can be changed using a participative process. What we don't know is the role that leadership (i.e., management style), size of the organization, and the existing culture play in making participation workable. We do know that employees have more data on the impact and consequences of a pay system than anyone else. Thus, their participation means that the design incorpo- rates features consistent with their needs and expectations. Finally, because their in- volvement gives them more understanding of the system, their commitment increases.

PERFORMANCE MANAGEMENT SYSTEMS

Organizations use a variety of processes and techniques to manage, evaluate, and de- velop the performance of employees. Three major ones are:

1. *Management by Objectives (MBO)*. This is a process, usually supported by a system of corporate forms and procedures, by which a manager and subordinate periodi- cally set and review the subordinate's goals (Ordione, 1965). **179**

2. *Performance Appraisal.* This is a process, usually supported by corporate forms and procedures, by which a manager evaluates a subordinate's performance and potential, and communicates these to him. The basis of appraisal may be achievement of objectives, or the extent to which a subordinate exhibits certain characteristics, or both.

3. *Performance Review and Development.* This is a process by which a manager and subordinate review the subordinate's strengths and weaknesses, develop understanding and agreement about them, and jointly develop a plan for the subordinate's development. This process is sometimes supported by paper systems designed to aid the manager in his discussions with the subordinate.

There seems little doubt that employees will be more motivated and the organization more effective if they work toward organizationally relevant goals (Beckhard, 1969; Lock, 1968) and they develop required attitudes, knowledge, and skills. The three performance management processes described above can help achieve these outcomes if they are regularly and skillfully executed by managers. Unfortunately, this does not always happen. Employees frequently report that they do *not* understand their goals, know where they stand, or get help from their managers.

For this reason personnel departments in organizations, particularly large organizations, have developed formalized procedures aimed at obtaining more uniform and effective application of performance management processes. New systems are continually being heralded as the ultimate answer to dealing with the difficult managerial and human problems associated with performance management. Yet few seem to have met their promise. At best, only moderate progress has been achieved. In some cases, rapid adoption of these systems has been followed by failure and the introduction of yet another system heralded to overcome the deficiencies of the former. In other cases, these systems have had unexpected side effects such as a decrease in autonomy, security, and a sense of competence, and an increase in employee turnover.

Reasons for Failure of Performance Management Systems

There are many reasons for failures in the introduction of performance management systems. Among these are:

1. *Misconceptions about performance management.* There have been some misconceptions about the processes and techniques themselves. One of the most frequent is evidenced in forms and procedures which "force" managers to engage in two or more of the performance management processes simultaneously. Since the processes themselves are different and have different goals, failure results. For example, appraising performance, an evaluative process, requires a different boss-subordinate dialogue than performance review, a developmental process (Beer & Ruh, 1976; Meyer, Kay, & French, 1965). Similarly, one process (for example, MBO), is often thought to achieve all performance management goals and no other processes and supporting techniques are developed.

2. *Standardization.* Not all organizations require the same formality or intensity of application of these tools. A research and development laboratory should have a different approach to MBO or appraisal than a manufacturing plant. The task and the people are different, hence the tools and their use must be different. The propensity of organizations to standardize procedures tends to undermine this reality.

3. *Not seen as culture change.* The application of performance management methods requires many different changes in behavior and attitudes up and down the organization. These are not merely techniques; they are ways of life and a philosophy of management.

Thus, just as with pay systems or job design, the introduction of performance management systems must come as part of a commitment by the organization to change its culture. Only top management commitment to a new way of managing, often triggered by a crisis, can support such a massive undertaking (Carrol & Tosi, 1973).

4. *Inadequate change strategies.* Even where such commitment might exist, the proper strategies for changing behavior patterns in large organizations have not been applied. The emphasis has been on training people in techniques rather than in changing ways of managing. Changing ways of managing requires a carefully planned process of cultural change.[2] Such an OD approach has rarely been used in creating these changes.

Strategies for Introducing Performance Management Systems

These deficiencies suggest that improving performance management processes and institutionalizing them will require the following interventions. First, it will require the development of systems that acknowledge the differences but also the interdependence of the three performance management processes. Second, more comprehensive organization development strategies will have to be applied to introduce such systems over a long period of time, if regression or unintended affects are to be avoided. In short, system design and organization development will have to be merged.

The example in Case 10-3 illustrates the kind of system-wide organization development strategies which must be used to introduce performance management systems. Of particular interest is the training of bosses and subordinates in interpersonal communication as applied to performance appraisal. It is typical for new performance management systems to be introduced without any training. If training does occur, it is typically in how to fill out the forms and to whom they must be sent. Equally important is the staged

---

CASE 10-3

Through a research and development process that spanned several years, a performance management system (PMS) was developed which had three interdependent components — MBO, performance development, and evaluation and salary review. Separate forms, procedures, and processes were designed for each and were to be executed by managers at different points in time. To introduce the system, a training program was developed which included skill training in interpersonal communication applied to performance appraisal and development. *All* salaried employees (bosses and subordinates) in the corporation eventually attended these training programs.

The strategy for change called for in-troducing PMS and training one division at a time, starting at the top. In this way early successes with managers who were motivated to implement PMS helped make the system more attractive to other less interested managers and divisions. The staged introduction also allowed the concentration of change resources in a few target divisions at a time. Training was followed with continual reminders and consulting by a staff of personnel development specialists. Finally, evaluation research was conducted to diagnose problems with the system and its introduction. After ten years, all parts of the corporation were using the system. (Beer et al., 1978; Beer & Ruh, 1976)

introduction of PMS starting with the most receptive divisions. The strategy follows this book's assumptions about the importance of dissatisfaction or readiness to the successful introduction of change. While this change strategy took longer than the typical corporate-wide introductions of such systems, it allowed early successes to develop readiness in other divisions, another change principle discussed in Chapter 3. Staged introduction also allowed better balance between the change task and change resources (trainers and follow-up by personnel specialists). Finally, the top-down introduction communicated important expectations to lower level managers and provided the modeling behavior needed from leaders.

We must disabuse ourselves of the idea that performance management systems can be introduced through corporate-wide forms and procedures. These systems must be supported by a system-oriented change strategy which relies on diagnostic, process, and individual interventions to create needed changes in attitudes, behavior, and culture. When managers are unmotivated to use performance management systems; when these systems are not valued by the top; and when managers are unskilled in interpersonal communication, no form can stimulate tough and realistic goal setting and open discussions about performance.

CONTROL AND ACCOUNTING SYSTEMS[3]

In view of the amount of time and energy managers spend reviewing financial information about their operations, it can be concluded that control systems have a very important impact on the attitudes and behavior of managers. Anyone who has lived in an organization knows that when the "numbers" look bad, managers respond. Bruns (1968) has shown that accounting information is used in decision making and, therefore, affects behavior when the information is relevant to problems at hand; when it is expressed in terms of goals for which people are rewarded; when it is seen as "perfect" and credible; and when it is available on a timely basis.

Problems with Control Systems

The problem is that the information managers respond to may not always result in decisions and behavior that is in the best short- and long-term interest of the enterprise. The financial data do not always reflect all the true costs and effects of decisions, particularly those relating to the human side of the enterprise. Because the data may reflect the performance of only one of several interdependent units, a unit manager might act in his own interests but not in that of the total enterprise. Finally, control systems may simply not include data relevant to decisions managers must make. These types of problems raise questions about the type of information that should be included in a control system.

An equally pervasive and important problem has to do with the validity of the information that goes into control systems (input). This is particularly a problem when managers are expected to provide realistic financial goals needed to measure their performance and control operations. Even a casual observer of organizational behavior will note that such goals are often unrealistic and that at least one of the causes of distortions is anticipation of rewards when goals are met and punishment when they are not. Thus, managers may budget low unless their estimates are closely checked by superiors. But superiors may be too far removed from the information to know if a goal is accurate or how to set realistic goals themselves, particularly when the organization operates in a changing environment. Generally, the more uncertain the environment, the less valid up-to-date information is available at the top of the organization. For this reason, extensive involvement in the goal-setting process by top management may distort financial goals even further. Thus, when accurate goals and forecasts are required for planning, many questions are raised about how goals should be set and their achievement rewarded. How much can participation in goal setting improve the accuracy of financial goals? What are the implications for the design and administration of control systems? Can rewards be attached to achieving financial goals without causing distortion in setting them? If so, what type of reward should these be?

Diagnosing Problems with Control Systems

At the core of these questions are financial accounting and control systems designed by accountants for accountants (Lawler & Rhode, 1976). The designers of these systems often do not take into consideration the human beings who feed information into the system and the human beings who respond to system outputs. The development of an organization in which behavior is congruent with the goals of the enterprise (economic and quality of work life) requires a close examination of control systems and their impact on behavior. A change agent must include this dimension in his organizational diagnosis since changes in control systems may be required to achieve changes in behavior.

There are no easy solutions to these problems. Each control and accounting system requires a diagnosis of its behavioral effects and redesign to enhance the desired behavior and minimize dysfunctional behavior. A recent book by Lawler & Rhode (1976), provided a comprehensive review of the considerations in diagnosing and designing a control system. There are, however, several key questions that a change agent might ask to evaluate the usefulness of a control system for planning, decision making, and motivation (Lawler & Rhode, 1976).

1. Does it provide decision makers with data relevant to the decisions they need to make?
2. Does it provide the right amount of information to decision makers throughout the organization?
3. Does it provide enough information to each part of the organization about how other interdependent parts are functioning or performing?
4. What is the extent of participation in setting financial targets and is the extent of participation consistent with the amount of change in the organization's environment?
5. What rewards (or punishments) are tied to control system outputs, what behaviors are they stimulating, and are these desired or undesired?
6. In particular, are extrinsic rewards (bonuses and promotions) tied to achieving financial goals, and if so, are they causing significant distortion in budgeted goals or in results reported?

The answer to these and other questions can lead to the identification of needed modifications in the control system, and/or the rewards tied to its outputs (see Case 10–4 for an example).

Human Resource Accounting

While many control systems might require some redesign in response to the questions above, almost all control systems would fall far short in their capacity to provide useful, **183**

CASE 10–4

In a company serving a competitive market, manufacturing plants were measured on plant profitability. This was calculated by subtracting the cost of manufacturing the products (variable costs such as labor and fixed costs such as facilities) from the sales dollars generated by products made at the plant (sales were calculated at market price). Plant managers' yearly bonus depended in part on their plant's profit performance. Furthermore, plant managers perceived that their reputation in the company and their promotability were also dependent in part on their plant's profit performance. The sales function on the other hand, was held responsible for sales volume and was rewarded for achieving budgeted goals.

Success in the business rested on being able to sell at a competitive price, on providing timely deliveries as promised, and on developing extensions of existing products. These new products might take from one to two years in development and required both product engineering and manufacturing engineering. In all these areas, the company was not doing well. Volume was dropping, service was poor, and new products were not being completed on a timely basis. In fact, significant conflict between manufacturing and sales occurred over selling price and service. Sales found manufacturing unresponsive to customer service needs because they wanted to minimize production runs to increase profits. The plants felt sales was not selling at a high enough price for them to make their profit goals. Marketing felt the plants were not doing their part in the introduction of new products

because it disrupted their operations, thus raising costs and lowering profitability.

A diagnosis of these problems led to the conclusions that the control system which held plants responsible for profits was causing at least some of the undesired behavior. The plant managers felt victimized by the system. Their plant profit was dropping because volume was shrinking and prices were being lowered. Yet they had little control over these factors. This led them to be hostile toward sales and affected their willingness to service customer needs. If anything, making exceptions in delivery dates increased their costs. Similarly, work on new products, which promised to increase sales and profits in the long term, took time and cost the plants money at the very time that their profits were dropping and managers were under pressure.

A change in the control system seemed warranted. If plant managers were held responsible for cost goals geared to expected volume, desired service levels, and planned product development, the squeeze in which they found themselves would be removed. They would now be more willing to provide needed service and support product development. But these benefits could increase costs unless goals were tough and responsive to the needs of the business. This required that top management provide cost objectives for the business and act as a check on cost goals submitted. The latter required good knowledge about the cost structure of the plant by top management and the controller.

relevant information about how quality of work life goals are being achieved or the efficiency with which human assets are being managed. Since OD focuses most on the organization's social system, this deficiency is particularly troublesome. How, for example, are managers to make the tradeoff decisions between economic and quality of work life outcomes referred to in Chapter 2?

There has been one innovation in accounting and control systems which bears brief mention here because it holds some promise of becoming widely applicable to organizations in the future. This innovation is called "Human Resource Accounting" (HRA). It is an attempt to translate the value of human resources into financial terms so that the impact on profits of decisions affecting these resources can be understood. According to Flamholtz (1974):

> Human resource accounting means accounting for people as an organizational resource. It involves measuring the costs incurred by business firms and other organizations to recruit, select, hire, train, and develop human assets. It also involves measuring the economic value of people to organizations.
>
> The primary purpose of a human resource accounting system is to help management plan and control the use of human resources effectively and efficiently. In addition, some human resource accounting information may also be reported in financial statements for use by investors and others outside the organization (p. 3).

One firm, R. G. Barry, began applying HRA in the late 1960s and included HRA data in its 1970 annual report. Other firms have recently begun to work on HRA. If human resource accounting can be developed to the satisfaction of accountants, accounting standard boards, and the financial community this innovation may have major impact. Even if this does not happen, however, the capacity to express the value of human resources in economic terms allows the use of a common standard for all decisions including those affecting people. This may make it possible for organizations to value organization development more objectively, particularly OD aimed at creating a healthy and adaptive organization. Of course, like any new accounting system, HRA also has the potential of some unintended effects. For example, nothing is known about its potential impact on people's perceptions of their financial worth to the firm and its implications for salary. These and other effects will have to be studied.

OVERVIEW OF STRUCTURAL INTERVENTIONS

This chapter has attempted to make concrete a very important tenet of this book, that organization development must include diagnosis of and intervention in the structures of the organization. These structures have short- and long-term effects on organizational behavior and performance. Thus, change agents (managers and consultants) must have a conceptual framework for understanding how various structures affect behavior and performance. With such a framework, they can diagnose problems and needed changes can be made. The change agent must also have an understanding of the problems in implementing structural changes and the intervention strategies which might be used to effect them. This chapter has provided an overview of the more important structural interventions being applied to improve organizational effectiveness and the key issues associated with their implementation. An extensive body of research theory and practice exists in each of the areas discussed and should be consulted by the reader who would like to pursue them in more depth.

Throughout the chapter, there has been an attempt to show the relationship between structural change and the other intervention methods and strategies discussed in earlier chapters. Structural change is not likely to work unless structural solutions are chosen on a basis of a sound diagnosis. Nor are they likely to work if there is little commitment to **185** them. Finding ways to combine the conceptual and analytic foundations of effective structural change with the collaborative traditions of OD presents an important challenge for the creative change agent. Early experiments with participation in pay system introduction are useful models of what might be done with other structural interventions. The use of participative diagnostic methods such as open systems planning, discussed in Chapter 8, is a useful example of what might be done in the area of organization design. Finally, as has been indicated throughout, the use of process interventions before and after structural changes holds the promise of adapting structures to people and people to structures. It is such a process of mutual adaptation that is the key to effective change.

The power of structural changes lies in the fact that they directly induce behavior. Changing organizational design, job design, control systems, or reward systems creates new stimuli and reinforcements to which people *must* respond. The problem has been that structural changes have often been introduced unilaterally following a rational/logical strategy as opposed to a normative strategy for change. If ways can be found to involve people appropriately, the powerful impact of structural interventions on organizational effectiveness will be obtained without the negative effects of resistance, resentment, and alienation.

NOTES

1. For a more extensive discussion of reward systems see Lawler and Rhode, (1976).
2. See the May Department Stores case (A) and (B) (1976) for an illustration of the length of time, difficulties, and resources required to introduce MBO even when the CEO is committed.
3. The reader interested in exploring this area further will find Lawler and Rhode (1976), a Goodyear Series book of particular interest.

INDIVIDUAL INTERVENTIONS 11

The importance of changing people to effect organization change can be seen in the social systems model presented in Figure 11–1. People's needs, expectations, beliefs, and abilities strongly influence all of the other social system components and interact with them. For example, people recruited into the organization or developed through education and other experiences become managers and ultimately members of the dominant coalition. Furthermore, values, beliefs, and skills directly affect the quality of interaction with others and therefore organizational behavior and process.

If effectively applied, many of the intervention strategies discussed in previous chapters also change individuals. When an organization's structure is changed, when jobs are redesigned, or when a group development meeting is held, people begin to perceive what new attitudes and behaviors they must adopt to fit with the emerging culture. They start to understand what personal changes they must make to succeed and some relearning begins.

But even major organizational transitions and the new expectations they communicate are often insufficient to effect needed changes in people. Additional strategies for helping people adapt to change are required. These might include counseling, training, and development of one kind or another. But when these do not result in individual change, replacement or termination of individuals may be required. Finally, a long-range organization development effort may include a plan for recruitment and selection of people whose characteristics will fit and enhance planned changes in organizational culture.

This chapter will describe these intervention strategies and methods and how they fit into an organization development effort. The chapter will end with a discussion of the broad problem of career development and its relationship to organization development and health.

THE PROBLEM OF INDIVIDUAL ADAPTATION

Individuals develop a relative state of equilibrium with respect to their social group and their role in the larger organization. As they learn the attitudes and skills required to fulfill **187**

FIGURE 11–1 A Social Systems Model of Organization

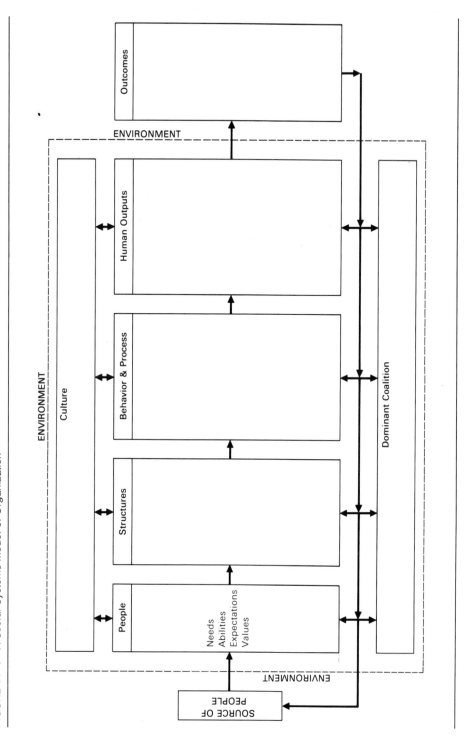

a role's demands, they receive recognition and other feedback which helps them begin to feel competent in their work. Similarly, they learn to establish a pattern of relationships that are both useful for getting the task accomplished and useful in fulfilling their needs for power and relatedness. Naturally, the degree of fit between the individual and the situation varies for different individuals, but unless some accommodation with the reality of the situation is developed, the person will perform poorly and be fired, leave voluntarily, or be a continual source of difficulty. In Chapter 2, we referred to this relationship between the individual and the organization as the "psychological contract," an implicit understanding by the individual and the organization about what constitutes an equitable and fair exchange of effort and rewards (extrinsic and intrinsic).

Major organizational transitions often mean a change in some people's psychological contract, particularly that of key managers. Their roles and relationships (social and power) are changed by new structures and processes and therefore their reality is changed. Particularly when individuals have not had an opportunity for extensive participation, they are forced to come to terms rapidly with two problems—learning a new set of attitudes and behaviors, and finding ways to meet their needs for competence, power, and relatedness.

Therefore, it is not surprising that individuals resist organizational change. If these individuals have limited ability, flexibility, and confidence they may defend themselves by projecting their frustration onto planned organizational changes. This will be seen in the form of hostility and resistance. These individuals may also distort reality in a number of ways. They may not be able to admit to themselves that a substantial gap exists between newly required behaviors and their current capacity. Or, they may claim to support the change and to be adapting when in fact large gaps still exist between actual and required behavior. In still other cases, individuals may accurately perceive the personal changes needed and want to change, but they simply do not know how to develop new behaviors. Often, all of these factors work together to slow individual adaptations and therefore organization development.

COUNSELING AND COACHING

The Goals of Counseling

If organization development is to proceed, the change agent (manager and/or consultant) must help key individuals adapt to change. He can do this by helping them understand the reality of the situation and their own attitudes and capacities to deal with it. *Individuals must be helped to answer the following questions about themselves:*

1. What changes in my own attitudes, assumptions, and behaviors are required if I am to fit with the emerging organization?
2. What skills and resources do I already have that fit with the change?
3. What new knowledge, skills, attitudes, and behaviors do I need to learn?
4. Do I want to make these adjustments? That is, will I get sufficient rewards for changing to make renegotiation of an acceptable psychological contract possible?
5. If yes (to number 4), what do I do to get started with the process of changing myself?
6. If no, what are my options and how do I go about exercising them in a responsible way? **189**

The reader will recognize that these questions constitute a self-diagnosis that helps an individual make informed choices and develop a program of personal relearning. When these issues are not confronted and dealt with, the individual may go through considerable personal pain as he resists, distorts reality, flounders, and ultimately fails to adapt. Similarly, if the organization does not come to understand the individual's needs and limits, it cannot modify change plans to accommodate him. The result can often be transfer to a lesser job or even termination. Both the individual and the organization need to know at the earliest possible time whether a fit between the individual and the organization is possible. A further question is whether adaptation can occur rapidly enough to satisfy the organization and slowly enough to allow the individual to reorient himself without undue discomfort and pain.

No dialogue between a change agent and an individual can result in a completely conscious clarification of all the questions listed above. Therefore, completely informed choice is impossible. But a counseling and coaching process can help the individual move toward informed choice. What are the basic ingredients of such a process?

Assumptions Underlying the Counseling Process

Counseling and coaching methods applied to organizational settings have their origin in various therapeutic models and methods. For example, in its first application in 1933, counseling at the Hawthorne plant of Western Electric was based on what Rogers (1942) later called nondirective counseling. Counselors listened, reflected, and sometimes interpreted what individuals said about themselves and their relationships with others, especially their supervisors. However, the counselors were not change agents and therefore did not see counseling as an intervention aimed at furthering planned change (Dickson & Rothlisberger, 1966).

In contrast, counseling within the context of OD does include this objective. The counselor is typically a manager or consultant engaged in changing the organization. Thus, he must bridge two roles, system change agent and counselor. This is difficult to do since the requirements of system-wide change may not be in the interest of the individual, and vice versa. However, if the counselor can relate equally to the demands of organization change and to the needs of the individual, he is in a unique position to help the individual and the organization renegotiate a new psychological contract.

There have been several applications of psychotherapeutic techniques and models to OD, including Gestalt Therapy (Herman & Phillips, 1971) and Transactional Analysis (Berne, 1964). However, a model which seems particularly appropriate to the problem of helping individuals come to terms with the realities of organization change is Reality Therapy (Glasser, 1965). In its simplest terms, the assumptions underlying Reality Therapy are that each individual must learn to meet his needs "in a way that does not deprive others of the ability to fulfill their needs (Glasser, 1965, p. 15)." This is the meaning of responsibility. In organizational terms, this would mean that an individual must balance his needs with those of the organization and the people who depend on the organization to maintain its efficiency and effectiveness (other employees, stockholders, management, etc.) Reality Therapy is a special kind of teaching or training which attempts to help individuals learn acceptable realistic behavior for fulfilling their needs in a relatively short and intense period. This means, of course, discarding distortions of reality and hostile behavior in favor of realistic and constructive adjustments. Or, if organizational changes are unacceptable, it means taking initiatives to influence the organization.

There are several principles for helping individuals accomplish this. The change agent must establish a completely honest, caring, and human relationship with the individual. Furthermore, the counselor must have one essential characteristic: "He must be in touch with reality himself [in OD this means organizational reality] and be able to fulfill his own needs within the world (Glasser, 1965, p.7)." By being in touch with reality, the counselor can ask questions which clarify for the person *what* he is doing and the consequences. The counselor might also help the person identify realistic alternative behavior which might lead to the satisfaction of both the organization's demands and his needs.

A basic tenet of Reality Therapy, which makes it particularly suitable to organization development, is that waiting to change attitudes stalls relearning. On the other hand, changing behavior leads quickly to a change in attitudes and in turn leads to fulfilling needs and further changes in behavior. Since most managers and consultants have neither the time or skill for more traditional forms of psychotherapy, this approach makes sense for organization development.

The Counseling and Coaching Process

The change agent must first establish a relationship of mutual trust with the individual. This means honest interest and caring but also a consistent toughness about the issues in question. One way for the counselor to establish trust is to be self-revealing about dilemmas and problems associated with the organization change. Covering up problems or mistakes he or management may have made will be counterproductive.

Having established a relationship, the change agent must help the individual *diagnose* the new situation in which he finds himself and *plan actions* that will lead to personal change or a decision to leave the situation.

The following are ways in which the change agent can help a person get in touch with the reality of the situation. They are listed in order of directiveness (the extent to which the counselor intervenes and attempts to influence) with nondirective interventions preceeding more directive ones. In this way, frustrations are vented early and the person is in a better position to discover reality or hear feedback from the change agent.

1. Ask nondirective questions such as "What are your views of the changes and what do they mean?" Listen, and let the person ventilate.
2. Ask questions which allow the person to listen to himself about things that he must clarify.
3. Reflect and restate what is said.
4. Provide feedback about the consequences of the person's behavior as felt by you (the change agent) or others.
5. Provide your evaluation of the person and your opinions as a change agent about his role in the organization's problems and in the change. If the change agent is not the manager (i.e., consultant), he is acting as a surrogate manager when he is doing this.
6. Help identify alternatives available to the person and their immediate and long-term consequences.

Having helped the person with a better understanding of reality, *the next step is to help the person plan actions* that will lead to further diagnosis, change, or self-initiated departure. The following are merely examples.

1. Provide advice about who to see, what to do, and what to say to obtain further data.
2. Provide advice on actual ways the person can change his approach to a situation. Tell the person what behavior he should try.

3. Help plan interactions and meetings which will induce new reality-based behavior, with the hope that it will be successful and thus reinforced.
4. Role-play situations to model attitudes and behaviors the person might want to consider and help the person practice new behaviors.
5. Provide feedback about the effectiveness of the person's attempts to change, their implication for the organization, and the person's next choices.
6. Help the person develop an action plan for training and developmental experiences outside of the organizational setting.

In summary, counseling and coaching individuals means helping them get in touch with new realities brought about by change and what it means for them. This should help them choose among behavioral alternatives and execute one of them. The counselor tries to stimulate alternative behavior. The relevant question is *what* will you do and *how, not why*. The more alternatives the person tries, the faster he will discover if relearning and influence on the organization are possible. Thus, the person and the organization will discover more quickly if the basis of a new psychological contract is in the making. If it is not, the alternatives of further development activities or replacement must be faced (see Case 11–1 for an example).

Unfortunately, managers and consultants underutilize counseling and coaching as a strategy for change. Managers in particular do not recognize the need to help individuals adapt. Too often, a mechanical assumption about change is employed. For example, if new expectations have been announced, people ought to and will respond. An effective counseling and coaching process cannot only help individuals change and grow, it can blunt the inevitable questions about fairness which arise when people who do not adapt are replaced or terminated. For this reason alone, counseling will become a much more important intervention in the future.

TRAINING AND DEVELOPMENT

Quite frequently, the counseling and coaching process can only help begin the process of relearning. Additional intensive learning experiences outside of the immediate work environment are needed for a person to gain a better understanding of himself and to acquire new knowledge, attitudes, and skills. An effective counseling process should help identify which training and developmental activities can best meet the individual's learning agenda. Indeed, a personal change plan should be developed jointly by the individual and the change agent.

Types of training and developmental experiences for key individuals may be differentiated on the basis of the following questions (Porter, Lawler, & Hackman, 1975).

1. What is the content of the program? Is it aimed at transmitting knowledge or is it aimed at learning new attitudes and behaviors?
2. What is the method by which the material is taught—lecture and reading or learning from experiences generated in the program?

Training Content

Experience in organizational change and development suggests that training which transmits knowledge (cognitive learning) and training which helps individuals diagnose

CASE 11-1

As part of an organizational diagnosis, substantial information was obtained about the effects of a general manager's personal style. His leadership was seen as weak and ineffective. Subordinates felt meetings were not effective. They felt that the manager, who was relatively new in the organization, did not understand their business. Finally, they felt the manager was not effectively representing their divisions to upper management. As one subordinate said, "He doesn't represent our case strongly enough." Dissatisfaction with the general manager was beginning to have a negative influence on the effectiveness of the top management group and the organization. Improvements in structure and process, introduced under the previous general manager, were beginning to lose their potency.

An OD consultant, working with the organization, began to meet with the general manager to help him become aware of how he was perceived and to explore ways to deal with the situation. An initial meeting was held in which the perceptions of subordinates were fed back to the manager. At the consultant's suggestion, the general manager met each of his subordinates to obtain direct feedback about their perceptions. Following these meetings, the manager and the consultant met several times to discuss the data. In these discussions the consultant also introduced relevant examples of the manager's behavior which he had observed directly. The

meetings between the consultant and manager spanned a period of one year.

After some considerable defensiveness in early discussions, a relationship of mutual trust began to develop between the consultant and manager. The manager began to explore more of his feelings and to reveal how his previous experiences had led to his particular approach to the job. Slowly, the demands of the current organization became clear. So did those things which the manager felt he could change and those which he could not. The consultant helped the manager identify specific things he could do in running meetings, communicating, and developing influence with top management. To learn about the business, the manager developed a plan to visit customers and plants. In places where he could not meet subordinates' leadership expectations, the manager and the consultant discussed ways of spreading the leadership responsibility.

Small personal and procedural changes reduced some of the frustrations among subordinates. The manager also articulated new expectations to subordinates for their involvement in the business. While the top management group became more effective, this did not come about through dramatic changes in personal style. However, the manager was left with a much clearer idea of his strengths and weaknesses as a general manager.

themselves and develop new skills are both needed. For example, a change to a matrix organization (see Chapter 10) requires that people affected by the change acquire knowledge about how that type of organization works (roles, patterns of interaction and decision making, reward systems, etc.). Without such knowledge, people do not have a road map of where the organization is going and how they are expected to live in it.

However, an intellectual understanding of a new model of managing does not neces- **193** sarily translate into the motivation or skills to execute newly required behaviors. This is the most difficult and important task in changing individuals. In the event of moving to matrix, people will have to adopt positive attitudes toward collaborating, confronting disagreements, and developing skills for working effectively with others. While these attitudes and behaviors may already exist in the repertoire of many individuals, many others will lack the attitudes and skills needed to make such an organization work. They will be the ones who will resist the organizational change because of the threat it poses to their competence.

For these reasons, finding or developing training experiences that help individuals acquire new attitudes and behaviors becomes an important task for the change agent. Traditional training programs which transmit knowledge through reading, lectures, and even group discussion have not proven to be very effective in accomplishing these goals (Beer, 1976; Campbell et al., 1970). They can provide knowledge about how to behave but they do not help individuals discover that they are the ones who need to change their behavior. Nor do these methods provide practice in new behaviors. Only successful experiences followed by attitude change can lead to further motivation for different behavior.

Toward Experiential Training Methods

In recent years, a number of experiential training programs have been developed, which have helped people learn from their own experiences with emotion-producing interpersonal or managerial events. The first and most well-known example of this type of training is the T group. In its original form, a T Group is a small, unstructured face-to-face group ranging in size from approximately eight to fifteen members who do not know each other. No activities or agenda are planned, but a trainer is present as a resource, guide, and model. The group members' struggle to deal with the lack of structure becomes the agenda. The "here and now" behavior of individuals and the group as a whole become the subject of learning. Members provide nonevaluative feedback to each other and help each other consider alternative attitudes and behaviors in dealing with others.

Research on T groups seems to show that it is a fairly powerful tool for changing individual behavior (Beer, 1976). In general, participants show increased sensitivity, more open communication, increased flexibility in role behavior, greater receptivity and awareness, greater tolerance of individual differences, less dependence on others, and less demand for subservience from others. In short, T groups help individuals become more interpersonally competent. Thus, they will positively affect managerial behavior and organizational effectiveness where these behaviors are required and where they are supported in the organization (see Case 11–2 for a personal account of a T group).

But despite the power of T groups, they have several problems associated with them. The lack of structure provides relatively little control over the content of what is learned and therefore the learning outcomes (Beer, 1976). It also increases the risk that individuals will receive feedback about themselves they can't deal with psychologically. Furthermore, the reliance on trainers for every group makes the training very expensive. To deal with these problems, a number of more structured laboratory training programs, as experiential training is sometimes called, have been developed. Some of these programs, like the Managerial Grid (Blake & Mouton, 1964), are also aimed at developing greater awareness of one's interpersonal or managerial style. They can also be aimed at increasing awareness and skill in other domains such as handling power, motivation to achieve (McClelland & Winter, 1969), decision making (Kepner & Tregoe, 1965) and career planning (Fordyce & Weil, 1971; Kotter, Faux, & McArthur, 1978).

194

About this time I attended my first T-group—an NTL President's Lab in Florida. It was led by Dr. Herbert Shepard and Dr. Jack Gibb. Although I had some deferential feelings toward the businessmen who were the principal participants in the lab, I personally felt that I was one of the best administrators in the whole federal government. Frankly, I was pretty satisfied with myself. I thought that I knew all of the problems, that I knew all of the answers, and that what I primarily needed to "straighten out the Department" was a group of loyal subordinates to carry out my policies and directives.

After a few days at the lab I was surprised, to say the least, by the feedback I was receiving. I recall sharing it with my wife Verla, who was there with me at the time, and curiously enough it was much like some of the feedback she had given me from time to time (which I had pooh-poohed as being just the usual "woman's bias"). To have a group of strangers tell me these things was tough to take. Among other things they said:

> You are devious and manipulative. . . . You are authoritarian. . . . You don't listen. . . . You intellectualize all feelings and refuse to deal with people on a feelings level. . . . You are sly, and we don't totally trust you, nor would we want to work for you.

At last it began to dawn on me that perhaps the problems we were having in gaining acceptance for our new programs and philosophies in the Department of State might, to some extent at least, be because of my own personal management style and how we were trying to bring them about. It was even more important that I saw (had mirrored for me) a side of myself and my behavior that I did not like and determined to change.

From W. J. Crockett, *Failures in Organization Development and Change* in P. H. Mirvis and D. Berg, (New York: Wiley-Interscience, © 1977), pp. 126–127. Reprinted by permission of John Wiley & Sons, Inc.

Laboratory programs hold several principles in common which appear to be important in reorienting attitudes and developing new behavioral skills (Bass & Vaughn, 1966; Hall, 1970; Porter, Lawler, & Hackman, 1975; Skinner, 1969).

1. Focus on behavior and attitudes as compared with cognitive learning. However, cognitive learning should be provided to support behavioral objectives.
2. Provide the learner active participation and involvement in tasks that demand the behaviors and attitudes which are to be learned.
3. Provide trainees an opportunity to examine these behaviors and attitudes and to obtain knowledge about their effectiveness (feedback about results).
4. Provide trainees with an opportunity to see modeling of desired behaviors which they can emulate (through role playing, videotape, films, or others' behavior).
5. Provide an opportunity to experiment with new behavior.
6. Provide an opportunity for participants to be reinforced for appropriate behavior.
7. Provide an opportunity to practice new behaviors so that they are overlearned.
8. Provide trainees with a rationale for the training experience and how it fits with their job situation and with organization development goals.

It is beyond the scope of this chapter to review the many experiential training programs which have been developed in recent years and what is known about their effectiveness. Some of them, like T groups, have been researched extensively while many
others have not. A change agent seeking to identify a program suitable to his organization
development objectives, or to development objectives of given individuals, must identify
whether the program focuses on the appropriate behavioral domain and whether it con-
forms to some of the principles outlined above. Where available, evaluation research
results should be consulted. But even if all of these criteria are met, the training experience will only be effective if it is planned in such a way that the typical fade-out phenomenon can be overcome.

Overcoming Fade-Out

Much of the research on T groups and other experiential training programs indicates that
their powerful effects on individuals can fade-out very quickly once they get back into the
organization (Beer, 1976). If the individual feels that new behavior will not be accepted
and rewarded by others, particularly his supervisor, he will not use these behaviors
(Fleishman, 1955). One study (Argyris, 1970) has shown that behavior learned in training
and not displayed on the job is not necessarily forgotten but rather is stored away for use
at a time when it is acceptable. Executives who had been through a T group did not use
what they learned on an everyday basis. They did use it when they were with others who
had also been through T groups. It seems clear that what has been learned in training
must be rewarded and supported on the job if it is to be used. This is, of course, a
restatement of the general premise outlined in Chapter 2 that culture has a pervasive
influence on attitudes and behaviors of people.

Fade-out becomes a problem, of course, when training and development are the *only*
interventions being applied in the organization and when they are applied to only a few
people. Unfortunately, millions of dollars are spent on training that has little effect on
behavior and organizational effectiveness because the training is not coordinated with
other organization development interventions. The thrust of this section has been to present training interventions as part of a broader strategy. If a broader change effort is
underway and if individuals receive counseling about the personal changes they must
make, they will be motivated to learn. This motivation, together with the more powerful
experiential training methods, is much more likely to result in relearning of more deeply
rooted attitudes and assumptions about managing. If individuals continue to be counseled and coached after their return to the organization, the chances of fade-out are
significantly reduced. This is the essence of OD and the reason why it is a more powerful
behavioral change strategy than other less systemic approaches. More will be said about
how to integrate individual interventions, such as training, with other interventions in
Chapter 12.

REPLACEMENT AND TERMINATION

It is the objective of counseling, training, and development to clarify for individuals what
they must do to adapt and help them do it. But what happens if these or other interventions
fail to change individuals sufficiently or quickly enough to be consistent with organization
development goals? What if the individual himself does not come to recognize that he
cannot or does not want to meet the new demands of the organization? There are few

major organizational transitions where managers are not faced with decisions about replacement or termination (Case 11–3 provides an illustrative example).

The replacement of key individuals can speed up changes in a group's and organization's overall effectiveness. However, it raises some important ethical and practical questions. How important are replacement and termination in change efforts and at what point in the change process does one employ them? Should counseling, team-building or interventions which encourage people to be open with each other be used as the springboard for replacement and termination decisions? What part should the OD consultant play in this process, given his unique role and relationship?

There is no question that replacement or termination of individuals can materially speed up organization improvement. This is particularly true of rapidly growing firms or underorganized firms in which a culture has not taken hold or is changing rapidly. Managers have, of course, known this and have been using these methods for a long time. Unfortunately, the process of replacing and terminating is not always open or direct. The "target person" is often given *indirect* messages through changes in title, withholding of bonuses, public ridicule, and other social pressures in the hope that he will leave voluntarily. When he does not, he is terminated suddenly and without prior discussion. The problem is not the outcome, painful as replacement or termination may be for the individual. The problem is in the process itself. Indirect messages and the lack of open discussion violate the individual's right for "due process" and are perceived by others as cruel and unfair. Thus, trust is reduced at a time in the organization's life when it is needed most as a basis for dealing openly and innovatively with difficult problems. This is particularly a

CASE 11–3

A top management team of a business unit was engaged in a group development process with the help of an OD consultant. In their first meeting they surfaced a number of individual and group issues blocking their effectiveness and discussed them for the first time. This process crystallized doubts for the general manager and others on the team about the competence of one of the key functional heads, doubts that existed before, but which had not been examined closely.

Following the group development meeting, the general manager and OD consultant met several times to discuss the functional head in question. Initially it was clearer to the OD consultant than to the general manager that this individual had weaknesses that were contributing to organizational problems and would slow planned change. With planning help from the consultant, the manager held a number of counseling and coaching meetings with the functional head. These reinforced and further clarified feedback in the group development meeting. They also served as a means of follow-up on a personal action plan developed at the group development meeting. Furthermore, the consultant met with the functional head several times and offered to help in solving some problems in his organization. This offer was never accepted.

As time progressed, it became clear that the functional head would not be capable of making the changes needed to improve his personal and his organization's effectiveness.

While some changes were evident in his personal style, the major problems were not being addressed. Nine months after the group development meeting, the general manager replaced him.

problem when an OD program, aimed at getting more openness in surfacing data and solving problems, is underway.

Because of the apparent contradictions between replacement or termination on the one hand and the building of trust and openness on the other, the field of OD has virtually ignored replacement or termination as possible interventions. Furthermore, the human potential movement has had strong influence on OD. Its views that people are capable of unlimited growth has blocked the field of OD from integrating these interventions into a strategy for organization development. There is *no* reason, however, why these interventions cannot fit into an OD strategy *without* reducing trust and openness significantly, compromising the role of the consultant, or violating professional ethics.

There is an approach that has promise for maintaining the OD consultant's relationship of trust with organizational members. He can consult with managers about the decision process leading to replacement or termination. The consultant can alert managers to the need for considering replacement and termination as important alternatives to development. Some managers back away from these interventions because of their discomfort with them. Helping managers develop a process of evaluation which includes the collection of valid data is useful. It is also constructive to help managers think through how they will discuss these issues with subordinates, whether they should attempt developmental intervention first and for how long, or whether they should discuss replacement and termination immediately. The consultant may offer his own evaluation about an individual's effectiveness if he is asked by the manager. But if he does so, it should be based on behavior that both he and the manager have seen together. In this way the consultant is not using data thay may have been obtained under the guise of confidentiality. Ideally, the consultant will want to share his evaluation with the individual when it can be helpful to him.

In general, the consultant can be helpful in planning an open, direct, and fair process for handling these difficult issues; one which will not reduce trust and confidence in the manager, himself, the organization, or the OD process. He can also act as a third party by helping both the manager and subordinate maintain a constructive dialogue and by helping them deal with personal and career difficulties arising out of replacement or termination.

Not only is the quality of the decision process important in maintaining trust and confidence, but so is what happens after the replacement or termination decision. If individuals are provided help in career planning and supported psychologically and economically as they search for alternative positions, others will perceive replacement or termination as a constructive intervention. Several large firms have experimented with developing an internal outplacement service that provides career planning and job search help for terminated employees. They have found that individuals leave the firm with more positive feelings when they get jobs suited to their needs and improve themselves materially (Thurber, 1975; see Case 11–4).

Effective outplacement can transform a personal crisis into an opportunity for personal growth. People in the firm who see this feel more secure, and their commitment to organizational change and improvement is maintained. Similarly, the existence of a constructive process for replacement and termination frees managers to use these interventions more often, thereby speeding up organizational improvement.

RECRUITMENT AND SELECTION

The discussion so far has been centered on interventions aimed at developing, replacing, or terminating existing people. In the short-term, these are the individual interventions that

CASE 11–4

When profitability problems required significant reductions in the salaried work force, a firm set up an outplacement center. This center, staffed by personnel specialists and OD consultants, was designed to help individuals with career planning and with mounting a campaign to find a new job.

The outplacement program lasted three days. After an introduction which described its purpose, individuals were given a ten-page questionnaire aimed at helping them think through their career objectives. They were asked to describe their ideal job, plot their earning goals throughout life, describe life style preferences, describe what their supervisor might say about the reasons for termination, and assess their own strengths and weaknesses. Participants were then asked to meet in small groups to discuss their responses and to profile the type of job they wanted. In some cases, a desire to make a major career shift emerged. When this occurred, one of the outplacement staff members was available for further discussion and counseling.

During the second and third days of the program, participants began to attend classes to help them plan and execute a job search. This included training in how to write a resumé, who to send it to, how to budget their income during the search process, and how to inter-view for jobs. Some of this training included role playing of job interviews and videotape feedback to assess their effectiveness. Participants learned to answer difficult questions such as "Why *were* you fired?"

By the end of three days, career goals had been clarified, resumés written, plans of action developed, and skills in interviewing developed. In general, participants reported coming to terms with the termination, getting new insights into performance problems which might have led to the termination, and developing confidence about the future. Periodic visits to the center continued to provide psychological support during the search process. Furthermore, the corporation invited recruiters from other companies to come to the center to interview terminated employees.

This intervention helped individuals with the difficult adjustments required by termination and energized them to action. It provided not only psychological support, but practical help in finding a job. A survey conducted one year later, indicated that terminated employees who had gone through the outplacement center compared favorably with those who did not in their attitudes toward the company, the time it took to get a new job, their adjustment to their new job, and their new salary.

can be implemented most quickly. However, in the long-term, major organizational transitions will also require a plan for recruiting and selecting new people into the organization whose characteristics are consistent with planned changes. Indeed, as the example in Case 11–5 illustrates, recruitment and selection can be used as a primary strategy for organizational change (Alderfer, 1971; Argyris, 1954).

Not surprisingly, the recruitment strategy in the bank caused a new set of intergroup problems. New employees came into conflict with older employees. Recruitment appears to have been the only intervention in the bank. If structural, process, or other individual interventions had also been employed, perhaps even employed first, older employees would have begun changing or leaving voluntarily or through termination. Intergroup conflict would probably have been reduced. This, of course, reinforces the "systems" **199**

CASE 11–5

It will be recalled that the bank had a tendency to recruit managers who were quiet and noncompetitive and who were quite willing to take orders but uneasy about giving them. The preferences of these individuals ("right types") for security, stability, and predictability had certain definite (and often dysfunctional) consequences for organizational effectiveness—for example, new sources of business would not be aggressively pursued. Further, the existence of the "right type" image tended to influence who applied (and who was selected) for management positions at the bank, thereby perpetuating its existing managerial style. The bank mounted a recruiting campaign to attract management trainees who were more aggressive, risk-oriented, and self-confident. A new management training program was instituted as well, designed to help the trainees ("new types") prepare themselves for positions of responsibility in the bank. The presence of the "new types" in the bank significantly changed how the organization functioned—it became much more oriented to growth and profit potentials, confirming the possibility of achieving organizational change through selection. In addition, however, an intergroup conflict emerged between the older "right types" and the "new types" which created a new and troublesome set of problems for the organization.

From L. W. Porter, E. E. Lawler, and J. R. Hackman, *Behavior in Organizations* (New York: McGraw-Hill, 1975), p. 441.

view of organizations and the interdependence between the intervention strategies discussed in this chapter and those discussed in previous chapters.

The example of the bank and others like it, suggests that recruitment and selection interventions should generally follow rather than lead other interventions. Until the organization has been diagnosed and the dominant coalition becomes committed to planned changes in organization culture, hiring different people can increase conflict and turnover. If changes in structure and process are planned and implemented first, the criteria for who to recruit will be clarified. A momentum of change will have been achieved by the time new people are recruited and their arrival will further support and speed up the change.

Unfortunately, recruitment and selection (internal and external) in most corporations is not integrated with OD efforts. One reason is that criteria and procedures are often developed at a corporate level without sufficient concern for the needs of specific units with unique cultures. When the corporation is highly diversified, selecting new people, particularly key managers, without regard to the unique requirements of each unit, can retard organization adaptation. A further problem is the state of art in the development of selection procedures. Many sophisticated techniques such as psychological tests and assessment procedures exist, but they are often calibrated statistically against narrow criteria of job performance. Little attention is given to the culture of the organization as a whole and its implications for types of people needed (Schneider, 1976). Finally, the performance criteria used to identify characteristics which distinguish good and poor performers are rooted in the past. If the organization is undergoing a major transition, the use of past performance as a criterion could easily mean that people hired will not meet the needs of the organization in the future.

All of this suggests that recruitment and selection procedures must be developed to fit with organization development objectives. These procedures must also be updated periodically as the organization continues to adapt to new environmental demands. New and more flexible techniques of selection and validation will be necessary, such as the *assessment center* (Bray, Campbell, & Grant, 1974; Byham, 1970), a technique which puts people through a number of managerial simulations (exercises). It emphasizes clinical observation of behavior and evaluation on general managerial characteristics. Thus, the relative weight of characteristics in selection decisions can be changed depending on organization development objectives. Furthermore, because managers are often trained as assessors, their competence in selecting people who will fit the organization development objectives is enhanced.

Career Development and OD

In closing this chapter, it is essential that we return to the central problem with which it opened—the problem of individual adaptation. Organization change requires that the organization be capable of obtaining newly required behaviors and attitudes as it changes and adapts to its environment. This means changing existing people, finding new ones, or optimizing existing human resources through manpower flows in the organization. There are several ways in which an organization can accomplish this.

1. It can hire and develop highly flexible people who have the capacity to learn and adapt as needed.
2. It can develop people, through training and multiple job experiences, to have a broad repertoire of behaviors capable of fitting a number of different jobs and subcultures.
3. It can loosen traditions and norms concerning career progression so that people can be moved up, down, and laterally within the organization, as needed.
4. It can loosen traditions of loyalty which lead to expectations of a lifelong career with the organization. Loosening these traditions can stimulate greater movement in and out of the organization as individual capacities and organizational demands change.

All of these career development and manpower strategies will be needed in the future if organizations are to adapt more easily to more rapidly changing environments. Unfortunately, career planning and development practices in many organizations are not consistent with these strategies. These organizations still do not encourage cross-functional transfers and end up with relatively narrow managers. Often, personnel development is seen as a relatively short-range strategy designed to help a person do his current job rather than learn skills and attitudes which the organization may need in the future. Organizations also have personnel systems and traditions which make flexible movement of people difficult. For example, pay and status are largely tied to a job rather than the person. Thus, high potential individuals resist moving into new roles or areas invariably seen as lower in status and power, where they may be needed to effect change. Finally, through an emphasis on loyalty and a lifelong career with one organization, barriers to confrontation of an individual's fit with the organization are created. Managers are reluctant to violate a psychological contract set at the time of recruitment and reinforced ever since. When people are confronted with the fact that they may not fit the changing organization, they become threatened and try even harder to protect their position in the organization. Moving on to another organization or another career, a strategy which may be adaptive for them and the organization, is not considered.

201

The individual interventions described in this chapter will be most effective in an organization where people are aware of their strengths and weaknesses, and are open to changing themselves or moving on to other careers or organizations. These attitudes toward self and the organization can only be developed by an organization that pursues the four strategies outlined above. This means innovation in reward systems, career planning and development, educational policies, recruitment and outplacement, and many other personnel policies and practices. These issues have been discussed elsewhere (Hall, 1976; Schein, 1978), and are well beyond the scope of this book. However, the reader is urged to see them as central to the problem of changing people to fit ever-changing organization development agendas.

STRATEGIC CONSIDERATIONS IN SYSTEM-WIDE CHANGE IV

OVERVIEW

Organization development can be differentiated from other strategies for organizational improvement by the fact that its target is the whole organization. It is generally recognized by organization development practitioners that a major cultural change requires an effective orchestration of diagnostic, process, structural, and individual interventions. Even when culture changes in one department or division, it cannot be sustained unless there are supporting changes in other parts of the organization. Indeed, this is why Chapter 1 defined OD as a system-wide change strategy. But if this definition is to be practical, change agents will need to be able to answer some important questions which typically arise in implementing system-wide change efforts.

1. How should multiple interventions be combined and sequenced to effect change?
2. What personal qualifications and role attributes must change agents have to orchestrate a system-wide change effort?
3. Where should an OD effort start in large complex multiunit organizations?
4. How can OD successes in one part of a large corporation spread to other parts and how rapidly should this occur?
5. What role should evaluation research play in the acceptance of OD and how should it be performed?
6. How can OD be institutionalized as a process for organizational renewal? That is, what structures and processes are needed to make OD an ongoing part of a large organization?

There is growing evidence that in the long run, these questions are perhaps the most important to the success of an organization development effort. They are also the questions about which we know the least.

Considerable evidence indicates that many of the intervention methods discussed in Chapters 8 through 11 can have an effect on organizations, at least in the short run. However, recent evaluation of a number of OD interventions several years after they were made, indicates that many changes that appeared to be successful and permanent when first reported have regressed or disappeared (Beer, 1979; Hinrichs, 1978; Walton, 1978). For example, in some plants innovation in job design and principles that guided these efforts have vanished without a trace. Some organizations that have adopted a management by objectives approach have dropped it. These and other interventions appear to serve an immediate need but do not stimulate a continuous process of organizational renewal.

Similarly, while many companies that have not previously used OD are now adopting it, some companies that pioneered in OD seem to have deemphasized or discontinued their efforts. In still other companies, problems have been created by too rapid an expansion of OD spurred by top management and/or a corporate staff group.

These experiences suggest that there is more to OD than successfully changing one organization unit or making one successful intervention. A number of strategic considerations must be understood in starting, orchestrating, and sustaining the thrust of organization development efforts in a large multiunit organization. The following three chapters will deal with these issues.

Chapter 12   Integrating Interventions: Systems Oriented OD
Chapter 13   Starting and Managing System-Wide Change
Chapter 14   Evaluating and Institutionalizing System-Wide Change

INTEGRATING INTERVENTIONS: SYSTEMS ORIENTED OD 12

If organizations are social systems defined by the interdependent components of people, structures, process, and environment, then it stands to reason that major cultural change cannot occur unless all of these components change. If there is one thing of which we can be certain, it is that major organizational change requires that multiple "levers" be pulled by the change agent. Organizational behavior is shaped by a multiple set of forces, and only congruence (see Chapter 1) among all of these forces provides the conditions for permanent and long-term change.

The four major categories of intervention methods described in Chapters 8, 9, 10, and 11 are the multiple "levers" available for changing organizations. But how are these methods to be integrated into a coherent strategy of change? This chapter will deal with this question. There are some preplanned OD programs which specify one sequence of interventions, and one of these, Grid OD, will be described and critiqued as a means of joining the issues. It seems apparent, however, that there are many possible ways to sequence interventions. Moreover, change agents seem to make choices about sequencing them based on a variety of intuitive considerations developed through experience. What is needed is an explicit conceptual framework which specifies the *considerations* change agents might use to make such strategic choices. This chapter will provide such a framework. The chapter will end with a discussion of the change agent's role in deciding on an intervention strategy and the intellectual and personal orientation required to do so.

PREPROGRAMMED INTEGRATIONS: GRID OD

Probably the most well defined integrated approach to changing organization culture is the "Grid Organization Development" program developed by Blake and Mouton (1964, 1968a). The Grid is a two-dimensional framework (see Figure 12–1) with one dimension representing a concern for production and the other a concern for people. A scale ranging from 1 (low) to 9 (high) makes it possible to quantify a manager's concern for people and production. Thus, a large number of different management styles can be represented **205**

FIGURE 12–1   The Managerial Grid®

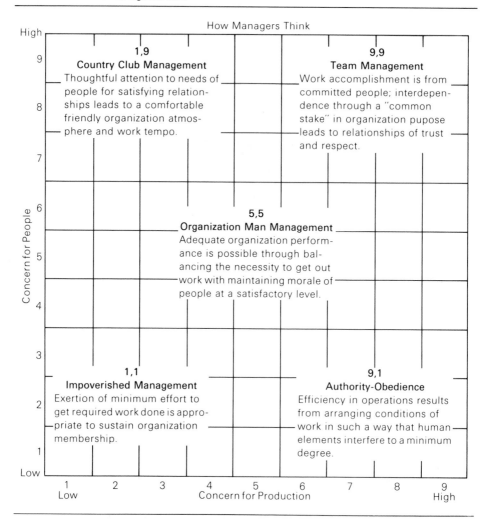

within the Grid framework by combining various amounts of the two concerns. For example, "9,1" describes a manager or organization with high concern for production and low concern for people. The framework can be used to diagnose personal style or organizational culture.

Grid OD includes a variety of interventions aimed at moving an organization to a "9,9" management culture, one that has a high concern for both production and people. Such a culture is characterized by shared goals, understanding of those goals by everyone, high commitment to work accomplishment, high collaboration, and high trust (Blake & Mouton, 1969). Blake and Mouton believe that a "9,9" culture leads not only to efficiency and effectiveness but also to organizational health. (See Chapter 2 for a definition of these systems-level criteria.)

A preprogrammed sequence of interventions for moving an organization to a "9,9" culture is recommended by Blake and Mouton. Six developmental phases, each featuring one type of intervention spread over a three-to-five-year period, are specified as the change strategy. The developmental phases are:

- *Phase 1:* A one-week laboratory training program for all organizational members in which they study the managerial grid concepts and use these concepts to learn about their managerial style, group decision making, and organization development (see Chapter 11). People at the top of the organization are expected to attend first.

- *Phase 2:* Team development for all groups in the organization, starting at the top. Each management team examines its own functioning and the behavior of individuals using managerial grid concepts. The procedure for a two-day meeting is specified in detail. In addition, questionnaires are provided to help move a group through the self-examination process (see Chapter 9).

- *Phase 3:* All major functional groups which must coordinate their activities are brought together in an intergroup laboratory. Using managerial grid concepts and predeveloped instruments, groups examine their relationships and develop plans for improved coordination (see Chapter 9).

- *Phase 4:* Using an agenda specified by Blake and Mouton, the top management group meets for several days to develop an ideal model of the organization (structure, process, and culture). They are assisted in this process by readings and data about the organization generated from diagnostic questionnaires, including the Corporate Excellence Rubric (see Chapter 8). A plan for organization development is developed.

- *Phase 5:* Temporary task forces and project teams are formed to implement the organizational changes specified in the plan. These task forces are made up of people throughout the organization who have knowledge or influence in the task force's target area.

- *Phase 6:* A program to measure changes that have occurred and to stabilize the achievements of all previous phases is activated. New goals for organization development are set.

The Grid program combines a variety of intervention methods described in Chapters 8 through 11. Indeed, Blake and Mouton themselves pioneered in the development of some of these methods. It begins with individual changes using laboratory methods, moves to group development, then intergroup methods, and ends with total organizational diagnosis and change.

The process starts at the top, moves down through the whole organization, comes back to the top for the development of a change plan, and again moves down into the organization for the implementation of the plan. With the help of predeveloped procedures and tools, managers guide this whole process.

A certain number of managers in the organization are trained to run "Grid Laboratories" and to help other managers with team building (phase 2) and intergroup interventions (phase 3). No outside consultants are used. The whole Grid program is aimed at moving the organization toward a "9,9" culture by creating a "critical mass" of individuals and groups who have been exposed to the same "cognitive framework" and who share the same beliefs and values about management.

Evaluation of Grid OD

There has been relatively little research on the effectiveness of the Managerial Grid Program. One reason is that few organizations have undertaken the full six-phase program. Another is that it is extremely difficult to evaluate the effectiveness of such a large-scale and multifaceted program, and the evaluations which have been performed have been contradictory. In some organizations, profit improvements and changes in attitudes were found (Beer & Kleisath, 1967; Blake et al., 1964; Blake & Mouton, 1978). In one, no changes in organizational climate were found because of lack of top management support for the Grid (Greiner, Leitch, & Barnes, 1968).

What constitutes success or failure, changes in profits or attitudes? If profits go up, is it because of the Grid, or some other technical or market factors? If profits do not improve and attitudes do not change, is it because of the ineffectiveness of the Grid concepts and programs, or because of top management's disinterest or ineptitude? In other words, is it a failure in the method, or a failure in the motivation or skill of managers to apply the method properly?

Clearly, success or failure is often a function of both of these; indeed, a program's effectiveness lies in a design that is compatible with managers' skills and motivation. For these reasons, we can evaluate the Grid only in the more general context of what is known about effective change strategies.

Strengths of Grid OD. Grid OD has many positive features which make it an effective system-oriented organization development program. It is the only prepackaged program based on assumptions supported by research and experience with organization change. Some of Grid OD's most important strengths are as follows.

1. *Provides a theory of behavior.* Managers are provided a theory of behavior which enables them to do their own diagnosis rather than being dependent on a consultant to tell them what their problems are. Furthermore, the two-dimensional theory of task and relationship orientation is supported by numerous research studies (Fleishman, Harris, & Burtt, 1955; O'Reilly & Roberts, 1978). Indeed, task and relationship orientation has been found to have explanatory power in other settings, including parent-child and marital relationships.

2. *Integrates individual and group development.* Individual education (phase 1) is integrated with efforts to diagnose and improve the effectiveness of the individual's work group (phase 2). Moreover, both of these interventions use the same cognitive framework. Though we do not know whether the Grid sequence is necessarily *the* correct one, research findings on the ineffectiveness of the laboratory training method, when used on its own (see Chapter 11), clearly support coupling it with group development.

3. *Intergroup interventions follow group development.* Groups that have gained skills in communicating and have cleared up internal issues are more likely to deal effectively with other groups with which they have conflict.

4. *Organization development starts at the top.* Starting at the top has been supported many times by research and experience in organization development (Beckhard, 1969). When top management begins the OD process, they model new behavior for lower levels and send signals that such behavior will be supported. Indeed, once committed to new behaviors, they have the power to reward them.

5. *Emphasizes diagnosis.* Diagnosis is an essential means for determining what improvements are needed. Throughout all phases, participants are asked to compare

their diagnosis of *actual* conditions with the *ideal* desired. This comparison unleashes motivation to overcome organizational problems.

6. *Examines strategy and structure.* In phase 4, Grid shifts from examining behavior to examining business strategy, as well as organizational policies and structures. In so doing, Grid OD recognizes the essential interdependence between organizational behavior and culture on the one hand, and organizational strategy and structure on the other. In effect, phases 4 and 5 are a process for open systems planning and make Grid OD a systems oriented strategy. Blake and Mouton argue (Blake, 1979) with some logical justification, that shifting into an examination of business practices *after* unsound behavior has been examined and acted on allows a fresh look at business practices. Management may see how their own personal values have guided business strategy and internal operations. Real adaptation may be possible for the first time.

7. *Involvement builds commitment.* Grid is a "shared approach" to change and thus tends to avoid the problems of "unilateral" and "delegated" change discussed in Chapter 3.

8. *Reduces dependence on consultants.* The use of a theory, the prepackaged process, and heavy reliance on managers to make interventions, all reduce dependence on external consultants. In fact, few if any consultants are called for and thus the possibility of regression after they leave is reduced. This has been a major problem with many OD programs.

9. *Relies on multiple interventions.* Grid's reliance on multiple interventions to create change in multiple components of the social system makes it a truly system oriented organization development program. However, there are some questions about the sequencing of these interventions which will be discussed next.

The strengths of Grid OD make it an attractive option for some organizations. It has been widely used by organizations in the public and private sector. Scientific Methods, which markets Grid OD, claims top managers of many organizations among its clients.

Problems with Grid OD. Despite its great strengths, there are a number of theoretical and practical questions which can be raised about Grid OD. Some of these questions could be asked of other OD efforts, but many are unique to Grid. For this reason, some of the assumptions on which it is based need examination.

1. *One culture is desirable for all organizations.* Is a "9,9" culture the most effective one for all organizations? While there is evidence to indicate that a style of management which combines high concern for people and production leads to greater motivation and satisfaction (O'Reilly & Roberts, 1978), it is not clear that all organizations require a "9,9" culture in order to be efficient and effective. As stated earlier in this book, a company's approach to management should depend on the nature of its business, tasks, and people.

2. *All organizations should develop adaptive human resources.* A "9,9" culture is probably consistent with the characteristics of organizational health described in Chapter 2: open confrontation of differences, participation, problem solving, and commitment. Thus, the assumption underlying Grid OD seems to be that all organizations should invest their resources in developing adaptive human resources. While this assumption is generally consistent with an ever-changing environment which demands adaptiveness, there are two reasons to question it. First, not all organizations can **209**

expect the same rate of change in their future environment. Investment in organizational health should be dependent on a forecast of the need for it as well as on a conscious choice that organizational growth rather than decline is desirable. Second, adaptiveness may also be obtained by maintaining liquid financial resources which allow diversification through acquisitions. This strategy for adaptation does not require adaptive human resources throughout the organization.

3. *OD should be approached through a long-term strategy.* Grid OD assumes that many short-term problems blocking efficiency and effectiveness will be solved by helping individuals and groups through a process of education and reorientation aimed at increasing adaptiveness ("9,9"). This is probably a correct assumption if the management can stick with the program long enough to achieve a "9,9" culture. However, this may not be possible in the face of short-term problems. First, the organization may not survive its more pressing short-term problems to have a future at all. Second, an organization in serious trouble may not have the slack resources (time, energy, and money) to invest in long-term culture development. Finally, a primary emphasis on long-term development as opposed to short-term problem solving, places an enormous burden on the vision and continued commitment of management to "9,9" ideas and values. This is highly unlikely since managers of organizations under pressure can only sustain their commitment and that of others if there are visible and relatively immediate successes (see Chapter 3). Indeed, this may be the reason why relatively few organizations can be found that have completed all six phases of Grid. All this means, of course, that corporations needing organization development the most may be the ones least likely to adopt or complete a program such as Grid.

4. *Managers will be motivated to follow standardized programs.* Grid OD relies on standardization of procedures to reduce consultant dependency. Experience suggests that managers do not respond well to standardized programs. Motivation is based on expected payoff. When managers must follow steps that they do not see as immediately relevant, they lose motivation. A lock-step procedure also reduces their freedom to shape a program and develop ownership and commitment to it. In one organization, a plant manager reported that the energy required to move through six phases of Grid in the face of shorter-term pressures, took so much out of him that he would never do it again. If the cure is more painful than the disease, can the patient be expected to adopt it?

5. *One sequence of intervention is appropriate for all organizations* Even if the Grid's "9,9" objectives are appropriate for an organization, it is not clear that its specified sequence of interventions is appropriate for *all* organizations. For example, in an organization where managers lamented that the most serious problem, intergroup coordination, had not yet been dealt with, OD was discontinued before phase 3 was reached. This example highlights the value of starting with a system-wide diagnosis of the problems that are preventing organizational efficiency and effectiveness, and directing early interventions to these problems. Could it be that Grid OD might not have been discontinued in the organization in question had such an approach been taken?

Early interventions dealing with problems identified by a system-wide diagnosis not only solve some immediate problems, but also result in early success experiences (see Chapter 3) that reinforce the OD process and its value to the organization. An approach which starts with such a diagnosis could lead to a variety of interventions but would introduce them in accordance with the problems of the organization and the felt needs of managers at the time.

6. *Organization change begins with attitude change* Finally, it is not clear that an organization development effort must start with individual interventions aimed at attitude and value change. First, there is substantial evidence to indicate that an individual's attitudes and beliefs about how he manages or ought to manage are not necessarily consistent with the way he in *fact* manages (Argyris & Schon, 1976). Thus, successfully training people in "9,9" management does not necessarily mean that changed behavior will follow. Second, there is increasing evidence from social psychological research that attitude change can and often does follow behavioral change. It is possible for individuals to adopt new behavior through watching others or by being put in situations that require or reward new behavior (for example, as a result of structural changes). New behavior is performed *before* any real attitude or belief changes occur (Porter, Lawler, & Hackman, 1975). Because people need to maintain congruity in their self-concept (Festinger, 1957), they often change their attitudes to fit their behavior. If attitudes and beliefs follow behavior, then an equally, if not more effective, change strategy might start a change program with structural changes of the kind that Grid OD does not introduce until phase 4 or 5.

Alternatives to Preprogrammed OD

This discussion of Grid OD has been aimed at providing an understanding of some of the issues that must be considered when integrating a variety of interventions into a systems oriented organization development effort. Blake and Mouton are pioneers in their recognition that system oriented change requires multiple interventions, a long-term program, top support, and process and structures for managing changes over a long period of time. In this regard, Grid OD still represents the only effective prepackaged systems oriented OD program. There are many managers who believe it has significantly added to the profitability and effectiveness of their organization. There are also some research findings to support this (Blake & Mouton, 1978). However, given its *primary* focus on long-term development of organizational health and its prepackaged form, Grid OD represents an attractive alternative for those organizations that are already relatively strong financially and organizationally. These organizations may have short-term problems too, but they also have sufficient slack to further invest in developing organizational health.

However, not all organizations are in this position. Strategies must be found for *many* organizations that have short-term problems. An OD strategy is needed that will focus on these and use this beginning to launch long-term development of organizational health. These organizations will require a more "organic integration" of interventions based on continual diagnosis, interventions, and reexamination of the appropriate next steps in organization development (Beer & Huse, 1972; Huse & Beer, 1971). With this approach, change can begin with any number of interventions as long as the choice of the intervention is based on valid diagnosis. This requires sophistication on the part of the change agent in diagnosis and knowledge of the many alternative interventions discussed in Chapters 8 through 11. In short, the change agent has to exercise "clinical judgment" based on information about the problem, the situation, and the change goals. A better understanding of the considerations that go into these judgments can improve the change agent's effectiveness in managing organic OD efforts.

ORGANIC INTEGRATIONS: DIAGNOSTICALLY BASED OD

A tailor-made program developed to fit the problems of a given organization is likely to be the most efficient and effective. A frequent problem with OD programs is that managers **211** feel much of their time is wasted in nonrelevant activities. But if interventions are designed to achieve the change objectives for their organization, managers will see them as relevant and will accept them, particularly if they have had a hand in their design.

A tailor-made program is also more flexible. It is inevitable that early interventions will lead to unanticipated consequences or that external events will change the nature of the organization's problem. Only an *organic OD effort*, one that continually changes to deal with current organizational realities, can handle these circumstances.

As we shall see, organic OD efforts aimed at systems change are comprehensive, complex, and therefore may appear more expensive in terms of time and money than more limited and traditional approaches. However, many "programs" developed by corporate staff groups, while cheaper and quicker, are ineffective and inefficient for reasons already outlined. A training program unleashed on an organization by the personnel department may not be relevant to problems many units or individuals face, and their lack of readiness to change will mean that the training effort is wasted. Long-range planning, performance appraisal, and other standardized programs are likely to fall short of their goals for the same reasons.

Fortunately, there is increasing evidence that in certain organizations organic OD efforts are being applied with some success (Beckhard, 1966; Beer & Huse, 1972; Dyer et al., 1970; Schmuck, Runkel, & Langmeyer, 1969; Seashore & Bowers, 1963). Perhaps one of the best-documented programs is reported by Marrow, Bowers, and Seashore (1967). Culture and performance of an acquired organization were successfully changed through the following interventions: (1) a new production system; (2) a vestibule training program; (3) coaching of substandard employees; (4) problem-solving meetings at various levels; (5) T groups for top management and supervisors; (6) a change in the compensation system; (7) termination of low performers; and (8) selection tests. See Case 12–1 for a description by Bowers (1976) which provides further insights into the nature of the program, the rationale underlying the integration of various interventions, and the effects of the program.

STRATEGIC CONSIDERATIONS IN SEQUENCING INTERVENTIONS

If most successful organization development efforts are an organic integration of a wide variety of interventions, what guidelines exist for the sequence by which they might be introduced? Successful change agents seem to have implicit guidelines by which they introduce interventions. Yet little research has been done to determine what those guidelines are, nor has their validity been tested. However, even if such research were conducted, the complexity of situational factors upon which sequencing decisions are made, make it unlikely that simple decision rules would emerge. However, based on experience with change and available research, it is possible to specify a series of considerations that ought to enter sequencing decisions.[1] The remainder of this section will list sequencing choices to be made and considerations that enter the decision process.

Diagnostic Interventions Should Generally Come First

Overwhelming evidence indicates that effective OD efforts start with one of many diagnostic interventions (see a description of some of these in Chapter 8). As the discussion in Chapter 3 indicates, the establishment of an effective relationship between the change

The organization and its settings are that of a pajama plant, in some difficulty both socially and technically, that had been acquired by a major competitor. To restore productivity and profits, more than a dozen different activities—some with most or all employees, some with specific groups—were employed in a carefully sequenced development program. Indeed, in the well-documented account of this effort, it is noted that the direct dollar costs of the change effort on the human organization side were about as large as the direct dollar costs of physical plant improvement. Furthermore, what was done was consistently tied to real on-the-job problems. That is, while sensitivity training was employed with supervisors, the interpersonal awareness thus gained was made relevant to the normal work world by having the supervisors, with guidance, then conduct problem-posting and solving sessions for groups encompassing all production workers. The outside resources brought to bear upon problems faced by the organization were carefully selected for their relevance, not

simply because of a persuasive pitch. Throughout, there was a careful imparting of knowledge and a demonstration of the ways in which to use it. Finally, the whole effort was very carefully evaluated—it has, in fact, been termed the best-documented study of its kind.

The results are well known. Operator productivity improved 43 percent. Operator turnover, which had been phenomenally high, declined nearly 90 percent, while absenteeism declined by 50 percent. The rate of manufacturing defects was reduced by 39 percent, and customer returns dropped by 37 percent. Return on investment improved and profits moved from a loss of 15 percent to a profit of 17 percent during the three-year period of study.

An analysis of operator performance statistics suggested that approximately one-fourth of their improvement was attributable to "social" or interpersonal events of an OD character, with the remainder attributable to technical change activities, to the combined effects of technical and social problems, and to unknown causes. Clearly, however, the broader picture of improved profitability is attributable to the whole program—custom-designed, as it was, to meet the organization's needs of both technical and social kinds.

From D. Bowers, "Organizational Development: Promises, Performances, Possibilities," in *Organizational Dynamics*, vol. 4, no. 4, Spring 1976, p. 57. Reprinted by permission.

agent and the organization, the development of motivation to change, and managers' feelings that the OD effort is relevant are all enhanced by an early definition of specific problems (Franklin, 1976). Regardless of whether it is simply a listing of problems by the top management group or an elaborate data-gathering process using interviews, questionnaires, and group discussions, some sort of diagnostic intervention must usually come first.

Diagnosis *first* allows the change agent to focus early intervention on pressing problems, and avoid spending substantial change resources on less important ones. Diagnosis screens out faddish interventions that fail because they do not fit the problem or individual's state of readiness. Furthermore, an in-depth diagnosis by a skilled change agent is likely to identify the real problems underlying the obvious ones people talk about. **213**

For example, when there is severe conflict between functional groups such as marketing and manufacturing, people often talk about personality differences as being the cause of the problem. Without a diagnosis, this definition of the problem might lead to counseling, third-party peace making, or replacement interventions. If the problem is stated as a problem of trust between groups, the intervention chosen might be an intergroup laboratory. However, none of these interventions will work if the real reasons for intergroup conflict are a poorly defined strategy or inadequate integrative structures such as project teams or meetings that bring people from different functions together. Only an in-depth diagnosis of an organization can surface these underlying problems.

Of course in some situations, such as when management merely needs help implementing major changes on which it has already decided, diagnosis should not be the first step in an OD program. Many OD efforts are triggered by these circumstances. When they are, the process and individual interventions described in Chapters 9 and 11 can be useful in helping people adapt to change. Starting with an elaborate systems oriented diagnosis under these circumstances would not be relevant to the immediate needs of the organization.

An example of the misapplication of a diagnostic intervention coming too late in the evolution of an organization development program, occurred when a railroad was undergoing decentralization (Baxley Railroad cases, 1977). A consultant was brought in after the decision to decentralize. It was clear to everyone that managers in the decentralized divisions needed help in working with subordinates who had previously reported to functional managers at headquarters and that problems were developing between those functional managers and new division managers. Instead of intervening directly with group development in the divisions and intergroup or interpersonal interventions at the interface between the divisions and corporate staff groups, the consultant took a year to work through a survey-feedback procedure using the Michigan Survey of Organizations (see Chapter 8). This procedure yielded no new data and only delayed needed process interventions. Organizational adaptation was slowed by an inappropriately timed and sequenced diagnostic intervention.

The reader should realize, of course, that process interventions in this example would also have provided diagnostic data. This data might have led to a modification in the organization development program or to a more elaborate diagnosis at a later time. This simply illustrates the iterative nature of diagnosis and the importance of understanding at what stage the OD program is before deciding on diagnosis.

Changing People and Process vs. Changing Structures

There are two schools of thought about the best way to create change in organizations. The first focuses on changing *individuals* through various training and educational programs (see Chapter 11) or direct intervention in the social process of the organizations (see Chapter 9). The second focuses more on changing structures of organizations (see Chapter 10) than with modifying knowledge, attitudes, and relationships.

Historically, at least, OD practitioners have adhered to the first school. However, as the discussion in Chapter 11 indicated, the effects of training programs generally "fade-out" over time. Individuals whose attitudes and beliefs change in a training program are often unable to maintain the change in the face of their supervisor's unchanged attitudes. To some extent, process interventions such as group development alleviate this problem by including the boss in the change process, but problems still persist. Organizational constraints may contradict new attitudes, or the flow of people within the organization erodes new norms and values.

Because of these drawbacks, OD programs have increasingly used structural interventions such as job design, changes in compensation, and changes in organization structure to create more permanent and pervasive change. Unfortunately, these kinds of changes often demand new attitudes and behavior from people who have insufficient guidance in how to behave. They then become frustrated by the confusion and difficulties they encounter. For instance, when work has been restructured in plants to enhance employee motivation, supervisors have had difficulty adjusting to inevitable role changes (Walton & Schlesinger, 1979).

Given what has already been said about the need for multiple interventions in a system oriented change effort, it should be clear that both kinds of intervention are needed. The question then is which should come first, structural or people and process change? The answer depends on the options the change agent finds acceptable and the situation surrounding the change. Structural interventions will change behavior very rapidly, but they will also create uncertainty and insecurity (Tushman, 1974). In this case, people are likely to direct their frustration and anger at both the source of the change, management or a staff group, and the change effort itself. Furthermore, they are likely to take little responsibility for future changes. On the other hand, people or process interventions, while slower, will result in a building of commitment. However, people may become frustrated as they try to apply new approaches and find themselves blocked by traditional practices. In this situation, they focus their anger on the organization rather than on the change agent or effort. Obviously, a change agent mixing these interventions must be aware of the different consequences a choice entails.

There is increasing evidence that structural interventions change attitudes and behavior faster and more permanently than more direct individual and process ones (Beer & Driscoll, 1977). If management is clear about the kinds of changes needed, solutions for some problems are needed immediately, and the organization has a low capacity for participation and involvement, it makes sense to start with structural change and follow it with supporting process and educational interventions. In this way, immediate problems in effectiveness and efficiency are attacked and people's capacity to cope with new structures can be developed later by educational interventions.

Since structural change tends to be a top-down approach and can result in hostility toward top management, it would be more appropriately used in organizations that are hierarchical and have an authoritarian culture (many business organizations). In such organizations, the amount of expressed hostility will be low, and management will be able to control deviations in behavior. For organizations with a "looser" structure or more participative culture (professional organizations, voluntary organizations, or academic institutions), it is probably wiser to begin with individual and process interventions to prepare people for change. Once attitudes have changed, people can be more easily involved in planning structural changes. The reader will recognize that this is the Japanese approach to change, in which structure emerges from a process of discussion and participation.

The important point is that structural changes must be accompanied by people and process changes and vice versa. The choice of a given sequence must be made on the basis of management's understanding of what changes are needed, the expected outcomes described above, and management's capacity to cope with the outcomes. If long-term organizational health is a desired outcome, process and individual interventions should precede structural change. In this way, people become more practiced in taking responsibility for change.

215

Process vs. Individual Interventions

In Grid OD, individual development through a laboratory training program is the first step in the change program and precedes process interventions such as group development and intergroup laboratories. It is clear that in any systems oriented OD effort, people will need to be developed and in some cases better-suited individuals selected (see Chapter 3), but should these individual interventions come before or after process interventions? Experience suggests that there are useful guidelines for these decisions.

In general, the more efficient approach is to make process interventions before individual interventions. For one thing, process interventions such as group development, not only affect group process and norms, but also affect individuals' expectations and behavior. For example, if a group decides that it needs to increase its teamwork, an individual who is not inclined to work collaboratively will recognize that this will mean change on his part. This realization will occur even if the individual does not receive direct feedback on his behavior. If the process intervention involves feedback about individual behavior, the individual will have an even clearer understanding of the group's expectations. Thus, signals about new expectations and individual action plans that are developed during various process interventions can be sufficient to create change in some individuals. Individual interventions are not needed for these people and therefore, starting with them in these cases is a waste of time and money.

Even in cases where process interventions must be followed by individual interventions, these interventions provide important diagnostic data for decisions individuals must make about their career development and managers must make about individuals. Process interventions clarify for individuals and managers what attitudes, behaviors, or skills will have to be developed and therefore help in the selection of appropriate training and developmental experiences. Those developmental experiences will also have more payoff when they follow process interventions. Individuals will see them as relevant, will be motivated to learn from them, and the new learning will be supported by group norms. Similarly, when replacement and termination decisions are made following process interventions, they are seen by people in the context of larger organizational changes and are better understood and accepted. This is particularly true if individuals have been given time and needed resources to change and develop themselves following process interventions.

The opposite sequence of individual interventions, before process interventions, is not likely to be as efficient in the case of training or perceived as fair in the case of replacement or termination. But when organizational change must occur rapidly and managers have concluded that certain individuals cannot adapt and will block progress, early replacement or termination decisions are warranted. Unfortunately, such early decisions are often made on the basis of inadequate information or shortly after a new manager has taken over. In these cases, acceptance is difficult to obtain and trust is lowered. Similarly, training and development may precede process interventions only when communication has clarified how these interventions fit into objectives for organization change and only when individual managers have sufficient diagnostic data to determine who needs training and what kind is needed. These conditions are only likely to exist in an organization that has an effective performance appraisal and development process, and are not likely to be met by most organizations requiring organization development.

Decision Rules for Sequencing Interventions

This section has provided recommendations about how interventions might be sequenced and a discussion of the considerations that enter these decisions. It should be clear that the discussion has oversimplified the actual decision process by dealing with only broad intervention categories as opposed to specific interventions and by generalizing about situational contingencies which might enter such decisions. Decisions about sequencing interventions are complex and require substantial clinical judgment.

Underlying the strategic considerations discussed are a number of decision rules which in some cases were made explicit and in other cases have remained implicit. These decision rules, which will now be summarized, can help a change agent focus on the relevant issues in making decisions about how to integrate a variety of interventions. They are rules for managing the implementation process.

1. *Maximize diagnostic data.* In general, interventions that will provide data needed to make subsequent intervention decisions should come first. This is particularly true when change agents do not know much about the situation. Violation of this rule can lead to choosing inappropriate interventions.

2. *Maximize effectiveness.* Interventions should be sequenced so that early interventions enhance the effectiveness of subsequent interventions. For example, interventions that develop readiness, motivation, knowledge, or skills required by other interventions should come first. Violation of this rule (leapfrogging) can result in interventions that do not achieve their objectives, regression, and the need to start a new sequence of interventions.

3. *Maximize efficiency.* Interventions should be sequenced to conserve organizational resources such as time, energy, and money. Violation of this rule will result in overlapping interventions or in interventions that are not needed by certain people or parts of the organization.

4. *Maximize speed.* Interventions should be sequenced to maximize the speed with which ultimate organizational improvement is attained. Violation of this rule occurs when progress is slower than is necessary to conform to all the other rules.

5. *Maximize relevance.* Interventions that management sees as most relevant to immediate problems should come first. In general, this means interventions that will have an impact on the organization's performance or task come before interventions that will have an impact on individuals or culture. Violation of this rule will result in loss of motivation to continue with organization development.

6. *Minimize psychological and organizational strain.* A sequence of interventions should be chosen that is least likely to create dysfunctional effects such as anxiety, insecurity, distrust, dashed expectations, psychological damage to people, and unanticipated and unwanted effects on organizational performance. Violating this rule will lower people's sense of competence and confidence and their commitment to organizational improvement.

These decision rules are not independent of each other and may call for contradictory sequencing decisions. Therefore, a change agent faces complex and ambiguous tradeoff decisions requiring sophisticated understanding of the change process and organizations as systems. Indeed, the effectiveness of an organization development program as opposed to a prepackaged program is heavily dependent on the capacities of the change agent to comprehend organizations as systems and to orchestrate the change process accordingly. (See Case 12–2 for an example of a change agent who is systems oriented.) For this reason, the remainder of this chapter will deal with the change agent's role in systems oriented OD.

I mentioned earlier that we changed the structure of the organization. When we established the system of Management by Objectives and Programs, it became evident that structural and procedural changes were necessary to make the whole organization function better. Just as we had learned that it was not enough to work on the structure without regard for interpersonal relationships we also learned that changes in the structure required changes in procedures and systems. In other words, people had to work within the structure (organization) and the structure could not be effectively changed without involving the people. In all cases, however, procedures and systems had to be changed for the system to work.

Procedures of work flow, decision making, and paper processing are so interrelated with structure, interpersonal relationships, and the procedures (the system) that all have impact on the overall goal of improving organizational effectiveness and all must be given attention almost simultaneously.

Therefore a "systems approach" was used extensively. By this means we tried to take into account not only interpersonal relationships but the whole life of the organization, the way the staff meetings were conducted, the way people were promoted and compensated, the way the organizational parts were linked, the way information flowed, the way decisions were made, who needed to see whom about what, and so on. We found out very early that a significant change in one part of the system directly affected another part, which would then require systems development. We discovered that the failure to bring about a procedural revision in one part of the system after we had changed another part seriously inhibited the whole process. Therefore, as part of the ACORD program, we had a group working only on systems and systems modifications. Their job was to ensure that the system *as a whole* was linked with common procedures and that all the interfaces required to make a complex organization work were provided for.

From W. J. Crockett, Chapter 5, pg. 136–137, in P. H. Mirvis and D. N. Berg, *Failures in Organization Development and Change*, New York: Wiley-Interscience, © 1977. Reprinted by permission of John Wiley & Sons, Inc.

THE CHANGE AGENT AND SYSTEMS ORIENTED OD

Because it is the change agent who directs the diagnosis toward certain dimensions of the organization, he is a major factor in the success of diagnostically. based OD efforts. The change agent influences the interpretation of the diagnostic data and the interventions that are chosen to create change. Thus he has enormous influence on the way problems are defined and the actions that are taken to deal with them. The manner in which change agents carry out their roles will determine the effectiveness of the OD effort. Attending to the wrong organizational dimensions in a diagnosis will cause a change agent to choose the interventions which will misdirect the organization development effort. Just how effective are change agents at carrying out their roles and can their effectiveness be increased?

Do Change Agents Employ Systems Models?

Chapter 2 described a social systems model of organizations that change agents could use to guide them in a systems oriented diagnosis. Unfortunately, it appears that many change agents (consultants and managers) have not internalized a systems model and are therefore not guided by a systems orientation. These change agents seem to diagnose organizations according to more limited models influenced by their values, unique competence, or past experience (Tichy & Nisberg, 1976). Thus, if a change agent is competent in group development or values working in teams, he may see all organizational problems in terms of inadequate group effectiveness. Structural, strategic, financial, or cultural elements may be left out of the definition of the problem (Tichy, 1974).

There is ample social psychological research to support the conclusion that people's perceptions of the world around them is a function of past experience, competence, and motivation. These general findings have been found to apply to the diagnosis of organizational problems. In one study, managers with different functional backgrounds (finance, personnel, production, etc.) analyzed the same business problem. Their diagnosis and recommendations for action reflected their functional perspective (Dearborn & Simon, 1958).

If we examine our experience, we will recognize that some consultants and managers are identified with one approach, one orientation, or one method. There are compensation consultants, process consultants, financially oriented managers, and people oriented managers. Each of them develops an approach to diagnosing and acting on organizational problems consistent with their background and competence. In short, many individuals who are placed in the position of being change agents do not have a systems or a general management orientation. If not a systems orientation, what types of orientation do change agents have?

Types of Change Agents

Individual characteristics such as functional background, type of organization in which one has worked, education, and other background factors may all influence the approach a change agent takes toward organization development. But these characteristics do not work directly to influence the change agent's behavior. Rather as Figure 12–2 indicates, these characteristics influence the individual's change model (Tichy, 1974). This model is composed of the change agent's values and beliefs, his cognitive framework, and his knowledge of intervention methods.

Recent research into the values and cognitive frameworks of professional agents of planned change (internal and external OD consultants, community organizers, business consultants, etc.) has revealed four main kinds of change agents (Tichy, 1974).

- *Outside Pressure Type (OP):* These change agents work outside the organization and use a variety of pressure tactics, including consumer-advocate work, mass demonstrations, civil disobedience, and even violence. Essentially, they seek to create change through outside pressure.
- *People Change Type (PCT):* These change agents use a variety of individual interventions (see Chapter 11) such as achievement training, behavior modification, assessment of individuals, and counseling.
- *Organization Development Type (OD):*[2] These change agents apply process consultation, team building, and data feedback to encourage problem-solving behavior. They primarily apply the process interventions described in Chapter 9.

FIGURE 12–2 A Framework for Understanding the Change Agent's Model of Change and His Practice

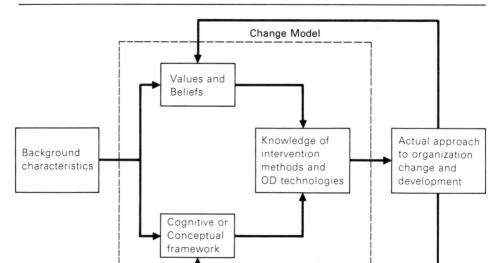

Adapted from N. M. Tichy, "Agents of Planned Social Change: Congruence of Values, Cognitions and Actions," in *Administrative Science Quarterly*, 1974, 19, p. 165. Reprinted by permission.

- *Analysis for the Top Type (AFT):* These change agents use operations research, systems analysis, policy studies, and other forms of analytical approaches to inform top management of needed changes. Their work most often results in structural changes of the type described in Chapter 10.

It is interesting to note that the change agent types identified by Tichy seem to specialize in diagnosing and intervening in one of several social system components outlined in Chapter 2 (environment, people, process, and structure), not the total system. Therefore, it is not surprising that when change agents were asked by Tichy and Nisberg (1976) to diagnose a problem and outline their change strategy, they asked very different diagnostic questions. These differences reflected their various cognitive and conceptual frameworks, and presumably (although the study did not determine this) influenced their organization development practice.

Change Agent Awareness of Their Change Model

If change agents were aware of the model they used in approaching diagnosis and action, their biases would not be such a problem. Unfortunately, in a study of professional consultants working in the area of planned change, Tichy and Nisberg (1976) found that these consultants had difficulty articulating their assumptions about organizational change. For example, in answer to a question about his model of organization change, one change agent responded:

I didn't think this out as formally as you want me to do on paper. If I were to do the task you ask me [develop and articulate his organizational model] to do, it would be something that is way back in the recesses of my head; it is not something I do consciously (Tichy & Nisberg, 1976).

If change agents cannot articulate their model or their assumptions, there is no way for them to understand whether they are systems oriented or how their values and assumptions influence their behavior as change agents. Without such awareness, they cannot attempt to broaden their perspective or to complement it with the views of others. In short, they cannot gain control over their practice as change agents. Ways must therefore be found to enhance their awareness of the assumptions and models underlying their practice, so that improvements can be obtained.

Developing Systems Oriented Change Agents

Given the evidence that most managers and consultants do not have a systems orientation, the outlook for systems oriented OD is pessimistic. However, at least two approaches have been effective in dealing with this problem.

The first way is through education. Fortunately, the research that showed that change agents can't articulate their diagnostic models also showed that the agents learned from working through the research procedure. Based on this finding, Hornstein and Tichy (1973) designed a workbook and procedures to assist line managers, consultants, and students in developing a model for diagnosing and selecting, as well as implementing, change strategies. The process of developing the model draws on the change agent's assumptions about behavior and organizations, as well as on research and theoretical work in the field of organizational behavior. The process is based on the assumption that all change agents have models that influence their approach to organization change. The workbooks make these assumptions explicit and subject them to collaborative examination.

This process and other educational approaches have recently been incorporated into executive education programs at Columbia and Harvard universities.[3] They show some promise for increasing the system orientation of change agents. In addition, many long-standing executive education programs aimed at developing a general management perspective have the effect of broadening the view of managers, though not all of these programs may explicitly recognize their task as developing a systems view. Even if educational programs such as these cannot permanently change an individual's orientation, they can clarify the change agent's orientation so that he can know how it might be complemented by others.

The second and perhaps the most important way for developing systems oriented change agents is the creation of roles that encourage such behavior. The creation of new roles has been a mechanism by which organizations have dealt with other problems. For example, where cross-functional coordination is required, organizations have roles for "integrators," such as project, program, or product managers. The role's definition and reward structure encourage the integrators to orient themselves to the welfare of a total project or business, rather than to the interests of one function (Davis & Lawrence, 1977; Lawrence & Lorsch, 1967b). There is no reason to believe that a systems oriented change agent role cannot be developed inside an organization.

But what should be the role and characteristics of a systems oriented change agent concerned with ongoing organization improvement? Experience in organization development suggests the following role and person characteristics are important. **221**

Generalist/specialist.   An effective systems oriented agent is a generalist in his organizational and administrative perspective and a specialist in the process of organizational diagnosis and intervention.

As a generalist, the change agent has an understanding of the management process and sufficient knowledge about various functions (i.e., marketing, manufacturing) and parts of the organization (technology, people, products, departments) to know their purpose and how they fit together. In this role, the change agent must have high levels of interpersonal competence and leadership skills to be a model and a change catalyst. He must balance a short-term and long-term orientation. Finally, as a generalist in organization development, the change agent has a broad knowledge of the administrative and behavioral sciences rather than in-depth knowledge of one theory or subfield.

As a specialist, the change agent is an expert in the process and techniques of organizational diagnosis. He is highly knowledgeable and skillful in process consultation, intervention theory and method, and the dynamics of planned change. He needs only moderate skills in performing the many interventions described in Chapter 8 through 11, and calls in specialists in these methods as needed. By avoiding a specialist's competence in one intervention method, the change agent is able to maintain the perspective of a generalist.

Integrator.   An effective change agent is more than a diagnostician and catalyst. He also performs integrating functions (Havelock & Havelock, 1973) by linking the target organizations with inside or outside resources appropriate to the situation or problem. For example, a plant-level effort to increase motivation and satisfaction of the work force might include a specialist (inside and outside the organization) in job design, labor relations, training, and compensation. The change agent as integrator also helps link the change target with top management and staff groups who can affect and are affected by planned changes.

Neutrality.   Ample evidence indicates that an effective change agent is seen as neutral in a number of dimensions. He has relatively low power over the fate of managers' careers in the target organization. He has no career authority over members of the organization and is not part of evaluating people for promotion or demotion (Franklin, 1976; Walton, 1969). The change agent does not have an ax to grind with respect to the solution to a problem. He has no aspirations for attaining a high position in the organization. However, he has fairly high power (through expertise) over the change process as it unfolds. Finally, the change agent is not involved as a primary party in conflicts that may exist among functions, levels, or coalitions within an organization—he is politically neutral (Franklin, 1976; Walton, 1969).

Taking a neutral and nonthreatening role allows the change agent to gather information about problems in the organization and to bring warring parties together to solve them. (See Case 12–3 for an example where this did not happen.) Clearly, the neutrality requirement conflicts with some parts of the manager's role. Managers often deal with these conflicting roles by mixing them or by working with a consultant who can fulfill the requirements of neutrality they cannot. Thus when the manager is the primary change agent, a manager-consultant change agent team is one means of meeting the neutrality requirement.

Credibility.   Effective change agents seem to have high credibility within the organization (Franklin, 1976). They have knowledge of the organization and its functioning. They have *not* been associated with failures, and preferably have been associated with

A brewery used my services to improve its marketing orientation. The change program was highly successful and over three years, the profits moved from $500,000 to $1,000,000 and the sole competitor's profit fell from $500,000 to $70,000. During this same period, the position at the top of the marketing team increased in power greatly, moving from what was essentially public relations officer to sales manager and then to vice-president of marketing. All this was very well, but was not viewed that way by the production department who had seen its considerable power and prestige erode. The OD emphasis should have then, or earlier, shifted to such interfaces within the firm and I made several unsuccessful attempts to achieve this. In the mind of the production department, I was the wicked consultant who had hurt them. In the mind of marketing, I was their man to use in the fight against production. All this might not be too bad, but twelve years later, very low trust still exists between the two subsystems to a degree that I even now discuss with the marketing vice-president whether he ought to move on.

From W. J. Reddin, *Group & Organization Studies,* March 1977, 2(1), 33–41. Copyright © 1977 by International Authors, B. V. Reprinted by permission.

some successes. They are regarded as having the competence to be leaders. Using authority vested in a position would reduce trust and collaboration needed for creating systems oriented change (see Chapter 3); the change agent will need credibility to generate influence.

Marginality. Effective change agents occupy marginal roles in relation to the organization they are serving and the disciplines which they are relying on for help (Margulies, 1977). The concept of marginality is similar to what some social scientists have called a boundary position. A boundary position is one in which the person is related to one particular work group but belongs to another unit or work group inside or outside the organization.

The discussion in Chapter 4 indicated that a successful intervention is based on maintaining an appropriate discrepancy in values and viewpoint between the change agent and change target. Such a discrepancy is particularly important in maintaining a systems perspective when members of the organization may have a narrow functional or short-range orientation. The change agent will also need to maintain values that encompass the characteristics of a healthy organization (openness, confrontation of conflict, inquiry, and innovation), while the members of the change target may not understand or value these organizational characteristics. He must maintain detachment in order to see the organization objectively and to confront elements of the culture that need changing. (See Case 12–4 for an example of a change agent who lost detachment.)

The change agent will need both an inside (organizational) and an outside (environmental) perspective, as well as an intermediate orientation to several disciplines and values. As generalist, he will have to be empathetic to the values of all four types of change agents listed earlier, so he can play all roles when appropriate or integrate the efforts of several roles. Thus, the change agent is in a marginal role with respect to several orientations and groups. It is this marginality that allows a change agent to maintain a **223**

After working with one U.S.A. client intensively for two years it became apparent to me that the client was talking change and had built a staff to implement it but that no change was taking place. For various reasons, I was emotionally involved with this client and

From W. J. Reddin, *Group & Organization Studies,* March 1977, 2(1), 33–41. Copyright © 1977 by International Authors, B. V. Reprinted by permission.

wanted the program to be a success. My style became abrupt and argumentative. Instead of trying to analyze resistance with the client, I was berating him for not changing. At the time, I put my change in style down to my innate style flexibility; after all, very few of us remain who are equally adept at Theory "X" and "Y" even when innappropriate (McGregor, 1960). Now I see it simply as emotional involvement leading to a lowering of effectiveness.

systems perspective—to see the organization as a complex interdependent system interacting with its environment.

Difficulties with the change agent's role. Four of the role characteristics—marginal, neutral, integrator, and generalist/specialist—are extremely difficult to maintain. There is the continued danger of becoming attached to one change model, one intervention, one theory, one group, or the views of an insider or outsider. Such a role is lonely, and it is difficult to maintain a sense of identity from which develops self-confidence and thrust. Only a very confident and interpersonally competent person can play such a role (Argyris, 1970). Even then, change agents require emotional and professional support. For this reason, managers or consultants acting as change agents must find ways to associate with others in similar roles through informal and professional networks. In this way, they can be exposed to relevant models, new ideas, and emotional reinforcement from others facing similar role problems.

Another difficulty with the change agent role is that of attracting credible people to fulfill it. Managers with high aspirations and potential may not see such a role as furthering their career. Indeed, if the role is carried out effectively, it will require loosening ties with political allies, confronting people in power, and taking neutral or marginal positions with respect to important organizational matters.

We now turn to the implications of these difficulties for the organization of change agent resources.

Creating New Roles for Organization Development

It is clear that as we examine contemporary organizations we do not often find roles such as the one defined above. General managers may be generalists, integrators, and command credibility, but they may fall short of the requirement for marginality, neutrality, and expertise in the administrative sciences and the dynamics of planned change. Personnel specialists may meet these requirements but may be too specialized in their orientation to training, selection, or compensation to have a truly systems orientation. Also, they often suffer from low credibility in not having had line management experience and success.

One way to meet all the requirements is to develop an organization development team composed of two or more individuals with complementary orientations. Such a team might be composed of a manager, a staff specialist in organization development or personnel, and other internal or external specialists. The change agent closest to a generalist/specialist orientation could act as the integrator for such a team.

Another way to meet the requirements is to create completely new roles and departments inside organizations concerned with organization change and development. In recent years, such organization development departments have emerged in some corporations (Union Carbide, Corning Glass Works, TRW, and Cummins Engine). These departments have adopted a staff change agent role which meets most of the requirements outlined above. They provide systems oriented change agent services to subunits of the corporation and, in some instances, to the corporation as a whole. Too often, however, these departments, while adopting the organization development label, provide much narrower and specialized services such as training, assessment, job enrichment, or survey-feedback.

If corporations are to have a systems oriented change capability, they will have to think about creating roles and departments that can attract credible managers and professionals. The role of these organization development specialists would be continuous diagnosis and intervention activities in various parts of the system and with the larger system itself. The OD specialist would be concerned both with bringing innovation in management into an organization and with the strategic responsibility of spreading these innovations.

These new roles are substantially different than traditional personnel roles and imply a change in thinking about the organization of the personnel function. Briefly, these roles would be concerned with integrating personnel activities and other functions and specialized groups into a systemic organization development effort. A person occupying such an OD role might work out of a corporate department or within a subunit of a larger system. The new role could be occupied by professionals or by high-potential managers to whom it would be an important development experience. New paths and reward systems will have to be developed to encourage the flow of good people to these new roles. With the creation of an explicit generalist change agent role or department, an organization is more likely to develop an effective systems oriented organization development capability.

Ultimately, organizations can encourage a systems perspective in organization development by creating policies, control systems, and training and reward systems that encourage such a perspective in their general managers. Balancing short- and long-term goals by giving bonuses for both is one way companies such as Pitney Bowes have attempted to do this. Another way is to hold managers responsible for both financial performance and quality of work life outcomes. The new development in human resources accounting discussed in Chapter 10 is one way organizations are attempting to do this. If general managers have a systems perspective, the generalist/specialist role is much more likely to be effective within the organization.

The prospect of creating a new change agent role or department for renewal raises strategic issues about where organization development activities should start, how they should be spread across an organization, and how they should be evaluated. It also raises the question of how such a new role fits into the power structure of the organization and the politics of its survival. Chapters 13 and 14 will deal with these issues. **225**

NOTES

1. The experience of many change agents with a variety of OD programs at Corning Glass Works, as well as other cases reported in the literature, are the basis of the considerations described in this section. Also see Beer and Driscoll, 1977.

2. The term "Organization Development" as used by Tichy is much narrower than the way it is used in this book. Using the terminology of this book, a more appropriate label for Tichy's OD type would be Process Consultant type.

3. The Columbia program is one for Senior Specialists in Organization Development given by the Business School. It includes a module designed to help participants make their model explicit. The Harvard program is called Managing Organization Effectiveness and is given by the Business School. It relies on the case method to help students practice a systems orientation in diagnosing organizational problems and recommending change.

STARTING AND MANAGING SYSTEM-WIDE CHANGE 13

WHERE SHOULD OD START?

A manager or OD consultant who would like to introduce OD to an organization and see it spread and encompass the whole organization, faces the choice of where to start change activities. Should the change begin at the top of the organization and work its way down? Should it start at the bottom and work its way up? Or, should the change start somewhere in the middle and work in both directions? Yet another consideration is with what kind of organizational unit is it best to start. Finally, what kind of problem is a good starting point for an OD effort?

Evidence indicates that change occurs and becomes relatively permanent when a number of important conditions are present in the target organization. The simultaneous presence of these conditions creates a "window" through which a change effort can move successfully (Franklin, 1976; Myerseth, 1977). The presence of only one or even two of these conditions may be sufficient to get a change started, but may not be enough to allow it to become institutionalized. If this is true, then the selection of the first change target is perhaps the most important decision for the long-term success of OD. If the first OD effort is not successful, the probability of success in other parts of the organization is significantly diminished.

Key Managers Must Be Dissatisfied

As Chapters 3 and 5 indicated, management's dissatisfaction with the current state of affairs is an absolutely necessary condition for a successful long-term organizational improvement effort. The whole thrust of the entry and contracting process is to ascertain if sufficient dissatisfaction and commitment exist to warrant investment of change resources in an OD effort. Consequently, OD should start in that part of the organization where the best OD contract can be negotiated. Such a contract is one in which management is able to identify specific problems and to commit themselves to becoming involved in the OD process. OD contracts in which the interventionist is given license to work with any **227** managers he can interest in OD or on a problem of his choosing, are likely to lead to failure.

Experience suggests that it is important to understand which of two major sources of dissatisfaction has triggered an interest in OD. Dissatisfaction may arise out of many internal and external pressures described in Chapter 3. These pressures and the crisis that they create comprise a *deficiency agenda* for OD. Under these conditions, OD is directed at eliminating deficiencies in organizational efficiency and effectiveness. However, dissatisfaction may also arise out of management's desire to introduce innovative and progressive approaches to management. This *growth agenda* for OD is motivated by management's desire to develop a new alignment between social system components closer to their values or capable of producing even greater efficiency, effectiveness, and health.

Most organization development efforts are triggered by both sources of dissatisfaction and include both agendas (Franklin, 1976). However, of the two, a deficiency agenda is more likely to have the attention of top management, lead to a good OD contract, and produce an early success. These are the preconditions that will lead to perceptions that OD can improve organizational effectiveness. The result will be its acceptance throughout the whole organization. For these reasons, OD should probably start with an organizational unit that has an important deficiency agenda.

Finally, the level of dissatisfaction with deficiencies in the organization may also be an important factor in choosing the first OD target. Very high levels of dissatisfaction may create so much anxiety that managers are incapable of entering a process of inquiry prior to taking action. Under these circumstances, they are not open to diagnosing problems and learning about new approaches. They tend to want to take control and are not willing to involve others in organization development. Therefore, a moderate amount of dissatisfaction may be the optimum for starting an OD effort.

The Top Manager Must Be Committed and Lead

A system-wide organization development effort must have the intellectual and emotional commitment of the target unit's top manager. Without this commitment the manager cannot provide leadership for the change effort. He cannot model new behavior and attitudes, and he cannot adequately confront traditional wisdom in the organization. In a period of transition, when traditional norms and structures are weakened, such leadership is crucial to the development of change momentum.

It will be possible to obtain commitment from the top manager if the direction of OD and its process are consistent with his basic values and assumptions about management. This does not mean that the manager must fully understand the new approach to management or be completely skillful in it. If he were, there would probably be no need for an organization development effort. It does mean that at a fairly fundamental level, OD goals and process are consistent with the manager's core values and beliefs about life and management.

For these reasons, the first OD efforts in a large multiunit organization should start with a unit whose key manager is friendly to the goals, process, and values of OD. Often managers support OD verbally but their behavior makes it clear that they will have difficulty with a collaborative process of inquiry and actions. The change agent must make an early assessment of the top manager on this issue before significant resources are committed to an OD effort.

Slack Resources Must Exist

Organization change and development requires "slack." That is, additional human and financial resources will have to be made available to execute a change plan while at the same time continuing with day-to-day operations. These slack resources are required to pay for training or consulting services, to staff the organization deeply enough so managers can have time and energy to learn new ways, and to provide a financial cushion if and when performance drops during the period of transition. Slack can be developed by improving the performance of the organization, by borrowing or budgetary allowances, or by lowering financial performance standards.

The need for slack resources, resources that the organization is not pressed to use elsewhere (other investments, contributions to corporate profits or dividends), suggests that whenever possible OD should start with an organizational unit that has these resources. Unfortunately, many organizations that need organization development do not have them. For example, a division of a large corporation found it difficult to budget for sufficient change resources. It could not obtain agreement from corporate headquarters for performance goals that would allow a significant investment in organization development. With pressures for profits, there was insufficient time and money for OD, people became disillusioned, and the thrust of organization development was blunted. The years of delay in achieving an OD success slowed and endangered the spread of OD to other parts of the corporation.

Naturally, the question of resources presents a dilemma. Organizations that have such resources are generally not dissatisfied and do not need OD. Those who do not have the resources can't fund such efforts. A system-wide change effort should start with a unit that is dissatisfied with its performance but also is able to free-up sufficient resources to mount a reasonably effective OD effort.

Political Support Must Exist

The need for slack resources also highlights the issue of political support for the top manager of the target unit. If he is to obtain the budgetary allowances and support needed for organization development, the key manager must be in a strong position with the executives above his level. These executives need not have an intellectual and emotional commitment to organization development, but they must support the key manager and his OD efforts. Such support may exist because the key manager has credibility or it may exist because the next level managers understand and agree with the goals and values of OD, but the support must be there or be developed.

No top manager can deal with potential resistance to innovations unless he feels secure with those who control his fate. Nor can a change agent be effective for long without an opportunity to discuss his efforts with those above him. Such discussions provide the guidance and acknowledgment that he needs to sustain his thrust as a change agent, when unanticipated problems develop and support is needed. For example, many of the new plant innovations in work design have resulted in a slower learning curve than expected. If upper management pressures the key manager unduly during the critical start-up period, or if the key manager is removed for unfounded reasons, regression in organization development is likely. Moreover, political support is needed to obtain the cooperation of staff and line managers who do not report to the manager of the change target, but whose support may be needed to introduce change in the target organization. **229**

Political support is more than a one-time directive to change or a one-time agreement to support innovation in management, an approach called a delegated approach to change in Chapter 3. The managers above the change agent must be willing to actively support him in the face of inevitable conflict and political in-fighting that surrounds most major change programs. It becomes important for the change agent to recognize early whether political support exists. The frequency and quality of communication about organization development between the change agent and upper levels is the best indicator of support. A distant and aloof stance is the best indicator that change is being tolerated but not supported. Case 13–1 contains an account of interchanges between a change agent and higher levels which indicates inadequate political support.

It is interesting to note that OD efforts in one large decentralized corporation were concentrated in several divisions and groups of the company and were almost nonexistent in others (Myerseth, 1977). Not surprisingly, the upper level managers in those parts of the company that did not have many OD efforts, were known to be unsympathetic to OD.

Change Resources Must Match the Size and Kind of Change

As a change effort unfolds it requires the time and energy of managers and the increasing support of consultants. Interventions must be made and followed-up. Some individuals may require counseling, others training. As unexpected problems arise, consulting help will be required. Finally, successful changes generally stimulate additional and more intense interest in organization development.

For a change momentum to develop, sufficient change agent resources must support OD initiatives. Furthermore, intervention skills and orientation of the change agents must be appropriate to the kinds of problems the organization is working on. Thus change agents should select the first target for organization development on the basis of the kind and amount of resources available. The problem should not be beyond the skill of the change agents nor should the size of the change target be larger than the available resources can handle.

It's unlikely that most corporations will be able to maintain an internal staff of OD specialists who have a full range of skills. Furthermore, organizations who are just getting started with OD may not have internal OD resources. Thus, when all the conditions for change are present, but *internal* resources are not, external consultants can be brought in. The external consultants can provide the skills and the effort needed to get things started, but they will have to train an internal staff to follow-up and support new initiatives. The timely availability of trained internal resources is critical to the successful evolution of an OD program.

The Organization Development Window

Where should OD start? It should start in that part of the organization that comes closest to meeting all of these major conditions for a successful change effort. When these conditions exist, the organization development window may be said to be open. The entry and contracting process outlined in Chapter 5 is intended to determine the extent to which this window is open.

If all of the conditions described above are met, then obviously the place to start an OD effort is at the top. Unless the top man is in a weak political position with other key executives or the board of directors, starting at the top eliminates the problem of political support for the change and increases the chances that resources will be made available. However, starting at the top without all of the preconditions present can create a very visible failure from which there may not be a recovery for a long time.

CASE 13–1

The following account, provided by a top administrative officer in the State Department, indicates inadequate political support for an OD effort in the State Department that ultimately faltered when he, the change agent, retired.

One of the first things that happened to me was a summons from Robert Kennedy, the Attorney General, to come to his office. There was no greeting, no small talk, and no chance for response by me except, "yes, sir" to his cryptic monologue. He said:

First of all, get your loyalties straight. No matter whom you think you work for, the President appointed you and he is your boss. He will expect your absolute loyalty. Second, get your job straight. The State Department must be made to be loyal and responsive to the President. It must become more positive and proactive. It must be made to assume a leadership position in the Foreign Affairs Community. Your job is to make this happen. And thirdly, do you know how to make this happen . . . ?

While I was trying to think up an answer, he held up his hand to silence my response and added, "You will make it happen by giving orders and firing people who don't produce." The discussion was ended,

From W. J. Crockett, "Introducing Change to a Government Agency" in P. H. Mirvis and D. N. Berg, *Failures in Organization: Development and Change* (New York: Wiley-Interscience, 1977), pp. 113-114. Reprinted by permission of John Wiley & Sons, Inc.

and although I had numerous calls from him later in which he asked for this and demanded that, I never saw him in person again.

It is interesting that neither the President, who appointed me, nor Dean Rusk, who was my nominal boss, ever discussed with me whether this was my primary objective or how I might best pursue it. Neither oulined a goal or a program. Rusk's favorite admonishment to his subordinates' inquiries for direction and feedback was: "Work up to the horizons of your job. If you get too far out I'll pull you back." In the six years that I worked for him he never "pulled me back." He never gave me guidance, directions, or goals, nor did he give me much support for my efforts or acknowledgment for my accomplishments. There was one other bit of ominous warning in the beginning, when he once told his staff, "I won't support you if you become embroiled in bureaucratic dog fights with other agencies."

At the time Rusk's warning didn't bother me; neither did the absence of direction. Thinking back on those early days of my new job I now wonder at the fact that I accepted the Robert Kennedy direction so calmly. His authoritarian recipe for bringing about change didn't seem to bother me at all. Having risen from the ranks, I felt that I not only knew the problems of the Department but also the answers, and I soon set in motion the changes for achieving the results that I had in mind.

In most organizations, however, the change window is not open at the top. In these organizations, OD consultants or personnel specialists will have to look for open change windows at the bottom or middle of the organization. Experience suggests that these are likely to be found in subunits which operate in rapidly changing market and technological **231** environments, or in situations where people's needs and expectations are changing. These units are likely to be struggling with problems of motivation or coordination for which there are known and effective intervention methods.

However, starting at the bottom or middle is not without its risks. The first OD efforts must generally start without political support since managers who understand the process have not yet risen to the top. Under these circumstances, the possibility of developing a viable system-wide organization development effort rests on the hope that managers who have experienced OD and support it will rise to the top.

MANAGING SYSTEM-WIDE OD EFFORTS

Where OD should start in a large organization is only the first important strategic decision. The second concerns sustaining changes in that unit over time. The third concerns spreading innovative solutions coming out of the OD effort and the OD process itself to other parts of the organization. The experience of several large corporations suggests that these are crucial issues that have not been addressed creatively or effectively.

These problems occur because a large multiunit organization is itself a system. The organizational units in which early successes occur are interdependent with staff groups at headquarters, with units whose help they require to get the task accomplished, and with top management which allocates resources, determines policy, and decides who is to be rewarded. This section will explore the strategic considerations in managing an OD effort from initial success to ultimate adoption by the larger organization as a total system.

Looking for Regression: The Problem of Sustaining Change

It is almost inevitable that the enthusiasm and energy associated with the "take-off" phase of change will diminish as the organization stabilizes at a new level. As time passes, there is an erosion in the innovations that were instituted with the OD effort. Structural solutions developed are modified and new managerial practices are less consistently followed or dropped entirely. Sometimes such modifications are warranted, given change in people, task, or business. But just as frequently, the modifications represent real regression from original change goals and must be dealt with if gains from the OD effort are to be sustained.

Let us look at the longevity of one plant-level OD effort that resulted in enriched jobs and a more open participative culture (Beer, 1979). Within approximately thirteen years after the organization development program began, substantial regression in patterns of communication occurred. A number of meetings, such as problem-solving ones between supervisors and production workers, and general information and product information meetings held by the plant manager, had been discontinued or occurred only sporadically. Regular performance appraisals for production employees no longer took place. A policy that recognized performance and seniority in identifying people to be laid off evolved into a policy that considered only seniority. Production employees felt poorly informed and saw themselves as getting the least attention from management as compared with the most attention shortly after OD began. Job design changes that gave workers responsibility for the assembly of the total product were, however, still in place. No assembly lines existed in the plant. Nevertheless, some job design elements, such as self-scheduling by groups making the same product, had disappeared.

Why should such regression take place when management viewed the original innovations in the plant as a great sucess? First, none of the management people involved in the original OD effort were there any longer. They had all been promoted or moved to other jobs inside or outside the corporation. New plant managers were not selected on the basis of their support for the innovations. Indeed, they were not convinced that the innovations at the plant were appropriate. Transferring managers from one unit to another is a normal part of the manpower flow in most large organizations and is needed to develop managers and reward them. But in this plant, it eroded a philosophical base that guided the OD effort.

Similarly, all OD consulting support to the plant ceased some three years after the change started. The OD effort came from local initiative and never became part of the corporate OD strategy. As a result, new plant managers were neither chosen according to the compatibility of their management philosophy with the new plant culture, nor encouraged or rewarded for sustaining the original changes. Indeed, one of the new plant managers saw continued OD work as potentially damaging to his career. Furthermore, a number of corporate staff units created pressures to apply corporate policies (job evaluation, labor relations, and pay practices) that were not consistent with the goals and philosophy of organization development at the plant.

Regression of the type seen in this plant has occurred in many other organization development efforts (Hinrichs, 1978). It might have been avoided at the beginning if the change agents and managers worked to obviate the potential causes of regression. The following conditions seem important in sustaining change (Beer & Driscoll, 1977; Walton, 1974).

1. *Manager replacement.* When key managers leave, they must be replaced with people who are compatible with the evolving culture of the change target. Similarly, managers in the change target who cannot keep up with the evolving culture need to be transferred to other units. One of the best ways to deal with the compatibility problem is to bring new people in at the bottom of the change target, develop them within the culture, and place them into key management positions only when they have been socialized into the culture.

2. *Management orientation and education.* New managers should receive orientation training on the history of the OD effort, the stimulus for its origin, and the rationale that has guided it. Often a lack of knowledge about previous events in the organization's evolution, particularly strategic decisions that guided the organization's adaptation, can cause regression (see Case 13–2).

3. *OD consulting support.* Because conditions and managers are continually changing, it is doubtful that OD's consulting support can ever be completely eliminated. This is contrary to much of the literature which stresses that termination of consulting support signals the end of a successful OD effort. Continued consulting support must be made available to an organization as it moves through new transitions. For this reason, appropriate corporate staff groups should follow-up and check for regression.

4. *Corporate interfaces.* To achieve their change goals, organizational units undergoing OD efforts often deviate from corporate policies and practices. Functions such as personnel, control, planning, and engineering can help OD efforts by allowing exceptions to corporate policy and practice. Encouragement for such exceptions can come from top management or through education of corporate groups.

5. *Periodic assessment.* Regression sometimes occurs because new and interesting approaches become familiar and routine. Periodic assessments of OD efforts and the development of action plans to further innovations can help sustain change.

233

Seven years after a consultant had played a major part in developing innovative work structures (see Chapter 10) in a manufacturing plant, he was asked to educate the plant's managers in the history and philosophy of this effort. Since none of the managers had been involved in the original innovations, none of them understood the theory underlying them. They had all heard about the OD program in the plant. They knew that workers in the plant tended to be managed differently than in traditional plants. They saw that assembly lines did not exist and wondered why not. They accepted a work organization in which individuals or groups took responsibility for assembling a whole unit. But they did not understand why this approach was undertaken or the theory behind it.

This lack of knowledge evidenced itself in the many questions they asked the consultant when he arrived. "Aren't assembly lines the best way to get efficiency? We hear from employees who have been here since the plant opened that the good old days were better. What do they mean?" This lack of knowledge reflected not only the complete turnover of the management staff but also the lack of a continual orientation program which briefed managers about the plant's history and philosophy.

The consultant's visit had been arranged by the current plant manager in an effort to revitalize the OD effort. The consultant described the history of the effort in some detail. He conveyed the assumptions underlying innovations, the many discussions that had led to their acceptance, early efforts to innovate, and the learning that came from these experiences. The struggles, problems, and successes of the OD effort in the first three years were described candidly. These descriptions served to give the current managers a "feel" for how the plant had evolved to its present state and why some employees talked about the good old days. The briefing and the discussions which followed lasted a half-day and were a precursor to a diagnosis aimed at starting a new cycle of improvement efforts.

6. *Rewarding new behavior.* Changes can only be sustained if managers in the change target are rewarded (promotion, formal recognition, and pay) for maintaining new managerial approaches. If managers perceive that there are career risks in continuing OD efforts, regression is a certainty. Formal organizational rewards to managers for sustaining change are even more important than those to early innovators. The latter group often obtains intrinsic rewards for getting change started. Furthermore, strong beliefs and values may carry them through the early phases of change despite potential risks. None of these conditions exist for managers who have to maintain change (see Case 13–3 for an example).

Developing and Maintaining Management Support

Top management can influence virtually all of the conditions just listed. They create reward systems, influence the policy of staff units, and make money available for OD consulting. Perhaps the most important condition under their control is the political climate for organization development. If managers perceive that OD is looked on favorably by top management, they will become involved in it and continue changes begun by others. If they perceive that top management doesn't support it, managers will find ways to discontinue these activities and avoid starting new ones.

If OD starts at the top and is successful, the problem of top management support doesn't arise. However, the vast majority of OD efforts have started at lower levels such as a plant, division, or branch. In these cases, the OD effort will be sustained only if at the very beginning, top management understands the goals and is kept informed about progress and results. Their involvement is likely to lead to their support. One reason to involve top management early is to find out if there are conflicts between its interests and values and ODs. It is better to discover a discontinuity during the planning stages, before too much effort has gone into the implementation of changes doomed to fail.

Organization development means changes in attitudes and behavior, which can be threatening to the values and beliefs of upper level management. Furthermore, changes in the status quo in a lower level unit can demand that upper management behave in ways of which they are not capable. This inability understandably threatens top managers' sense of competence.

Numerous times, the failure to communicate with top management and develop their understanding have resulted in a lack of support for organization development. In one instance, a laboratory training program undertaken by lower level management was abruptly terminated when the top manager learned about it (Bennis, 1977). Evidently, the top man had not been told about the change program and the values underlying sensitivity training conflicted with his own.

In another instance, a program was started by the head of a department, and was continued with the support of a vice-president, despite the failure of a two-day conference to gain the support of the president and a hostile corporate management group. Sometime later, shortly after the vice-president left the company, top management discontinued the program, even though it was going full swing (Buchanan, 1967).

The second case illustrates the importance of top management commitment even when middle management is already supportive. One never knows when a middle management's protective umbrella might disappear as a result of transfer or turnovers. Both

---

CASE 13-3

A manager who had taken over a division which was on the leading edge of OD applications, described his reasons for slowing down these efforts. "I basically believe that the managerial approaches being used in this division are the right way to go. But frankly, I don't think they are being supported by the corporation. Some of the staff groups think this approach is poor and I have to work with them. I also don't believe the president thinks we are on the right track. I was at a meeting at corporate headquarters the other day, and during a break the president and I began talking about the approaches taken in my division by my predecessor. He pointed to several problems these approaches might create. I could sense immediately that he had reservations. He didn't say stop, but I know he didn't say go. I have to watch out for my career. It won't be helped by pushing ahead. I am just letting the current approach to management continue because I know changing it would result in a lot of resistance from my people. But I am not putting a lot of effort into further innovation and change. Why should I?"

cases illustrate the importance of early communication and the need to weigh the risks of continuing changes not supported by upper management.

Obtaining top management support for a change effort can sometimes blind change agents to the need for getting the support of middle managers immediately above the subunit in which an OD effort is being undertaken. For example, a middle level manager terminated a new and innovative pay incentive plan that had significantly reduced absenteeism soon after the external change agents had ended their personal involvement in the project. A retrospective analysis showed that this manager had not been helped sufficiently to gain an understanding of the project (Porter, Lawler, & Hackman, 1975; Scheflen, Lawler, & Hackman, 1971). His intolerance for the project led him to take the relatively risky step of reversing the change, even though it had been successful, and top management (who initiated the project) had supported it. Clearly, "management support" means the support of managers at all levels above the subunit undergoing OD.

Efforts to gain the support of as many key management people as possible is important for other reasons as well. As the first OD effort achieves the prominence often accorded successful innovations, factions unsympathetic to the changes taking place will attempt to block, consciously or or unconsciously, the people supporting change from achieving their objectives. Detractors can take subtle, but potentially damaging, political steps to discredit and weaken the leading edge organization and its supporters; corporate constraints, that the leading OD unit needs lifted to move change along, don't budge; negative information about the OD effort is publicized and blown out of proportion. In any case, conflict between the innovative unit and some key people in the larger organization develops and escalates. This conflict has negative consequences, not only for the spread of innovations, but also for the innovators (Marris & Rein, 1973).

In one plant, which undertook major innovations in work restructuring, several key managers associated with initiating the OD effort found themselves no longer employed by the company. The plant manager was asked to leave, the manager of organization development, who was associated with this and other similar innovations, was "forced" to leave. Several other managers left voluntarily because they did not see advancement opportunities. The terminations occurred despite the fact that the plant's financial performance was significantly better than an older plant making the same products.

How could this happen, given the success of the plant? A pattern of conflict between change agents and the larger organization has been noted in other OD efforts and, indeed, in the introduction of most significant innovations (Pettigrew, 1976; Walton, 1974). The managers who are involved in OD often have different beliefs from top management about how to manage. These beliefs drive them to innovate, and success leads them to deepen their beliefs. Their commitment to OD sometimes approaches religious zeal. Thus a value gap develops between the subunit undergoing OD and the larger organization. This gap leads to the negative cycle of attitudes typically found in any severe intergroup conflict. Secure in their beliefs, the plant people communicate disdain and arrogance to corporate people who do not share these beliefs. Corporate management's negative reaction leads the plant's managers to feel unappreciated and underrecognized, especially given the results and high interest by outsiders in their innovations.

In these circumstances, each side sees itself as right and develops negative stereotypes about the other. At a time when it is most needed to create a positive political climate, frequency and quality of communication decreases.

If changes brought about by organization development are to be sustained and adopted by other parts of the larger organization, the relationships between the innovators and the supporters of the status quo must be managed effectively. Because of the

dynamics described, the change agents associated with leading edge OD effort will probably not be capable of managing these relationships. While we do not yet know how to deal with these dynamics more constructively, some kind of integrator is probably needed (Lawrence & Lorsch, 1967b). This person can be a manager, or a corporate OD group could act in that role. The integrator needs to have a corporate perspective, credibility, and the trust of all constituencies. Such a person or group can facilitate the communication process and help the change target and management deescalate their conflict.

Spreading Organization Development

In a system-wide OD strategy, early change efforts are spread to other parts of the company until eventually all units and levels are in some way engaged in the process. The spread entails the whole organization, adopting (1) innovative solutions to management and organizational problems that have emerged from early OD programs and (2) the process and methods of OD.

When OD has spread, intervention methods such as team building and survey-feedback will be increasingly used as means for solving and preventing organizational problems. An increasing cadre of change agents will be found working and living in various parts of the organization. It is important to recognize, however, that these change agents may not and should not always be professional behavioral scientists identified by the title OD consultant. They may be line managers, personnel specialists, corporate planners, or external consultants.

Unfortunately, evidence indicates that organization development does not spread very easily from one part of an organization to others. Walton (1974) investigated twelve plants in eleven companies that undertook innovations in work design and management at the shop-floor level. In three of the cases, there was regression back to more traditional states, and in several others the innovation in the experimental plant was sustained but did not spread to other parts of the corporation. In the few large corporations that have had OD efforts for at least ten years, there are still many divisions and subunits not engaged in organization development.

If OD is to survive where it started, a system-wide organization development strategy must find ways to spread OD to the whole organization. A momentum of change must develop across the whole system so that some of the conditions for sustaining innovative changes, listed earlier in this chapter, can develop. If OD does not spread, the units where it started become more and more isolated. Those opposed to OD begin to successfully marshall their opposition. Managers of compatible managerial philosophy, needed to replace those in leading edge units and/or needed to start OD in new units, will be hard to find.

An effective system-wide OD strategy must include a plan for how to spread organization development. Such a plan would include the following elements (Beer & Driscoll, 1977; Walton, 1975).

1. *Communication about OD.* Research on the spread of innovations has shown that it depends on communication from innovators to potential innovators about the new approach (Havelock & Havelock, 1973, Rogers & Schoemaker, 1971). Similarly, the leading edge unit must mount an active program of communication about its organization development activities. Preferably, this communication comes from credible managers. Regular forums of communication, such as company meetings, may be used or special conferences for those interested might be organized. **237**

However, merely communicating knowledge has been found to be insufficient (Myerseth, 1977). In order for other managers to seriously consider involvement in OD, they will need to get a "firsthand feel" for what it is like. Arranging visits for these managers to organizations leading in OD applications is one way to do this. Talking to managers who have experienced team-building or other OD interventions is another.

2. *Top management involvement.* An earlier discussion highlighted the importance of developing top management understanding so that leading edge innovations can be sustained. To spread OD, top management involvement in the development of a strategy is a key factor. A statement of policy, support for expansion of OD resources, approval for lifting traditional constraints, and a periodic review of progress are all needed. Without these, OD is not likely to spread. If it does, it is likely to regress when top management belatedly becomes aware of its substantial impact. Yet, top management involvement cannot be so heavy-handed as to force managers into OD. Such OD efforts, not meeting the conditions of readiness and internal commitment that are so important, would result in failure.

3. *Continued use of the contracting model.* The importance of readiness and internal motivation in the target unit is no less important for later OD targets than it was for early ones. This fact is often forgotten by change agents who have experienced early success. They fall prey to the lure of success, try to spread OD too rapidly, and rely on top-down pressure to open new doors. This can often result in failure, resentment, wasted time and resources, and a slowed momentum of change. Continued use of the entry and contracting model is important.

4. *Manpower flows.* The most effective way to spread OD and to create readiness in other units is to transfer experienced OD managers to other parts of the organization. The careful seeding of these people can be the single most important step in spreading OD, provided they are supported when they get to their new location.

5. *Preventing religious fervor.* The tendency of early innovators to acquire religious zeal and commitment to new approaches has already been discussed. This is a natural by-product of successfully creating change against resistance and constraints in the larger organization. However, this zeal polarizes believers and nonbelievers and prevents managers unfamiliar with OD to make an informed choice. Such religious fervor must be prevented at all costs if OD is to spread.

6. *Removing bureaucratic barriers.* Units undergoing OD will develop more and more congruity within themselves, but this will run headlong into standard practices and procedures that usually pervade large organizations. As OD spreads, staff groups—who often create these standard practices—will have to be persuaded and/or directed to make more and more exceptions. Top management's support is critical for making this happen.

7. *Rewarding the application of OD.* If OD is to spread, managers must perceive involvement in it as beneficial to their careers. If early users of OD are promoted and recognized, other managers will be more prone to explore the potential benefits of organization development. In one company, the promotion of an early OD user and advocate to the presidency of the corporation created a climate of acceptance in which OD flourished. While this climate is desirable, change agents must be careful that managers do not become involved in OD for political reasons. Such OD efforts are likely to fail because the motivation and readiness to create real change will be lacking.

238

8. *Organizing change agent resources.* The spread of OD, particularly in the early phases of a system-wide strategy, depends on the effective development and organization of change agent resources. Many of the conditions for spreading OD that have been discussed in this section can be created or managed by an effective network of OD consultants and managers. The change agents, often located in different parts of a large organization, must meet regularly to review the status of OD and develop a system-wide strategy. Such a strategy assumes that the needed specialists will be hired and developed so that the rising demand for OD services can be met with effective consulting resources. If such resources are not available when managers need them, the "window of conditions" which make these managers and their organizations potential clients, will disappear. Similarly, meeting these demands with ineffective change agents will result in failures that will close these windows.

In the long run, organization development cannot succeed in a large multiunit organization unless it spreads to many parts and levels. As the numbered triangles in Figure 13–1 show, OD may start (1) in the middle and move to other parts of the organization before it finally reaches the top (8). But it must ultimately reach the top and help managers at that level with their problems. Similarly, spread to a critical mass of divisions, departments, branches, or plants is important to ensure both sufficient influence on corporate policy and a pool of managers who can fill top positions in the increasing number of units undertaking OD.

Centralized vs. Market Strategies in Spreading OD[1]

The discussion in the previous sections has emphasized the importance of managing a system-wide OD effort. Finding an appropriate first target, sustaining change in this and other change targets, and spreading change through manpower planning and other methods requires some degree of planning and coordination aimed at developing a wider and wider circle of success. In the end, organization development becomes an integral part of the organization's adaptive coping process. There are different strategies for achieving this final goal.

At one end of a continuum is a *centralized approach.* This approach would probably include a staff OD department at headquarters reporting to the chief executive offices (CEO) or the corporate vice-president of personnel. The OD activities would be initiated and budgeted by the larger system and they would be planned and reviewed with close involvement of corporate management (the CEO or the vice-president of personnel). Such an OD effort is essentially an arm of the corporation. The problems and parts of the organization which receive attention, do so as a result of top management's definition of priorities and problems. With this strategy, OD spreads primarily because top management is committed and only secondarily because of its perceived benefits at lower levels. The advantage of this approach is faster spread and better management of all the forces that shape culture change. The disadvantage is that commitment to OD at lower levels may be questionable and OD takes on a top management perspective rather than a systems perspective.

At the other end of the continuum is a *market strategy* for managing OD. With this approach, subunits are encouraged to undertake OD efforts, but they must find their own consultant (internal or external) and pay for their own programs. There is no corporate OD department nor is top management heavily involved in planning and reviewing OD activities. If a corporate OD staff group exists, its services are bought and paid for by line **239**

FIGURE 13–1   Typical Diffusion Pattern for OD

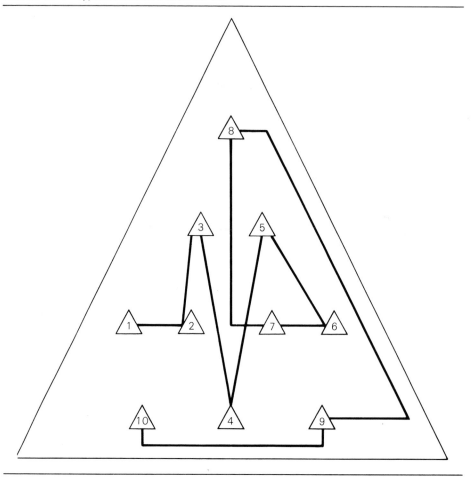

NOTE: Numbers indicate sequence of entry into various parts and levels of the organization.

and staff units on a charge-back basis. Top management's assumptions are that people ought to be held accountable for results, but not for how they manage their organization. Centralized review and guidance of OD activities is thus seen as inappropriate meddling in the personal affairs of lower level managers. The advantage of the market approach is that it is quite consistent with the values of free and informed choice. Thus if OD spreads at all, it does so because of its perceived value. The disadvantage of this approach is that OD will spread extremely slowly, if at all, because there is minimal management of the many forces so important for sustaining and spreading it. A market strategy is essentially a decision not to actively manage the cultural development of the corporation.

Of course, these two approaches represent extremes that are not likely to be found in pure form in many corporations. Nevertheless, they clarify the strategic choices which top management must make about its posture toward OD. Like other management dilemmas there is no one answer. Some of the situational factors that must be considered in arriving at an appropriate balance between these two strategies are listed below (Coleman, 1973; Morris, 1964; Rogers, 1973).

1. **To what extent is the organization authoritarian, hierarchical, controlling, and centralized?** If it is authoritarian then a more centralized strategy for managing OD is appropriate.

2. **Do all parts of the organization have common goals and values?** If the organization is homogeneous in terms of values and goals, a centralized strategy is possible without incurring resistance and hostility.

3. **To what extent do people in the system desire freedom and participation?** If people desire participation, a market strategy is more appropriate.

4. **To what extent are the costs of delaying the adoption of OD greater than the costs of low commitment inherent in a centralized strategy?** If delay is more costly, a centralized strategy, which spreads more rapidly than a market strategy, is desirable.

5.. **To what extent are various subunits of the organization (divisions, groups, etc.) similar in their tasks, people, and problems?** If subunits are dissimilar, a market strategy is more appropriate because each unit requires unique solutions.

6. **To what extent is OD likely to threaten the power elite's basic values and power?** If OD is potentially threatening to management, a more centralized strategy with early involvement is appropriate. When the top begins to feel threatened, it will squash a successful market strategy.

7. **Is the organization centralized in its operations?** A centralized organization requires a centralized strategy, while a decentralized organization requires a market strategy.

Relative emphasis on a centralized or market strategy is likely to shift and should shift according to changes in the situational factors listed above. For instance, in a highly centralized and authoritarian environment, a market strategy is not likely to get anywhere. In such an environment, managers are not mature or sophisticated enough to make informed choices. Only after extensive involvement in OD would a market strategy be more appropriate than a centralized one. The reverse can also occur. In one company, as the structure became more centralized, the market strategy was dropped even though it had been successful when the company was decentralized. Before the change, the OD department provided services to line divisions on a charge-back basis; afterward, the personnel division was in charge of its budget and its activities.

How Fast Should OD Spread?

From the perspective of the change agents interested in moving OD across an organization, the spread of OD should be as rapid as possible. Much of what has been said, however, implies that OD should spread at a rate consistent with its successes, the availability of competent OD resources, understanding of top management, and their willingness to become appropriately involved. That is, those who manage a fledgling OD effort must make sure that their plans for spreading OD activities are consistent with management's readiness and the availability of OD resources.

Controlling the growth and spread of OD is critical. If it spreads too rapidly, its emergence as a major force for change in the organization can become extremely threatening. Rapid spread means that some managers are not involved while others are pressured to change without sufficient involvement. Large budgets (for internal or external consultants) and large OD staff groups become targets for an anti-OD constituency. Pressures for cuts in OD resources build, particularly during periods of poor profitability. In one recent example, top management arbitrarily cut a large budget for external OD **241**

CASE 13-4

It is of little import that there was a grand design and that all the changes fitted together neatly into the mosaic of the final objective. The important thing is that far too much was attempted. We did not have the time to oversee them all. We did not have the energy to nurture them all. We did not have the power to push them all. We did not have the insight to involve all the people who should have been made a part of them. It was far too ambitious an effort for the organization to digest and implement.

If I were to do it over, I would be more

From W. J. Crockett, "Introducing Change to a Government Agency," in P. H. Mirvis and D. N. Berg, *Failures in Organization Development and Change* (New York: Wiley-Interscience, 1977), p. 143. Reprinted by permission of John Wiley & Sons, Inc.

patient with the process. I would involve a great many more people and groups. I would include all the interested constituencies from the inception of the problem and try to make it their problem for their solution. Instead, I thought that I knew all the problems and had all the answers (which I probably had), but this attitude does not elicit broad support. I met my needs—not theirs.

I would have started earlier to ensure that my personal assistants and those responsible with me for bringing about change also worked through the participative mode instead of the authoritarian: "the boss wants so-and-so to be done." I suspect that there was much of that by fine, loyal subordinates who fell into this trap as a means of getting things done for me.

consultants when it became aware of its size. Case 13-4 illustrates one change agent's account of rapid change.

There are several ways to deal with this problem. Perhaps the most basic is to spread OD efforts more slowly than the needs of change agents and clients dictate. The problem with this approach is that professionals and managers engaged in OD work often thrive on change, and look for progress as a sign of hope. To these groups, the measure of success is the degree to which OD has penetrated the larger system. Slow or moderate progress becomes frustrating and does not meet their needs. McClelland (1978), in a discussion of an analogous problem, has suggested that many social scientists developed feelings of failure about the social change program of the 1960s, because they raised everyone's expectations, including their own, about immediate success.

To avoid these frustrations, change agents must spend much more time setting realistic goals (given the constraints outlined in this chapter) for change. They need to learn to derive satisfaction from small achievements rather than from impact on the whole organization. One way is to set goals for the research and development of more effective organization development methods. Unrealistic goals for penetrating the organization can only result in disillusionment. The many cycles of growth and decline in OD efforts are likely to be a function of the "mismanagement of hope."

The importance of change agents managing hope more effectively, raises issues about the selection and career development of change agents. For example, is it realistic for innovative plant managers or consultants, who pioneer the introduction of work restructuring, to stay in the same corporation for their whole career? If this is desirable, what career goals and paths make the most sense for them and the corporation? What help can they be given to mesh their own career needs with the reality that organizations change slowly? Their needs for progress and success must somehow be met. The career issues that OD creates for professional change agents and managers may explain in part the repeated rise and decline of OD efforts in several large corporations over the last twenty years.

Thus far the discussion has centered on what change agents and organizations can do to limit the rate of OD growth. An alternative is to manage rapid growth wisely. Political realities suggest that visible entities, like large staffs and budgets, are more likely to come under scrutiny and be cut in difficult times. It would seem wise, therefore, to disperse OD resources throughout those parts of the organization that use their services.

This scattering of OD resources not only makes them less visible, but it places responsibility for those resources in the hands of managers who derive the most direct benefit from OD and have the most valid data about its effectiveness. Giving these managers such control enhances the quality of decisions made about OD resources and increases commitment to OD. This course is entirely consistent with the intervention strategy described in Chapter 5, which stresses valid data, informed choice, and internal commitment.

Summary

This chapter has dealt with the question of where OD should begin in a large complex organization and how it might be spread. If OD is a fundamental managerial process by which an organization can maintain its vitality, then institutionalization of the process, not just the innovations which it delivers, becomes an important goal. The emphasis in this chapter has been on the kind of commitment, communication, involvement, political support, education, manpower planning, and rewards that are needed to start and spread OD. However, research aimed at evaluating OD programs can also help spread and sustain OD. Furthermore, specially designated departments, sensitive to the politics of managing change and innovation, can be a major force for institutionalizing OD. Chapter 14 will deal with these important subjects.

NOTES

1. This section is based in part on Beer and Driscoll, "Strategies for Change" in J.R. Hackman and J. L. Suttle, *Improving Life at Work, Behavioral Science Approaches,* (Santa Monica, Calif.: Goodyear, 1977).

EVALUATING AND INSTITUTION- ALIZING SYSTEM- WIDE CHANGE 14

One of the key questions facing the field of organization development is how to sustain the process of OD and the innovations which come from it. There are more than a few cases in which the spread of OD has been followed by its decline (Crockett, 1977). Just as OD seems to be at the height of its success, resistance builds to its increasing application. Managers opposed to OD openly question its effectiveness and value to the organization. When the organization falls on hard financial times or when there are changes in political support at the top, OD activities and resources come under scrutiny. There may be cuts in budget, and organization development specialists and managers involved in leading OD efforts may leave. The vitality of the OD effort is sapped as availability of effective change agent resources diminish.

This chapter will deal with two major strategies that might help institutionalize OD. The first strategy is research to evaluate the effectiveness of OD. We will be particularly concerned with the role of research in sustaining OD and in how evaluation research should be conducted. The second strategy is the establishment of a credible renewal function. The role, management, and politics of such a function will be discussed.

EVALUATION OF OD

Evaluation of organization development involves planned information gathering and analysis undertaken by those responsible for the management of change. It should result in a satisfactory assessment of the effects and/or progress of the change effort (Beckhard & Harris, 1977).

While this definition of what constitutes evaluation may seem simple and straightforward to the reader, it is a controversial subject among change agents and scientists (Beer, 1971c; Dunnette, 1970). The reason for this has to do with the interpretation of a number of key elements of this definition. What is satisfactory assessment? What does one measure to determine if change has occurred? What constitutes sufficiently valid information gathering and analysis activities?

At the root of the controversy about these questions are different goals for evaluation and different views about how effective various research methods are in meeting these goals. Managers, OD specialists, and behavioral scientists have quite different perspectives when it comes to these issues. By examining these we should arrive at a better understanding of the multiplicity of goals an evaluation can serve and how one or more of these might be met within the context of a system-wide strategy.

Different Perspectives and Purposes

Managers are generally concerned about the impact of OD on organizational performance or on specific symptoms that might have led to the introduction of OD. For example, they may be interested in the impact of OD on profits, costs, turnover, or labor relations. These are important and visible measures of organizational functioning. Data about their improvement can be used to justify further investment in OD to higher management or to sell them on becoming involved themselves. Unfortunately, managers typically assume that the effects of OD on these indices will be self-evident and they lose sight of the complexity of factors that might cause change in them. For this reason, they rarely push for a systematic evaluation. Thus, by the time hard questions about its effectiveness have arisen, OD has been in progress for some time. It is too late to collect baseline measures (measures taken before OD started) needed to determine if current attitudes and performance are an improvement. With no systematic evaluation, managers rely on the opinions of other managers.

OD specialists are typically more concerned with evaluation than managers, but their perspective is different. While they share an interest in measuring the impact of OD on results, OD specialists are more keenly interested in its impact on organizational process and behavior. They intervene in this component of the organization directly and hope to see immediate changes. Similarly, they are interested in evaluating the impact of particular interventions so that they can learn from their own practice and improve it. Typically, they are also interested in obtaining this data frequently enough to allow modification of the change strategy or method. This sometimes requires ad hoc measurement when unanticipated events occur and it means staying in close touch with the people experiencing the interventions. In contrast to managers, OD specialists are more interested in data that will help them intervene more effectively now and in the future.

Change agents are themselves behavioral scientists or involve them in evaluating OD programs. Yet a third orientation is then added to the problem of evaluation. Behavioral scientists are interested in adding to knowledge about organizations. Therefore, they would like to generalize about their findings in the target organization (this is called external validity). For this reason they are interested in both process and outcome measures. But they want to be sure these measures are not biased and contaminated in any way by organizational members who might want to meet the expectations of the investigators. Their concern for scientific objectivity causes behavioral scientists to distance themselves from people in the organization through structured measures (questionnaires, interview protocols) and plans for applying them (research designs).

Given these perspectives, it is not difficult to see why behavioral scientists have been critical of both managers and OD specialists for not doing comprehensive research and evaluation of interventions and their system-wide effects (Dunnette, 1970). When evaluations have been done, they have criticized them for lack of scientific rigor in measurement methods and experimental design. For example, they say that many evaluations of OD efforts lack control or comparison groups, thus making it difficult to generalize about the effectiveness of OD interventions. OD practitioners and managers argue that there are no two organizations exactly alike and that in any case, they are only interested in whether OD had an impact on the target organization.

OD specialists have been critical of behavioral scientists' preoccupation with scientific methods which they do not see as relevant to field settings and to managers' decisions about OD. They are supported in this argument by the fact that there is little evidence to prove that OD efforts have been terminated because "rigorous and scientific" assessment of a change was not carried out. Similarly, rigorous evaluation research by itself has not been shown to add to the momentum of system-wide change. Indeed, the very fact that OD has grown and spread as widely as it has without sophisticated research suggests that managers simply do not use that type of data in deciding to continue or discontinue OD.

All of this raises serious questions about what the role of evaluation is in a system-wide OD strategy and, if it has a role, what research methods should be used. If evaluation does not enhance the spread of OD and if managers do not pay attention to rigorous evaluation, why do them? Perhaps managers simply prefer to use their direct experience. On the other hand, managers probably do not pay attention to evaluations because they are not properly involved and informed by change agents about their value to them early in OD programs. One purpose of evaluation could be to help managers become more sophisticated consumers of action research.[1]

It is not the purpose of this book to resolve these questions, if indeed they can be resolved. It is likely that each perspective has some validity. The important point is that various partners in an organization development effort have different interests, orientations, and purposes for evaluation:

1. determining the impact of OD on organizational behavior and performance
2. determining if an OD strategy or intervention method should be modified
3. collecting data that will be useful in selling OD to decision makers
4. upgrading intervention skills and methods
5. contributing to knowledge about organization behavior and change

All of these goals are legitimate, but none of them can be fully met by any single evaluation plan. What is important is that evaluation plans be developed during the entry and contracting states so that measures of organizational functioning and outcomes can be obtained before OD begins. It is equally important that these evaluation plans be developed and executed jointly by all parties to the evaluation so that the evaluation meets everyone's objectives. Case 14–1 provides a manager's account of how research was used and conducted to achieve several of these goals.

Joint Planning of Evaluation

Too often there is a tendency to turn the evaluation over to a scientist. The scientist accepts this opportunity because it allows him to choose *his* method, measure things of interest to *him*, and provide feedback of results at times that fit with *his* research design. Because managers and OD specialists are not involved they do not feel ownership of the evaluation. The result is that they place little credibility in the findings and they do not use them for decision-making purposes.

An example of this occurred in a nonprofit organization sponsoring work restructuring programs involving several companies and unions. They invited a research institute to evaluate these OD efforts to determine if anything had changed and if so, what. They **247**

Another ingredient that played an important part in the program was research. A general body of theory, which we put vigorously into practice, required some research to give us knowledge of our progress. It also gave us quick recognition of whatever new problems our organization was causing. We felt a need for carrying on a variety of action-oriented research efforts in conjunction with the programs themselves. These activities included such things as pre-meeting interviews, open discussions by participants in off-site meetings, and written surveys to determine the effect of major organizational changes on people. Research gave us help in diagnosing the real-life situations we faced in fulfilling our program objectives and provided specific targets at which we could aim in our meetings to solve problems without wasting time or without beating about the bush. This research effort was carried on under contract with the Center for Research on Utilization of Scientific Knowledge, Institute for Social Research, The University of Michigan.

From W. J. Crockett,"Introducing Change to a Government Agency," in P. H. Mirvis and D. N. Berg, *Failures in Organization Development and Change* (New York: Wiley-Interscience, © 1977), p. 137. Reprinted by permission of John Wiley & Sons, Inc.

insisted that the research and intervention process be separated to increase objectivity. While the evaluation package was indeed scientifically rigorous and objective, it did not always meet managers', unions', or the change agents' needs for timely and relevant information. The enforced separation of the researchers from the change agents created tensions between the two groups and probably led to poor communication between them. Effective communication between change agents and researchers might have guided the change program at crucial points. It might also have provided more in-depth data about the organization to the researchers. One also wonders whether managers and union leaders saw the evaluation as relevant to their needs for communicating with constituents about the program.

If the needs of change agents, managers, and behavioral scientists are to be met, all parties must be involved in planning the evaluation (Alderfer, 1977). Joint planning will, however, require social scientists to significantly change their view about what constitutes valid evaluation. Accepted research procedures in the behavioral sciences predetermine and structure methods and periods of measurement. They place heavy emphasis on separating the researchers from their subjects. Thus, to involve managers would be unscientific.

These traditional scientific methods have been called *mechanistic* by Argyris (1970). He argues that mechanistic research makes the client organization more dependent and submissive and thus makes data less relevant and essential to the client. If evaluation research is to be seen as truly important and relevant to decisions, Argyris argues that it must be defined jointly by managers and the scientist or interventionist. He calls this approach *organic research*. As Table 14-1 shows, it is different from mechanistic research in that the client organization helps define what is to be measured, how frequently it should be measured, and what methods are to be used. The change agent and behavioral scientist are resources to management on these questions but they do not control these decisions.

In one organization, an ongoing feedback system that included both performance and work attitude data was developed in this way (Nadler, Mirvis, & Cammann, 1977). Rather than impose their ideas and questionnaires on the organization, the researchers worked with a task force of employees to design a questionnaire that met *management's* needs for relevant information. Consultants and clients together designed a system that brought back feedback to the organization on a monthly basis. It is precisely this approach that is needed if evaluation research is to be utilized and politically relevant.

The organic research orientation would dictate that those responsible for the management of change must be intimately involved in planning and implementing the evaluation. Unless this occurs, the evaluation will contribute little to the momentum of change and may be ignored completely. Yet given the specialized knowledge and skill required in designing and implementing evaluation research, what should management's role be?

Unless managers are themselves knowledgeable about research design and methods, they should obtain staff assistance or consulting help to plan and implement the evalution research. Managers, however, must be involved in deciding about the purpose and focus of the evaluation. They must define the questions they want answered and the

TABLE 14–1   A Comparison of Mechanistic and Organic Research

Mechanistically-oriented Research	Organistically-oriented Research
1. The interventionist takes the most prominent role in defining the goals of the program.	1. The subjects participate in defining goals, confirming and disconfirming, and modifying or adding to those goals defined by the professionals.
2. The interventionist assumes that his relationship of being strictly professional cannot be influenced by the clients. He maintains his power of expertise and therefore keeps a professional distance from the clients.	2. The interventionist realizes that, in addition to being a professional, he is a stranger in the institution. Subjects should be encouraged to confront and test their relationship with him. His power over the subjects, due to his professional competence, is equalized by his encouraging them to question him and the entire program.
3. The amount of client participation in the entire project is controlled by the interventionist.	3. The amount of participation is influenced by the subject and the interventionist.
4. The interventionist depends upon the clients' need to be helped or need to cooperate as being the basis for their involvement. He expects clients to be used as information givers.	4. The interventionist depends upon the clients' need to be helped for encouraging them to control and define the program so that they become internally involved and feel that they are as responsible as the interventionist.
5. If participation is encouraged, it tends to be skin-deep, designed to keep the subjects "happy."	5. Participation is encouraged in terms of instrument design, research methods, and change strategy.
6. The costs and rewards of the change program are defined primarily by the interventionist.	6. The costs and rewards of the change program are defined by the clients and the interventionist.
7. The feedback to subjects is designed to inform them how much the diagnostician learned about the system, as well as how professionally competent the diagnosis was.	7. The feedback to subjects is designed to unfreeze them, as well as to help them develop more effective interpersonal relations and group processes.

From Chris Argyris, *Intervention Theory and Method: A Behavioral Science View* (Reading, Mass.: Addison-Wesley, © 1970), pp. 104–105. Reprinted by permission.

information they want gathered. They can be involved in developing some of the specific questions that may be asked of organizational members, but their primary role is to direct and control the evaluation. This should not be left to staff groups or consultants.

An evaluation planning and review committee composed of the top managers of an organization plus the change agent and research specialist should supervise the evaluation. This group develops the purpose and design of the evaluation in general terms. A task force composed of middle or low level organizational members aided by a research specialist can develop an implementation plan and carry out the evaluation. While a staff group could do this alone, the involvement of middle and lower level people in the implementation adds credibility and validity to the evaluation. Knowing the data will actually be used, motivates organizational members to respond. Furthermore, middle and lower level managers can interpret the meaning of data that may be abstract and meaningless to others. They know the organization and its recent history in a way that staff people or researchers do not. An evaluation that follows this kind of process is less likely to be ignored or underutilized. It is much more likely that such an evaluation process will add momentum to the change itself and to the sophistication of managers about the role of action research in organizational renewal. Case 14–2 gives an example of organic research.

A Framework for Planning and Evaluation

A joint planning process can be helped immeasurably by a framework of thinking about alternative strategies for evaluation and how they relate to the various purposes listed earlier. Unless the purpose and focus of the research are clarified, criteria such as ease of getting data and the use of interesting questions becomes more important than the search for relevant data. The framework can help different constituents in the evaluation relate their goals to a research strategy. It can help settle the broad question "What should we be evaluating?"

There are several evaluation strategies from which one can choose (Beckhard & Harris, 1977; Beer, 1971c).

1. *Evaluation of total system effectiveness, efficiency, and health.* The focus of this evaluation is on whether the organization as a whole has changed. This would include those dimensions of a social system (discussed in Chapter 2) which are to be affected by the change program. It is likely to include an assessment of all social system dimensions and collection of data from a cross-section of the whole organization.

2. *Evaluation of attitudes toward the change process itself.* The focus here is on people's attitude towards the way change has been managed. For example, do they feel sufficiently involved or have there been any dysfunctional and unanticipated side effects to the change (i.e., anxiety, rising expectations, new problems, etc.).

3. *Evaluation of a specific intervention.* The focus here is to evaluate the effects of a specific intervention, such as team building or job design. The evaluation would examine only those organizational dimensions that the intervention is expected to affect. The evaluation would collect data from those directly participating in the interventions and perhaps those that might be indirectly affected.

4. *Evaluation of performance outcomes.* The focus here would be on the "hard" or "soft" performance outcomes that social system changes are likely to affect. Productivity, sales, profits, turnover, absenteeism, customer attitudes, and customer returns would be examples of the things that might be looked at. It is important to remember that

Several years after the start of an OD program aimed at improving productivity and quality of work life, a new plant manager wanted to evaluate its impact on the organization and to determine what steps might be taken to revitalize OD. He called in a behavioral scientist from the corporation's organization research and development department.

In a series of meetings between the plant manager, his staff, and the behavioral scientist, objectives for the evaluation were developed. Since most OD interventions had occurred at the first-line supervisory level and below, it was decided that evaluation would focus on the hourly work force. A number of dimensions such as satisfaction with work itself, supervision, and involvement in scheduling and planning were identified by the plant's management as targets for data collection. In addition, turnover, absenteeism, and productivity data were to be collected. These were targets of the original OD interventions. It was agreed that a task force of supervisors and hourly workers were to be appointed to develop a questionnaire and a procedure for implementing the evaluation and feedback process.

The behavioral scientist became a resource to the "diagnostic task force." He trained the group of hourly employees and first-line supervisors in the fundamentals of interviewing and questionnaire construction.

With this technical training, the task force interviewed a sample of hourly employees, developed a questionnaire, pretested it, and presented it for review to the plant manager and his staff. They also recommended a questionnaire administration and feedback procedure.

At a designated hour, work in the plant stopped and everyone filled out the questionnaire with instructions from the task force. When all the questionnaires had been collected, the behavioral scientist took responsibility for delivering a statistical analysis to the task force. He then met with task force members to help them interpret the data and develop their report to management. When the research analysis was complete, the task force met with the plant manager and his staff to report on their findings and to recommend further OD activities for the plant.

Throughout, the behavioral scientist was a resource on how to conduct the evaluation, analyze data, and interpret it. While he did not withhold his opinions about how to conduct the evaluation or his interpretation of the findings, control of the evaluation process stayed in the hands of the plant.

these variables are affected by many other factors and that social system changes may not be felt for a long time.

Table 14–2 shows the relationship between the four research strategies and the various goals of an evaluation. The "X's" indicate the strategies which are appropriate for a given goal. For example, if the purpose of the evaluation is to sell upper levels on the effectiveness of OD, performance data such as profits, number of new products developed market share, and so on are likely to be the most convincing. A desire to learn if modification of a change strategy is needed will be served best by data about changes in social system characteristics, attitudes toward the change process, and the effects of specific interventions. To determine the impact of OD on the target organization, one requires data about all the social system variables and about performance outcomes. Professional **251**

TABLE 14–2   The Relationship Between Strategy and Purpose of Evaluation

Purpose of Evaluation	Research Strategies			
	Evaluation of Total System Functioning	Evaluation of Interventions	Evaluation of Change Process	Evaluation of Performance Outcomes
Assessing OD impact on the target unit	X			X
Modifying change strategy	X	X	X	
Selling OD to upper levels				X
Upgrading intervention skills and methods (professional practice)		X	X	
Scientific knowledge	X	X	X	X

NOTE: X indicates the research strategy likely to be needed for a given purpose.

practice, on the other hand, is likely to be improved by data about the effectiveness of specific interventions and the change process. Naturally, more than one research strategy serves each evaluation goal.

What Data, What Method, What Sample?

With the purpose and strategy of evaluation decided, questions still remain about what information is needed, who should be asked for the information, and what methods should be used. The following questions must be answered.

1. *What dimensions of the social system (people, processes, outcomes, etc.) will be affected by the OD program?* A model such as the one presented in Chapter 2, can serve as a guide to answering this question.
2. *What people and departments in the organization are likely to be most affected by the change or the particular intervention?* The answer to this question can guide where in the organization and from whom data should be collected.
3. *What method is best suited to the purpose and strategy of the evaluation?* There are choices between questionnaires, interviews, observations, and organizational records and reports. (See Chapter 6 on diagnosis and the literature on research design and methods.[2])

By definition, an evaluation of how the total system functions must include data on all the dimensions of a social system (described in Chapter 2) collected from a large cross-section of people. The most efficient method for this is likely to be the questionnaire, using one or two general questions per dimension. However, a more focused evaluation is possible if relatively narrow and specific OD objectives have been defined. On the other hand, evaluation of how the change has been managed or its dysfunctional effects may be best obtained through change agent observations or interviews. Questionnaires are inappropriate because it is not clear ahead of time what questions could be asked. Furthermore, interviews are more likely to reveal emotional reactions to the change process. An evaluation of one intervention might focus on only one or two dimensions of the social system. These might be measured in more depth and with greater precision using interviews and questionnaires. Only the group involved in the intervention or those who are expected to be affected indirectly would be asked to provide data.

Evaluations of large-scale OD efforts are likely to include multiple dimensions, multiple methods, and quite a cross-section of the organization (see Case 14–3 for an example). The real danger is in collecting too much information and creating data overload. Behavioral scientists will be interested in as much data as they can get (see Table 14–2), but managers will not be inclined to wade through it all. Similarly, long questionnaires and many interviews will sap time and energy away from making change happen. A good evaluation is likely to include a series of compromises between the various purposes, strategies, methods, and targets of the evaluation—particularly early in the evolution of OD. Naturally, as management becomes more sophisticated about action-research, the discrepancy between their needs for evaluation and those of the change agent and behavioral scientist will be reduced.

INSTITUTIONALIZING SYSTEM-WIDE CHANGE

The purpose of organization development is not merely to solve immediate problems in one organizational unit or introduce a single innovation. It is also meant to create an organization that is continually adaptive to changes in people and environment. Such a renewing organization would be a hospitable place for a continuous stream of appropriate innovations emanating from a process of data collection, problem solving, and planned change. Traditional wisdom in OD has been that managers can do this on their own. It is thought that once an OD effort is over, change agents should terminate their relationship with the target organization leaving it with ongoing mechanisms for diagnosis and action planning. Some examples of these mechanisms are:

1. *Survey-feedback*. Surveys and feedback meetings are conducted throughout the organization (see Chapter 8).
2. *Group development meetings*. Groups in the organization, particularly top management, meet on a regular basis to review how they are working together, evaluate the organization's effectiveness, and update plans for organizational improvement (see Chapter 9).
3. *Sensing meetings*. Meetings between various members on top management and lower levels in the organization are held periodically to find and diagnose the state of the organization (see Chapter 8).
4. *Management conferences*. Management conferences involving the top two or three levels of the organization are held once a year. Their purpose is to solicit information about current or anticipated problems, set priorities, and develop action plans for improvement (see discussion of confrontation meeting in Chapter 8).
5. *Parallel and collateral organizations*. Horizontal task forces and teams are given the responsibility for examining certain problems the organization may face in the future **253**

CASE 14–3

A system-wide OD program aimed at influencing a variety of structural and process dimensions was evaluated with several of the purposes and strategies listed in Table 14–2 in mind.

The major reason for the OD program from management's point of view was the improvement of coordination between functional groups. The specific performance outcome of concern was low product development output. To evaluate the effects of OD, from management's point of view, information about new product introductions was collected. This meant counting the number of new products that had achieved certain sales and profit goals before and after the OD program. Since the relationship between functions was also of concern, perceptions of these relationships were obtained by questionnaire *before* and *after* the OD program.

In addition to new product development performance, the OD specialists were interested in measuring the effects of the OD strategy on a number of cultural and behavioral dimensions. These were ones their interviews and observations had revealed were responsible for poor product development performance. They included relative power of the functional groups, their perception of each other, and the willingness of people in the organization to confront conflict. Based on the interviews, questionnaires were developed and administered to a large number of people in the organization involved in new product development activities. These were intended to provide quantitative data on specific organizational dimensions identified as important by the interviews. Measurements were taken before the OD program started and again two years later.

OD specialists were also interested in measuring the impact of several intergroup laboratories (see Chapter 9) on the relationship between specific pairs of groups. They wanted to determine if these interventions added to improved relations between groups beyond structural and role changes which had been made early in the OD effort. A specific research plan was developed for evaluating this intervention. It included a special questionnaire administered to a group just before, immediately after, and six months after the intergroup laboratory. Interviews at the end of six months with key members of these groups were also conducted. Since part of the evaluation process was aimed at improving professional practice and adding to knowledge, questionnaires about perceptions of intergroup relationships were obtained from several pairs of groups in other divisions of the company at about the same time.

Comparison of changes in relations between groups who went through the intergroup laboratory and those who didn't, showed the interventions had indeed contributed to an overall improvement in relationships. The data on the rate of new product development showed that it had improved after structural changes had been made but before the intergroup laboratory had been applied.

Multiple methods and measures had made it possible, not only to measure the overall effects of OD for managers and OD specialists, but to learn about the effectiveness of an OD intervention. The latter helped improve OD practice and contributed to behavioral science knowledge. (See Corning Glass Works (B) case in appendix for further detail.)

and making recommendations to management for change (Carlson, undated; Zand, 1974).

6. *Performance management systems*. The practice of reviewing individual performance and behavior is institutionalized through the installation of formal procedures and supporting training programs (see Chapter 10).

Problems in Institutionalizing OD

Unfortunately, evidence is increasing that mechanisms such as those listed above do not seem to be sustained by management over time (Beer, 1979). Thirteen years after a successful OD program had been started, a number of the mechanisms listed above were no longer in place. Regular sensing meetings, which had been the practice, ceased as did performance reviews, particularly upward appraisals of first-line supervisors. Similarly, the use of surveys as a means of periodically collecting data had been discontinued. Not only were old mechanisms, installed to institutionalize change, discontinued, but there seemed to be no effort to introduce new mechanisms or to push for further management innovations. The process of organization development and renewal seemed to have stopped and the organization was regressing to more traditional practices. Of course, regression in the target unit also prevented spread of innovations to other units. As the introduction to Part IV indicated, there are many other examples of this phenomenon (Hinrichs, 1978; Walton, 1978). Several reasons for the atrophy of organization development efforts can be cited.

1. *Transfer of managers*. Managers who were part of getting OD started are transferred to other organizational units within the company. When they leave, their collective learning about OD and the mechanisms that have been created to sustain OD are lost to the organization.

2. *Time pressures*. Other demands compete with organizational development for managers' attention. Not the least of these are short-term pressures for profitability and a continual stream of new crises.

3. *Linking requirements*. The systems nature of organizations requires a tremendous amount of linking, communication, and coordinating to prevent bureaucratic barriers from slowing down organization development.

4. *Management defensiveness*. Like most people, managers tend to be defensive about their behavior and ideas and have difficulty seeing these as barriers to change and renewal. Thus feedback mechanisms left behind by a change agent tend to atrophy as subordinates find that confronting management is not paying off.

5. *Power differentials*. Even if management wants feedback and is not defensive when it is received, the power differentials in most contemporary organizations prevent people from being completely open in their upward communication. It will take much longer than traditional OD wisdom has held, to change this condition.

As the list suggests, the process of system-wide change and renewal is extremely complex and requires a long-term developmental perspective that many managers seem to find difficult to adopt, or which natural forces in the organizations tend to discourage. For these reasons, it is likely that organizations will only be able to maintain a renewal process if a network of permanent change agent roles, described in Chapter 12 is created. We now turn to a discussion of how such a network might be organized and its relation to the power structure.   **255**

Organizing OD Resources—A Power Perspective

Many years ago, John Gardner (1963) suggested that each organization needs a department for renewal and that such entities could prevent "dry rot" from developing. His view was that such departments could challenge the established order. They could stimulate innovation in the organization because they would be given a specific responsibility for doing so. They would give managers freedom of thinking and action.

The need for internal change agents who live and work inside the target organization and are exempt from certain of its constraints is supported by a number of research findings. In an attempt to introduce innovations in a large number of community mental health centers, Tornatzky (1976) found that on-site involvement of a change agent resulted in faster adoption of these innovations than merely providing written information or do-it-yourself manuals. Additionally, the momentum of change was sustained in those units which were visited periodically by a consultant who was associated with the change program but did not live in the organization. Presumably, these individuals were not as constrained by the culture of the organization and were able to support internal people in confronting the organization. Similarly, research findings about the importance of continual follow-up in successful team-building and survey-feedback interventions tend to support the need for a permanent change agent role (Friedlander, 1968; Frohman, 1970). Finally, research on companies that have been successful in developing new businesses has shown that they have done so through the creation of special self-contained entrepreneurial units exempt from corporate policies and practices. Entrepreneurs in these companies can interest any part of the organization in their ideas without going through regular channels. Only a single review at the top is needed to approve capital for new projects (Roberts & Frohman, 1972).

These research findings and experiences in OD provide the outlines for the organization of change agent resources. A corporate OD group with an entrepreneurial charter to innovate in organization and management can be the hub for renewal activities in the larger system. Change agents in this unit must find clients for new innovations and must be equipped to deal with the same forces for status quo experienced by internal entrepreneurs. They may be supported in this by external consultants who can help them maintain their innovative thrust and an appropriately discrepant position with respect to traditional values. Change agents will also have to be located in each of the subunits of the larger system targeted for a major organization development effort. Their effectiveness will be heavily dependent on the professional, emotional, and political support they obtain from the more entrepreneurial and innovative corporate OD unit or from outsiders. Thus, the relationships within the change agent network become very important. Large companies who have been successful in organizing and maintaining a network of change agents have done so through regular meetings of the network used for professional development, role clarification, relationship building, and emotional support. See Case 14–4 for a description of how external and internal change agents functioned as part of a major change program in the Department of State.

Even a well-organized network of change agents must relate to the power structure of the organization in a way that allows them to maintain a system perspective, challenge the system, and survive. The biggest barriers to organizational development and renewal are top managers who support the status quo. They may believe that their way of doing things is the "right way," and their position of power prevents others from confronting them, even though substantial data may exist to support a position for change. In rapidly changing environments, data about the need for change are likely to exist first at lower levels, at the boundaries of the organization (sales, R&D, unions, certain staff groups, etc.), and with

AN EXTERNAL CONSULTING TEAM

An important ingredient in ensuring the effectiveness of the ACORD program was building an external consulting team, a professional group of behavioral scientists that could come in to work with us as we needed them. This association of top-flight social and behavioral scientists from the NTL network with the State Department was an important part of the program.

In addition to serving as a training staff at special seminars and team-building and problem-solving sessions, these professionals worked closely with line operators to help form a strong link between *training* and *follow-up* action within the organization. They were available to attend problem-solving meetings and were on hand to observe the process of the group in other operational modes. They would often stop the group in its work to have it focus its attention on the process within the group as well as on the problem under discussion. They coached and counseled with the leader and members.

INTERNAL CHANGE AGENTS

As a part of the ACORD project we also developed internal change agents or consulting teams. Staff members of the ACORD program were identified and trained to act as internal consultants. They were assigned to our program managers and assisted them in all kinds

From W. J. Crockett, "Introducing Change to a Government Agency," in P. H. Mirvis and D. N. Berg, *Failures in Organization Development and Change* (New York: Wiley-Interscience © 1977), p. 136. Reprinted by permission of John Wiley & Sons, Inc.

of organizational development matters. They were available on a full-time basis to meet with operators and their staffs, to talk with them about their problems, do research with their people, and then feed this research back to the manager so that he could see what he was doing and how it was affecting his internal operations. This permitted an increased involvement and a better continuity between the individual consultants from the outside and the organizations to which they were assigned on the inside.

various constituencies in the organization. If top managers impose their own models of management, don't solicit this data, or are defensive when they receive it, the organization cannot adapt. The essence of OD is to help facilitate the flow of data from these sources and to create conditions where they will be dealt with in a problem-solving manner.

For all these reasons, change agents with a *systems perspective* must be completely free to work with a variety of levels and constituencies in the organization, to represent these views to those in power, and to help others confront those in power as needed. This suggests that effective change agents *do not only* follow a top-down strategy for change. They also attach themselves to and develop relationships with a variety of other constituencies and power centers such as the union, minorities, government agencies, customers, the community, subsidiaries, and various functional groups (Brown, 1976). Unless **257** they do this, powerful top managers can easily influence them to take on management's perspective of the organization. If this happens, change agents will adopt similar attitudes and behaviors as those in power and like them, run the risk of growing distant, aloof, and controlling in their relationship with people. Their own capacity to confront problems would be blunted. See Case 14–5 for a description by Reddin (1976) of this process.

If he is overly influenced by top management the change agent can't be helpful to top management in bridging the hierarchial gap. This loss of neutrality can be disastrous if the problems in the organization are communication, delegation of responsibility, or upward influence. Indeed, a change agent cannot help the client view the organization from a systems perspective without ensuring that various constituencies influence the solution to the problem.

A top management that wants a truly system-wide renewal process must encourage its change agent group to develop relationships with various constituencies. The change agent's role is to understand the constituency's views and help it influence top managment's decision-making process. In effect, management sets up a force for change by which they will be confronted. For example, an OD group might develop an independent relationship with a union so that it can improve union-management relations as a third party. Such a role can be threatening to management because it means that they may be confronted with the need to change. In one instance, the Vice-President of Industrial Relations told an OD group to stop all communication with the union, despite the fact that interventions in union-management relations in two plants had significantly improved those relations. The success of these interventions threatened the traditional approaches and role of Industrial Relations. The directive prevented the OD group from responding to the union president's request for help in improving participation and communication in the union—an activity that could only have improved total system effectiveness.

Some companies are trying new ways to include multiple constituencies in planning for change. For example, union-management committees have become a common mechanism for planning innovations in work structure at the plant level. Similar *representative models* (Brown, 1976) by which change agents bring a variety of groups into the change process, are certain to emerge in the future. Within this framework, effective OD groups are ones that attach themselves to multiple coalitions and formally or informally adopt the representative model.

The threat of a confronting OD group which represents multiple constituencies can result in its decline even after periods of success and growth. This has happened in a number of corporations. Yet if OD is to be an ongoing force for renewal, these cycles of growth and decline must be prevented. This means that OD groups must be more aware of organizational politics and consolidate their power base more effectively than most OD groups have to date. The next sections will deal with this problem.

The Politics of OD[3]

Staff groups usually develop power in organizations by obtaining the support of top management. This usually means supporting them with services that they require and see as crucial. Often it means avoiding head-on confrontations with their core values and beliefs. The OD group cannot follow this model if it is to be trusted by multiple constituencies and maintain a systems perspective. The problem then is how to achieve neutrality and independence, even with respect to top management, while developing enough power to be effective and survive.

Since it cannot rely on top management or any other constituency for its only source of power, an OD group must develop additional sources of power. This can be done by
developing credibility based on competence and ability to provide clients with help that

they need and request. An OD group can do this by developing a reputation for serving system needs rather than being self-serving. Research by Pettigrew (1976) on how specialty staff groups gain influence and power suggests the following six sources of power an OD group can consciously develop.

1. *Competence*. The first and foremost source of influence for the OD group is their own competence and effectiveness. They must be seen by the line organization, the union, or any other group of employees as professionally capable. This means that they are acknowledged experts in organization behavior and in the process and techniques of change agentry. But it also means that they must be interpersonally competent and model effective ways of managing conflict—ways which they often encourage in their clients. The OD unit must also demonstrate competence as a group, operating efficiently internally and operating effectively in their relations with various parts of the organization. This means meeting deadlines, achieving goals, following-up, keeping people informed, and so on.

2. *Political access and sensitivity*. The OD group can increase power by developing multiple relationships in the organization with key power figures (not only management, but union leaders, heads of minority groups, etc.). These relationships are informal and informally developed. They allow the change agents access to key individuals who know what is going on in the organization. Relationships with key power figures allows the change agents to determine what is important to them and gear their services to meet felt needs. Relationships also allow the OD group access to information about their reputation so they can detect early on any political activity aimed at reducing the influence of the group or eliminating it.

3. *Sponsorship*. Substantial research literature supports the general proposition that innovations (technological or managerial) are adopted at least in part because there is a strong and powerful sponsor in the organization who supports the innovation. In the product development area, these people have been called product champions. Organization development groups will gain power to the extent that they have sponsorship, preferably multiple sponsorship, in powerful places. This means vice-presidents, presidents, or union leaders, respected elder statesmen, etc. For example, it is likely that Irving Bluestone's sponsorship (he is vice-president of the United

Auto Workers) of the quality of work projects at General Motors is an important source of power for the OD group. Multiple sponsors can be obtained by successfully completing OD projects in support of powerful people. Thus, past clients who are powerful become sponsors and some may even get more powerful as they move up in the organization. The key is not to rely on a single sponsor or power center (e.g., management).

4. *Stature and credibility*. Power accrues to people and groups who develop a reputation for success and effectiveness. For the OD group, this stature must come first and foremost from line management's view that OD efforts have paid off. If key line managers spread the word that OD helped their organization to increase profits, reduce turnover, or in some other way improve effectiveness, stature and credibility are assured. Assuming they are capable of providing and delivering successful OD projects, OD groups can help themselves by encouraging their clients to communicate and spread the word. Organization Development groups can also enhance their stature by developing a positive reputation in their professional community so that feedback comes back into the organization from other sources. This secondary strategy must be carefully managed so that the group does not become viewed as so "professionally" oriented that they are seen as unconcerned with the organization's primary goals.

5. *Resource management.* Power accrues to those who control resources. If OD groups can deliver services to clients when they need to solve problems, they enhance their influence and reinforce interest in OD. Flexibility in assignment of OD specialists is one way to achieve this. A second way is to develop a pool of line and staff people in the organization who are capable of doing OD work, thus freeing the corporate OD group to shift their focus as new requests are made. A third way is for the OD group to bill their services to line managers. In this way the availability of change agent resources is geared to the demands of clients rather than to an arbitrary budget of dollars or people. Resources would be added when a client is ready. This stance is also consistent with the idea that change resources are likely to be most effective when the managers are motivated to use them (see Chapter 3). It is important to recognize, however, that this market strategy has downside risks because it makes the OD group more independent than some managements would like.

6. *Group Support.* Groups that are cohesive are more powerful. OD units that are able to work out internal differences, agree on common goals and strategies, share a philosophy of OD, and support each other are more likely to be effective. OD work involves a lot of stress and risk taking. It becomes easier when there is an internal atmosphere of supportiveness. Furthermore, internal strife takes up energy that could be spent in task-related activities and in determining future direction. For this reason OD groups, like other specialist groups, need to spend a substantial amount of time in team-building activities. For this they may need an external OD consultant of their own. But this must not be done at the cost of bringing an OD group into conflict with other staff groups whose missions overlap with OD (e.g., personnel). A frequent problem for OD in many corporations has been conflict with the personnel function, generated in part by the cohesion and arrogance which OD groups develop.

An OD group that tries to have a systems perspective is constantly balancing two relationships. It must maintain influence with multiple constituencies through the means just described. Unless the OD group can maintain its credibility, its effectiveness in serving the organization as a total system is reduced. When this happens, its capacity to generate enough influence to prevent its own destruction at the hands of a threatened constituency is diminished. On the other hand, the OD group must not allow the process of developing an independent and credible position to become so threatening to the power structure that the group is reduced in size or eliminated. This is likely to happen when top management feels the group has become too independent and systems oriented and not enough management oriented. Political access and sensitivity, sponsorship by key members of the power structure, and direct services for members of the power structure are important means of avoiding this outcome.

The essence of this complex political process is simultaneous maintenance of independence from the power structure and the development of dependence by the power structure on the OD group's services. This is a function of both political skill and luck. For example, hard financial times can occur just when the OD group is developing its power base but has not yet attained it. Or sponsorship can be withdrawn for reasons beyond the group's control. However, a combination of competence, political access, and multiple sponsorship can reduce the probability that the occurrence of these events will eliminate the OD group.

Despite all of its best political efforts the OD group is likely to go through predictable phases in their development and relationship to the larger organization which not only they, but top management must understand. We now turn to an examination of these phases.

Predictable Phases in the Evolution of OD Activities

Establishing an OD activity is a form of long-range planning for organizational innovation and renewal. Unless such a perspective is taken by top management and the managers of the OD and personnel function, the OD activity is likely to go through a predictable cycle of rise and decline (Pettigrew, 1975a).

This cycle is inherent in any innovative activity within an organization. But because of its threat to many power centers, the OD group is particularly vulnerable. The very forces that cause an OD group to rise in visibility and have an impact will also be the forces that cause its ultimate demise. If OD groups are to have the longevity needed to manage a system-wide strategy, a strategic orientation is needed in looking at the relationship between the OD group and the larger organization of which it is a part.

The OD group is likely to go through distinctive yet connected and interdependent phases as it moves from conception to a number of outcomes, ranging from demise to renewal. Figure 14–1 provides an overview of these phases, and we now turn to their description.

Conception phase. All the external or internal pressures described in Chapter 3 are reasons for setting up an OD group. However, these very same forces, because of their crisis nature, also make the conception of OD an unplanned act. As needs are felt, a sponsor in a power center (vice-president of personnel, line manager, corporated president, etc.) pushes for hiring a manager for the new group. A protegé of the sponsor may find himself appointed. Occasionally, outsiders are brought in to head the new function. The unplanned nature of the conception phase is the root cause of the drift into a later phase of "self-doubt."

Entrepreneurial phase. With the appointment of a manager and the hiring of OD specialists, the new unit moves into the entrepreneurial phase. The group scans the organization to find potential clients, begins to define projects, and, if it is competent **261**

FIGURE 14–1   The Evolutionary Phases of OD Units

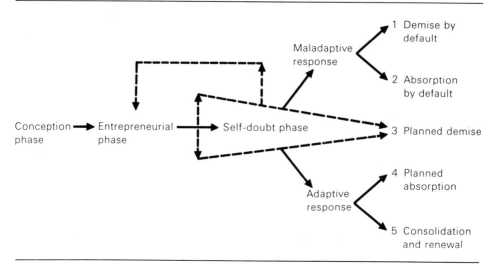

Adapted from A. M. Pettigrew, "Strategic Aspects of the Management of Specialist Activity," *Personnel Review*, vol. 4, no. 1, 1975, p. 12. Reprinted by permission.

in performing the change agent role, begins to chalk up successes. These successes, as has already been pointed out, are the fuel that further feeds the OD activity. They are essential to the rise in the OD group's visibility, stature, and power in the organization. Success provides a multiple set of constituencies, clients, and sponsors (managers, whole organization units, union leaders, and individual employees at all levels).

But as these successes multiply, events unfold within the OD group that can be the seeds of later difficulty. OD groups develop some of the characteristics commonly found in other innovative groups: high involvement and commitment to the values and goals to OD; high energy output as new managerial approaches are developed; a strong sense of identity, *esprit de corps,* and even arrogance; group cohesion and a lot of social contact by members; rituals; a special language and the intensive application of the OD process to the group itself.

All these characteristics serve the useful purpose of helping the group increase its self-awareness and help it to develop a unique identity. This may be reinforced by the unit's leader who may become internally oriented, defensive, and protective of the group in his interactions with others in the organization. The pull to spend more time inside the group is sometimes reinforced by the need to resolve tensions within the new OD group. Cleavages may express themselves along lines of old versus new, strategists versus pragmatists, or along differences in professional orientation.

Despite the conflicts in the group, it is during this phase that the OD group feels strongest. The excitement of a growing activity, an increasing number of successes, and the development of a group identity override the internal tensions. But the group's internal orientation prevent it from spending enough time on its relationships with key managers and groups in the organization, particularly those who are not involved with OD. This is the beginning of the unit's later political support problems.

Self-doubt phase.   At some point, often when the organization hits hard financial times or a major OD failure has occurred, questions will be raised about OD's value to the organization. Powerful executives who have not become involved in OD, demand its reduction or elimination on value grounds or because they think the activity does not contribute to the bottom line. During the entrepreneurial phase, these executives could not openly fight success after success or the increased political support from clients and sponsors. But in a time of crisis, power shifts to advocates of economy. The difficulty in measuring the contribution of OD to profits is a major weak spot in defending against doubt about its value. This is particularly a problem if systematic and ongoing evaluation of OD activities have not taken place. Even if events do not unfold quite this way, the ultimate event that triggers the self-doubt phase is withdrawal for whatever reason (departure, decline in power, political upheaval in the organization) of support by the group's original and/or most powerful sponsor. This withdrawal of sponsorship may occur over an extended period of time, but only becomes visible in a crisis.

The way in which the OD group and its supporters cope with these stresses is critical to the group's credibility and continued survival. The group's tendency is to overreact to threat and start to question its own effectiveness. Every new piece of information is seen only in terms of its negative implications for the group. Sometimes, the differences that have existed right along within the unit create divisions that occupy the group's energies. Some of the earliest pioneers and/or the leader leaves. With their departure, members of the group are left without a buffer between themselves and their environment. Perhaps for the first time, they get a realistic picture of their environment, and this causes confusion and self-doubt.

OD groups can respond poorly to this crisis by adopting an increasingly inward orientation. Sometimes the group tries to differentiate itself from other staff groups, particularly the personnel function of which it is a part. Often, additional OD specialists leave, further weakening the group. Just at the time that the group must take risks, form links with power centers in the organization, and define new projects, the group becomes passive. When the group does initiate, it does so unilaterally rather than in cooperation with potential new sponsors.

Adapting to the crisis, on the other hand, means diagnosing the causes of the problem and then formulating and implementing new strategies. The key to adaptation is for the group to redefine its identity, reexamine its staffing mix and needs, offer appropriate new services, and continue efforts to reestablish a power base through new contacts and sponsorship.

Advance knowledge of these phases can help an OD group and its sponsors be more effective when they occur. Although these phases may not always occur as described here, self-doubt will occur sooner or later. Only adaptive responses will move the OD group through this phase to a renewal of its identity and effectiveness. Maladaptive responses will lead to its absorption by another staff group—("No one wants them, so let's let so-and-so have them.")—or its demise.

Adaptive responses are not the responsibility of only the OD group. They are also the responsibility of top management or other power centers in the organization (clients, unions, etc.) that want to maintain an organization renewal activity. These groups need not only respond to political resistance in adaptive ways, but they must also anticipate that it will occur and plan for it.

Implications for Organizing a Renewal Activity

If there is one single trend in OD today, it is that top management and OD specialists alike lack vision and strategic perspective about the nature of organization development and its potential contribution to the enterprise. Typically, they see it as a set of techniques that **263** help deal with certain human and organizational problems. It is rare that managers see OD as a long-range strategy for organizational innovation and renewal. This perspective would acknowledge OD as a renewal activity that has important political implications. Such a perspective would lead top management to establish an OD activity in a way that encourages multiple relationships with constituents for change. It would recognize that by its nature all innovation, and OD in particular, incurs strong resistance by the very individuals and groups who need it most and, therefore, are threatened by it most.

The key is to organize an OD group responsive to internal market demands and pressures but protected from arbitrary power by small or unrepresentative groups. This might be done by setting up a planning and review board for OD activities composed not only of top management representatives but also of representatives from various constituencies (client systems, unions, special interest and minority groups, the community, customers, and suppliers). The OD activity would be funded by constituents, but long-range direction would come from the review board. The OD group could not be abolished unless there was substantial agreement by the review board to do so. In this way, continued organizational renewal would be ensured even when some power centers are threatened by change and its agents.

We do not yet know much about this or other mechanisms needed to ensure organizational renewal. Organizations that recognize the strategic importance of OD and want to institutionalize it, will have to develop them.

NOTES

1. Action research refers to a cyclical process of social science investigation which begins with research aimed at identifying problems and ends with research to evaluate the effects of actions taken. The process then recycles as action leads to new problems.
2. See in particular, Campbell and Stanley (1966) and Bouchard (1976).
3. The next two sections of the chapter are based on research by Pettigrew (1975a, 1976).

APPENDIX: SELECTED CASES

The cases included in this appendix have been selected for two reasons. First, they represent real life organization development cases. They provide a substantial amount of detail about the situation and people's thoughts and feelings before, during, and following an organization development effort. Secondly, the cases are teaching cases and thus provide the reader with a test of his or her diagnostic skill. They also provide an opportunity to test skills in developing a change strategy and a program of interventions. Finally, the cases provide an opportunity to evaluate the actual change strategy taken by the change agent and to learn from success and failure. The Corning Glass Works (A) case presents the problems facing a division of a large company and allows the reader to engage in a diagnosis. The (B) and (C) cases present the actions taken by management with the help of OD consultants and the effects of the OD effort. The Datavision (A) and (B) cases provide an in-depth description of a team building intervention, the problems which led to it, and its consequences. The May Department Stores (A) and (B) cases describe the efforts of a chief executive officer to introduce a management by objectives system as the centerpiece of a strategy to professionalize the management of his company.

If the cases are being used for class discussion the reader is cautioned *not* to read the (B) and (C) cases until the instructor has said to do so.

Corning Glass Works (A)
The Electronic Products Division

In July of 1968 Don Rogers, Vice-President and General Manager of the Electronic Products Division (EPD) of Corning Glass Works met with Corning's Director of Organization Development at his request. He began the discussion by reflecting on the state of his organization.

I asked you to get together with me so that I could discuss a serious problem. We have had some difficult times in my division over the past two years. (See Exhibit 1 for EPD's operating data.) Sales have been down due to the general economy and its effects on the electronic industry. But our problems are greater than that. Our business is becoming fiercely competitive. To deal with the downturn in business we have reduced the number of people and expenses sharply. This has been painful, but I think these actions have stemmed the tide. We are in control again. But, the business continues to be very competitive, morale is low, and there is a lot of conflict between groups that we can't seem to resolve. There is a lack of mutual confidence and trust. The organization is just not pulling together and the lack of coordination is affecting our ability to develop new products. Most of my key people believe that we are having conflicts because business is bad. They say that if business would only get better we will stop crabbing at each other. Frankly, I am not sure if they are right. The conflicts might be due to the pressures we are under but more likely they indicate a more fundamental problem. Can you and your group determine if the conflict between groups is serious and if so what I might do about it? . . .

THE LARGER CORPORATION

Corning's Business

The Electronic Products Division was one of eight line divisions in Corning Glass Works (CGW). (See Exhibit 2.) Corning was recognized as a leading manufacturer of specialty glass. Its growth and reputation were based on a strong technological capability in the invention and manufacture of glass products. This technological capability was supported by a Technical Staffs Division which conducted basic and applied, as well as product and process research in glass and related technologies. The company had been the first to establish an industrial laboratory in the early 1900's and by 1968 its investment in R&D as a percent of sales was quite significant when compared with other companies in the industry. The company's growth, which had been running at an average of ten percent a year over the previous ten years, was based on its capacity to invent new glass products which had a technological uniqueness or capability its competitors' products did not have. Many of these products were invented in response to a request from original equipment manufacturers (OEM's) who wanted Corning to apply its research and development strength to meet their needs. The technological edge was not limited to its product capabilities as it also had strength in manufacturing. Thus Corning was in the unique position of growing profitably without substantial competitive pressures. Patents, technological know-how in manufacturing, and the requirement of substantial capital investment prevented others from offering serious threats.

Corning's R&D capability led to major businesses in the manufacture of glass envelopes[1] for incandescent lamps and television tubes. Other businesses included glass lenses for optical and opthalmic use, laboratory glassware, refractories for glass and steel furnaces, and many other specialty glass items sold to a wide variety of industries in a wide variety of markets. A major exception to its OEM business was their position in the manufacture and sale of household consumer products for use in the kitchen. Pyrex® pie plates were an early entry into this business, followed in the 1950's by the development of Corning Ware® (heat resistant cook and serve ovenware) and Centura® (break resistant tableware).

---

[1] Glass envelopes are glass bulbs that encapsulate the electrical wiring and filaments which make up an electric light bulb or television tube.

Corning's unique technological strengths resulted in very profitable growth for the firm in the 20 years preceding 1968, though this growth was uneven due to a dependence on invention in the laboratory. In 1968 Corning was in a strong financial and profit position. (See Exhibit 3 for financial history.)

How the Corporation Operated

The trend of growth through technological breakthrough led to a number of unique corporate characteristics. The Technical Staffs Division (R&D) was regarded as very important by top management. Its V.P. reported directly to the Chairman of the Board. Next to R&D, Corning's strongest functional area was manufacturing. Many of the company's top executives had been promoted from the manufacturing ranks and it was widely regarded as the function through which one could advance to the top. To complement a strong manufacturing orientation, the company had developed a control system in which plants were viewed as profit centers. Thus bottom line results were measured by gross margin (plant sales less cost of manufacture) at plant level and operating margin at the divisional level (total gross margin for the division less selling and administrative expenses). Financial results were reported every 28 days and were reviewed 13 times a year. These period reviews were conducted at all levels of the corporation.

The nature of Corning's business called for most divisions to maintain relatively small sales departments where a few salesmen would service key accounts. Because there were only a few key customers, virtually all the information needed by a division about its markets could be obtained by these salesmen who maintained close relations with their customers. Thus many of the divisions had limited marketing efforts. Major sales transactions between Corning and its customers were conducted at high levels of the Corning organization since major investments were often involved for Corning. Similarly, decisions about new products were also made at a high level in the division or the corporation.

Corning Glass Works was established in Corning, New York in the mid 1800's. For many years all of its operations were based in Corning but as the company grew plants and sales offices were located throughout the country. In 1968 most of its 40 plants were located east of the Mississippi River. Headquarters for all but two of its divisions were located in Corning, New York. Therefore, in the case of most of the divisions, business problems could be discussed on a face to face basis. People from the several divisions saw each other frequently on Corning's premises, on the streets of Corning, and on social occasions. In a sense, the corporation operated like a relatively close knit family. People at all levels and from diverse parts of the corporation interacted informally. Even top officers were addressed on a first name basis. It would not be uncommon for top level corporate officers to meet divisional personnel in the main office building and to engage them in informal discussions about the state of their business—asking about orders, shipments, sales and profits for the period.

HISTORY OF EPD

The Business

The Electronic Products Division (EPD) manufactured passive components[2] for several markets. More than half of EPD's sales in 1968 were OEM's who bought resistors and

---

[2]A device used in electrical circuitry which does not perform an electrical function by itself but does act upon or modify an external electrical signal. **267**

capacitors in large volume for use in a variety of their products. The remainder of the division's sales were to distributors who resold the components in smaller quantities.

Much like other Corning businesses, the components business grew based upon Corning's unique capabilities in glass, which when used as a substrate[3] gave the components desirable electrical qualities. Corning's knowledge base allowed them to develop and manufacture highly reliable components for the military market. The growth of the space program and the growing reliance in defense on missiles in the late 1950's and early 1960's demanded components that had a low probability of failure in order to ensure the integrity of very sophisticated and expensive systems. The government customer, however, was willing to pay premium prices for components that met its very strict specifications. In response to market demands EPD expanded its plant operations in Bradford, PA and in the early 1960's built a new plant in Raleigh, NC. Bradford, manufactured resistors and Raleigh produced capacitors.

In the early 1960's the nature of EPD's business began to shift. As the military market leveled off, new commercial markets were developing and growing and EPD concentrated more of its efforts in these. For example, color television was emerging as a significant market and color sets required a larger number of components with more stringent specifications than those for black and white televisions. The growth of the data processing industry also provided a new market for EPD components. EPD, using its unique technological capabilities in product development and manufacturing, was able to enter these new markets and quickly establish a major position in them. In 1965 EPD built a plant in Wilmington, NC to supply high volume demands in the consumer electronics and data processing markets. By 1968, sixty percent of EPD's sales were to the data processing, consumer electronics (primarily TV) and telecommunication (telephones) markets.

Between 1966 and 1968 the needs of commercial customers for low cost components resulted in increased and often fierce competition among a number of firms. As companies competed for large volume contracts from major OEM's, prices fell severely with resultant pressure on costs. Often it appeared that EPD was in a commodity business.

In addition, there was continual pressure on component manufacturers for extensions of existing product lines as OEM's developed new end use products for their growing markets. Thus added to the price competition for large contracts was a need to respond to customers with new products which met their unique specifications. A component manufacturer could not bid on a contract until his product had passed tests conducted in his and in the customer's laboratory. Often it was also necessary to meet military specifications since commercial customers sometimes ordered against these specifications.

EPD's response to customer needs with new products was necessary because new products commanded higher prices in their early stages of development and thereby offered an opportunity for growth. As the technology of integrated circuits was introduced in the early 1960's, top management in EPD feared that the total volume of components sold would decline, making an increase in market share mandatory for survival. EPD's poor performance in 1967 and 1968 was a reflection of a major shake out in the electronic components industry compounded by a weakening of demand. A large number of component manufacturers were competing for what they perceived to be a declining total market in the future. Competition was on price, but quality and service were also important. Customers were giving special consideration to manufacturers which could assure short delivery lead times (usually no more than four weeks) while manufacturing operations depended on long lead times. Stricter quality standards were also being demanded because poor quality often could shut down an OEM production operation.

---

[3]A substrate is the material (carbon, glass, etc.) on which various coatings are deposited to make a resistor or capacitor of given electrical quality.

The intense competitive pressures within a declining economy came at the time the Wilmington plant was completed in 1965. The future looked bleak indeed and some managers in EPD wondered whether the division would survive and if so, whether it could meet Corning's high expectations for profitability and growth.

Management History

Prior to 1966 EPD was headed by Joe Bennett. Bennett had been in charge of the division in its infancy and nurtured it into a significant business for Corning. He was an entrepreneur who was always seeking to get EPD into new businesses. Recognizing the importance of the new integrated circuit technology in the early 1960's and its threat to the passive components business, Bennett prevailed on Corning to purchase Signetics Corporation, a small company which at that time was on the forefront of the new integrated circuits technology. Similarly, EPD had started a major effort to develop a new product and market using microcircuit technology—a technology that bridged both passive components and integrated circuits, and offered opportunities for further growth.

Scott Allen, the division's controller until 1966, described the division's strengths by pointing at Bennett.

> We always try new things. We always experiment. We set a fast pace. There is a feeling of urgency and commitment and dissatisfaction with the status quo. As an example, we are 1 1/2 steps ahead in computer applications. This stems from Bennett and the dynamic industry we are in.

The entrepreneurial spirit, the desire to grow, and the spirit of experimentation fostered by Bennett created an air of excitement and anticipation about the future. People talked about growth and opportunity being "around the corner." These expectations were not always met. Signetics had been acquired but was operating as a separate organizational entity, resulting in relatively few promotional opportunities for EPD personnel. An even greater disappointment was the microcircuit project. It had been dropped as a failure after large sums of money were spent in development.

Joe Bennett

Joe Bennett was 48 years old in 1966. He was a big man with a quick and creative mind who ran the division almost single-handedly. Many of the key decisions were made by him and none were made without consulting him and gaining his approval. People respected yet also feared him.

Tom Reed, Product Development Manager for capacitors and the new microcircuit project described Bennett and his style:

> Joe is very authoritarian with me and others. As a result those working for Bennett who are most successful are political and manipulative.
>
> People around here do not extend themselves very much to disagree with Bennett. The way to disagree with him is in a manipulative way. If he wants something done, tell him you'll do it and carry it out immediately. Then after a period of time go back to him and tell him that following through on his suggestion is going to cost us X number of dollars and we could make more the other way; but if he still wants to do it his way, it will be done.
>
> Bennett has a significant impact on our organization with all of us reflecting him in our managerial styles. We are all more authoritarian than before. I am less willing to **269**

let my people make mistakes even though I think it is important that people learn from their mistakes. The pressure and unrealistic standards are transmitted down to people throughout the organization. This results in our commitments often being unrealistic.

There is little group activity and decision making by the top team except where there is a specific problem. It is not a natural group. We are never together. I don't think we have been together, except at formal managers' meetings once in the last three months or so. There is no cohesiveness in the group reporting to Bennett.

Joe Bennett was a man of paradoxes. Although he was widely recognized as being extremely directive in his management style, he also had an intense interest in the behavioral sciences and their applications to management. He was widely read in the field. Mark Bell, Corning's industrial psychologist claimed that Joe Bennett was better read in the field than he was. In addition to reading, Joe Bennett also attended a number of sensitivity training sessions where participants spent a week in an unstructured group learning about themselves through the eyes of others.

Participation in the Managerial Grid Program

Bennett's interest in the behavioral sciences stimulated a number of attempts to apply behavioral sciences to management within the Division. In 1965 EPD undertook a division-wide management and organization development program called the Managerial Grid.[4] The program was to include an examination of individual management styles, group effectiveness, intergroup relations and organizational-wide problems. In all phases action plans for improvement were to be developed.

The Grid program was to span a three year period. It was discontinued following Joe Bennett's untimely death due to cancer. Dr. Don Rogers, a Director in Corning's Technical Staff Division, took over as Vice President and Division Manager. Upon taking over the Division he asked for and received a report on the current state of the Managerial Grid in EPD. The report indicated that Grid had a positive impact on the division but that Phase III dealing with the improvement of intergroup relations, which was yet to come, was particularly needed.

In light of business difficulties and his relative newness to the division Rogers decided to discontinue the program.

EPD IN 1968

The Division Manager

Don Rogers' promotion to V.P. was considered unusual given his lack of line experience, but his knowledge and background were relevant to EPD's business and he had a number of qualities which indicated his potential for a top management position.

As Director of Physical Research Don Rogers had responsibility for all research and development work going on in Technical Staffs in support of EPD's business. He was therefore knowledgeable about EPD's technology. He often sat in on EPD's meetings and

---

[4]For more information on the Managerial Grid see Blake, R. R. and Mouton, J. S., *The Managerial Grid*, Gulf Publishing, Houston, Texas, 1964 and *Corporate Excellence Through Grid Organization Development*, Gulf

Publishing, Houston, Texas, 1968.

had a general knowledge of their business. He had even served as a member of the board of Signetics, which manufactured integrated circuits and which Joe Bennett had urged Corning to purchase.

Don Rogers also had considerable personal assets. He was very bright and quick thinking. EPD managers were impressed with his capacity to grasp a wide variety of complex problems ranging from technical to managerial. He was always very pleasant and friendly and was able to get people to be open with him. This openness was stimulated by his readiness to share information and his own thoughts. In fact, he often surprised people with the things he was willing to reveal and discuss. He also involved people in problems and consulted them on decisions.

Despite these very positive attributes and managers' genuine liking and respect for Rogers, people did have some criticisms of Rogers. His personality and his superior intellectual capabilities almost always assured that he was a dominant force in meetings. There were also some questions about how much confronting Don did or tolerated or how much leadership he took in difficult situations. Managers' comments about Rogers included:

> He does not listen too well. His interruptions of others prevent him from hearing others' opinions and make it seem as if he really does not want criticism. What's more he has been too soft on me. He should be holding me to my goals. I have not met some of these goals and he should be climbing all over me.
>
> He is not involved enough in the problems that arise from differences in the goals of functional departments. This may be because he spends too much time away at Ion Physics and Signetics. But it doesn't change the fact that he is not involved enough.
>
> You get the same record back from him regardless of what you say. It is safe to be open with him and tell him what's on your mind but he does not listen.
>
> Rogers is too gentlemanly, is not tough enough, has not demonstrated risk-taking, and is encumbered by Corning Glass Works philosophy and standards. I am not sure how well he fences with others in the company.
>
> Wave makers are not wanted in the division and are being pushed out. People at the top do not create and confront conflict.

EPD's Organization

In June of 1968 EPD employed 1200 people, 250 of whom were salaried managerial and professional employees. It had three plants and four sales districts, and with the exception of some R & D support from Corning's laboratory, was a self-contained multifunctional organization. Reporting to Don Rogers were a controller, a manufacturing manager, a marketing manager, a sales manager, and a product development manager. (See Exhibit 4 for organization of EPD.)

EPD's organization was representative of a typical division with two exceptions. First, the marketing and sales functions were separated by Rogers shortly after he became division manager. As he said later:

> It seemed to me that Marketing and Sales had sufficiently different responsibilities to justify their separation. Sales, I felt, should be concerned with knocking on doors and getting the order while marketing should be concerned with strategies for pricing, new products, and the identification of new opportunities for the future. Marketing is a strategic function, as opposed to a day-to-day function.

271

A second difference was the existence of a Product Development group. Most other divisions relied totally on the Technical Staff division for technical product development support and only had engineering groups for manufacturing staff support. EPD's Product Development Department was responsible for developing new products although they also relied on Technical Staffs for research and development support. In addition to product development, the Product Development Department often became involved in manufacturing process development.

Don Rogers made a number of additional organizational changes shortly after his takeover.

1. EPD headquarters had been in Raleigh, NC. Joe Bennett had prided himself in EPD's difference from the rest of Corning, EPD being one of only two divisions not head-quartered in Corning, NY. At the urging of top management Don Rogers moved the headquarters to Corning, NY. He believed that EPD had to learn to relate more closely to the corporation.

2. Prior to 1966 the division had been geographically decentralized. The Raleigh, NC plant, which manufactured capacitors, not only housed the plant, but also had located on site a Market Development group and a Product Development group for capacitors. Similarly the Bradford plant had on site a market development group and a product development group for resistors. The Product Development managers had reported to Bennett, the Market Development managers to the General Sales and Marketing manager. In 1968 product development was consolidated under Ted Moss, who was located in Corning, New York though the groups themselves remained at the plants. The Market Development groups were brought back to Corning, New York.

3. Rogers also replaced all of his key managers with the exception of Ted Moss, the Product Development Manager. Ben Smith, the new Manufacturing Manager had held a similar job in Corning's Laboratory Products Department. Bill Lee, the new Marketing Manager, had held positions in manufacturing in Corning's other divisions and had recently been in charge of Corporate Market Planning. Frank Hart, the new Controller, had worked in plants in Corning's Lighting Products Division. Of the new division staff only Jack Simon, the new Sales Manager, came from within EPD. He had been a District Sales Manager. (See Exhibit 5 for a listing of key managers and their backgrounds.)

4. Prior to 1966 a Market Planning function had reported to Joe Bennett. As part of the cost cutting efforts in 1967 and 1968 this function had been eliminated and its responsibilities given to the new Marketing function.

5. One of EPD's major problems in 1966 and 1967 had been service to customers. The number of missed commitments was very high; EPD's reputation for delivery and service was slipping. Under Rogers' direction EPD undertook a successful program to improve service. The Manufacturing Manager held plant managers responsible for meeting delivery commitments and shortening delivery lead times based upon specific goals that were developed. In addition an information system was developed by the sales service function in an effort to improve service.

EPD and the Corporation

Don Rogers reported to the President of Corning (See Exhibit 2) and was responsible for managing all aspects of the division's operations. He was held responsible for achieving profitability and growth goals. These goals were established at the end of each year

(September-October) for the following year through a process of negotiation. The division would generate its sales budget through a bottoms up process in the Sales Department, using price guidelines from Marketing. The plants would then generate their gross margin budget based on their estimate of plant sales and costs. These would be consolidated at the top of the division and submitted to corporate staff. Invariably corporation staff would return to the division and, based on its corporate forecast of sales and profits, ask the division to modify its sales and profit plans. If corporate sales were forecasted to be lower than desired the division might be asked to increase its sales goals. The same was done with profits. This process often caused great consternation at the division level as budget proposals, which took a lot of time and energy to generate, were modified by corporate needs.

EPD, along with the other divisions, was expected to grow at an average rate of ten percent a year, the corporation's historic average growth rate. In the area of profits the EPD was expected to approach the profitability levels the corporation had come to expect of its more traditional OEM businesses. These typically were higher than the prevailing profitability levels among electronic component manufacturers. The ability of EPD to attain these objectives was a subject of much discussion and controversy in the division. A number of key people wondered whether both growth and profit objectives could be met. Volume could always be increased by taking low price business, but this reduced profitability. Most people within EPD looked to new products as a major source of both new volume and profits.

THE FUNCTIONAL DEPARTMENTS IN 1968

Manufacturing

Resistors and capacitors were manufactured in high volume at three plants located in Wilmington, NC (resistors), Bradford, PA (resistors) and Raleigh, NC (capacitors). Each of these plants had a plant manager and a full complement of manufacturing functions including production, engineering, quality control, purchasing, accounting and control, and personnel. With all manufacturing operations under him, the production superintendent had the greatest power in the plant. The head of engineering was second in line of influence. The plants (as other plants in Corning) were held responsible for gross margin and thus were profit centers.

The plant managers, with one exception, had grown up in EPD. Their performance was evaluated on gross margins and assorted other manufacturing variances including delivery lead times and missed commitments to customers. Plant accounts were closed every 28 days and the plant's performance was reviewed in meetings in Corning, New York 13 times each year.

The plant managers' reputations and therefore their promotability were perceived by them to be dependent on plant growth and good gross margin performance. All saw their future advancement within the manufacturing hierarchy of the company leading to the possibility of promotion to general manager of a division. Since manufacturing was the dominant function such an expectation was not unrealistic.

Because plants were profit centers their performance was well known around the corporation. There were many opportunities for exchanges at plant managers' meetings and the corporation had established an informal system for comparing plant performance. All of this heightened the individual plant manager's concerns about plants gross margin and growth.

EPD's plant managers were extremely upset with the lack of growth in the division's business. In the last two years their volume had shrunk and, through price cuts, their dollar volume had dropped substantially. This put enormous pressures on them for cost reduction in order to maintain their gross margins. While they were able to reduce some costs, gross margins still declined. With some exceptions, EPD's plants had the lowest gross margins in the company. Plant managers expressed the following statements:

> We're experiencing price erosion in our product lines and I don't see a large number of new products. We need something new and unique. I don't see growth potential in our existing products.
>
> We need direction on resistors. We cannot afford two plants. We need a process to allow us to make low cost resistors.
>
> There are no operational objectives. I get the feeling that everyone is concerned but no clear objectives are set.

The frustration experienced by the manufacturing people was expressed most in their attitudes toward Marketing and Sales. They viewed Sales as being concerned exclusively with volume with no concern for gross margin. They blamed Sales for getting low gross margin business and not fighting hard enough to get better prices. Sales, in other words, was giving the store away at the plant's expense and sales wasn't penalized for it as they saw it.

A Production superintendent:

> There is a breakdown in common agreement when it comes to pricing. Sales will sell for anything and the plant won't buy it unless 40 percent margin is involved.

The Manufacturing manager, Ben Smith:

> There is a feeling of mutual distrust between sales and manufacturing because manufacturing believes sales is not putting enough of a price on the products. This is a typical problem that results when two groups have different goals.

Manufacturing's negative feelings about Sales were only exceeded by their feelings about Marketing. They felt that it was Marketing's responsibility to provide direction to the division for profitable growth and that such direction was not apparent. They particularly blamed Bill Lee, the Marketing manager, for lack of "strong leadership." They were upset by what they called the "disappearing carrot syndrome." As Manufacturing saw it, Marketing would come to the plant and project a several million dollar market for a new resistor or capacitor (the carrot). Manufacturing, based on the projection, would run samples and make other investments in preparation for the new product only to find out six months or a year later that Marketing was now projecting much smaller sales and profits for the product. Manufacturing's explanation of this situation was that marketing lacked the ability to forecast marketing trends accurately and was generally incompetent. They saw a need to replace the Marketing manager and many others in Marketing.

A Production superintendent:

> What is slowing down EPD is weak marketing, lack of marketing direction, and a very narrow product base. You can't sell what you do not have and if you do not have it and you do not know where you are going to be in two years, you probably will not sell what you have.

A Production superintendent:

The last five years have left people quite cold as far as strategies are concerned. For example, Marketing does not have the same strategy as we do and they give us no direction.

The Manufacturing manager, Ben Smith:

No one has confidence in Marketing people. Plant managers don't believe them now since they have been wrong so many times.

Manufacturing was also unhappy with Product Development. They felt that Product Development had not always given them products that would run well on their production lines. They looked to Product Development to develop low cost components and saw nothing coming. When Product Development requested special runs on their manufacturing lines to develop new products, they wondered what the benefits were for this sacrifice in their efficiency.

Marketing

Marketing included several functions such as customer engineering and advertising. However, its most important function was Market Development under Glen Johnson. It was Market Development's responsibility to develop sales projections for the next year, market plans for the next three years, analyses of market share, and plans for improving market position. One of the primary means for increasing market share was the development of new types of resistors and capacitors. It was Market Development's responsibility to identify these new opportunities and to assure the development of new products in coordination with other functions. Marketing specialists reporting to Johnson had responsibility for scanning and analyzing different market segments and for developing new products in them. Measures of profitability and growth by market segment were used by them to assess their progress. Because the identification of new market opportunities was primarily Marketing's responsibility (with help from sales), as was the development of the new product plan, they felt the pressure for new product development was on them.

The marketing function had many new people as it had been established as a separate function just a year earlier. Most of the people had transferred from the Sales department where they were salesmen or in sales service. Johnson, for example, had been a district sales manager himself. The marketing specialists were generally recent technical or business graduates with one or two years of sales experience.

The Marketing people felt overwhelmed with the tough job of forecasting, planning and strategizing in a very turbulent market place and felt that no one appreciated their difficulties.

The Marketing Manager, Bill Lee:

We have not defined the resistor business. When the government business dropped, we did not face up to a need to produce at lower cost.

A Marketing specialist:

You can't be stodgy in this business. You must be fast moving and quick acting. You must be decisive, adaptable, a long-range thinker and deal with a very ambiguous situation.

275

Some felt that Corning had such high standards for profitability on new products that it was impossible to meet them in the components business.

The Marketing Development Manager, Glen Johnson:

> While corporate financial people will admit that we need a different set of criteria, they informally convey to us that we are doing a lousy job, and it makes us run conservatively. The corporate environment is not a risk taking one. We tend to want to bring a proprietary advantage to our business which we cannot do. This is slowing us down.
>
> Glass K (a new product) took seven years in product development. Technological development of unique characteristics is not an effective strategy in a dynamic environment. There were some original conceptions, but these quickly passed by the boards as the development process took seven years instead of the original three years projected for it.

Marketing people were also critical of Product Development and their responsiveness to divisions needs. As Marketing people saw it, Product Development's priorities were wrong and their projects were always late. According to the Market Development Manager, Glen Johnson:

> Moss bootlegs projects. There are no ways to establish priorities in development; no criteria have even been set up. Seventy percent of his time is in process development.

Marketing felt most resentful about manufacturing's lack of cooperation and the continual sniping which came from them. They saw the plants as conservative and unwilling to take risks. This was particularly aggravating because many of them saw themselves spending inordinate amounts of time dealing with the plants which they felt took time away from their primary task of marketing. Glen Johnson indicated that he would not have taken the Marketing job had he known that it would involve the many frustrations of getting manufacturing and others to do things.

Sales

The products produced by the plants were sold through a direct selling force of approximately 25 salesmen organized into four sales districts. Each district was managed by a district sales manager who reported to the national sales manager. The direct sales force visited manufacturers who used passive components in the end products they manufactured. Their job involved learning about manufacturers' needs by talking to purchasing agents and design engineers, and then obtaining contracts for resistors or capacitors.

In addition to direct sales, products were sold in small lot sizes through distributors. Distributor strategy and relations were the responsibility of the Distributor Sales Manager who reported to Jack Simon, the National Sales Manager. It was his job to coordinate the efforts of field salesmen in support of his objectives.

A sales service manager reported to the distribution manager. The sales service group was split geographically, with a sales service group located in each plant. It was their job to work with the plants to expedite order processing and keep the plant informed about customer needs for delivery and service.

The sales force consisted of college graduates interested in sales or marketing careers and older and experienced salesmen who had worked in this industry for a long time. Salesmen identified strongly with their industry. Jack Simon, the sales manager had come up through sales as had all of the district sales managers.

The sales task in EPD differed from that of other Corning divisions even though they also served OEM customers. They served a much larger set of customers in several markets. They had to develop a large number of relationships with purchasing agents and engineers and relied on good relationships to obtain market intelligence and an opportunity to bid on contracts. But, salesmen also had to negotiate with these same people to obtain the best possible price.They were measured on sales volume and worked hard to beat their budgeted sales target in order to obtain recognition from top management. They were not paid on a commission basis though this had often been a point of some discussion and discontent.

Jack Simon, the Sales Manager in 1968 reported mistrust, gamesmanship, maneuvering and politicking between Sales and Marketing:

> Most people (in Marketing) do not believe that sales competence is high. On the other hand we in Sales do not believe that the information Marketing gives us is the best.

Simon reported that major conflict developed in budget-setting sessions. This came in part because Sales developed their forecast from customer canvassing while Marketing developed theirs based on analytical tools. He said:

> Conflicts are not resolved based on facts. Instead there are accusations. I don't trust them (Marketing) and I don't trust that they have the capability to do their jobs.

Simon's view of manufacturing was somewhat more positive:

> Relations with Manufacturing are personally good, but I have a number of concerns. I do not know and no one knows about actual cost reductions in the plant. I don't think Manufacturing gets hit as hard for lack of cost reduction as Sales takes it on the chin for price reductions. Another problem is Bradford's service. It's putrid! There is constant gamesmanship in the Bradford plant.

At lower levels of the organization relationships between sales and manufacturing were viewed as even worse. There were shouting matches over the telephone between the midwest district sales manager and the Wilmington, NC plant manager. In one instance Sales wanted quick delivery to meet a major customer's needs. They felt that EPD's position with the customer would be hurt if it were not provided. The plant said they could not provide delivery on such short notice without upsetting plant operations.

The Sales Service Manager:

> The relationship with the Bradford plant is bad. Measurement for plant managers has to change. They are not really measured on service. Things have improved somewhat, however, and they are a bit more concerned about service.

Product Development

Product Development was responsible for the development of extensions to the current product line. There were generally between 10 and 12 new product development projects underway and they often required significant technological development. To handle this work, the development group was divided into two parts—a development group for resis- **277** tors located in the Bradford, PA plant (which manufactured resistors) and a development group for capacitors, located in Raleigh, NC. No product development group was located in Wilmington, NC. The manager of product development was located in Corning, New York along with the rest of the divisional staff.

The product development group was composed of technical people who had spent their careers in research and development work. While some of these people had come from the corporate R&D group, many had worked in the division for most of their careers or had held technical positions in other companies in the electronic industry.

Ted Moss, Manager of Product Development described his relationship with other groups:

> In general my department's relations with the plants are pretty good although some problems existed at Bradford. My biggest concern is with Marketing. I do not feel that Marketing provides detailed product specification for new products. In addition, Marketing people do not understand what is involved in specification changes. I think that writing specifications jointly with Marketing would help this problem. Another problem is that Marketing people have to look ahead more and predict the future better. They always need it yesterday. We need time!

Ted Moss was also critical of Corning's Technical Staff division which also did some product development work for EPD.

> It is difficult to get a time schedule from them. Their direction is independent of ours since they report elsewhere. They will not wring their hands if they are behind schedule. They will more quickly try to relax requirements for the development if it is behind schedule. I need more influence on specifications when it comes to things they are working on. I often have to go upstairs to solve the problems that occur with this group.

Moss also cited problems with the Sales group.

> We need comments from the Sales group on our new products. I wanted to get the call reports they write and asked Simon for copies. His argument for not giving them to me is that the Marketing Department has the responsibility for interpretation. I finally had to go to Rogers to resolve the problem.

The Controller

It was the division controller's responsibility to maintain all accounting records for the division, provide a financial summary every 28 days and report the performance of the division to the division staff and the corporate controller. It was also his responsibility to develop quarterly forecasts of business performance.

Frank Hart, the division's Controller:

> In most cases three period forecasts are extremely inaccurate. It is very difficult to forecast the business this way. Our forecasts are always off. Yet it is a corporate requirement.

Not only did EPD find it difficult to forecast its business but they had difficulty explaining
278 the reason for upturns and downturns.

The New Product Development Process

While there were several attempts to develop completely new components or products beyond components, such as the microcircuits effort—most of the new product development effort concentrated on developing product extensions. These were resistors and capacitors with different technical characteristics than existing products which were intended to meet new market needs.

Product development was going far from smoothly in the division. In one case, the focus divider, a new product for the television market, was killed and resurrected four times with different parts of the organization having differing knowledge of its status at given points in time. Marketing clearly thought that this was an opportunity and Product Development saw it as feasible from a technical point of view. Yet as far as Sales was concerned, Manufacturing's cost quotes called into question EPD's ability to compete in the market place. As discussions progressed on needed product modifications to reduce costs, Marketing's estimate of the potential market changed and Product Development's estimate of technical feasibility changed. Thus each function's management made its own estimate of the viability of this product and, at different points in time, told people in their function that the project was on or off depending on their optimism at the time. At one point, salesmen were obtaining orders for samples of the product at a time when Manufacturing and Marketing had decided that the product was not feasible and had killed the idea. Similar problems occurred on other projects because it was not uncommon for Product Development to bootleg samples for Sales people for products that did not have the commitment of Manufacturing or even Marketing.

In another case severe conflict between marketing and plant personnel erupted over a new coating for resistors. Marketing had determined that a new and uniform coating was needed for competitive and efficiency reasons. They presented their views to the division's management and received what they thought was a commitment to change resistor coatings. Yet no significant progress had been made by Marketing in getting plants to convert their operations. The plants questioned whether Product Development had proved that the new coating would work and could be manufactured to meet product specifications at no additional cost. Since they also completely distrusted Marketing on the need for this change they dragged their feet on this project. In 1968 two years after this project had started, there was still no project completion in sight. The Marketing specialist in charge of this project would return from meetings at the plant angry and completely discouraged about his ability to influence plant people to do things to advance the project.

The forum for the product development process was the two day meetings held once each accounting period (28 days) in Corning, New York. One meeting was for new capacitor developments. The other meeting was for resistor developments. In all, approximately 20 people attended each meeting including the division manager, his immediate staff, plant managers, and a few other key people in the other functions. The purpose of the meetings was to discuss, coordinate and make decisions about new products. In 1968 the division was working on approximately 12 of these new projects.

The meetings were chaired by Glen Johnson, the Market Development Manager. He typically sat at the head of the table. At the other end of the table sat Don Rogers. Johnson would publish an agenda ahead of time and would direct the discussion as it moved from one project to another. For each project, progress was checked against goals as they had been agreed to by each function at the previous review. Each function would describe in some detail what had been done in their area to support the project. For example, plant managers might describe what equipment changes had been made in their plant. If the **279** goals had not been met by a function, as was often the case, new dates for the accomplishment of the goal would be extracted. While problems encountered were always described the issue of slippage in goals and the underlying reasons for it were rarely discussed. When differences in opinion on a project did surface, there was great difficulty in resolving them. People would end them by agreeing to disagree and moving on to the next item on the agenda. While tempers flared occasionally there was rarely any open hostility or aggression expressed in the meetings. However, after meetings, people were often observed meeting in pairs or smaller groups in the hallways, over coffee, or in others' offices to continue the debate.

There was a continual stream of people in and out of these meetings to obtain information from subordinates in their functional area about a project's current status. It was not uncommon for a plant manager to leave the meeting to call an engineer in his plant for details about a project's status. On one occasion Ted Young, a Marketing specialist, was continually mentioned as the person who knew the most about a project under discussion, yet he was not at the meeting. On other occasions marketing specialists would be called into the meetings, (which was possible since they all were located in Corning, New York) to provide information about a project. Plant people and product development people were sometimes brought to Corning for parts of the meeting if their input was thought to be needed.

Prior to 1968, product development meetings had not been attended by the Division Manager. In 1968 Marketing asked Don Rogers to attend these meetings to help in moving decisions along. Rogers became very active in the meetings. He often became involved in the discussion of a new product, particularly its technical aspects. He could be seen explaining a technical point to others who did not understand it. His viewpoints were clearly heard and felt by others and people thought that meetings had improved since he had decided to sit in. Despite these improvements in June of 1968, Glen Johnson still dreaded the product development meetings.

> I never sleep well on the night before the meetings. I start thinking about the various projects and the problems I have in getting everyone to agree and be committed to a direction. We spend long hours in these meetings but people just don't seem to stick to their commitments to accomplish their objectives by a given date. Projects are slipping badly and we just can't seem to get them moving. In my opinion, we also have some projects that should be killed but we can't seem to be able to do that either. Frankly, if I had it to do over again, I would not take this job. After all how much marketing am I really doing. I seem to spend most of my time in meetings getting others to do things.

The Outlook for 1969

As 1968 was drawing to a close Don Rogers and the top management group were preparing for their second GLF meeting (Great Leap Forward). This meeting had been instituted the year before to discuss major problem areas and to develop commitment to division objectives for 1968. Now it was time to look ahead to 1969.

In a memo to the key managers he summarized what he viewed as the problems which needed to be addressed in the coming year:

> It is obvious that division growth is our major problem and that we need to develop new products to get growth. Achievement of budgeted operating margin is a close second. Morale has become a more acute problem and the need for communication,

coordination, and the proper balance of long and short range efforts continue to require our attention.

As the top managers in EPD prepared for the two-day meeting in Ithaca, New York, it was clear that they had survived the shake out in the industry. But it was also clear to them that many major problems remained. They all wanted growth and saw it as their major problem, but they were not developing new products fast enough to meet this objective nor were they in agreement about strategies, priorties, or what constituted acceptable criteria for profitability.

To complicate matters, morale was low, risk taking was down, and significant problems in communication and coordination existed. All of this was occurring in an environment where the price/cost squeeze was continuing and competition was as fierce as ever.

As key managers prepared for their GLF meeting the Corning Organization Development Staff was preparing to present the findings of their study of EPD to Don Rogers.

EXHIBIT 1   Electronic Products Division Sales and Operating Margin in Thousands (1961–1968)*

	61	62	63	64	65	66	67	68
Sales	12,723	21,745	22,836	20,036	25,320	26,553	23,852	24,034
Operating Margin*	3011	5449	5826	2998	5075	4170	1559	1574

*Operating margin equals sales less manufacturing, administrative and sales expenses

EXHIBIT 2   Corning Glass Works Organization Chart

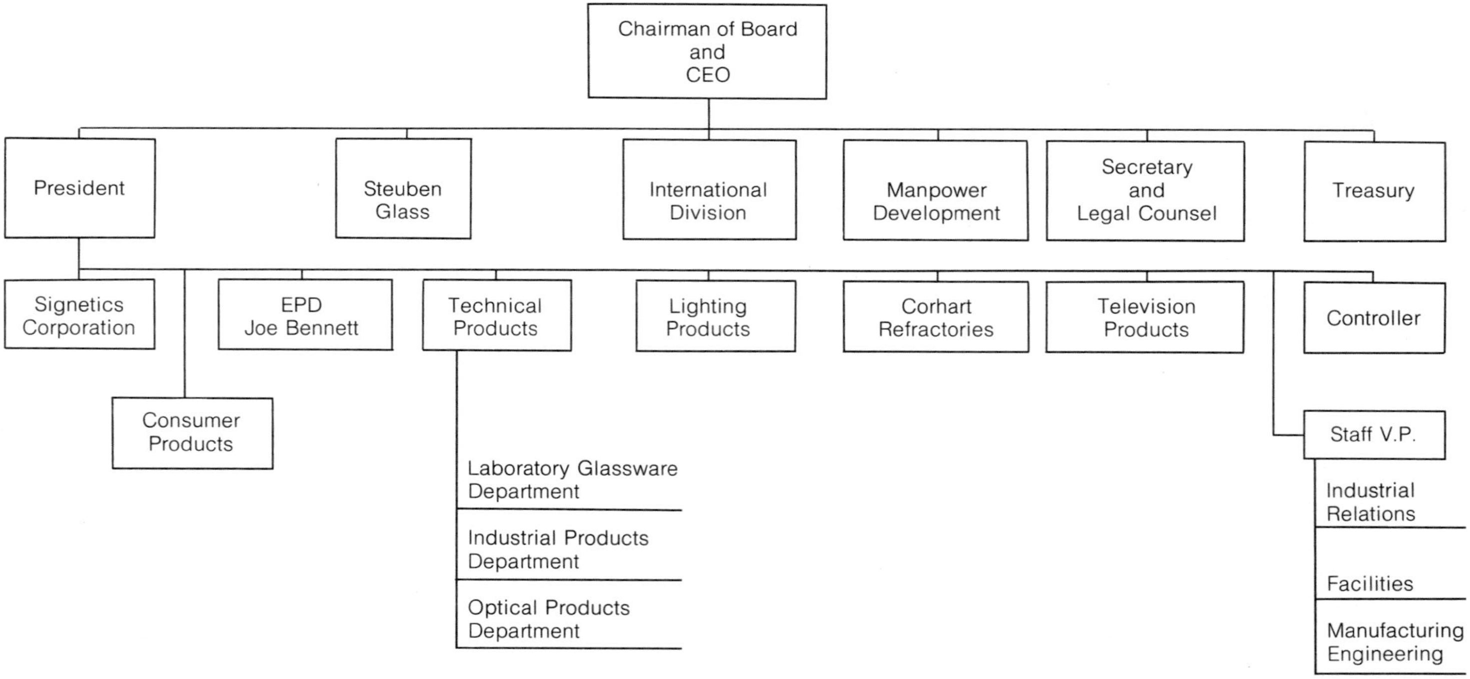

- Chairman of Board and CEO
  - Treasury
  - Secretary and Legal Counsel
  - Manpower Development
  - International Division
- President
  - Steuben Glass
  - EPD Joe Bennett
    - Technical Products
      - Laboratory Glassware Department
      - Industrial Products Department
      - Optical Products Department
    - Lighting Products
    - Corhart Refractories
    - Television Products
    - Controller
    - Staff V.P.
      - Industrial Relations
      - Facilities
      - Manufacturing Engineering
  - Signetics Corporation
  - Consumer Products

EXHIBIT 3   Corning Glass Works Financial History (1959–1968)

Consolidated Statement of Income	1968	1967	1966	1965	1964	1963	1962	1961	1960	1959
Net Sales	$479,089**	$455,220	$444,139	$340,471	$327,612	$289,217	$262,200	$229,569	$214,871	$201,370
Dividends, Interest and Other Income	17,733	15,639	15,404	12,489	10,093	10,554	9,593	8,835	10,160	8,071
	496,822	470,859	459,543	352,960	337,705	299,771	271,793	238,404	225,031	209,441
Cost and Expenses:										
Cost of Sales	335,957	310,798	291,669	237,048	229,432	199,211	184,100	160,773	158,293	138,128
Selling, general and administrative expenses	67,251	63,253	61,172	45,612	44,525	40,012	35,088	28,972	25,538	25,380
Interest, state taxes on income and other charges	8,961	9,210	6,333	2,622	1,505	1,708	1,408	1,243	1,119	1,297
U.S. and foreign taxes on income	37,886	37,779	47,195	28,989	27,221	27,264	23,100	21,490	18,026	20,300
	450,055	421,040	405,369	314,271	302,683	268,195	243,696	212,478	202,976	185,105
Net Income	$ 46,767	$ 49,819	$ 54,174	$ 38,689*	$ 35,022	$ 31,576	$ 28,097	$ 25,926	$ 22,055*	$ 24,336

*Exclusive of non-recurring net gain of $1,279,499 in 1965 and net loss of $2,334,024 in 1960 on contribution and sales, respectively, of investments in associated companies.

*All figures in thousands.

EXHIBIT 4   Electronic Products Division Organization Chart

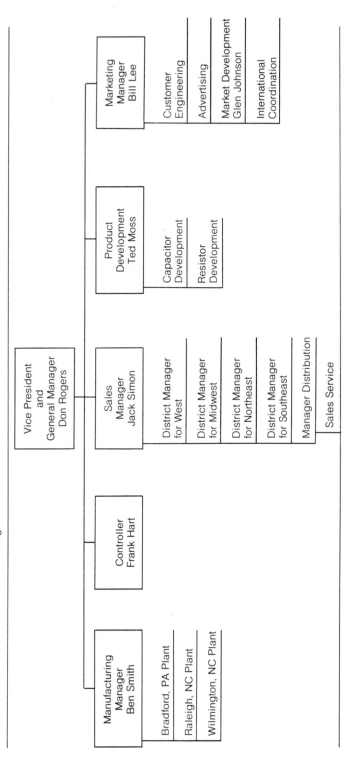

EXHIBIT 5   Background of EPD Executives

Don Rogers—Vice President and General Manager—Electronic Products Division, 40 years old: He received a Ph.D. in Chemistry from the University of Cincinnati, a Masters in Chemistry from St. Johns University, and a B.S. from Queens College in New York City. He joined Corning in 1957 as a Chemist in its Technical Staffs Division (R&D). In 1961 he became Manager of Electronic Research and in 1964 Director of Physical Research in the same Division. He was appointed as EPD's division manager in June of 1966.

Bill Lee—Marketing Manager, 39 years old: He received a B.S. in Chemical Engineering from Rutgers. He joined Corning Glass Works in 1950 as a staff engineer. This was followed by several engineering and supervisory positions in glass plants. Following an assignment in corporate market planning he became Manager of Marketing in EPD in 1967.

Ben Smith—Manufacturing Manager, 43 years old: Received an engineering degree from Clarkson College. He became EPD's Manufacturing Manager in 1967 following numerous manufacturing positions in Corning's Lighting Products and Technical Products Division. He had started as a plant engineer, Department Foreman, production superintendent, and plant manager in several glass plants in these divisions. Just prior to moving to EPD he had been Manufacturing Manager in the Laboratory Glassware Department.

Ted Moss—Product Development Manager, 45 years old: After receiving a degree in Mechanical Engineering from City College in New York City, he joined Corning Glass Works as a staff engineer. After five years in other divisions he joined EPD in its early infancy. He served as a project engineer first and then held several managerial positions in product and process development. He became Manager of Product Development for EPD in 1968.

Frank Hart—Division Controller, 31 years old: He joined Corning Glass Works in 1962 after completing a B.S. in Industrial Administration at Yale, serving in the U.S. Army, and completing an M.B.A. at the Harvard Business School. Prior to joining EPD as its Division Controller in 1967 he served in a variety of plant accounting positions in Corning's Lighting Products and Television Divisions.

Jack Simon—Sales Manager, 34 years old: He went to St. Bonaventure University where he received a degree in Sociology. He joined Corning Glass Works in 1960 as salesman in the Electronic Products Division. All of his experience with Corning was with EPD where he became a District Sales Manager before taking over as Sales Manager in 1967.

Datavision (A)

Datavision, a small computer company, had grown rapidly since its birth in 1969. By 1977 the organization was a leader in the process control monitoring industry. Despite the fact that Datavision's business was flourishing, its President, Dr. Larry Campbell, was concerned with some existing and potential problems inherent in rapid growth situations. He was particularly concerned about Datavision's high turnover rate, the lack of collaboration between functional areas, and "morale" problems within the organization. In general, Campbell was disturbed by a lack of sense of vitality both in the executive wing of Datavision's office building and across the organization. To deal with these issues specifically and to improve their ability to manage organizational issues generally, Campbell and his Vice President of Finance, Matt Leona, enrolled in a two-week executive education program. This program was called Managing Organization Effectiveness and was held in August 1977 at the Harvard Business School.

At the seminar, participants met in large classes as well as in small, 8 to 10 member, action planning groups. By the end of the two weeks Campbell and Leona had gained perspective on Datavision's needs and identified an appropriate course of action. The focus of their plan was to set in motion a process designed to get problems out on the table, increase the executive group's ability to communicate, and plan more effectively. They did not have any clear ideas about what particular changes in management, in managerial roles, or in organizational structure might result, from this process. At the suggestion of other managers in their action planning group, they planned to use an organizational development consultant to play a catalytic role in their effort to identify and address issues.

DATAVISION'S BUSINESS

Datavision Incorporated is an organization involved in the design, development, manufacturing, and marketing of process control monitoring systems; such systems provide real-time visual feedback of process type manufacturing operations. Datavision has pioneered the use of color graphic displays in process monitoring. Their mini-computer based systems replace older dial and strip-chart recorder monitoring methods.

Process control monitoring systems are used in a number of different industries. Datavision has directed its marketing and sales efforts towards large companies in the chemical processing, food processing, and utility plant industries. A Datavision system sells for approximately $250,000.

HISTORY OF DATAVISION

Datavision began in 1969 when Larry Campbell, Walter Jackson, Luther Beale, and Paul Winters, four engineers from Lincoln Labs at MIT, decided to go into business for themselves. Campbell became president, Jackson, Beale and Winters became vice presidents, four other people were hired and headquarters were set up in Campbell's living room. Datavision's engineers worked closely that first year and in 1970 introduced the first color graphic process monitoring system ever to appear on the market. The systems were well received, particularly in the food processing industry, and by 1972 Datavision was growing at a rate of 50% per year. In 1977 Datavision was a very different organization than it had been initially. Campbell and Jackson were still involved in company management. Beale, however, returned to MIT in 1972 and in 1976 Winters went to work for another computer company. As Datavision grew, it relocated and finally was housed north of Boston in six separate buildings within 15 minutes of each other. In the spring of 1977, the company employed a total of 470 people.

Despite rapid growth and profitability, the company was not without problems. In an industry where the average turnover rate is from 12 to 15%, Datavision experienced a 30% rate in 1975, a 25% rate in 1976 and, still, in 1977 was troubled by 18% turnover. Although the top management team was stable, except for the resignation of Winters, engineers, programmers, technicians, and marketing people would come and go quickly. Datavision's business is characterized by high and ever-changing technology. Employee loss can be a serious problem in that type of situation because qualified people are in high demand but limited supply. The process of recruiting, interviewing, and hiring costs the company both time and money.

Despite the turnover problem Datavision has a 31% share of the current graphics processing market. Its five major competitors have 37%, 14%, 9%, 3%, and 6% of market share, respectively. As mentioned previously, the graphic system industry is characterized by a rapid rate of technological advancement. As a result, the industry is highly competitive. To continue to grow, gain market share, or simply maintain its position in the marketplace, Datavision must actively market its product to generate sales. Active marketing is also important to build up order backlog. The organization aims for a steady $5 million backlog of orders. In addition, an organization in the process control industry must constantly develop more efficient, more advanced, and less expensive products. According to one manager,

This is a highly pressurized and competitive industry. To survive you have to be one step ahead of everyone else. Every 6 months there is a significant change in our market place. That kind of activity puts a lot of pressure on everyone, engineering, but particularly sales. People simply don't wait in line to buy a $250,000 computer. **287**

BUSINESS STATUS

Since 1973 net sales at Datavision have grown at a compound rate of a little less than 50% per year. (See Exhibit 1, Consolidated Statements of Income, 1973–1977.) When Campbell and Leona left their offices to attend the executive seminar, results of the first quarter of fiscal 1977 were in. (See Exhibit 2, Consolidated Operations Report.) Actual total revenues were slightly less than predicted. Income before taxes, however, was slightly higher than predicted for that time of year. By the time the seminar had ended and Leona and Campbell had returned to Datavision there was decided concern about the financial situation. According to Matt Leona (V.P. Finance),

> In April 1977 we had just finished a very big year. By August though we were behind our predictions. We hadn't thought the summer doldrums would affect business that year but apparently they did. We had to readjust our thinking and cut down our forecasts for fiscal '78. We had originally predicted a year with $25 million in sales at that point in time (August 1977). We had to cut that forecast down to $22 million.

Datavision's managers were also concerned with company financials. According to a manager in the manufacturing department,

> We all know in an industry like this we need a backlog. By the end of the summer of 1977 we had really eaten away and were continuing to eat away at the backlog we had. At that point our backlog was only $2 to $3 million and, from what I understood, we just weren't getting orders.

THE ORGANIZATION

Twenty-nine of the 470 employees at Datavision were executives and managerial staff. The organization was housed in six separate buildings in an area north of Boston, Mass. The President, Vice Presidents of Finance, Engineering, Marketing, and their respective staffs had their offices in building #1. The Vice President and staff of the Manufacturing Department were located in building #2. The Customer Service Department and its functional head, a manager, were housed in building #3. Buildings #4 and #5 were primarily manufacturing. Building #6 housed mostly the N.E. regional sales office. Five of the six buildings were within walking distance of each other. The sixth (a manufacturing building) was only 15 minutes away by car.

Datavision was headed by President Larry Campbell, who was responsible to a 12-member Board of Directors of which he and the other Vice Presidents were members. Reporting to Campbell were five functional managers. (See organization chart and personnel profile, and Exhibits 3 and 4.)

To maintain contact and disseminate information about departmental and company activities, Campbell's staff met weekly for several hours. Typically, Campbell ran the meeting. He'd ask for informal reports of department activities and problems. Then he would present an idea for some kind of corporate plan or organizational idea and ask for input which he would use to make decisions. According to Campbell,

> I generally make most of the organizational decisions around here. When we first started the company I did everything. I made all the decisions and didn't really explain to anybody why I made them. I was in a position though to have a very

complete picture of the organization and was the only one in a position to make good decisions. Things have changed since the beginning though and there are just too many decisions to make. I've been adapting to our growing organization and trying to change. I let certain people make decisions but I don't feel right now that I can delegate all or even most of the decision making. I tend to be a bit of a perfectionist and expect an awful lot. I feel as though I'm a little ahead of the organization in terms of knowing or thinking about where we are going, where we ought to be, and what ought to be done. I have a tendency to figure things out, make assumptions, and make decisions. That confuses people sometimes but I think it's what we need right now. I use the information I'm given at executive meetings but really make final decisions mostly myself.

Following Monday staff meetings each V.P. met with his own department managers to communicate organizational plans, decisions, or discuss company or department activities. Such meetings gave managers the opportunity to formally meet with their area V.P. and communicate with him and with each other.

The monthly written report was another important communication tool used at Datavision. Each Vice President was responsible for preparing a monthly activity report for the President. Once he received all five reports he consolidated the information into one report for the Board of Directors and each Vice President. In order to best prepare such reports, Larry Campbell met with each V.P. and his managerial staff, for several hours, during the week before the reports were to be written.

The atmosphere at Datavision was friendly. Simultaneously a formality was emerging. In earlier days doors were always open. Managers felt comfortable dropping in to chat with V.P.s and the President. As the organization grew the atmosphere changed and, although managers usually met their V.P.'s whenever necessary, Campbell was seen by appointment.

THE INTERVENTION

On September 16, 1977, approximately one month after completing their executive seminar, Campbell, Leona, and Personnel Manager Harold Wheeler had a luncheon meeting with Dave Brennan. Brennan was an organizational consultant recommended to Campbell and Leona by both a seminar faculty member and fellow participant. (See his personnel profile, Exhibit 5.) Larry Campbell explained,

We attended MOE generally because there was a feeling on the part of some people that our hang-ups (turnover, morale problems, people feeling overworked) were organizational and somehow we weren't managing the organization to be effective. As a result of our seminar experience, we decided to hire an organizational development (OD) consultant to come in, do some work, help us bridge the gap between many different parts of the organization. We expected he would do that by talking to different people, sensing feelings and attitudes, and bring them forth in a way that doesn't offend people. We had had a sense of this OD need before going to that program, about a year earlier, and in fact hired someone who came on for a day. Anyway, after the summer program we, Matt and I in particular, were really motivated to do some OD work. Brennan seemed like the right guy.

During their three-hour lunch Brennan explained himself and his ideas to Campbell, **289**

Leona, and Wheeler. He outlined a possible action strategy for Datavision. Dave Brennan recalled,

> I spoke with the three of them back then and told them that I was interested in new and developing organizations. I've done a lot of work with high technology companies in rapid growth situations where there are very bright people, usually engineers. I thought that I could help the V.P. group work together more effectively. Larry and Matt referred to that as "team building."

As a result of that meeting Brennan was hired to help Campbell's staff work more effectively as a managerial team. Brennan planned to initiate the "team building" effort in three phases. To begin, he would interview each member of Campbell's staff individually. Next, on November 3 and 4, 1977 he planned to meet with Campbell and the staff at a resort in Rhode Island for an off-site session. Finally, Brennan suggested that after Rhode Island he hold a meeting with company managers reporting to the staff. Dave planned to meet with those managers, about 25 in all, by himself and then have Larry and the V.P.'s join the session for a question and answer period.

Interviews With Top Management Group

On October 18, Dave Brennan spent the day at Datavision interviewing the top staff. These interviews served two major purposes: (1) by introducing himself to the staff, Dave was able to explain his goals, Larry's goals in hiring him, and his plans for carrying out the team building task. (2) In addition, by questioning each manager Brennan could learn more about the operating environment at Datavision. He reported,

> I started all my interviews by saying, "I'm Dave Brennan. I'm here to interview you but before we can do that I need to know what kind of expectations you have and what you've heard about me." I got five different stories from those five different guys. The theme was basically that Larry had gotten a hold of me because he went to Harvard, he (Larry) thought I could help them work together better, and that they needed it. Although initially people were a bit formal and stiff I was received very well.

The idea of a consultant was not new to Datavision executives. Approximately a year before Dave Brennan was hired another O.D. consultant came to Datavision, interviewed executives and managers, and made some recommendations to Campbell. Datavision executives were also used to two-day off-site meetings. Characteristically each quarter, executives and their wives went to a resort for a combined business meeting and social gathering. One Vice President commented,

> We were relieved to meet Dave. We all felt that Datavision needed something. We'd probably all mentioned our interest in having outside help to Larry independently. We hoped Dave would give us what we needed. I wasn't so sure that anything would change, but I was willing to give it a try. If nothing else I was sure he could act as referee when we started yelling at each other at the off-site meeting. We were in the habit of getting pretty excited at those sessions.

After introducing himself, Dave asked questions about Datavision's strengths and weaknesses and about Larry and their fellow V.P.'s. He was particularly interested in assessing problem areas which might be preventing the top management group from

290

working together as a team. As a result of his interviews Brennan identified six recurrent and key issues.

1. Lack of trust among the top level people and across the organization,
2. Confusion about company goals,
3. Poor decision-making policy and too much decision unmaking.
4. Lack of clarity regarding organizational structure,
5. "Cronyism",
6. Conflicting management styles at the executive level.

Dave designed a flip chart presentation for the two-day session which included a list of the six problems and illustrative quotes gathered during the interviews. After laying the meeting's ground rules he planned to use the charts to introduce the issues and help promote discussion. His agenda for the off-site meeting included convening on Thursday, the 3rd, at 8 a.m., working until 12:00, and working again from 4 p.m. to 8 p.m. The first day would raise problem issues and "clear the air." On Friday, the 4th, Dave scheduled meetings from 8 a.m. to 12:00 and 3 p.m. to 6 p.m. Dave expected that on Friday the group would be ready to devise strategies for dealing with Datavision's weaknesses.

The Off-Site Meeting

On Thursday morning Dave began the session, by explaining his agenda and the ground rules for the two-day meeting. According to one V.P.,

> There were several rules Dave suggested we follow. First, he said that we should try to stay on the topic of conversation and not bring in other issues when we were concentrating on one issue. Next he suggested that if we were discussing or criticizing the behavior or style of a particular person then we had to look that person in the eye. Also, you had to give the person being discussed a chance to talk and respond. Finally, the receiver of criticism also had the power to control the flow of conversation. If he was upset, offended, or uncomfortable he had the option to say stop—I'd like to discuss something else.

As part of the ground rules Dave also described the role he would play at the meeting: an unbiased outsider whose primary function was to help people listen, talk, and hear each other more effectively. According to another V.P.,

> To be honest, when we were beginning that meeting in Rhode Island I was thinking to myself, we've been trying to get along for years, we've had a consultant, we've met together at off-site gatherings. I was discouraged and didn't think it would work. I was also convinced, though, that I would try and because Dave had come across so straightforward and capable, I had a glimmer of hope. I trusted him and wanted this to work out for us. I felt willing to do what had to be done and even put myself on the line.

Another V.P. recalled,

> I thought that we all really had a good feeling at the start of that session. Larry was behind the effort. I really thought it could work.

After setting up the rules, Dave unveiled his flip chart presentation. The first chart included a list of all six problems and quotations illustrating each issue. He focused on each problem one by one trying to elicit additional comments and discussion. Participants were hesitant initially, but began to contribute by clarifying their ideas.

Trust was a major concern around Datavision. Nearly each V.P. had criticized other executives. According to one V.P.,

> We've developed strict territories around here, we stay out of each other's departments mostly because we don't trust or approve of what the other guy is doing. I'd like to question someone on their department's activities but I'd have to let them do it to me and I'm not sure I want that.

Apparently these feelings were particularly true between Marketing and Engineering. It was not unusual for Walter (V.P., Engineering) and Bob (V.P., Marketing), to argue and blame each other for missed deadlines. Bob was quite vocal in blaming the slippage in orders on the inadequacies of the Engineering Department. Each V.P. took great pride in his own department and seemed to feel that, "things are operating real well in my department. If everyone else took care of his area like I take care of mine things would be teriffic around here."

Another problem related to trust was that no V.P. seemed to feel he could confront another V.P., or could discuss negative feelings about another V.P. or manager openly to Larry. In some ways they didn't feel that Larry would listen and in other ways they didn't want to diminish another man's reputation.

Confusion about company goals was a problem related to the trust issue but presented separately. One commonly held feeling was that no one around Datavision was skillful enough to plan for the company's future. Each Vice President had confidence in the organization's technical competence but felt that no one was really in touch with the marketplace and realistic enough to make some good planning decisions for the business. One V.P. explained at the meeting,

> We are all, except Scott (V.P., Manufacturing) relatively new at managing. We are probably all experts in our own areas but because we don't really trust each other we don't pool our information. That kind of coordination isn't the norm around here. Another reason for the confusion is that the company may have outgrown whatever managerial skills and planning skills some of us had.

One major focus of planning criticism was the Marketing Department. One representative sentiment participants recalled was,

> There are many places our system can be used. We haven't figured out what's happening in the marketplace. Our competitors seem to know. We are, or have become very weak in that area. Our sales are dropping and we've been eating away at the backlog. There are some real doubts about the skills in that department. The V.P. in Marketing had made some particular blunders we all knew about, blunders that especially affected the Engineering and Manufacturing Departments. He'd talk to a customer, find out what the customer wanted and promise a system. That would have been a good move except sometimes the product wasn't designed or produced yet.

To a lesser extent the Engineering Department was criticized for not developing products quickly enough or not effectively designing a less costly product. During the session V.P.s initially became defensive when criticized this way, but learned, as the session went on, to listen to the criticism and try to deal with it constructively. Dave commented,

> They were all putting a great deal of effort into working hard at listening and abiding by the ground rules. Bob Fowler, who took the most criticism tried especially hard to sit quietly and respond rationally.

Decision Making and Unmaking was related to the goal issue and a source of complaint. Several V.P.s commented to Dave, "It seems that no one is willing to take a stand on long range goals." Not only did V.P.s worry that no one, particularly Larry, was willing to take a stand on long range goals but sometimes when a stand was taken it would be reversed quickly. Several of the V.P.s had mentioned this during their interviews and again during the Thursday session.

> Sometimes these Monday Staff meetings we had were more confusing than not having them at all. Sometimes we'd talk for eight hours straight and leave without having a real sense of what had gone on. Other times Larry outlined some very definite plans and ideas. We left the meeting assuming our policy was one way. You'd tell your managers and make sure the policy was understood. Soon you'd get a memo that the policy was changed. Larry did that all himself. That kind of change of plans was very confusing and irritating for Datavision employees. It was also pretty embarrassing for the V.P. who made a statement that was reversed or negated a week later.

Perhaps the decision-making problem attributed to Datavision executives by each other was, in part, related to the nature of a high technology business. During the meeting, several V.P.s were irritated as they recalled leaving a meeting committed to a marketing, engineering, or manufacturing course of action which would be changed when the Finance Department discovered a new piece of data. One V.P. commented, "It is apparent when Matt goes to Larry with some new information because we are all told to stop what we are doing and proceed a different way." The V.P.s felt that this type of situation was frustrating and costly. Engineers who had to stop one activity and get geared up for another lost valuable thinking time. Manufacturers also became angry when they set up shop to proceed one way and then had to close down to restructure activities.

During Thursday's meeting several V.P.s confronted Larry with comments like, "sometimes it seems you make decisions for reasons of your own, unmake them for reasons of your own, and don't bother to communicate to us why or what is going on. You make decisions without involving people who have a right to be involved."

Voices became raised during these kinds of confrontations although participants consciously tried to control tempers. Dave contributed only to add a comment like "Well Larry, did you understand exactly what Bob was saying? Why don't you rephrase that." "Does anyone else feel the same way. How about you, Scott?" By questioning that way, Dave helped Larry, the V.P.s, and Tom better understand the criticism and avoid one-to-one hostile confrontations.

Lack of Clarity was a problem related to organizational structure. Participants recall feeling angry as the group began to discuss this topic. The consensus among the V.P.s was that Larry made all the organizational decisions and in many ways they didn't make sense. "One day a certain service group is a member of one department and the next day it's been moved and reports to another department." One particular irritant to several V.P.s was the fact that Tom (Manager, Customer Service) reported to Larry. The V.P.s were **293** angry because Tom had been elevated to an executive level and had managers reporting to him. During their interviews, several V.P.s told Dave that they felt Tom didn't have the title or experience to be a member of the top staff. At the meeting they confronted Tom with these feelings. Tom remembered that at the off-site meeting he,

> . . . was really shocked to hear that people, Matt in particular, doubted my credibility. I had trouble relating to them, but I just thought that was because I was a friend of Larry's.

Cronyism was the fifth problem which Dave found to be recurrent. In thinking back about the meeting one V.P. expressed the sentiments of the rest when he reported, "Tom Sisco didn't belong there. We told him we tolerated him but didn't trust him in the company and didn't trust him to be there. He was a tennis buddy of Larry's which is why he was there in the first place."

Active discussion took place around the cronyism issue. The V.P.s felt that the friendship between Larry and Tom stood in the way of business because around the company, people felt that you got promoted if you were Larry's friend. Tom recalled,

> Those kinds of feelings were surprising to me because I really thought we played down our friendship. It was good to get it out in the open though because I knew where I stood, we all did, and that was good.

When first discussing these five issues the group had been somewhat subdued. As the hours went by they grew more willing to participate. Matt, Walter, Bob, and Larry were the most vocal participants. Tom and Scott were fairly reserved. Dave attempted to include them and elicit their comments when they were "watchers" for too long. When introducing the sixth issue, however, Dave had a difficult time getting anyone to comment right away.

Conflicting Management Styles was an issue that each staff member discussed with Dave during their respective interviews. As a result Dave was keenly aware that Bob's (V.P. Marketing) management and decision-making style was completely different than each of the other V.P.s. Bob himself was aware that he had a different approach and a different philosophy than his peers. Bob described himself as "the kind of person who is caring, feeling, people oriented and intuitive. I have a gut feel for a project or procedure and am often right. No one else around here feels that way. Larry and Matt in particular are logical and analytical, it is a very different style."

Dave Brennan remembered that after interviewing the staff,

> It became obvious that Bob was perceived as the center of many other of Datavision's problems. Before the meeting on Thursday I had breakfast with Bob. I wanted him to be aware before the session that his management style was seen not only as different but in conflict with the management styles of other Datavision executives. He was upset about that, didn't like it, but said that he wasn't surprised. When we got to the issue in the meeting, people started denying it. At that point I had to confront them and said, "Bullshit, these are your quotes right there. I said let's not monkey around, we've only got two days and there's a lot of hard work to do. I really need your help." After being straightforward in that way a couple of the guys admitted to their feelings and their quotes. After that point, for the rest of that day the discussion centered around Bob.

At this point Walter and Matt in particular, became vocal. Even Scott entered into this part of the discussion. Each perceived Bob as having a caustic, hostile, angry approach. Scott expressed the opinions of Walter and Matt when he commented, "We all felt that Bob was into winning and losing. He was confrontive and angry. He raised his voice and was very aggressive. That was just not necessary to get the job done. It wasn't our style here."

At the session Matt remembered expressing the idea that,

Bob and I had a very different approach to decision making I knew he was certainly aware of it. He just fought me on it all the time. I believe in reality; facing it, living with it, and making well thought out logical decisions based upon it. Bob couldn't give me data to back up his ideas, or wouldn't and that annoyed me and at the meeting I let him know how I felt.

Another serious criticism directed at Bob related to his "empire building" and salesmanship attitude. More specifically, Bob was seen as someone who needed to feel important and powerful and would approach customers as if he was in control of everything at Datavision. He promised customers products and then would ask Engineering to develop them. He'd promise customers deadlines which were impossible for Manufacturing to meet. Scott Palmer recalled,

It really boiled down to a lack of trust in Bob. At the meeting we all took turns and confronted him on these issues. He didn't seem to be getting the marketing job done. Our sales were down, we were eating away our backlog. He was probably feeling some pressure but as a result he'd take things out on Walter or try to put blame somehow on Engineering or Manufacturing.

When issue number six came out into the open all subsequent discussion became focused on Bob. Every other issue was related back to Bob's inabilities and personality style. Although Dave helped maintain calm, and the criticism was delivered constructively, Bob was subjected to several hours of direct confrontation. Walter commented,

For a long time Bob and I had had problems. This was a forum for expressing my feelings about those problems and getting them out on the table. We all tried to explain ourselves pretty calmly. He may have perceived it as an attack.

Bob said later that he had perceived the session as an attack. At the time he did not react defensively or with hostility. Although he admitted feeling initially that the whole session was a setup to confront him he listened to everyone's comments and tried to understand them. He also redirected some of the criticism if he thought he was being unfairly blamed for something or that others could benefit from similar criticism.

Scott Palmer stated,

Because Dave was there, I guess we were able to voice complaints we had never voiced before. For the first time I was able to tell Bob that it really irritated me that he never listened. That kind of honesty caught on and Bob and Larry went back and forth about individual management styles and things about each other that bothered them. Bob said Larry always turned around his (Bob's) decisions. Larry expressed the feeling that Bob was too dogmatic. It was refreshing in a way because people had things buried for five years that they were able to express then. As positive as it was though, in some ways it was brutal. Bob sat there, through criticism that was mostly **295** directed at him and maintained his cool. I give him a lot of credit, we all did. He was open and made no attempt to stop the flow of conversation. We all learned a lot about each other during that time. We all wanted this thing to work and all appreciated Bob's willingness to listen and take criticism pretty calmly.

Larry commented,

You could almost see the improvement. Bob was really trying. He did quiet down and acted much calmer. He tried not to raise his voice and seemed to really hear what everyone else was saying.

As the first day ended people were energetic and exhausted simultaneously. Participants remember having positive and negative sentiments about the day. They were relieved to get their feelings about problem issues, particularly Bob, out into the open. However, it was upsetting for most of them to imagine what Bob must have been going through during the day. All credited Dave Brennan for being an effective coach, moderator, and guide. They perceived Dave as helping keep decibels down, fists from flying, and the conversation flowing. When the meeting adjourned, the group went to dinner feeling that they worked hard and made some good progress.

Although the schedule for Thursday did include a four-hour break in the afternoon, the group stopped only two hours for lunch. They were as energetic Friday morning. Friday's meeting was to run from 8 a.m. to 6 p.m. with a quick break for lunch in the middle of the day. Larry and his staff agreed that corporate planning would be the topic of discussion for day two. The group discussed their planning methods, how to make efficient use of their meeting time, how to communicate individual department needs, and set up ground rules for meeings.

Larry ran most of the meeting on Friday and together the group developed a planning procedure for Datavision. The plan excited everyone because it seemed to integrate functional area needs. The session on Friday was characterized by energy and activity. Overall, Scott and Tom remained less vocal than the rest of the group but seemed as enthusiastic about what they were accomplishing. Walter recalled, "Our feelings were very different on Friday than they were on Thursday. We seemed more committed on Friday. Larry was listening more carefully and Bob was almost low key. He only spoke his fair share of the time."

The group worked steadily, all day, Friday. They seemed invested in preparing planning strategies together. Dave was less involved Friday than he had been Thursday but, apparently, his presence was a catalyst for discussion. One V.P. recalled,

On the second day Dave had the effect, even when he didn't say anything, of helping us talk without ignoring each other or becoming argumentative. He wasn't involved as an obvious leader but he did promote honesty and openness on our parts; the first day especially but even the second day. Even when he was quiet we did need him in the room. That became obvious when he left to make some phone calls in the afternoon on Friday. After a few minutes, I guess when we realized he was gone, no one said a word. Apparently, we needed him there to really help us communicate, team build, or whatever.

At about 5:00 in the afternoon Larry suggested cocktails, which had not been served Thursday or before 5:00 on Friday and initiated a feedback session. He wanted to hear

perceptions of his meeting behavior and asked Matt, Walter, Bob, Tom, and Scott to take turns commenting. They mentioned strengths like "you seemed to be listening more," "you seemed to take our suggestions seriously," "you were trying hard to get our input." They also asked him to try to maintain some of these behaviors back at the office. Larry enjoyed the feedback process and suggested they continue to comment on each participant. On the whole, the feedback was positive and related to listening skills and the high levels of honesty. At least overtly, the group was proud of itself. At 6 p.m. the meeting ended and because he had plans Friday night Larry headed back to Boston. Those who stayed on, had an informal post-meeting dinner.

After the session participants reflected about what had been accomplished and what might be accomplished as a result of their efforts. Feelings about the meeting ranged from very positive to very negative. Tom Sisco stated,

> I came out of that meeting feeling very high. So many things came out in the open as a result of those two days I felt we could all be much more open and honest with each other and had a very good idea about who the Vice Presidents were and where they stood on certain issues. I learned a lot about Walter and Matt. I felt I could work with both guys much more efficiently as a result of those sessions.

Another positive, yet less enthusiastic opinion shared by several staff members was,

> When we first heard about going to Newport we all had a certain amount of skepticism about being able to work together well and about our planning capabilities. We had consultants before that, we were used to off-site meetings. I wasn't convinced that this guy (Dave) on this team thing would be any different for us. The first day was very encouraging though. We didn't have fistfights and didn't yell too much. We had all been so open that there was a collective feeling that things might really change. We were all hoping for it anyway.

There were a couple of participants who, despite overt enthusiasm were doubtful that the session had changed anything or would act as a catalyst for future change. Their comments were,

> We have a pattern of leadership, decision making, and management style here that we are used to. We've had consultants before who pointed out the same problem issues to us that Dave did now. We didn't listen a year ago, why should we listen now?

Meeting with Next Level Down Managers

Dave scheduled a meeting with company managers who reported to session participants for the week following the session. The meeting would let the managers know what had taken place in Newport and would run for about an hour. For the first half, Dave would meet with the managers alone and after about thirty minutes the officers would join the session.

On Monday, November 7, 1977 Campbell sent a memo to the 25 managers that were to be included, announcing that a meeting would be held November 8, 1977 at 11:00 in the conference room of Datavision's main building. Dave Brennan stated,

> I wanted to do three main things at that meeting. I wanted to present an overview of the idea of team building, gain credibility, and give a brief description of the Newport meeting. I didn't plan on describing comments or anything like that but I did want to **297**

explain the process, major issues raised, and the sense of excitement and commitment that came out of that meeing. I hoped that would promote questions that I could
answer and that the officers could answer when they entered the room.

There was some confusion surrounding that November 8 meeting. Not all the managers were aware that any special off-site meeting had taken place. Some thought it was to
be a typical managers meeting during which Larry would announce some kind of change
in the organization. One manager recalled,

Some of us were blasé, others curious, others pissed off. No one really knew what was
up. Those of us who knew that the meeting was about consulting were, for the most
part, unimpressed. We had spoken to consultants before and hadn't seen any results.
There was no reason to think this would be different.

Larry began that November 8 meeting. He explained briefly that the officers were "all
fired up" about new corporate goals, strategies for planning, increasing market share, and
profits. Next he pointed to Dave as the man who was going to help achieve those goals.
Several managers remembered:

Dave began his presentation by saying something like, "Well I'm sure you're all
curious about the weekend we spent in Newport." Someone spoke out at that point
and said, "Frankly we don't give a damn about what happened in Newport because
lots of us don't even know they went to Newport." At that point there was silence. Dave
handled it well. He explained and proceeded as he had planned. He probably
thought we had a better idea about what was going on than we did.

As the meeting progressed Dave talked mostly about organizational development
and Newport specifically. He outlined general problem issues. Managers at that meeting
agreed that Dave seemed credible, likeable, and genuinely committed to changing things
at Datavision. They were less convinced that things could, in fact, be changed. They were
hesitant to confront Dave with those feelings. As he spoke many managers felt doubtful
and whispered among themselves. As reconstructed later by participants at that meeting,
the ideas going through people's minds and being exchanged were:

We don't have a team work problem in the company. The only problem is at the
top. The rest of us work together fine because we know we have to. The troops
communicate across departmental lines. It's just the generals that don't.
We've heard all these promises before, nothing will change now.
If they'd get together and take a stand maybe something would get done. Larry
sends a memo to go ahead and proceed a certain way on a product, or something.
The next thing you know he sends another memo that says with more information the
project stops.
It is going to take a lot for most of those guys to improve as managers because,
first of all they are all engineers and second of all, they never had to manage anyone
before they managed us. They just were never taught how to do it.
The officers go off to the woods for a couple of days and think they are a team
now. Its just not true. It can't be. They can't be a team when they all have such strong
personalities.

About 45 minutes into the meeting one manager asked Dave a question. In doing so,
298 he raised a volatile issue, one that every manager reported remembering and worrying

about. The question was "Don't you think that, at the top, there may be a couple of people who won't change because they don't really want to and, in fact don't have the capacity?" Dave responded with a flat "No." He explained that Newport convinced him that all the officers were committed to changing and were willing to work very hard at integrating, planning, and acting as a team. Until that point Dave was viewed as a competent ray of hope for Datavision. At that point, however, several managers became discouraged. They remembered,

> Dave really lost credibility points. It was no secret that there were attitude, capability, and personality differences and problems at the top. Bob Fowler was very different from the rest of them and there were bad feelings about that filtering through the company. We couldn't believe that Dave hadn't picked up on that or wouldn't tell us. If he didn't figure that out then he wasn't so skillful or had been lied to.

A wave of cynicsim and doubt spread through that conference room after Dave's response. Feelings of frustration, anger, and discomfort permeated this meeting. One manager commented,

> We wanted things fixed very badly, we wanted Brennan to be able to give us solid evidence that things could improve. Instead his efforts seemed like they would almost have to be fruitless. It was almost like a joke after that. We were all very very skeptical.

Another manager reflected,

> We all felt pretty awkward after that. When the officers came in it got worse. People asked a couple of questions trying to assess their (the officers) real commitment to organizational development, Dave Brennan, and team building, but the tone was disbelieving and doubtful. The people who were relatively new to the company were more hopeful than those who had been around for four years or so. Generally though even those of us who were new weren't convinced that it would change, I don't really think we expressed our doubts or questions very honestly during that meeting. We became even less open and honest, though, after the officers came in.

Campbell's Perspective

After the officers' session in Newport, Larry Campbell felt committed to O.D. work and team building at Datavision. He was enthusiastic and felt that his fellow officers were similarly excited. His spirits were dampened after the managers' meeting. He stated, "It was really the first time I was aware of such widespread skepticism. That disappointed me and discouraged me."

He became even more discouraged when, after the meeting, he approached several of the managers individually. Such discussions convinced Larry that many managers at Datavision were certain that the officers could never work together as an effective team and that, given who they were, no O.D. consultant could help change things.

Simultaneously, other events disturbed Larry. Financial results for the company's second quarter were in, and both revenue and income were well below prediction (see Exhibit 6). In addition, it was two weeks into November, sales were down, and the backlog was becoming smaller and smaller. Dave Brennan reported,

> Larry called me with two major problems. He was very upset by the amount of **299**

skepticism felt by the managers. It seemed to him that they didn't believe anything the officers said. He also mentioned that he had approached a couple informally and, it seemed to him, that the whole team building and planning effort would fall by the wayside if he didn't come to grips with what he saw to be the major issue. He continued and reported that, he felt, there was no confidence in Bob. He was convinced that, if he didn't deal with that then "we can plan ourselves to death and nobody is going to believe the planning process."

Larry was distressed and discouraged. He was not sure how to proceed. He recalled,

It all of a sudden became obvious to me—Bob was an outsider in the organization —I don't think he was viewed as a competent marketing guy. His style was troublesome for some people too—I had a realization. Everyone was against Bob. Morale was very low. I wasn't 100% sure what to do. Whatever it was though, it had to be done quickly.

EXHIBIT 1   Datavision (A) Datavision Incorporated and Subsidiary Consolidated Statements of Income for the Years Ended April 30, 1973, 1974, 1975, 1976, 1977 ($000's)

	1973	1974	1975	1976	1977
NET SALES	$3,457	$7,265	$9,461	$10,183	$16,640
COST OF SALES	1,976	4,236	5,759	5,661	9,471
Gross Profit	$1,481	$3,029	$3,702	$ 4,522	$ 7,169
OPERATING EXPENSES:					
Engineering, Marketing, General, Administrative & Other	$1,280	$2,609	$3,309	$ 4,254	$ 5,253
Income (Loss) from Operations	$ 201	$ 420	$ 393	$ 268	$ 1,916
INTEREST EXPENSE, net of interest income	12	87	230	302	265
Income (Loss) before provision for for Federal and State Income Taxes	189	333	163	(34)	1,651
PROVISION FOR INCOME TAXES:					
Federal	$ 76	$ 123	$ 59	$ (12)	$ 860
State	17	21	4	—	—
Income (Loss) before extraordinary credit	$ 96	$ 189	$ 100	$ (22)	$ 791
EXTRAORDINARY CREDIT—Federal Income Tax reduction resulting from net operating loss carryforward	76	123	—	53	—
Net Income	$ 172	$ 312	$ 100	$ 31	$ 791
NET INCOME PER COMMON SHARE:					
Before extraordinary credit	$ .09	$ .15	$ .08	$ (.02)	$ .50
Extraordinary credit	.07	.09	—	.05	—
Net Income (primary)	$ .16	$ .24	$ .08	$ .03	$ .50

EXHIBIT 2   Datavision (A) Consolidated Operations Report Quarterly Comparison

	First Quarter FY 1978			First Quarter FY 1977		
	Budget	Actual	Percent	Budget	Actual	Percent
Revenues:						
System and Upgrade Shipments, Customer Funded Eng. Shipments, Less Discounts— Syst. & U/G Cust. Fund. Eng., Net Shipments, Customer Services, Application Development, & Other Revenue						
Total Revenue	$5,014,000	$4,721,764	100.0%	$3,324,857	$3,397,296	100.0%
Cost of Sales:						
System and Upgrade at Standard, Manufacturing Variances, Color Plotter Development, Customer Funded Engineering, Customer Services, Application Development						
Total Cost of Sales	$2,797,932	$2,503,704	53.0%	$2,019,429	$1,980,898	58.3%
Gross Profit	$2,216,068	$2,218,060	47.0%	$1,305,428	$1,416,398	41.7%
Operating Expenses:						
Engineering, Marketing, Corporate Administration, & Other	$1,621,770	$1,602,761	33.9%	$1,115,161	$1,143,888	33.7%
Income from Operations	$ 594,298	$ 615,299	13.0%	$ 190,267	$ 272,510	8.0%
Interest Expense	60,000	37,305	0.8	78,000	83,677	2.5
Foreign Currency Exchange	—	2,768	—	—	—	
Income Before Tax Provision	$ 534,298	$ 575,226	12.2%	$ 112,267	$ 188,833	5.5%
Provision for Income Taxes	283,000	335,000	7.1	60,000	85,000	2.5
Net Income	$ 251,298	$ 240,226	5.1	52,267	103,833	3.0%
Net Income Per Share	$ .14	$ .14		$ .04	$ .08	

EXHIBIT 3   Datavision (A) Organization Chart

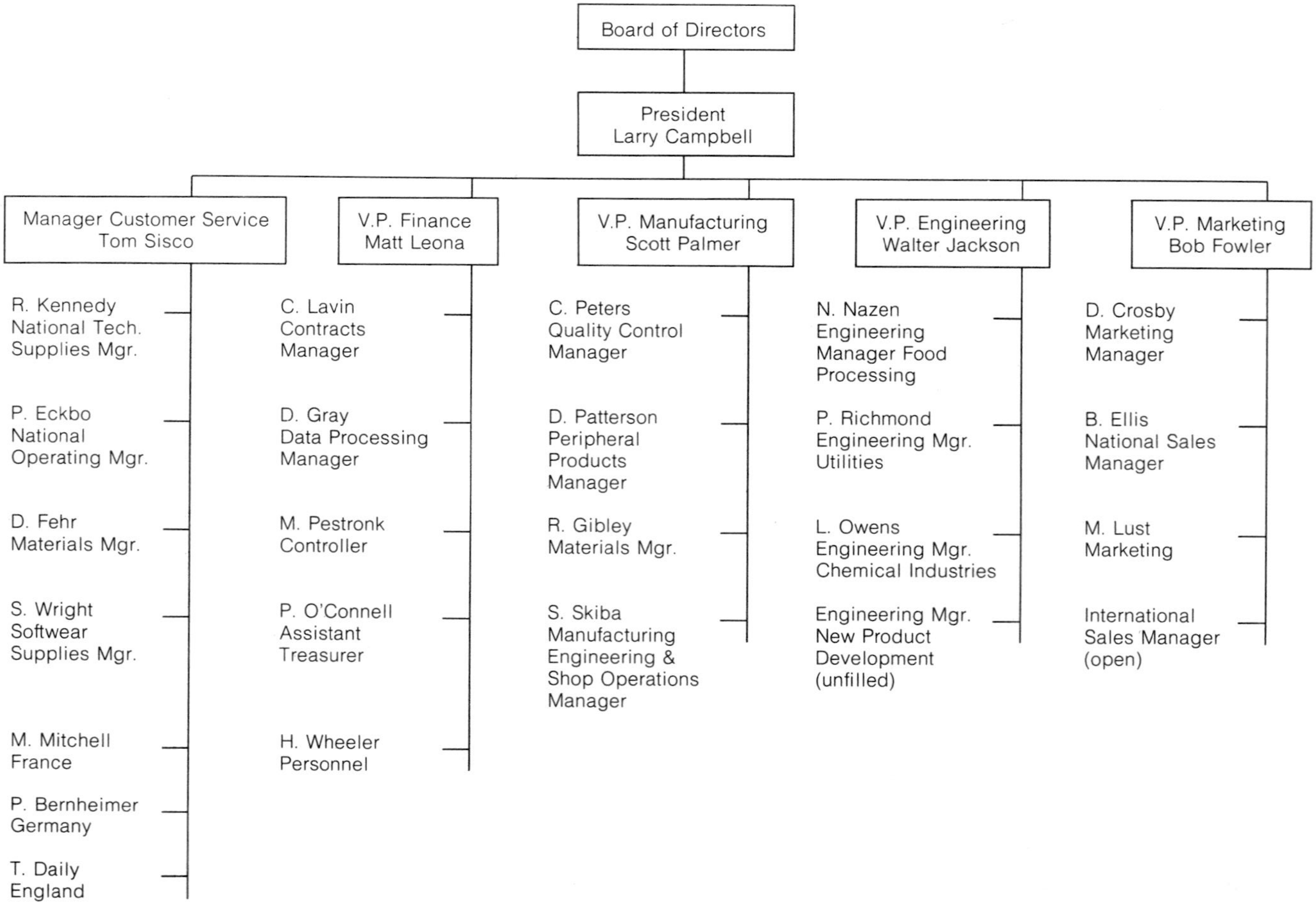

Board of Directors

President
Larry Campbell

Manager Customer Service
Tom Sisco

- R. Kennedy
  National Tech.
  Supplies Mgr.
- P. Eckbo
  National
  Operating Mgr.
- D. Fehr
  Materials Mgr.
- S. Wright
  Softwear
  Supplies Mgr.
- M. Mitchell
  France
- P. Bernheimer
  Germany
- T. Daily
  England

V.P. Finance
Matt Leona

- C. Lavin
  Contracts
  Manager
- D. Gray
  Data Processing
  Manager
- M. Pestronk
  Controller
- P. O'Connell
  Assistant
  Treasurer
- H. Wheeler
  Personnel

V.P. Manufacturing
Scott Palmer

- C. Peters
  Quality Control
  Manager
- D. Patterson
  Peripheral
  Products
  Manager
- R. Gibley
  Materials Mgr.
- S. Skiba
  Manufacturing
  Engineering &
  Shop Operations
  Manager

V.P. Engineering
Walter Jackson

- N. Nazen
  Engineering
  Manager Food
  Processing
- P. Richmond
  Engineering Mgr.
  Utilities
- L. Owens
  Engineering Mgr.
  Chemical Industries
- Engineering Mgr.
  New Product
  Development
  (unfilled)

V.P. Marketing
Bob Fowler

- D. Crosby
  Marketing
  Manager
- B. Ellis
  National Sales
  Manager
- M. Lust
  Marketing
- International
  Sales Manager
  (open)

EXHIBIT 4   Datavision (A) Personnel Profiles

Larry Campbell: President, 38 years old. Dr. Campbell received a BS, MS, and Ph.D. in Engineering from Berkeley. During his graduate studies, Dr. Campbell consulted for several organizations in the area of process control. After a brief period as a professor at Berkeley he went to work in research at Lincoln Labs at MIT. He worked there for two years and founded Datavision in 1969. Dr. Campbell is a member of Datavision's Board of Directors.

Bob Fowler: V.P., Marketing, 37 years old. Mr. Fowler received an undergraduate degree from Fordham and an MBA from New York University. After his graduate education he went to work for Exxon, then Pitney Bowes in Sales. He was recruited by a search firm and came to Datavision in 1972. Fowler is also a member of Datavision's Board of Directors.

Walter Jackson: V.P., Engineering, 36 years old. Jackson received a BS in Engineering at the University of Arkansas. He continued his education in engineering at the University of Illinois and received a Ph.D. After finishing his doctorate Jackson went to work at MIT, stayed there for one year and left to begin Datavision in 1969. He is a member of Datavision's Board of Directors.

Scott Palmer: V.P., Manufacturing, 38 years old. Mr. Palmer received a BS in Engineering at the University of Rhode Island. He continued his education at Wharton and earned an MBA. After graduate school Mr. Palmer went to work for General Electric in manufacturing where he worked for 10 years, before being recruited and joining Datavision in 1973. Mr. Palmer is also a member of the Board of Directors.

Matt Leona: V.P., Finance, 39 years old. Leona earned a BS in Electrical Engineering from Case Western Reserve and an MBA from Harvard. He went to work for IBM directly out of Harvard, in finance and pricing. He stayed with IBM for several years before joining and working with an investment banking firm for one year. His next job involved venture capital work at General Electric. While at GE he invested GE's and his own money in Datavision. He became a member of the Board of Directors in 1975, left GE to join Datavision.

Tom Sisco: Manager, Customer Service, 34 years old. Sisco earned a BA from St. Anselms College, went to work in the Peace Corps and then spent 8 years as a manager at the United Parcel Service Company. Sisco and Campbell were neighbors and friends. Sisco was personally recruited to Datavision by Campbell.

EXHIBIT 5   Datavision (A) Personnel Profile

R. David Brennan: 38 years old. Brennan received a BA in psychology at the College of Wooster, an MS, and a Ph.D. from Case Institute of Technology. His Ph.D. was in Organizational Behavior. In 1966 he began working as a self-employed consultant in the area of organizational training and development. He has worked in a variety of settings including large and small businesses, government and community agencies, and educational and health institutions. Simultaneously, since 1967, Brennan has been on the faculty of the Whittemore School of Business and Economics at the University of New Hampshire. He has taught a variety of courses in the organizational behavior area. In 1977 he was promoted to full professor. At that time he decided to work primarily as a consultant but is still affiliated with the University as an adjunct professor. Brennan has had additional business experience. Between 1973 and 1975, while on leave from UNH, Brennan was employed by Digital Equipment Corporation in Switzerland as the European Personnel Manager.

EXHIBIT 6   Datavision (A) Consolidated Operations Report Quarterly Comparison

	Second Quarter FY 78			Second Quarter FY 77		
	Budget	Actual	Percent	Budget	Actual	Percent
Revenues:						
System and Upgrade Revenue	$4,466,000	$3,986,298	90.4%	$3,300,000	$3,294,611	89.6%
Customer Funded Eng. Revenue	478,000	423,405	9.6	467,000	382,761	10.4
Total	4,944,000	4,409,703	100.0	3,767,000	3,677,372	100.0
Less Discounts—Syst. & U/G	401,000	224,445	4.9	343,500	319,006	8.2
—Cust. Fund. Eng	43,000	21,659	.5			
Net AGS Revenue	4,500,000	4,163,599	82.8	3,423,500	3,358,366	86.9
Customer Services	774,000	800,249	15.9	434,000	438,160	11.3
Application Development	138,000	58,526	1.2	52,500	66,586	1.7
Color Plotter	37,000	—		—	—	
Other Revenue	—	4,693	.1	—	4,584	.1
Total Revenue	5,449,000	5,027,067	100.0	3,910,000	3,867,696	100.0
Cost of Sales:						
System and Upgrade at Standard	1,696,000	1,677,761	33.4	1,400,000	1,441,325	37.3
Manufacturing Variances	—	106,944	2.1	—	(53,933)	(1.4)
Customer Funded Engineering	304,000	257,798	5.1	231,000	254,251	6.6
Customer Services	810,568	764,647	15.2	423,918	422,995	10.9
Application Development	103,352	32,375	.7	52,987	57,562	1.5
Color Plotter	97,503	111,299	2.2	—	—	
Total Cost of Sales	3,011,423	2,950,824	58.7	2,107,905	2,122,200	54.9
Gross Profit	2,437,577	2,076,243	41.3	1,802,095	1,745,496	45.1

Operating Expenses:

Engineering,						8.1
Marketing,						16.4
Corporate Administration,						7.7
Other	1,797,620	1,829,601	36.4	1,223,754	1,246,904	32.2
Income from Operations	639,957	246,642	4.9	578,341	498,592	12.9
Interest Expense	79,600	41,059	.8	84,100	83,639	2.2
Foreign Currency Loss (Gain)	—	8,445	.2	—	(3,397)	(.1)
Income Before Tax Provision	560,357	197,138	3.9	494,241	418,350	10.8
Provision for Income Taxes	297,000	135,000	2.7	243,000	209,000	5.4
Net Income	$ 263,357	$ 62,138	1.2	$ 251,241	$ 209,350	5.4
Net Income Per Share	$ .14	$ .03		$ .18	$ .15	

The May Department Stores Company (A)

I was hired by Stanley Goodman in 1967 to bring professional management to the May Company. At that time Stanley said we'd have an MBO program in place in 3 years; I said somewhere between 6 and 7. That was 9 years ago—and we're not done yet.

In May 1976, Dave Babcock, Chairman of the Board of the May Department Stores Company, reflected on the progress of his program to introduce professional management into the May organization. Recognized as the "father of MBO" in retailing, Babcock employed his own version of Management by Objectives, which he described as "a simple, organized approach to the manager's job." Babcock was preparing for a second time to lead MBO seminars for top management at each of May's twelve discount and department store companies. In reviewing his thoughts on MBO, he tried to assess a number of issues: how far down into the May organization the program had extended since his first seminars in 1967; what the present level of commitment was to MBO in the store companies; and what implementation problems still had to be addressed.

BACKGROUND OF THE MAY COMPANY

The May Company operated in five areas of retailing: department stores, discount stores, catalog showroom stores, shopping centers, and trading stamps. (See Exhibit 1 for size and location of May's companies.)

With 1975 sales of $2.017 billion and earnings of $67 million (See Exhibit 2 for May's ten-year financial performance), the May Department Stores Company was the nation's second largest department store organization. In 1976, the May companies had 59,000 employees, an increase of 4,000 over the previous year. May's management accounted for 12 percent of the total employment, and salesworkers for 49 percent; the remainder were sales supporting employees.

The May Company utilized a tandem structure (i.e., a team composed of a chairman and a president) for the top management of most of its retail operations. According to Babcock, the ideal tandem would have one top manager (termed a principal in retailing) with a strong administrative or sales supporting background and a second with a strong merchandising background. In the first corporate tandem, initiated in 1972, Babcock was President and Stanley Goodman, the veteran merchant who hired him in 1967, was Chairman. When Goodman retired in 1976, Babcock became Chairman and Dave Farrell, merchant and president from one of the May companies, became President. (See Exhibit 3 for a typical store company organization chart.)

THE COMPANY IN 1967

Dave Babcock described the May Company as he found it in 1967 and the history of his initial contract with Stanley Goodman:

> By 1967, when Stanley Goodman took over the presidency, the earnings per share had dropped from $3.10 in 1966 to $2.50 in 1967. Stanley knew that he had to change the company's merchandising mix and make it more fashion-conscious. He also had to improve operations. But in order to do these things, he had to totally revamp the management of the company. So he called me at the Dayton Company, where for 17 years I held the position of Vice-President of Personnel. During that time I had introduced professional management and my MBO system. Stanley asked if I would come to May and help him get the job done.
>
> Before I took the job, Stanley made two commitments: first, to develop the most professionally managed retail organization in the country; second, that all of the principals (presidents and chairmen) of all of the May Company stores would attend the American Management Association's six-day Management Course for Presidents. I asked for this stipulation because I wanted to make certain all of the company presidents understood what I meant when I talked about professional management. I agreed to join the May Company as a Vice-President for Organization Planning and Development, and as a member of the Executive Committee and the Board of Directors. On March 13, 1967, I joined the May Company.

Dave Babcock described the organization's problems as he saw them in 1967:

> Until the middle '60's the May Company was, with a few exceptions, dominated by highly profitable "one-man" stores run by strong, individualistic merchants. These men were very good at manning one downtown store, but didn't know much about how to maximize opportunities for growth in branch stores. There was little or no growth of managers inside the corporation and little mobility of executives within it. There were three corporate offices, and virtually no long range planning.
>
> Personnel practices were unsophisticated. There was no manpower planning and no one knew on a corporate basis what our manpower "inventory" was. There was a complete bypass of supervisory levels in salary and performance appraisals. Store presidents and general merchandise managers would review a buyer's performance, leaving the divisional merchandise manager to whom the buyer reported completely out of the picture. In most stores, bonuses were based on a formula related to that **307**

year's profit dollar and there was no distinction between a quality profit—which means one that was achieved while maintaining a high level of store and merchandise quality—and a short term profit that was based on merchandising and service level policies that would end up hurting a store image over time.

In 1967, the company was still dominated by career merchants—in the traditional sense. The contrast between them and the newer breed was illustrated by one of the company's executives:

Today's multi-store culture means that demands on buyers are more complex, that they need more sophisticated business skills. The old-time merchants operated by instinct and experience in a kind of general store atmosphere. They didn't need EDP to tell them when to reorder—they could see, feel, touch their merchandise. They knew it was time to reorder when they saw an empty shelf or a dwindling supply of something. It wasn't important for them to be skillful in communicating with their employees because they made their decisions independently: they determined both the quantity and quality of merchandise for their relatively small group of consumers. The one-store environment meant they didn't have to determine what, or how much of an item would sell at Store A versus Store B. They didn't have to understand rate of sale by item by store or how to balance stocks in a multi-store operation. They were independent, and they were generalists.

One of the company's buyers also commented on the traditional merchants:

I think the days of the fly-by-the-seat-of-your-pants merchants are gone. I've seen older buyers who bought by their gut feeling, because they liked something, and I think all merchants have do some of that. But today we're more scientific people, we're better educated, we're a different breed, especially the younger executives. We do things for a reason, scientifically. It's important to me that I have some basis on which to make decisions rather than I *feel* this is going to be a good item. I've never been very good at making decisions on gut feel.

BABCOCK'S MBO

The MBO program introduced at the May Company was a management technique that brought the employee and his or her supervisor together to agree on work to be done for the coming year. The MBO process involved four steps, each initiated by the employee and then discussed and negotiated with his or her supervisor.

1. A job description was formulated detailing responsibilities and authority.
2. Objectives for the job were determined annually. This process included specifying performance standards that stated clearly when each responsibility was being satisfactorily met, and establishing dates for the periodic review of progress in meeting objectives. (See Exhibit 4 for a buyer's sample objectives.)
3. Work progress and review meetings were held throughout the year, sometimes quarterly, sometimes less often. If necessary, objectives were revised.
4. Results were measured against the standards and objectives set and against the results of other retail companies. The employee initiated his or her own review by

providing the supervisor with a written self-appraisal of how well or poorly objectives had been met. The self-appraisal was reviewed in a meeting between the supervisor and the employee after which the supervisor wrote an evaluation of the employee. The supervisor discussed the evaluation with his or her own supervisor before it was presented to the employee.

The MBO program involved a time commitment for everyone. Corporate planners and members of the executive committee developed corporate objectives and determined each store company's contribution to the overall corporate objectives. One month was reserved out of the corporate and store company calendars for the review of each of the store companies' previous year's performance and its objectives for the coming year. For an individual manager, writing and negotiating objectives with a supervisor might take as long as four meetings spread over several weeks. Time was also allotted for progress and review meetings throughout the year and for the self-appraisal meeting at year-end.

In addition to a commitment of time, the MBO program called for specific and, for many people, new forms of behavior. The process of negotiating objectives required a willingness on the part of the supervisor and the subordinate to confront differences of opinion. Both were responsible for the objective: the subordinate manager for its achievement, the supervisor for ensuring that the objective was consistent with corporate and store company objectives. The supervisor was also responsible for assisting the subordinate in achieving the objective. Both, therefore, had to be fully committed to the objectives they finally agreed on. Many newly promoted managers also had to learn how to calculate and work with a variety of statistical measures of performance. Finally, all managers had to learn the process of self-appraisal; that is, how to evaluate their own performance in an objective fashion and to recognize their strengths and weaknesses. The self-appraisal process also required managers to acknowledge and discuss differences between their own performance assessment and the supervisor's evaluation.

May's Introduction to Professional Management

Within two months of Babcock's arrival, Stanley Goodman and two other May principals attended the American Management Association's Course for Presidents. Goodman's reaction was enthusiastic: "This is great, Dave, but we're already wondering how we can get this down to people who report to us." Between March and October 1967, Babcock supervised three levels of executive training as well as a program for buyers:

1. Store principals from all of May's operating divisions were sent to the AMA Presidents' Course.
2. Seventy corporate and company vice-presidents attended three-day seminars that had been created by Babcock and Fred Schwartz, head of the University of Wisconsin's Management Institute. Designed as a "poor man's AMA presidents' course," participants included operating vice-presidents, personnel vice-presidents, controllers, and general merchandise managers. According to Babcock, "damn few" of the vice-presidents had been very excited about attending the seminars, but in the end, their reactions were identical to Goodman's: "How can I get this down to my people?"
3. The response to the vice-presidents' enthusiasm was the development by Babcock and Jack Boyd, his new assistant, of a three-day middle management seminar, which 400 employees ultimately attended. The middle managers, who reported directly to corporate or company vice-presidents, were exposed "not just to MBO, but to all of professional management." Members participated in groups of 30–40 each from **309**

different store companies and included divisional merchandise managers, downtown store and branch store managers, assistants to vice-presidents of personnel, control, promotion, and advertising, and middle managers from the May Merchandising Corporation in New York. Jack Boyd described the process of the seminar:

> There were three elements of professional management that we wanted to introduce: job descriptions, standards of performance, and objectives. First, Dave talked about the three elements. Then we divided the group into small work groups by job category and asked them to come up with examples of each of the three elements, which they wrote on transparencies. We asked for a volunteer to show his group's transparency for one of the elements and then the whole group discussed it. Having a seminar group that had representatives of various functions lengthened the process considerably: people had to learn the specifics of the different jobs. But, we got a lot of side benefits from bringing all of those people together.

> There was almost no controversy or disagreement with MBO that showed up during the seminars, but people's response to Dave was mixed. On the one hand he was seen as a real hero on a white horse. People felt his strong personal interest in MBO, and they saw his involvement in the seminar as a signal of top management interest in the system. On the other hand, since Dave *was* top management, people felt they had to be on "top behavior." So they might not have said *all* that they were thinking.

Babcock described his approach to the middle management seminars:

> I gave eleven seminars in 1967, and doing them gave me a fantastic view of the 400 people who were really the guts of our business. Also, this was really my chance to get across my thinking and philosophy. I did a lot more than just talk about MBO. I talked about professional management and how MBO tied into it. I talked about personnel issues such as salary administration and college recruitment. I talked about management development, McGregor's Theory X and Theory Y, and some of Peter Drucker's concepts.

> As for resistance to the professional management approach, I didn't see a single sign. The most typical response was "I can see that this is going to be the first time that my boss and I agree on what the priorities are!" Also, you have to understand that this was a corporation in which the stores wanted to have little or nothing to do with the corporate image. They all considered their own image better than the corporate image. This was the first time most of them had met as a corporate group, and I believe that it was like a breath of fresh air to them. People were thinking, "My God, maybe we are going to do some of the management things that we know other companies do." There was also a bit of halo effect. I was new to the company—an outsider—and already had a reputation in the industry as someone who understood professional management. And I had come from Dayton's, a company with an excellent reputation.

4. A final step in the 1967 introduction of professional management and MBO was a one and one-half day seminar for buyers, which Jack Boyd presented on site at each of the May Company stores.

The First MBOs

The culmination of these introductory actions was to write in October 1967 the first corporate and company MBOs for 1968. All management personnel through the middle management level were involved. Gerald Boyne, a Vice-President—General Merchandise Manager, who was involved in the initial objective setting, reported:

> In doing the thing for the first time we tried to move too quickly. Instead of one or two good, solid objectives we just set out the whole lot. And we never had any choice. Once MBO setting was started, you *had* to write objectives.
>
> Still, writing my first MBO wasn't very hard at all. At the time, we used the same financial statistics that we used to evaluate performance at year-end: sales volume, gross margin on sales, turnover, etc. What was new was the chance to discuss with your boss what you thought you could do from *your* point of view. That was different.

Many managers felt that the generally positive reaction to the MBO program was largely due to its usefulness for a business as quantifiable as retailing. Richard Sherwood and David Elmo, two store company presidents, commented:

> In this business we get a report card every day in the form of our sales reports, which means that we have a lot of ways of statistically measuring progress. This is important because in writing MBOs you have to be very specific and get measurable objectives.
>
> Also, MBO is inherently a much fairer program for determining compensation than what the old-time retailers used. There used to be pre-set formulas for bonuses, like one percent of your increase in sales for the year. But that was inequitable, because there was no way to take into account market changes over which you had no control. MBO lets you use all of the statistics, but you can add to your evaluation an understanding of how well an individual did given the market in his area. But it's still hard to use MBO to evaluate performance in functions for which there aren't good statistical measures, like advertising. MBO is strongest where performance is measurable—it's not as effective in what Dave Babcock calls weasel areas.

The sales supporting side's view of MBO was related by Mike Wittrup, a Vice-President for Operations:

> The response to MBO was very favorable from the start. There had never been any monetary incentive for sales supporting to do well before, because traditionally in retailing it was the merchants who were measured by profit dollars and had bonuses tied to profit. The performance of store managers and other operations people who control expenses and sales volume was never separated from the profit performance of the store, which is a function of the merchant's buying skill and the mark-downs they decide to take. So sales supporting people were being penalized for bad profit years for which the merchants were responsible. MBO gave us a way of separating out our achievement from the profit fate of the store. It also gave us an inroad to being part of management. And by separating out what we needed to do, it helped us attain our goals.

Bob Barnett, a Vice-President—GMM, commented on the necessity for credibility in tying MBO to compensation:

> I think it's a great way of making sure that people are judged fairly—but that's also one of the possible weaknesses of MBO. If a person is not evaluated properly on the basis of his MBO it can destroy his whole belief in the system. Recently someone who **311**

had done poorly on his MBOs was better rewarded than a number of people who had done well on theirs, which illustrates how we sometimes compensate people more on their potential than on their performance. If a person is remunerated for a bad performance he ends up laughing at MBO and that kind of news travels fast.

Babcock described some of the problems that cropped up in writing the first MBOs:

We started out with eight corporate objectives to which each store company's principals would add eight company objectives, to which each manager would probably add another eight objectives of his own. No one could work with twenty-four objectives.

We also learned that developing standards of performance wasn't as easy as it looked. We were weak in having the tools to measure standards. For example, a store manager might have an objective to control shortage, but if he didn't have accurate, separate stock records, there was no way to measure his results.

Revamping Management

As part of the program to introduce professional management, Dave Babcock also began in 1967 to recruit new top-level executives for May's store companies, a task that had been established as one of his major responsibilities in his contract with Goodman. With twenty years' experience as a personnel executive in retailing, Babcock was well prepared for the job of rebuilding the May Company's management.

I knew everybody in retailing, and I knew where the people were that I wanted. So Stanley and I set up two rules: number one, we didn't hire anyone we didn't know anything about. And number two, we didn't hire anyone who was looking for a job. If somebody's looking for a job, you don't know if they're looking because they're unhappy or because they were fired. You can always quit and get a job in this business. But if you're fired, it's different, and it explains why you really have to be careful about who you hire.

Between 1967 and 1970, May's management was almost completely rebuilt. Eleven of twelve store companies had new presidents and new general merchandise managers. Babcock described the criteria he used for their selection:

One of the things I decided to gamble on was hiring people who were taking a big jump. For example, instead of taking an Executive Vice-President of Merchandising and promoting him, I'd find a good soft-line GMM and make him a store company president. The lower-level GMMs were more in the age bracket I wanted, and also I knew I'd have a better chance of attracting the younger people in retailing. I also wanted managers who were easier to train and not as set in their ways. We sent each newly hired or promoted principal to the American Management Association's Course for Presidents—something we're still doing.

The approach we used in recruiting was to sell the hell out of them on what we were going to try to do with the May Company. We did our best to convince them that this was going to be a professionally run organization. MBO was definitely part of what we sold them. Everyone we talked with knew that we were going to operate with very clearly established objectives and that we were going to evaluate results against those objectives. There's no way that the May Company could have hired the people we hired from 1967 on without the MBO program.

312

In addition to emphasizing the benefits of professional management and the MBO program, the company also began a trend of higher compensation to attract and keep its top executives. Also, publicity in retail trade journals provided a great asset in recruiting. Sam Feinberg, who wrote for *Women's Wear Daily* (the major trade publication of the retail industry) and who was a friend of Dave Babcock's, based a series of articles on his attendance at one of the three-day seminars in 1967. In the first article, "May Company Is Building Up Its Human Resources," Feinberg described the range of training programs offered. "May Company's New Direction: Professional Participation" was a blow-by-blow account of one of the middle management training seminars. The third article featured a model job description for a store president taken from Babcock's manual on professional management. The final article detailed the May Company's plans for the further implementation of the professional management program, which included extending it to the buyer and assistant buyer level by Spring 1968 and having "total programs" in individual stores by 1970.

Babcock commented on his use of the articles and their effect:

> The decision to allow Feinberg to attend the seminars was deliberate. I wanted retailers to know what we were doing, and I wanted people to understand Stanley's and my commitment to run May in as professional a manner as possible. The articles opened up a lot of doors to me and several people got interested in coming to the May Company as a result of them.

The appointment of new company principals and general merchandising managers resulted in many top management changes in each store company. Some existing store presidents who were merchants functioned effectively in the administrative side of the tandem (as chairmen) and provided a smooth management transition. Some older managers were given short-term assignments until they reached normal retirement age or elected early retirement. At any rate, in a reasonably smooth manner, all of the company presidents of 1967 had been replaced by 1970.

The appointment of new company principals also set a new standard for other top management positions. By 1976, of the thirty-six operating vice-presidents, controllers, personnel directors (three per store company), only two were in their original positions.

The middle and lower management levels were also characterized by change. In addition to the typically high turnover rate in the retailing industry as a whole, the May Company's growth contributed to the creation of new or specialized positions and increased mobility for many managers. In 1975, for example, the overall turnover was 16.1 percent, and 30 percent of the company's buyers were new at their jobs. Tenure in some lower management positions such as merchandise counselor or store manager might be as brief as five or six months.

This continuing turnover in management positions had some negative effects on efforts to implement the MBO program. According to one DMM:

> Interim promotions tend to wipe out formal objectives and the whole evaluation process. After five years in this company I had my first review this April. Every other time my promotion *was* my review. And when I had my review, it wasn't even with the boss I'd been working for all year. In fact, I've found that in this business you always seem to be reviewed by someone who had nothing to do with your performance. I've had seven bosses in five years.

Positions were also redesigned as part of Babcock's program, particularly that of personnel director. Historically, they (with few exceptions) had reported to the operating   **313** vice president. To upgrade this position, the new people reported directly to the chairman or to the president, and their responsibilities were augmented.

The final step in organizational restructuring was at the Board of Directors' level. Outside directors of top quality were recruited and by 1976 there were four outside directors who played major roles. MBO was also used with the Board: members wrote objectives as well as an appraisal of year-end results, which were fully discussed.

IMPLEMENTATION OF THE MBO PROGRAM: 1968–1976

In addition to the wholesale turnover of management in the store companies by 1970, changes in top corporate management and in May's financial performance continued through 1976. In 1969, Dave Babcock rose to senior executive vice president and chief administrative officer, and in 1972, when Stanley Goodman was elected chairman, he became president of the May Company. The downward financial trend which had begun in 1967 had not halted by 1970, as Babcock reported to a group of senior executives at a May Company store:

> Under the brilliant leadership of Stanley Goodman and myself, May's EPS dropped from $3.10 in 1966 to $1.88 in 1970. We swore at that time that that was the lowest we'd go; and our earnings have been climbing ever since.

Corporate Involvement in Implementation

After its 1967 introduction, responsibility for implementing the MBO system was transferred to the store companies. Corporate involvement was generally limited to producing training materials (e.g., videotapes) and to disseminating an MBO manual written by Dave Babcock.

When the first objectives were set in 1967, each company store designed its own forms, a deliberate decision by Babcock:

> I decided to start out with no forms, because I guessed that if I started out with a complete system we would never get to first base trying to introduce MBO. So we got twelve different forms and twelve different ways of doing MBO. It wasn't until 1974 that standard forms were introduced throughout. Most of the ones we ended up with were developed by the companies, including our format for writing narrative-type objectives. Only a few of the forms we use today are mine.

Each year after 1968, corporate objectives were written and reviewed. The store companies wrote objectives on the basis of the corporate objectives, and in individual stores objectives were written through at least the vice-president level. In March of each year, the previous year's accomplishments were reviewed and the next year's objectives were determined. Store company principals then sent Babcock and Goodman their own self-appraisals and objectives and those of their managers. Each pair of principals then went to corporate headquarters to review their goals and hear Goodman and Babcock's reactions to them.

Wendell Mayer, Chairman of one of the May companies, commented on the dilemma inherent in the goal-setting process:

314   Early on, we didn't have a good handle on how to have top-down objectives. Two or three years ago objectives were written from the bottom up and we ended up with a hodge podge that didn't add up to the corporate objectives. Now the company's management arrive at company objectives, and what the president and chairman say they'll do has to go down the line. Our MBOs are more top-down than they were before.

Another point of view was expressed by a DMM:

Our MBO program is still not on the right track because we don't set our objectives the right way. Objectives should be mutually agreed on, but here they are set from the top down, and where the objectives start is not open for discussion. There's no opportunity for personal input—we say we have input, but we're handed our objectives. I think when you're working with mature businessmen you should work from the bottom up.

Although Babcock perceived no resistance to the introduction of professional management during the 1967 seminars, he did find skepticism when it came time to evaluate year-end performance:

The resistance came from a lot of old timers who, in effect, were saying, "Oh, Christ, this is the fourteenth program that someone has put in with a bang! Let's not get too excited about it—it will go away." It took a while for them to realize that it wasn't going away. The first time they realized it was in 1969 when I said, "O.K., we're ready to appraise results against our 1968 objectives. And here's how we're going to do it: you're going to have one day with us, *your* day, when we want you to come in and tell us how you think you did."

The first year we formally appraised results we fell into a great trap that I had fallen into years ago as a personnel director, which was to only appraise objectives. You might have nine responsibilities on your job description, but your objectives would only be on the four of them that would make the biggest impact on profits. *This* year's profits. So that's what we appraised. But some of those other responsibilities could be damned important. So, after we went through about two years of appraising only objectives we learned to first appraise the objectives and then to appraise the whole job.

The other big mistake I made was in emphasizing a standard of performance for every aspect of every job description. People struggled to develop standards, but the whole process just confused them.

Despite the continuous use of the MBO program after 1967, Dave Babcock acknowledged a lull in corporate involvement in implementing the professional management program:

I let the companies flounder for a couple of years. Having me do the 1967 seminars was a big plus. And having me continue to be the guiding light on MBO was a real plus. The minus was I didn't have the time to do it. I was still a hobby rider. I wouldn't turn MBO and the whole professional management thing loose, because I wanted to do it myself. At the same time, though, I was busy recruiting and hiring probably twenty people at salaries in excess of $75,000 to $150,000 a year. I just didn't have time to go to the store companies and sit down and say, "Where are you having trouble with objectives?" or "Don't overproceduralize and get them so complicated." **315**

Stewart Clark, a store company principal, described what he saw as signs of increasing top corporate interest in the MBO program after 1973:

> During the last three or four years, I've sensed a new initiative that's been gaining momentum. There are lots of new personnel directors now who are really the glue that holds the MBO program together. And now, if corporate doesn't think our objectives are strong enough, or if they don't back up total corporate objectives, they send our objectives back for us to redo. Corporate has also developed new forms which ask for specific information about how and when objectives will be attained.

Direct corporate involvement in implementing the professional management program was recommended in 1973 when the first companywide training program since 1967 was held for ninety branch-store managers. Vice-presidents of branch stores served as leaders for the three-day seminars, and both Goodman and Babcock participated in several sessions.

In August 1974, two articles on the May Company appeared in Sam Feinberg's *Women's Wear Daily* column. The first, "May's Way of Life," described the MBO program and summarized its introduction. In the article Babcock asserted: "If we two were not running the company today, we believe that Management by Objectives would continue as a management style." The article concluded with Goodman's comment, "All we can report is that we in May's top management have embraced it, each of our companies sees the value of playing the game, and it's worked out very well for us."

The second article described May's tandem structure and reported on the personnel changes in the company, including Goodman's plans to retire in 1976, and Babcock's promotion to the chairmanship at that time.

Training in the MBO System

Because corporate involvement was minimal, approaches to training varied from store to store. Some companies held seminars for managers at a single function level; others relied principally on written materials. (See Exhibit 5 for an excerpt from one store company's training materials.)

Beyond the formal training session or materials distributed, most newly promoted managers learned about the MBO system from their supervisors (one of their formal responsibilities since 1968). As a first step the new manager would be given a copy of her predecessor's and supervisor's objectives for the year. She would then be asked to develop her own objectives, occasionally immediately, most often after a month or two on the job. The process of writing objectives was one way of learning about the new job, as Joe Stone, a buyer, explained:

> When you sit down to write objectives you will learn things about the retail business in a couple of days that took me years to learn. For example, I might have an objective to reduce inventory shrinkage, but how do I know how *much* I can reduce shrinkage? So I have to start asking questions to find out what affects shrinkage—what I can do to reduce it and how much of a reduction is reasonable.

The usefulness of supervisor training in writing objectives depended on the supervisor's understanding of the objective-setting process. Lack of understanding could lead to "incomplete" objectives as Bill Matthew, Vice-President for Operations, explained:

There are definite tricks to learning to write objectives, and I'd say it takes at least three years to get good at it. The most important thing is to learn where the loopholes are. For example, it would be easy to achieve a high sales volume if you sacrificed gross margin, which means that a merchant's objective has to contain some sort of markdown and shortage objective. In the sales supporting group you would have the same situation if in writing an objective to increase credit sales you didn't include an objective stipulating that bad debt write-offs were not to exceed some percent of credit sales. You have to learn where the loopholes are.

The supervisor's attitude toward MBO affected the amount of training given and the commitment of subordinates to the program. Mark Jackson, a divisional merchandise manager, commented on his experience with the program:

The level of commitment to MBO varies widely among GMMs, and DMMs take their cues from their GMM about how important MBOs are. It took me four to eight days to develop my MBOs for one boss, who wanted very detailed objectives on volume, gross margin, presentation of merchandise, development of personnel, etc. My current boss and I wrote my objective in ten minutes; all he was interested in was volume and gross margin, he didn't really care about anything else.

MBO in Three May Company Stores

Because MBO was introduced simultaneously to all of the store companies, Babcock was interested in the differences in its application among them.

Store Company #1. This was a turn-around assignment for the new principals, who came from another May Company in 1974. After its introduction to all managers in 1967, the application of MBO had been checkered. It was soon eliminated at the buyer level, reportedly because of management's lack of belief in the system. Although store principals, vice-presidents, and some DMMs wrote objectives, by 1974 the system was not actively used or encouraged.

Soon after his arrival, the Chairman hired a new Vice-President for Personnel, who was made responsible for educating managers in the use of the system. Their goal was to bring all DMMs into the program within one year and all buyers within two years. Training meetings were held for DMMs in 1974 and 1975, and by 1976 all DMMs were writing objectives and formal MBO reviews were being instituted. Bonuses for achieving MBOs existed at the vice-presidential level and above, but were not used for middle management (though it was planned that they would eventually include all participants in the program). Plans to include buyers in the program were postponed for a year when, it was felt, DMMs would understand the program better. Also, the high degree of buyer turnover necessitated a more intensive training program than had initially been planned.

Bill Brown, Chairman:

May bought this company ten years ago, and its family managment wasn't focusing on any of the financial areas we try to achieve in. If nothing else, MBO lets people know what I think is important and what areas we have to concentrate on. While I did decide to go after the MBO program more actively and aggressively than the previous management, introducing MBO was not in the forefront of my mind. The real credit for making MBO a part of our normal management routines goes to the Vice-President of Personnel.

Ralph Pines, Vice-President—GMM:

We talk about a lot of things, but no one ever talks about objectives. Originally we were told that MBOs have to be reviewed quarterly, but we only review them annually, and even then there isn't a lot of discussion of them. MBO is basically a one-shot proposition here.

Store Company #2. A generally held perception at store company #2 was that interest in the MBO program had increased recently at both the corporate and the store company levels. Between 1967 and 1975 the store's involvement with the MBO program had been sporadic. Store company objectives had been written each year since 1967, but the seriousness with which the MBO program was regarded, particularly in the merchandising side of the organization, depended on the opinion of MBO held by the company's top executive. In 1975, the President departed. He was described as "more from the old school than the new school of professional management." Two local executives were promoted, one a self-described believer in MBO, and a second who was seen as "increasingly interested, particularly when he saw the results MBO could produce." Other executive changes took place and in 1976, only two of the eight DMMs and four of the eight branch store managers had been in their positions for over twelve months.

Buyers were first introduced to the MBO system in 1975. Training was left up to the GMMs and DMMs, some of whom held training meetings for the buyers who reported to them. Many, but not all, buyers wrote objectives for 1975. The goals of store managers were also formalized in 1975, and by 1976 all store managers and merchandise counselors had written objectives. 1975 was also the first year when written year-end self-appraisal of objectives was done by all members of management through the buyer level, a major accomplishment according to the Vice-President for Personnel. He hoped that discussions of self-appraisals would soon be instituted. In 1976 an MBO bonus for DMMs was introduced, providing as much as $5,000 for the accomplishment of their objectives.

Connie Howard, Buyer:

The sooner we really have an MBO program, the better the morale will be. The MBO program gives me a chance to put down in writing what I should be evaluated on at the end of the year. But so far I haven't seen any signs of real commitment to the program. There haven't been any presentations by management or any meetings about it. Our only information is in the bulletins we get. I'm really excited about what the MBO program could do, but it's still being treated as just another piece of paper.

Store Company #3. May's chain of discount department stores was started by the company in 1970. According to a store manager who had been with the chain since its creation, MBO was introduced to all of the managers "from day one." Objectives based on industry trends were written before a single store opened and were used to guide the new chain's development. Jack Boyd, who was promoted in 1970 to Vice-President for Personnel, described the new chain as a laboratory for the MBO program and "as a way of life for people who know no better because they know no other way to manage." The MBO program extended through store department managers and buyers in the merchandising side of the organization. Training was done by distributing a manual to new executives and by the new executive's supervisor. All elements of the MBO system were in use at all levels covered by the program: objectives, work progress reviews, self-appraisals, and

318 review of performance against objectives.

John Lundegard, President:

MBO gets a lot of emphasis here because I use the technique a lot and find it effective. The amount of use MBO gets depends on the people at the top of the company.

Jack Boyd, Vice-President for Personnel:

We have virtually no formalized training in MBO at this point. We have a memo and manual that we use for new executives, but we made a conscious decision to downplay MBO as something you just talk about. We just say, "Now here's the way you plan your work for the year and we call the plan 'objectives,' and here's how we review, it's called 'self-appraisal.'" In companies that made too much of MBO, the thing fell of its own weight. To work, MBO has to be a line activity—bosses have to use it. It's a way of life with us, which is why we don't have to do a lot of training: managers will learn how to use it because their supervisors use it.

DAVE BABCOCK'S 1976 TRAINING SEMINARS

The Need for Training

Dave Babcock retained control over the corporate personnel function until 1974, when he appointed Roy Paulsen, a 25-year veteran of Federated Department Stores, head of Operations and Personnel. He and Paulsen agreed on the need for a complete audit of the state of May's MBO program. Also, before his retirement, Goodman had asked Babcock to conduct a new round of training seminars at each of the store companies. He and Paulsen agreed on the need for the training seminars and decided to make the MBO audit part of the training process. Paulsen commented:

The degree of skill in doing MBO varies. Some of our companies do a great job of training on MBO, others do not. I received one set of objectives that was twenty-one pages of paper—that overwhelms you. And this person's MBOs were approved by his supervisor.

A lot of new executives have a wrong idea of what MBO is all about, and that's where it can break down. If you want to hire a high-level executive from the outside who does not have formal training in the system he won't understand it. And if he doesn't understand it, he can't ask his subordinates to use it.

Babcock felt that MBO was not being used as effectively as it could as a common training tool for new employees, and he saw its biggest potential contribution as a way of training new people in the specifics of their job and introducing them generally to how the May Company organizes its business. But Babcock wanted to work for a while with Dave Farrell, the newly elected President, before committing himself to conducting seminars in each of the department and discount store companies. After he felt confident that Farrell would continue to use the system, he agreed to conduct the seminars.

Executives in the store companies expressed different reactions and interpretation of Babcock's decision to conduct the MBO seminars. One buyer stated:

I have no doubt that the recent increase in interest in MBO that I've seen at our store is **319** because he's coming. Basically, it sounds to me like the corporation is set on making the MBO program work, and that Mr. Babcock's the club that will help them do it.

A vice-president of personnel saw the renewed corporate interest as a positive reaction by the company's principals:

I prefer to think that the reason Mr. Babcock is making his trips out to the stores is in response to a VP-Personnel meeting at which we expressed our strong desire to put MBO in our stores. We feel frustrated because we can't get any leverage on our principals to push MBO. My idea of utopia is having Dave Babcock come around to the stores talking MBO. What better reinforcement could we get?

A Typical Seminar

AT 9:00 on a Wednesday morning in 1976, fifty executives, from store principals to divisional merchandise managers and store managers from one of the May Company stores were assembled in a training room. In front of each of them was a name card and pad of paper. For many it would be the first time that they had seen Dave Babcock. He began:

I have two goals for the seminar today. One is to reinforce MBO and the concepts of professional management in general. Second, is to convince you that MBO is not a procedure piled on top of your job, but is just a simple way to do your job. In doing these seminars I'm the staff guy—I have no authority. When I walk out of here your President and Chairman will run things the way they want to, which is the way it should be. I'm not close enough to run a business. But, I do have some general concepts I'm going to try like hell to sell.

During the morning, Babcock lectured on a wide variety of topics: the history of the introduction of MBO into the May Company; a definition and description of the principles of professional management; a history of management and management techniques in American business; a description of the manager's job (planning, organizing, directing, controlling, appraising results); thoughts on motivation. During the afternoon he described the MBO process: creating job descriptions; setting objectives; defining performance standards; conducting work progress and review sessions; appraising results.

Babcock solicited audience response once during the seminar, when participants were asked to indicate which area of the manager's job they felt their store handled the worst. "Planning" received the most votes, and Babcock asked, "What element of planning are we missing? And I want to hear from a DMM or a store manager, not one of your principals." Two divisional merchandise managers pin-pointed the problem as stemming from the fact that planning moved from the top down, rather than the bottom up. Babcock asked how many people agreed, and then commented, "I see that people don't want to raise their hands. I promise I won't let the president or chairman look."

Throughout the day, Babcock expressed opinions on a wide range of issues, from his own philosophy of management to the relationship between MBO and the business environment. He stated:

As a top company, we don't have a lot of choice about our financial objectives. The multiple that determines our stock price depends on what the financial analysts say we'll do in the future. We have to meet the standards for performance that get set by the market if we are going to be a growth company. This means that the parameters of negotiation regarding our financial objectives are narrow. The only way for the corporation to make our numbers is for you guys to make your numbers. But how you decide to achieve your statistical objectives is negotiable, and that's where participation comes into the MBO process.

The seminar concluded with the distribution of the corporate questionnaire on the MBO program. Babcock anticipated that it would provide feedback for planning changes in the MBO system: what the program consisted of (i.e., which of the four steps of the MBO process were used); how far down in each store organization the MBO program reached; whether and in what way participants found the program useful; how effective the individual thought the MBO program in his company was; and in what areas of the program additional training seemed to be necessary.

EXHIBIT 1   The May Department Stores Company (A) May Company Divisions as of 1975

Store Companies	Principal Locations	Number of Stores
May Company	California	25
The Hecht Company	Washington D.C.	11
	Baltimore	7
Famous-Barr	St. Louis	10
Kaufman's	Pittsburgh	7
The May Company	Cleveland	7
Meier & Frank	Oregon	5
G. Fox & Co.	Hartford	5
The M. O'Neil Co.	Akron	9
May—D & F	Colorado	9
Strouss	Youngstown	9
May—Cohens	Florida	5
Venture Stores	St. Louis	11
(discount stores)	Kansas City	6
	Chicago	3
Consumer's Distributing Co.	N.Y.–N.J.–Conn. area	58
(catalog showroom stores)	San Francisco area	
May Shopping Centers		16
The Eagle Stamp Company		

Other Divisions

May Merchandising Corporation
   —market strategy advisor
May Department Stores International, Inc.
May Design and Construction Company

EXHIBIT 2   The May Department Stores Company (A) Ten Year Performance Record (thousands of dollars, except per share)

Operations Fiscal Years Ended:	January 31, 1976	February 1, 1975**	February 2, 1974*** [1]	February 3, 1973	January 29, 1972
Net Retail Sales	$2,004,057	$1,748,645	$1,574,102	$1,467,931	$1,310,798
Rental Revenues	13,309	11,297	10,963	10,053	7,280
Earnings before Income Taxes	134,719	93,680	98,208	97,730	86,667
Percent of Sales and Revenues	6.7%	5.3%	6.2%	6.6%	6.6%
Earnings	66,706	46,775	48,186	47,867	41,981
Percent of Sales and Revenues	3.3%	2.7%	3.0%	3.2%	3.2%
Dividends Paid on Common Stock	23,838	23,883	24,064	24,148	24,104
Earnings Retained in the Business	42,413	22,395	23,625	23,222	17,380
Capital Expenditures	77,717	91,967	70,767	53,724	52,338
Depreciation	41,119	33,944	30,360	28,567	26,702
Rentals of Real Property, Net	16,017	11,795	10,923	10,298	9,521
Interest and Debt Expense, Net	27,864	24,407	19,262	16,175	15,010
Per Common Share					
Net Earnings	$4.41	$3.08	$3.16	$3.13	$2.75
Dividends	1.60	1.60	1.60	1.60	1.60
Common Stockholders' Equity (Book Value)	35.64	32.84	31.28	29.68	28.20
Return on Common Stockholders' Beginning Equity	13.4%	9.8%	10.6%	11.1%	10.1%
Financial Position					
Accounts and Notes Receivable, Net	$427,227	$406,664	$377,142	$324,659	$293,519
Merchandise Inventories	261,247	193,118	186,826	195,519	186,370
Working Capital	373,574	343,770	323,514	327,157	281,600
Property, Plant and Equipment, Net	552,769	520,791	464,495	427,609	410,391
Long-Term Debt—Real Estate and Finance Subsidiaries	249,507	237,598	193,999	199,897	153,780
—Parent Company	114,426	118,047	123,547	78,406	90,713
Common Stockholders' Equity (Book Value)	530,843	487,821	466,983	447,161	424,094
Store Facilities					
Number of Stores—Department and Discount Stores	129	118	109	102	97
—Catalog Showroom Stores	58	57	53	—	—
Number of Square Feet of Store Space	29,900,000	28,400,000	27,200,000	25,500,000	24,800,000

**Net retail sales and interest and debt expense have been restated to include CD (see Note 9) in order to conform with 1975 presentation.

[1] Company changed to LIFO method of accounting.

Operations		January 30, 1971	January 31, 1970	February 1, 1969	January 31, 1968	January 31, 1967
Fiscal Years Ended:						
Net Retail Sales		$1,174,834	$1,134,237	$1,086,242	$1,017,014	$979,093
Rental Revenues		6,639	6,306	5,829	5,193	4,870
Earnings before Income Taxes		64,195	61,804	71,946	70,952	73,095
Percent of Sales and Revenues		5.4%	5.4%	6.6%	6.9%	7.4%
Earnings		31,873	28,919	34,006	36,287	38,416
Percent of Sales and Revenues		2.7%	2.5%	3.1%	3.6%	3.9%
Dividends Paid on Common Stock		24,111	24,164	23,856	23,748	23,584
Earnings Retained in the Business		7,264	4,257	9,106	11,309	14,180
Capital Expenditures		48,869	60,500	42,500	33,700	38,100
Depreciation		25,735	23,995	21,849	20,576	19,490
Rentals of Real Property		9,156	8,530	7,914	7,379	6,813
Interest and Debt Expense, Net		14,969	12,597	8,478	7,706	8,285
Per Common Share						
Net Earnings		$2.08	$1.88	$2.21	$2.36	$2.50
Dividends		1.60	1.60	1.60	1.60	1.57½
Common Stockholders' Equity (Book Value)		27.12	26.63	26.36	24.99	24.27
Return on Common Stockholders' Beginning Equity		7.8%	7.1%	8.8%	9.7%	10.7%
Financial Position						
Accounts and Notes Receivable, Net		$279,766	$280,186	$260,433	$239,605	$238,081
Merchandise Inventories		172,483	176,338	166,847	161,334	156,147
Working Capital		291,542	255,911	241,754	258,977	271,023
Property, Plant and Equipment, Net		387,553	368,361	334,416	319,023	310,419
Long-Term Debt—Real Estate and Finance Subsidiaries		151,934	99,447	57,538	60,067	63,642
—Parent Company		101,112	105,827	112,598	118,674	127,528
Common Stockholders' Equity (Book Value)		407,741	400,923	398,386	370,445	360,373
Store Facilities						
Number of Stores—Department and Discount Stores		89	85	84	78	75
—Catalog Showroom Stores		—	—	—	—	—
Number of Square Feet of Store Space		23,400,000	22,600,000	21,500,000	20,500,000	20,100,000

EXHIBIT 3   The May Department Stores Company (A) Typical Store Company Organization Chart

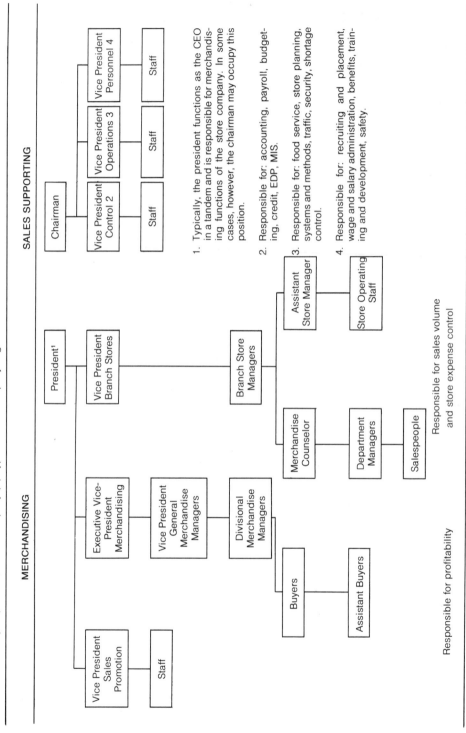

MERCHANDISING   SALES SUPPORTING

Chairman

President[1]

Vice President
Control 2 | Vice President
Operations 3 | Vice President
Personnel 4

Staff | Staff | Staff

Executive Vice-
President
Merchandising

Vice President
Sales
Promotion

Staff

Vice President
General
Merchandise
Managers

Vice President
Branch Stores

Divisional
Merchandise
Managers

Branch Store
Managers

Buyers

Merchandise
Counselor

Assistant
Store Manager

Assistant Buyers

Department
Managers

Store Operating
Staff

Salespeople

Responsible for profitability

Responsible for sales volume
and store expense control

1. Typically, the president functions as the CEO in a tandem and is responsible for merchandising functions of the store company. In some cases, however, the chairman may occupy this position.

2. Responsible for: accounting, payroll, budgeting, credit, EDP, MIS.

3. Responsible for: food service, store planning, systems and methods, traffic, security, shortage control.

4. Responsible for: recruiting and placement, wage and salary administration, benefits, training and development, safety.

EXHIBIT 4   The May Department Stores Company (A) Sample Objectives for Buyer

Obj. No.	Objective (Include Means of Measuring)	Specific Plan for Achieving (Include Completion Dates Where Applicable)	Touch Base Sessions Scheduled	Actual
1.	Improve existing, and further develop, private label program for Department "X" to produce a $45,000 sales increase over last year.	**SAMPLE FOR BUYER** 1. a) A list of those categories considered appropriate for private label consideration are submitted and approved by my GMM. (By March 1, 1974)	2/15/74	
		b) The market research has been completed and items for consideration have been sent out for laboratory analysis. (By April 1, 1974)	3/15/74	
		c) The laboratory results of product analysis are consistent with Venture's product label quality standards; thereafter private packaging will be developed by the Advertising Department by August 1, 1974.	6/15/74	
		d) Package designs are finalized and vendor commitments are made by September 1, 1974.	7/15/74	
		e) New labels have been designed and implemented. (By July 1, 1974)		
		f) Signing that improves product identification is implemented. (By March 1, 1974)		
		g) The store organization is supplied with a detailed schematic for product display. (By April 1, 1974)		
		h) An outline of the entire year's advertising program has been developed. (By March 1, 1974)		
		i) Increase private label sales of the "widget" line by 35% over last year.		

325

EXHIBIT 5   The May Department Stores Company (A) Guidelines for Preparing Personal Objectives

An objective is a statement of what *you* want to accomplish in the coming year for *your* specific area of responsibility. In other words, it describes the work to be performed in order to achieve your goals.

1. Gather pertinent data:
   a) Review the company objectives to be certain that your personal objectives will contribute to their completion.
   b) Review the statistical plans and budgets for your area of responsibility.
   c) Analyze the present weaknesses in your area.
   d) Consider the opportunities which will improve your operation.
   e) Consider, and include as you see fit, any appropriate personal development objectives that may or may not fall within your specific and immediate job responsibilities.

2. Some personal objectives will be primarily comprised of numerical goals (sales, margin, expenses, etc.) and others will be primarily verbal (training, special projects, operational, etc.). For both kinds, be certain that they are *verifiable* in some manner so that there can be no dispute as to whether or not they have been accomplished.

3. Avoid "weasel" words because they are not measurable. Avoid using the following or similar words or terms: acceptable, adequate, approximate, efficient, generally, maximum, minimum, normal, necessary, optimum, proper, reasonable, relatively, satisfactory.

4. Make the objectives "stretchy" so that their completion will represent your true capabilities. In other words, buffer your goals and dates realistically to allow for a safety factor. Remember, your annual appraisal is primarily based on the accomplishment of objectives. However, don't "shoot for the moon" to the point that your objectives become unrealistic.

5. The number of personal objectives generally will range from six to twelve; however, there is no "magic number" for acceptability.

6. Be sure that the combined objectives of the executives who report to you are compatible and that they collectively portray the major "thrusts" within your function.

7. Write objectives on the forms provided.
   a) Beside each personal objective, under the column headed, *"Specific Plan For Achieving"*, describe *what conditions will exist when the objective is completed.*
   b) Indicate specific means for measuring objectives and specific dates for the completion of each.
   c) Under the column headed, *"Touch Base Session"*, place a *tentative date* in the "Scheduled" section to review progress on the objective during the year.
   d) The *actual date* of the progress session should be entered when it is actually conducted.

8. Your personal objectives must be negotiated and subsequently approved by your supervisor and his/her supervisor (two levels).

9. After personal objectives have been negotiated and approved, one copy is to be retained by the individual and one copy by the immediate supervisor.

Corning Glass Works (B)
The Electronic Products Division

In January 1969 Tom Noles, Director of Organization Development for the corporation, met with Don Rogers, Vice President of the Electronics Products Division (EPD) to present his diagnosis of the problems facing Rogers' division. In July of 1968 Rogers had asked Noles to study his division to ascertain the root causes of a number of problems Rogers felt existed and to recommend solutions. The division's sales and profits had declined drastically in 1967 and 1968 from previous levels (see Exhibit 1) and severe cost-savings measures had been taken. Despite these measures, Rogers had been concerned about the continuation of fierce competition in the components market, low morale in the division, and the lack of mutual confidence and trust between groups which often led to conflicts that were difficult to resolve. He had been particularly concerned about the impact of poor relations between functional groups on business decisions, product development, and divisional performance as a whole.[1]

Noles and two members of his department had agreed to undertake a three month study of the division and to feedback the findings and recommendations. The study included several phases. In the first phase Noles and his associates became acquainted with EPD's business and the key members of the organization by sitting in on a variety of meetings held at the divisional and plant level. This included a two-day product development meeting held each month.[2] During this phase the consultants also had many informal conversations with individuals. In the second phase some 40 in-depth interviews were conducted with individuals at the top three levels of the organization in all functional areas and plants. The final phase involved the administration of a questionnaire aimed at measuring more precisely certain salient findings which were emerging from the interviews. The process had taken longer than anticipated and now four and one-half months after they started, Corning's Organizational Development (O.D.) department was ready

---

[1]See Corning Glass Works (A) for the situation in the Electronic Products Division in late 1968.

[2]Ibid.

with its diagnosis and recommendations. Flip charts were prepared and Noles was about to begin the presentation to Rogers. Bits and pieces of the internal consultant's observations had been discussed throughout the four months, but Rogers now waited in anticipation for a comprehensive report.

The Diagnostic Findings

The presentation was long and provided a detailed review of the findings. It came as no surprise to Rogers when he was told that there were serious problems in cross-functional conflict and coordination in the division when compared with other industries studied (Exhibit 2). These poor relations had an effect on the division's performance through their impact on new product development, service, morale, and decision making. Some on Rogers' staff had held that the conflict in the division was due to declining market conditions and poor divisional performance. They felt that if business would only get better they would stop "crabbing" at each other. The O.D. staff felt otherwise. They saw the poor relations between functional groups as a symptom of some fundamental organizational problems which had been building in the division for a long time and were associated with changes in the division's markets and recent changes in management. A summary of their major conclusions about the causes of intergroup problems is presented below:

1. EPD markets have been shifting as a result of a decline in space and military spending by the Federal government and the growth course charted by the division. The result has been increasing sales in the data processing, telecommunications, and consumer electronics markets which required the rapid development of product extensions at competitive prices and good service — not unique technological advantage in product, which was the original vehicle for entry into the components business. These changes had made EPD's environment more uncertain than in the past. EPD's management had rated the predictability of the division's environment as very low (see Exhibit 3). Other indicators of uncertainty were the inability to forecast and the inability of marketing to accurately project market size for new products.

2. EPD operates in an uncertain environment — much more uncertain than many other Corning divisions. Yet, the way it is managed and organized is very similar to other Corning divisions in much more certain and stable original equipment manufacturing businesses, where Corning has a technological advantage, and where capital requirements have prevented serious competition. This is not surprising, given the fact that all but one of EPD's key managers have spent most of their careers in some of these other division. [The research of Lawrence and Lorsch[3] was presented as a conceptual framework for understanding EPD's problems and led to the following interpretations of the root causes of the problem.]

3. The division has larger differences (differentiation) between functions than most other Corning Glass Works divisions — differences in structure, goals, time horizons, and personal orientations of people. These differences are needed to cope with the business. Rogers' decision to split marketing and sales reflects an intuitive understanding of this. The need for a product development group and corporate R&D support are other examples. Yet in some places there is not yet enough differentiation. Market Planning as a function has been eliminated as a cost-saving step, and Product Development in the division is working on similar projects as corporate R&D.

---

[3]Lawrence P. R. and Lorsch, J. W., *Organization and Environment: Managing Differentiation and Integration* (Cambridge, Mass.: Harvard University, Graduate School of Business Administration, Division of Research, 1967.)

4. High levels of differentiation have placed a greater demand on the division for coordination (integration). Yet, there are no mechanisms for integration in the division other than the organization's hierarchy and Rogers' own involvement in many decisions. The two days of product development meetings are an example of how most integration and decision making is handled at the top. But this mechanism is being frustrated by the relatively large number of new product projects and the diversity of information required to make decisions. This information simply does not exist at the top.

5. Poor integration is heightened by the demise of mechanisms that have existed in the past. Marketing groups previously located at the plants have been moved to Corning, reducing opportunities for communication. Bennett, Rogers' predecessor, achieved some coordination through his singlehanded management of the division. Now this is no longer appropriate, nor is Rogers the type of person who is inclined to do so.

6. The natural differences between groups, the absence of mechanisms for bringing them together, and the historic competitive atmosphere of the division has led to some very poor relationships between groups. [The consultants presented questionnaire data which showed that groups like Manufacturing and Marketing, which people perceive as requiring high levels of coordination, have the poorest relationships. There were other examples like this in the data (see Exhibit 4).]

7. Marketing is already attempting to coordinate (Integrator role) the work of other functions in developing product extensions and other profit-oriented projects (Marketing chairs the product development meetings). But, Marketing is staffed by young and inexperienced individuals; they are seen as sales-oriented and incompetent, and they are *not* formally acknowledged as having the responsibility for integrating. This makes it difficult for Marketing to get other functions to do things in support of product development. The perception that Marketing is not competent, together with the fact that they are seen as having high influence on what happens in the division (see Exhibit 5), creates great resentment against them. This is particularly true of Manufacturing, the function which historically has been most important and most powerful in the division and in Corning Glass Works.

8. Product Development and R&D have relatively low influence in the division (Exhibit 5). Yet, EPD needs to develop products to meet its growth and profit objectives.

9. Marketing is not measured on profit. The absence of this measure reduces their sensitivity to cost/price tradeoffs in managing new product introductions and reinforces their tendency to be sales-oriented. On the other hand, Manufacturing's responsibility for gross margin gives them a final "club" in any conflict with Marketing, thus worsening the relationship between the two and reducing problem-solving.

10. The culture of EPD, shaped by Bennett's singlehanded management style, is one in which differences are ignored (smoothing) or resolved by pressuring the other party to one's will (forcing). There is relatively little use of the open dialogue and problem-solving (confrontation) that has been found in other successful companies in uncertain environments. The questionnaire data (Exhibit 6), observations, and interviews confirmed this.

11. People do not have a common understanding of division objectives, strategies, and business philosophy — even at the top. There are disagreements about what the primary markets are and about realistic profit and growth expectations. This contributes to poor integration.

12. The differences between EPD's business and Corning's traditional glass business create some problems. The division's goals, strategies, and managerial approaches **329**

need to be different in certain areas, yet the close physical proximity and control by Corning's management and staff groups leads to some difficulties.

As Noles finished his presentation of findings, he knew that he had captured Rogers' attention and interest. There had been many incisive questions, typical of Rogers' intelligence and grasp of complex issues, and Rogers was now sitting forward in anticipation of the recommendations which were to come. There were both short- and long-range recommendations for what the consultants viewed would be major change in the division's structure and management process.

As Noles proceeded, he wondered how the recommendations would be received. He had been strong in his conviction to be direct and make specific recommendations despite some concern by his staff that this might create resistance, particularly among those in Rogers' staff most affected by the findings and recommendations. Their view had been that recommendations should be jointly forged with EPD's management after a presentation of the findings.

O.D. Department Recommendations[4]

A project team organization was recommended, especially for new product development tasks. It was suggested that members of these project teams be selected differently, depending on the function represented. For example, functions such as Research and/or Development would be represented by bench scientists or development engineers, while Manufacturing would be represented by individuals at higher levels in the organization such as the Production Superintendent or the Manufacturing Engineer.[5] Sales, it was recommended, should also be represented, but it was less clear who in Sales would be appropriate. Sales was organized geographically and not by product, as were Manufacturing and Product Development (see Exhibit 7). There was a further question about whether salesmen or district managers should represent Sales on the team. The Controller function was to be represented by the controller of the plant associated with the given product.

Marketing, it was recommended, should be the integrating function. Specifically, it was suggested that the Marketing Specialists in the Market Development Department under Glen Johnson (see Exhibit 7) should serve as project team Integrators. The consultants made this recommendation despite the findings, which they had just presented, that people in the division, particularly Manufacturing, had great concerns about the competence of Marketing's personnel, their inexperience, and their sales-orientation. Project team Integrators were to receive training in their roles through seminars and group discussions. Additionally, O.D. specialists would sit in on the early project team meetings as process consultants,[6] observing the functioning of the team, feeding back their observations, raising issues, and facilitating the confrontation of conflict. They were also to provide feedback to the Integrators on their effectiveness and help train them.

It was further recommended that Rogers and his staff modify their roles by withdrawing from the detail of product development projects, delegating project planning and action responsibility to the teams, and reserving for themselves review of projects and

---

[4]Parts of the next three sections are based on a paper by Dr. Gerald Pieters. Pieters, Gerald R., "Changing Organizational Structures, Roles and Processes to Enhance Integration: The Implementation of a Change Program," presented to Division of Industrial and Organization Psychology of the American Psychological Association, September 3, 1971, Washington, D.C.

[5]These people were generally regarded as having the two most important positions in the plant in the order listed.

[6]See Schein, E. H., *Process Consultation: Its Role in Organization Development* (Reading, Mass.: Addison Wesley, 1969).

resource allocation. They were to be referred to as the Resource Allocation Team, or RAT. A director from the corporate R&D Laboratory who was responsible for electronic research was to be asked to join Rogers, staff for these reviews.

The project teams were to develop their own objectives for their projects, plan the project (it was recommended that PERT[7] be used as a program management tool), and report to the top team on a quarterly basis through the Integrator. These quarterly meetings would replace the monthly product development reviews. At these quarterly meetings, the progress of the projects would be reviewed along with money and manpower resource requirements.

It was recommended that the top group should spend some time (several days away from the office) developing itself into an effective management team that would be able to provide unified direction to the division. There were two parts to this. First, they were to re-examine the present strategies and direction of the division and develop a set of commonly agreed to goals, strategies, and business philosophy to be communicated to the division's membership. At a later date they were to spend time looking at how they functioned as a group, the quality of their meetings, how individuals' behavior impacted group effectiveness (including Rogers), and what and who had to change. These meetings were to be attended by Noles as a facilitator and were referred to as Team Development Meetings.

It was recommended to Rogers that he adopt a stronger management style. It was suggested that he motivate through budgeting more time for direct contact with his subordinates and other key people, molding a cohesive staff by clarifying his expectations, setting a tone and direction as well as settling conflicts, and by inspiring enthusiasm for projects and the direction of the division by "talking them up." At the same time, more listening and receptiveness to conflict was required on Rogers' part. The consultants offered Rogers help on these personal agendas through further feedback as the program of change developed.

To deal directly with the intergroup relations problems, it was recommended that "intergroup laboratory meetings"[8] should be held for those groups experiencing the worst relations. In these meetings (typically two days) pairs of groups were to come together to exchange perceptions of each other, obtain clarification of these perceptions, and develop an action plan for improving relationships. The intent of the meetings would be to develop better mutual understanding and trust between groups and improve integration.

There were a number of longer range recommendations that were also made:

a. A program would have to be developed for identifying potential Integrators and consciously developing them through cross-functional work experiences and various types of training. Laboratory training, Kepner Trego rational problem solving training, and technical Marketing seminars were recommended.

b. For the long-range development of greater interpersonal competence and collaboration, it was suggested that many of the salaried personnel in the division who had to work on teams should receive laboratory training (sensitivity training or a more structured program called the Managerial Grid).[9]

---

[7]PERT is a program management technique invented and used by the U.S. Navy during the development of the Polaris submarine.

[8]See Blake, R. R., Shepart, H.A., and Mouton, J.S., *Managing Intergroup Conflict in Industry* (Houston: Gulf Publishing Company, 1964); and Beckhard, R., *Organization Development: Strategies and Models* (Reading, Mass.: Addison-Wesley, 1969).

[9]For information on these or other techniques referred to, see Beer, M., "The Technology of Organization Development" in Dunnette, M. D. (ed.), *Handbook of Industrial and Organizational Psychology* (Chicago: Rand McNally, 1976).

331

c. The division should consider hiring a full-time organization development professional to carry on these activities and help the division make the changes recommended.

Although not part of the formal recommendations, the O.D. consultants did present
their views that the accounting and control system which placed gross margin responsibility (sales less cost of manufacture) at the plant should be changed in the future. Their
view was that Marketing should be the profit center and plants cost centers. There was a
discussion of these views with Rogers but the consultants did not press their views, nor
did Rogers encourage them. He and the O.D. consultants knew how committed the corporation was to the plant profit center concept and the near impossibility of obtaining an
exception for EPD.

Implementation

By the time the presentation of the recommendations had been completed, it was clear
that Rogers was not only receptive but enthusiastic. Through frequent questions and
discourses throughout the presentation, he had shown an understanding of the analysis,
its conceptual foundations, and the rationale for the actions recommended. He was less
enthusiastic about the consultants' analysis of the relationship between the division and
the corporation and the implication that the corporation was somehow responsible for part
of EPD's problems. Rogers was also in disagreement with the implication of this analysis
that the division should maintain some differences (profit objectives, types of people,
control system, etc.) between itself and the corporation. His view was that the division
would be "dead" without corporate support and that maintenance of differences would
interfere with that support. However, he supported the bulk of the recommendations and
suggested that they be presented to his staff. When Noles asked if this presentation
should include the findings about Marketing and his (Rogers') own style, he quickly said,
"Yes!"

The presentation by the O.D. group to Rogers' staff took place in February and went
smoothly. There were many questions about the findings, particularly those relating to
how Marketing was perceived. Throughout the discussion, the Marketing Manager did not
behave defensively and asked questions, while the Manufacturing Manager remained
fairly quiet. On occasion someone would come to Marketing's defense, but no one used
the negative data about them to attack them further. There was relatively little discussion
of the feedback on Rogers' style of management. When the meeting ended, Rogers'
enthusiasm seemed to have carried the day, and the staff committed itself to getting to
work immediately on the development of a strategy and implementation of the project
organization. The other recommendations also appeared to be accepted, although no
specific steps were planned to deal with them at that meeting.

Subsequently the top management group met off-site for two days to examine and
reestablish the goals, strategies, and direction of the division. This meeting took place in
March and surfaced the fact that they all had slightly different views of what the division
direction should be. With the very strong guidance of Rogers, the meeting ended with
setting priorities for markets (i.e., data processing, military, etc.) based on their growth
and potential profitability, and a list of those projects that reflected these priorities. In yet
another meeting they considered which of these projects should be handled by a project
team, and selected nine projects to begin with. They identified members for each team
including the Integrators from Market Development and, where appropriate, a representative from Corporate R&D. In addition, several "Evaluation and Recommendation" proj-

ects were identified which required study and analysis on the part of a cross-functional team. These teams would report to the RAT with their analysis and recommendations on whether the division should launch a full-fledged project.

During April and May the decisions reached by Rogers and his staff were communicated widely. Rogers personally briefed Corning's president about what he was intending to do in EPD. All of the salaried exempt employees of the division in all plant locations, sales districts, and in Corning, New York, plus members of related staff groups (Corporate R&D, Controller's Division, Manpower Development Division, etc.) were exposed to a three-part presentation lasting up to four hours. Most of Rogers' staff were present for each of these presentations. They covered:

1. The division's redefined objectives and strategies presented by Rogers.
2. The diagnostic findings and recommendations of the O.D. Department, including the perceptions of Marketing and Rogers, presented by Noles. This part included the conceptual framework of Lawrence and Lorsch, which had guided the diagnosis and recommendations.
3. Bill Lee, the Marketing Manager, presented the nine projects which had been identified as high priority and the project team members which had been identified. He emphasized the Marketing Specialists' role as Integrators and what that meant. He also talked about the changing role of Rogers and his staff from a direct detailed involvement in development projects to a review and resource allocation role, with specific project responsibility delegated to project teams.

Following the presentation, extended informal meetings were held for discussion and clarification of the actions being initiated. These were often followed by drinks and dinner with at least the key people at each location. The formal and informal give-and-take sessions resulted in a number of reactions to the proposed changes.

1. There were a lot of sharp questions in the formal meetings at the plants about why Marketing had been chosen to integrate project teams and about the advisability of the project team concept. The questions and comments reflected a deep distrust of Marketing and concern about loss of influence by Manufacturing:

    "Will anyone in Manufacturing have a chance to head up project teams? Why should it be just Marketing?"

    "What does this Integrator concept in Marketing mean for the role and importance of Manufacturing?"

    "What is in it for a plant person to be on a project team. Why should I go to meetings and put in a lot of time? As far as I can see, I still get evaluated on the same thing I have always been evaluated on within the plant."

    "It looks to me as if the members of the project team are going to be dependent on the Marketing Integrators' ability to sell the project to the Resource Allocation team. If he can't sell it effectively, the project fails and we all fail with it."

    "How do we get projects started now? In the past, if we saw an opportunity to consolidate products or make some changes in order to reduce costs, we would get our Manufacturing Engineering department to start work on the project. Now it looks like we have to go through Marketing to get a project started. They can screen out a lot of projects that we think are important to increasing our gross margin."

2. In several of the meetings with Sales personnel, District Sales Managers indicated **333**

considerable concern about the impact of the organization change on the Sales group. One District Manager said:

> "Why can't salesmen be Integrators on the project teams? They have as much contact with the customer as Marketing people, and we have some pretty good people who can do the job. If salesmen are not made Integrators, they will feel that the sales function has been downgraded. Anyway, I don't feel that the Market Development people have done that good a job. Why should they be given this assignment?"

3. Over drinks and dinner in Wilmington, North Carolina after one of the presentations, several plant people opened up on the Marketing group and indicated that they felt the group was weak and lacked the ability to take on the responsibility for integrating. Rogers and his staff responded by saying that the people in Market Development were going to be given the chance to do this job and that many could. Those that couldn't would not stay. Rogers said, "We have to start some place, and Marketing appears to be the logical group to pull things together because of their role and position in the organization."

4. The presentation in Corning, New York which included the Market Development Department surfaced considerable concerns on the part of the Market Specialists who were to be the Integrators. These concerns were best reflected in what Roy Stone had to say:

> "I am very anxious about the changes you are talking about. Frankly, I don't know if I can do the job, if I have the capability. This job is going to put me in the spotlight. What happens if I don't succeed? We have several strikes against us already, judging by what people have said about us. Also, how are we going to get the plants to do what has to be done? Those idiot Manufacturing people can't get the costs down."

A corporate staff manager who had recently been a production superintendent in EPD said in an informal discussion after the presentation:

> "The whole thing might fail if you don't get heavyweights into the Integrator jobs."

The communication meetings took two months to accomplish. Rogers and his staff made 14 different presentations and travelled to eight different locations from Wilmington, North Carolina to Los Angeles, California. Everywhere the same presentation was given and reactions were obtained. Rogers took charge in these presentations and in the meetings that followed, answering questions as candidly as he could. The management of EPD and the O.D. specialists came away from the presentations chastened. At the conceptual stage, the ideas seemed right and sensible. But, the reactions to the communication meetings had indicated that a lot of people would have to change to make it happen. The enormity of the change for EPD became apparent. Now it was time to see if it would all work.

The First Year of Change

By June of 1969 the project organization was in place. Project teams were beginning to meet and the first review with the Resource Allocation Team were being scheduled. People were beginning to understand how the new organization was to function and were changing their approach to running EPD's business. Rogers himself was strongly supportive of the changes and was seen as providing the impetus for the changes. Despite this progress, there were problems.

In the early stages of implementation, a number of meetings were held by the O.D. specialists with the project Integrators to explore and discuss the implications of the role of Integrator. In these meetings their anxieties about the "additional load" they had been assigned surfaced. It seemed like this was a job on top of their exisiting Marketing job. They were also uncomfortable with the label of "Integrator." Although they recognized that successful performance of the role, with its additional visibility, promised added growth potential, they were equally aware of the strikes against them; e.g., youth, inexperience in the division, existing negative perceptions of the Marketing function, and concerns, particularly by Manufacturing, that Marketing was too sales-oriented and had no concern for costs and profit. In addition, the idea of them managing a cross-functional project team without formal authority boggled their minds. They had a hard time understanding how to develop other sources of influence and how to handle non-responsiveness by other functions.

Some frustrations developed in many of the project team members. When project teams first met, they would get into extended discussions in team meetings about the background of the projects in the functional groups represented. They had trouble getting to the stage where they could set goals and outline the task. People wondered if project team management meant long and, what seemed to them, unproductive meetings where nothing got accomplished.

Several of the people on Rogers' staff became uncomfortable about not having frequent, detailed feedback on project status. The Manufacturing Manager, Ben Smith, specifically requested copies of all the memos that were generated by teams. In another instance, Rogers and his staff received rather sketchy information which appeared to identify a catastrophic problem. They quickly scheduled a meeting to "resolve the problem." The Integrator of the team voiced his concern that this would undermine the activities of the team and not give the team concept a chance to work. Rogers and his staff held the meeting, and the Integrator was asked to describe the situation. He related what was going on and what the team was doing about it. Management seemed to go away from the meeting satisfied that something was being done.

As teams began to form, it became apparent that not all of the people who had been designated to be on the teams were going to have and/or make the time. For example, Production Superintendents and Manufacturing Engineers soon delegated their role on the team to lower level people in the plants. District Sales Managers delegated their responsibility to salesmen — although in most cases these were senior salesmen. Sometimes the senior and junior people from a function would come to a meeting and the meeting would become large and unwieldy.

Soon after the change to a project organization, plant managers, who had been involved personally in planning and decision making for all projects in their plants, began complaining that they were uninformed and "out of the loop." Project teams were planning and making decisions affecting the plant with the understanding and consent of the plant representative, but the plant managers and, in some cases, others in the plant often learned about it after the fact. This increased the plant managers' concern about the organizational change, and their complaints about Marketing continued to be voiced and, if anything, seemed to increase because they were talking about it more openly. These complaints were often carried to Ben Smith, the Manufacturing Manager, who would raise these concerns with Rogers and his staff.

For a period of time after the implementation of the new organization, it seemed as if every situation requiring coordination between two or more departments was perceived as requiring a formalized project team. As the Distribution Manager in Sales said, "It seems as if we form a team every time we go to the Men's Room." He, for one, began to **335** complain that people weren't taking responsibility for making hard decisions. There were also complaints that decisions were taking a long time to be made. As one individual said: "Previously I could make a decision and run with the ball; now I have to sit in a meeting for a day and get six other guys to agree that I ought to do it before I can go ahead. This slows things down."

As the year of change progressed, a number of problems surfaced in the relationship between EPD and the corporation. The job of Marketing Specialist had increased in scope and responsibility with the addition of the Integrator role to the point where people in Marketing felt that it wage and salary level should be reevaluated and raised. They felt this was needed to pay Market Specialists equitably and to attract into the job the kinds of experienced people everyone agreed were required in the long run. Marketing's management ran into problems, however, as they tried to explain their reasoning to the Wage and Salary Department in Corning's personnel function. This department had not run into this type of role before (they had heard the presentation by Rogers and staff), did not fully understand it, and weren't at all sure that the Market Specialist's job in EPD should be rated higher than similar jobs in other divisions.

There were other problems too. As Rogers and his staff began to delegate more and more responsibility to lower levels, two aspects of their relation to the corporation began to emerge as somewhat troublesome to some members of this group. Several people began to point to the inconsistencies between their efforts to delegate within the division and corporate management's formal and informal requests for information about what was going on in EPD. As the Marketing Manager, Bill Lee, said, "I run into top corporate people in the lobby, in the cafeteria, or on airplanes, and they ask me questions about projects, customers, shipments, and orders that require more details than I feel I should have, given our new approach to management. They are important people and expect me to know these things, and so I will continue to try to have the information at my fingertips, but it runs counter to what we on staff are trying to do when we say we want to be more strategically oriented." The frustration with this phenomena was often directed at the O.D. consultants when they reminded Rogers' staff about their commitment to delegation. A similar type of inconsistency was seen by Jack Simon, the Sales Manager, with respect to budgeting. He complained that yearly sales budgets, which were increasingly developed through a bottom up process within Sales, were being changed at a corporate level and a request for an increase or decrease made based on corporate estimates and needs. He wrote a long memo to Rogers on this issue, expressing his concern about asking salesmen and District Managers to come up with budgets only to change them later arbitrarily. Though this concern had been there earlier, its intensity seemed to increase.

But project team meetings continued throughout 1969. Rogers and his staff set aside two or three days each quarter for reviews of project team activity. Project team Integrators in Marketing, though initially poorly prepared for these reviews, began to improve their presentation. They liked the exposure that their new role gave them with top management. They saw the project team concept as providing visibility for their problems and getting top management support for the directions they were proposing.

The project team organization also gave lower levels more exposure to what was going on at the top as they interacted with Rogers and his staff during the reviews. People sometimes came away from these meetings feeling that the RAT did not always solve problems openly. They were not always confronting conflicts, and weren't operating as much as a team as they should be. More criticism of the top group began to be heard in the form of lack of direction and teamwork at the top. It was felt that they were not allocating resources as they were expected to do. Project Integrators still had problems getting people they needed to work on their project because of the competition of other activities. This came out in comments like:

"They are not setting priorities and communicating these."

"I don't know what they do in RAT meetings."

Throughout 1969, the O.D. consultants sat in on project team and RAT meetings, counseled with Integrators and individual managers, and kept Rogers and his staff informed on the progress of the whole change effort. But, this too was behind schedule. Rogers and his staff had not had a second meeting to deal with how they worked as a group (Team Development). The intergroup meetings for pairs of groups that were having difficulty had not yet been held because there wasn't enough time given the demands of working with project teams and the RAT. Similarly, no change in the control or evaluation system had taken place. The plant was the profit center, and there was no way to account for profit by products. Individuals on teams were evaluated by their functional bosses. No laboratory training for people on teams had taken place, and no plans for upgrading the people in the Integrator role had been developed.

By December of 1969 when Rogers and his staff met for their annual GLF (Great Leap Forward) meeting, EPD was operating as a project organization. Project teams and the RAT were meeting as scheduled. Marketing people were enthusiastic about the impact of the organization on their role and influence in the organization, but negative voices about them were still being heard from Manufacturing in particular. Occasionally, the Marketing Manager, Bill Lee, would come under attack for providing no direction and for weaknesses in the Marketing function. Throughout, Rogers held firm to the concept of the project organization and supported Bill Lee and the Marketing function in their efforts to adopt the Integrator function and exert more influence in the management of the division.

EXHIBIT 1   Electronic Products Division
SALES AND OPERATING MARGIN IN THOUSANDS
1961–1968

	61	62	63	64	65	66	67	68
Sales	12,723	21,745	22,836	20,036	25,320	26,553	23,852	24,034
Operating Margin*	3011	5449	5826	2998	5075	4170	1559	1574

*Operating margin equals sales less manufacturing, administrative and sales expenses

EXHIBIT 2   Comparison of integration in electronic products division in 1968 with other high and low
performers in three industries[1]

Industry	Organization	Average Integration
Plastics	High Performer	5.6
	Low Performer	5.1
Foods	High Performer	5.3
	Low Performer	5.0
Container	High Performer	5.7
	Low Performer	4.8
Electronic	Electronic Products	
	Division	4.3

[1]Comparison scores from three industries obtained from Lawrence, P. R. and Lorsch, J. W., *Organization and Environment: Managing Differentiation and Integration* (Boston, Mass.: Harvard University, Graduate School of Business Administration, Division of Research, 1967).
NOTE: All ratings were on an eight point scale with high score indicating high integration.

EXHIBIT 3   Ratings of EPD's environment by people in division, 1968

High Stability, Predictability and Certainty						Low Stability, Predictability and Certainty
:	:	:	:	:	⊗ :	:
1	2	3	4	5	6	7

Mean = 5.7 (X)

EXHIBIT 4   Required and actual integration as seen by people in EPD, 1968

Groups	Required Integration			Actual Integration		
	Rank	Mean	Standard Deviation	Rank	Mean	Standard Deviation
Sales & Marketing	1	6.6	.60	16	4.4	1.10
Product Development (capacitors) & Manufacturing	6	5.5	1.01	17	4.3	.75
Fluidics* & Controller	18	4.2	1.03	2	5.0	.74
Technical Staffs (R&D) & Marketing	11	5.0	1.16	15	4.4	.90
Controller & Sales	16	4.5	1.15	3	5.0	.84
Marketing & Fluidics	12	5.0	1.71	14	4.5	.96
Manufacturing & Sales	5	5.6	1.09	19	4.1	.91
Product Development (resistors) & Technical Staffs (R&D)	8	5.3	1.10	9	4.6	.98
Manufacturing & Controller	9	5.3	1.28	1	5.3	.84
Sales & Product Development (capacitors)	15	4.6	1.60	5	4.7	.79
Marketing & Controller	17	4.4	1.14	10	4.6	1.00
Product Development (resistors) & Controller	19	4.0	1.12	8	4.6	.73
Technical Staffs (R&D) & Fluidics	13	4.6	1.14	13	4.5	.83
Product Development (capacitors) & Controller	20	3.8	1.00	4	4.9	.87
Manufacturing & Marketing	7	5.5	1.24	21	3.8	1.02
Product Development (capacitors) & Technical Staffs (R&D)	10	5.2	1.05	6	4.7	.91
Manufacturing & Product Development (resistors)	4	5.8	.97	20	4.1	.99
Marketing & Product Development (resistors)	2	6.4	.79	18	4.3	1.37
Technical Staffs (R&D) & Manufacturing	21	3.1	1.25	12	4.5	.83
Marketing & Product Development (capacitors)	3	6.3	.78	7	4.7	1.00
Product Development (resistors) and Sales	14	4.6	1.36	11	4.5	.68

NOTE: All ratings were on a seven point scale with high scores indicating high required or actual integration.
*The Fluidics Department was a small, $2 million business which reported to Rogers, but was not part of the components business and operated independently of it.

EXHIBIT 5   Influence of functional groups in EPD and corporate R&D as seen by people in division, 1968

Function	Influence Score
Marketing	4.1
Sales	3.9
Production	3.8
Controller	3.1
Product Development	2.9
Technical Staffs (Corporate R&D)	2.0

NOTE: Ratings were on a five point scale with a high score indicating high influence.

EXHIBIT 6   Modes of conflict resolution in EPD as seen by people in division, 1968

Confrontation	2.9
Forcing	3.1
Smoothing	3.0

NOTE: (a) All scores are on a five point scale. (b) In organizations studied by Lawrence and Lorsch, Confrontation was almost always rated significantly higher than Forcing or Smoothing—even when the company operated in a certain environment.

EXHIBIT 7 Electronic Products Division Organization Chart

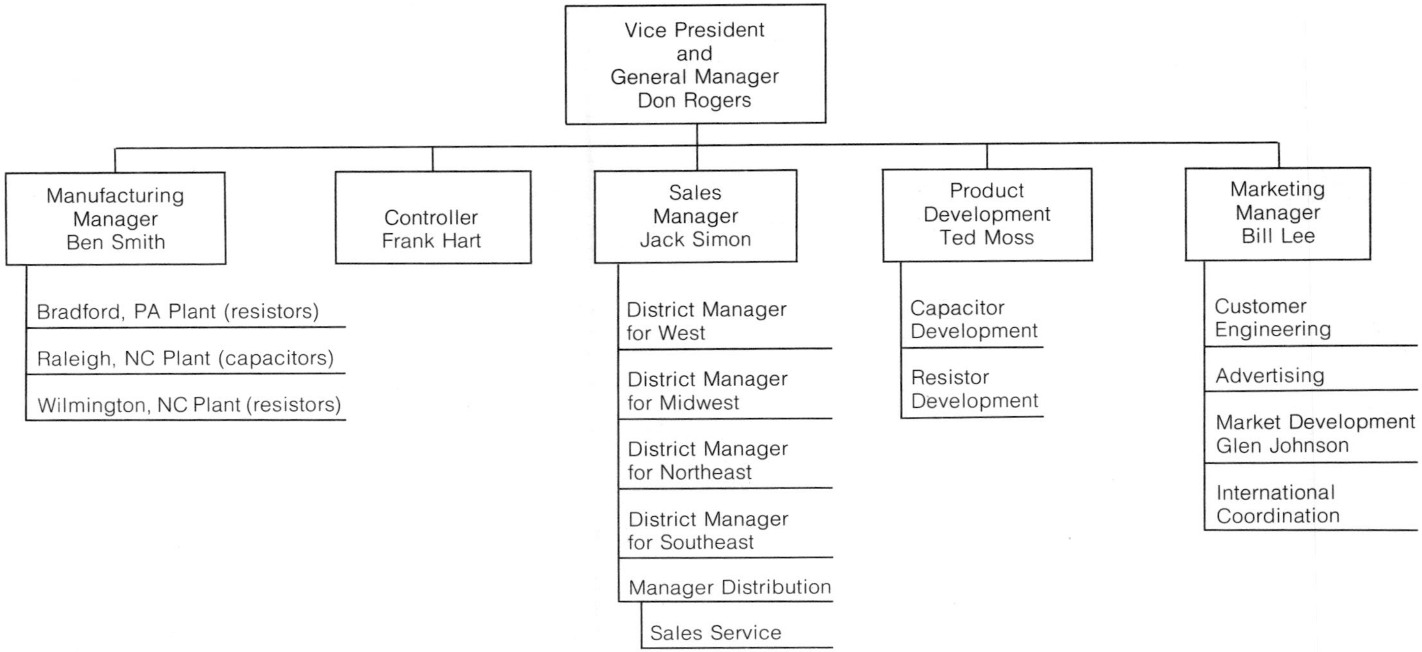

Vice President
and
General Manager
Don Rogers

Manufacturing
Manager
Ben Smith

- Bradford, PA Plant (resistors)
- Raleigh, NC Plant (capacitors)
- Wilmington, NC Plant (resistors)

Controller
Frank Hart

Sales
Manager
Jack Simon

- District Manager for West
- District Manager for Midwest
- District Manager for Northeast
- District Manager for Southeast
- Manager Distribution
- Sales Service

Product
Development
Ted Moss

- Capacitor Development
- Resistor Development

Marketing
Manager
Bill Lee

- Customer Engineering
- Advertising
- Market Development Glen Johnson
- International Coordination

Datavision (B)

After talking with Dave Brennan, Larry spoke individually with Datavision's board members. By the third week in November 1977, Campbell decided upon a course of action. On November 29, 1977, he asked Bob Fowler to hand in his letter of resignation. Bob agreed upon a monetary settlement and resigned with little argument.

Since that time Larry has been acting as V.P., Marketing. He decided to recruit outside the company and, as of February 1978 hired a search firm to help find Fowler's replacement.

The May Department Stores Company (B)

By July, 1976, Dave Babcock had conducted MBO training seminars in over half of the May Company's department and discount store companies. Babcock talked about what he had learned in the process.

Well, for one thing, I can see much more clearly the lull we talked about between 1968 and the early 1970's. All of the people in the stores have been asking, "Why did you wait so long to do this?" If I ask myself, "Should I have done MBO seminars three years ago?"—the answer is yes. "Should I be doing them now?"—the answer is yes. And I expect that I will do the seminars again in four years, during my last year in the company. I am more convinced than ever that the CEO should do MBO training if he believes in it, and if he wants to keep people thinking of how they can improve it. The store principals agree. A number have said, "We think you must break down what you're saying there into four or five sessions and videotape them so we can use them for new trainees."

Another thing I now recognize is that I sold MBO so hard that I ended up selling a program and a procedure rather than a concept, which is not at all what I tried to do. We went through such a long period of struggling with the procedural aspects of MBO that we lost sight of the fact that it's basically a concept—a way of approaching the manager's job. I've gotten a lot of good feedback from the seminars around the idea that you can't do MBO by mail or memo—that it has to be a dialogue, and to be a dialogue MBO need not be long and highly proceduralized. So I'm going to try to simplify it even further.

Finally, I've discovered a problem related to training. A lot of our present personnel directors came on board after I did the 1967 seminars, and I now see that I'm going to have to take them and train them in MBO, if they are to teach it to people in the stores. I also think they could be very useful in giving me information about the stores' problems with MBO. I'd like them to run meetings three months after these seminars and say, "O.K. it's now been three months since Dave Babcock's been here. What do you think now about what he said? What makes sense? Where is he all washed up? What problems do we have that he doesn't recognize?" That would be a great way for me to get feedback after people have had a chance to chew over what I've said.

Corning Glass Works (C)
The Electronic Products Division

By the end of 1970, the change process moving EPD to a project/matrix organization had been underway for 18 months. The organizational changes introduced in 1968 were still in place. The division had a banner year in 1969. Sales were the highest in the division's history, and profits had improved significantly (see Exhibit 1). In 1970 sales had dropped slightly but profits continued to be much better than the pre-1968 levels.

The management of the division was becoming very committed to changes in organization and management that they had introduced in 1969. At the request of the President of Corning Glass Works, Rogers made a presentation to all officers and key executives of the company about what had been done in EPD and how, in his (Rogers') view, it had contributed significantly to improvements in the division's performance. Rogers' staff was equally enthusiastic about the changes, although there were differences between individuals in degree of enthusiasm. Despite their enthusiasm, the top group wanted an objective reading on the impact the new organization was having on EPD. They commissioned a re-diagnosis of the division by the Organization Development Department. A number of significant improvements in EPD's management process and performance were found.

The target of the change program had been to improve integration in the division with a clear expectation that such improvements would effect better product development performance. Prior to 1968 the division had developed five (5) new products. This was considered inadequate if the division was to maintain or improve its position in the market place. In 1970, nine (9) new products were introduced, more than in the previous five years (see Exhibit 2).

Questionnaire data and interviews showed an increase in overall integration between functional groups. People all over the division felt that teams had greatly facilitated coordination and that intergroup relations were improved. As one person, representative of many others, said: "Problems are shared and understood. If things don't happen, I don't start placing blame. I have a better understanding of why it didn't happen. Now I ask how I can help to make it happen. It is important to have empathy for the other guy, but not sympathy." Despite these overwhelmingly positive reports of change, the relationships between Manufacturing and Marketing had not improved significantly.

People reported that higher quality decisions were being made because "the team supports openness, and all relevant information is being pooled for decision making." The locus of decision making shifted dramatically after the introduction of project teams. Responsibility (as it related to product development and other cross-functional profit improvement programs) was being delegated from upper management to project teams who had the information and data necessary to solve the problems and make decisions. People thought that teams facilitated the development of a more objective approach to problems. More commitment to decisions was also reported.

An unexpected but positive outcome of the change was that people on project teams felt that the experience had been the best and the most management development they had received since being with Corning. Many felt that they understood for the first time how different functions operated and the complexity of business problems and decision making.

The handling of conflict in the divison changed dramatically. Confrontation/problem solving increased and in 1970 was the primary mode of resolving differences. Forcing dropped to second in frequency of use, and Smoothing dropped significantly and was third in the frequency with which it was used (see Exhibit 3). The following anecdote illustrates the type of changes that took place:

> In June 1971, one of the O.D. consultants received a telephone call from Joe Black, a Marketing Specialist and Integrator of a major product team working on the development of a new product. The team had been in operation for less than a year and had both technical and organizational problems. The following is the gist of his remarks:
> "Sam, our team has been having some problems and I have decided it is time to get to the causes. We are just not working together effectively, and we all see a need for improvement. For example, I find myself 'going around the system' to get things accomplished. Instead of going to a team member to get something done, I am going over his head." (Other symptoms of an unhealthy situation were given.) "I think we should all get together and put the technical tasks aside and take a closer look at our 'process' (his word) . . ."

If Joe Black were in the same situation in 1968, he would most likely have continued to go to his boss to get pressure exerted on people in other functions.

Another area where noticeable change had occurred was in the recognition of Marketing as the integrating function. Marketing was now more involved in the communication network related to product development and introduction and played a more central role in business decisions. The young Integrators were seen as having matured over the 18 month period, and their legitimacy and acceptance by others had increased. Those who could not handle the increased responsibility were moved out of Marketing. However, some people in the division still had concerns over the competence of the Integrators and Marketing in general. Manufacturing in particular was still critical of Marketing and the lack of direction they gave. They still viewed the Integrators as too young and too inexperienced, and indeed they still were. Bill Lee, the Marketing Manager, increasingly came under attack for his lack of leadership in moving the division into profitable product lines. Other influence patterns did not change. Product Development continued to be low in influence and Manufacturing and Sales high. Of all the functions, Manufacturing was still the most powerful and dominant function.

The improvements in integration extended beyond EPD to the corporate R&D group. This came about through participation on project teams by R&D people. One comment heard over and over again was that ". . . scientists are now out of their labs and know how their work fits into the overall project." As one scientist said, "My blinders have been taken off."

Coordination at the top was seen as improved. Integrators felt that they were getting most of the resources they needed and liked being exposed to the top group. However, some concerns about the top group continued. People wondered what they did at RAT meetings since there were often no visible products or communication to the division. Some felt the top group was not together, confronting conflict or operating as a team.

On the whole, however, there had been many positive changes in the division, and these outweighed continuing and new problems. Increased numbers of new products introduced; improved integration and intergroup relations; high degree of commitment to decisions made; improved morale; improved problem solving; increased use of confronting as a means of resolving conflict; Marketing in a stronger position to integrate and seen by some at least as doing a better job; and a better interface with corporate R&D.

In 1970 Rogers was promoted to be a Group Vice President of Corning's Technical Products Division — a much larger and more important division. A new Vice President who had been sales manager in EPD in the early 1960's and was known to be a directive and tough was taking over. Many in the division were quite concerned about the impact this would have on the changes in management which had taken place in EPD.

EXHIBIT 1   Electronic Products Division sales and operating margin in thousands 1961–1970

	61	62	63	64	65	66	67	68	69	70
Sales	12,723	21,745	22,836	20,036	25,320	26,553	23,852	24,034	31,100	26,900
Operating Margin*	3,011	5,449	5,826	2,998	5,075	4,170	1,559	1,574	6,400	1,400**

*Operating margin equals sales less manufacturing, administrative, and sales expenses.

**Two million dollars were expensed by EPD out of component profits for the development of a new business unrelated to components. Thus profits from components were actually $3,400,000.

EXHIBIT 2   Electronics Products Division Introduction of New Products**

Year	Resistors	Capacitors
1966	1	0
1967	0	0
1968	4	0
1969	0	0
1970	6	3

**New Products are defined as those which meet the following three requirements:

1. Produced within the last five years.
2. Have major significance to customer.
3. Not an obvious one-for-one replacement.

EXHIBIT 3   Conflict Resolution Styles in EPD Before and After Changes

	1968	1970
Confrontation	2.9	3.5
Forcing	3.0	2.8
Smoothing	3.0	2.5

REFERENCES

ALDERFER, C.P., "Organizational Diagnosis from Initial Client Reactions to a Researcher," *Human Organization,* 1968, 27, pp. 260–265.

ALDERFER, C. P. "Effect of Individual, Group, and Intergroup Relations on Attitudes Toward a Management Development Program," *Journal of Applied Psychology,* 1971, 55, pp. 302–311.

ALDERFER, C.P., "Organization Development," in M.R. Rosenzweig and L.W. Porter (eds.), *Annual Review of Psychology*, vol. 28, 1977, pp. 197–223.

ALDERFER, C.P., "Boundary Relations and Organizational Diagnosis," in L. Meltzer and F. Wickert (eds.), *Humanizing Organizational Behavior.* Springfield, Ill.: Charles C. Thomas, 1976.

ALDERFER, C.P., "Organization Development," in M. R. Rosenzweig, and L. W. Porter, (eds.), *Annual Review of Psychology,* vol. 28, 1977.

ALDERFER, C.P., and L. D. BROWN, *Learning from Changing: Organizational Diagnosis and Development.* Beverly Hills, Calif.: Sage, 1975.

ALFRED, T.M., "Checkers or Choice in Manpower Management," *Harvard Business Review,* 1967, 45 (1), pp. 157–167.

ANDERSON, J., "Giving and Receiving Feedback," Procter & Gamble Co., Internal Document, undated.

ARGYRIS, C., "Diagnosing Defenses Against the Outsider," *Journal of Social Issues,* 1952, 8 (3), pp. 24–32.

ARGYRIS, C., *Organization of a Bank.* New Haven, Conn.: Labor and Management Center, Yale University, 1954.

ARGYRIS, C., *Interpersonal Competence and Organizational Effectiveness.* Homewood, Ill.: Dorsey, 1962.

ARGYRIS, C., "T-Groups for Organizational Effectiveness," *Harvard Business Review,* March–April 1964, pp. 84–97.

ARGYRIS, C., "Some Unintended Consequences of Rigorous Research," *Psychological Bulletin,* 1968, 70 (3), pp. 185–197.

ARGYRIS, C., *Intervention Theory and Method: A Behavioral Science View.* Reading, Mass.: Addison-Wesley, 1970.

ARGYRIS, C., *Management and Organizational Development: The Path From Xa to Xb.* New York: McGraw-Hill, 1971.

ARGYRIS, C., *Behind the Front Page.* San Francisco: Jossey-Bass, 1974.

ARGYRIS, C., and D. SCHON, *Theory in Practice: Increasing Professional Effectiveness.* San Francisco: Jossey-Bass, 1976.

BANDURA, A., and R.H. WALTERS, *Social Learning and Personality Development.* New York: Holt, 1963.

BARNARD, C.I., *The Functions of the Executive.* Cambridge, Mass.: Harvard University Press, 1938.

BASS, B., "When Planning for Others," *Journal of Applied Behavioral Science,* 1970, 6, pp. 151–171.

BASS, B.M., and J.A. VAUGHN, *Training in Industry: The Management of Learning.* Belmont, Calif: Wadsworth, 1966.

BAUMGARTEL, H., "Using Employee Questionaire Results for Improving Organizations," Kansas Business Review, December 1959, pp. 2–6.

BAXLEY RAILROAD (A) & (B) cases, Graduate School of Business Administration, Harvard University, 1977.

BECKHARD, R., "An Organization Improvement Program in a Decentralized Organization," *Journal of Applied Behavioral Science,* 1966, 2, pp. 3–25.

BECKHARD, R., "Planned Change in Organizational Systems." Invited Address, American Psychological Association, Miami Beach, September 1970.

BECKHARD, R., "The Confrontation Meeting," *Harvard Business Review,* 1967, 45, 2, pp. 149–155.

BECKHARD, R., *Organization Development: Strategies and Models.* Reading, Mass.: Addison-Wesley, 1969.

BECKHARD, R., and R. HARRIS, *Organizational Transitions: Managing Complex Change.* Reading, Mass.: Addison-Wesley, 1977.

BEDDOWS, R.; H. LANE; and P. LAWRENCE, *Managing Innovations and Adaptation.* Book in progress, undated.

BEER, M., "Organizational Climate: A Viewpoint from the Change Agent," in B. Schneider, *Organizational Climate,* a Symposium, American Psychological Association Convention, Washington, D.C., 1971(a).

BEER, M., "Organizational Diagnosis: An Anatomy of Poor Integration," in *Improving Integration Between Functional Groups: A Case in Organizational Change and Implications for Theory and Practice.* Symposium presented at the American Psychological Association, Washington, D.C., September 1971(b).

BEER, M., "Evaluating Psychological Programs in Industry: Trials, Tribulations, and Prospects," in a Symposium, *Evaluating Psychological Programs in Industry.* Bowling Green University, 1971(c).

BEER, M., "The Technology of Organization Development," in M.D. Dunnette (ed.), *Handbook of Industrial and Organizational Psychology.* Chicago, Ill.: Rand McNally, 1976.

BEER, M., "Using Surveys and Feedback in Organization Development," paper presented to the American Association of Training Directors, Atlanta, Georgia, 1977.

BEER, M., "The Longevity of Organization Development," in B. Lubin, L.D. Goodstein, and A.W. Lubin, *Organization Change Sourcebook I: Cases in Organization Development.* La Jolla, Calif: University Associates, 1979.

BEER, M., and S.M. DAVIS, "Creating a Global Organization: Failures Along the Way," *Columbia Journal of World Business,* vol. 11, no. 2, 1976, pp. 72–84.

BEER, M., and J.W. DRISCOLL, "Strategies for Change," in J.R. Hackman and J.L. Suttle (eds.), *Improving Life at Work: Behavioral Science Approaches to Organizational Change.* Santa Monica, Calif.: Goodyear, 1977.

BEER, M., and E.F. HUSE, "A Systems Approach to Organization Development," *Journal of Applied Behavioral Science,* 1972, 8 (1), pp. 79–101.

BEER, M., and S. KLEISATH, "The Effects of the Managerial Grid Laboratory on Organizational and Laboratory Dimensions," in S.S. Zalkind (Chm.), *Research on the Impact of Using Different Laboratory Methods for Interpersonal and Organizational Change.* Symposium presented at the American Psychological Association, Washington, D.C., September 1967.

BEER, M.; G.E. PIETERS; S.H. MARCUS; and A.T. HUNDERT, "Improving Integration Between Functional Groups: A Case in Organization Change and Implications for Theory and Practice." Symposium presented at meeting of the American Psychological Association, Washington, D.C., September 1971.

BEER, M., and R.A. RUH, "Employee Growth Through Performance Management," *Harvard Business Review,* vol. 54, no. 4, 1976, pp. 59–67.

BEER, M.; R.A. RUH; J. DAWSON; B.B. McCAA; and M. KAVANAGH, "A Performance Management System: Research, Design, Introduction and Evaluation," *Personnel Psychology,* vol. 31, Fall 1978, pp. 505–535.

BENNETT, E.B., "Discussion, Decision, Commitment, and Consensus in Group Decision," *Human Relations,* 1955, vol. VIII, pp. 251–274.

BENNIS, W.G., *Changing Organizations.* New York: McGraw-Hill, 1966.

BENNIS, W.G., *Organization Development: Its Nature, Origins, and Prospects.* Reading, Mass.: Addison-Wesley, 1969.

BENNIS, W.G., "Bureaucracy and Social Change: An Anatomy of a Training Failure," in P.H. Mirvis and D.N. Berg, *Failures in Organization Change and Development.* New York: Wiley-Interscience, 1977.

BENNIS, W.G.; K.D. BENNE; and R. CHIN, *The Planning of Change.* New York: Holt, Rinehart and Winston, 1961.

BENNIS, W.G., and P. SLATER, *The Temporary Society.* New York: Harper & Row, 1968.

BERNE, E., *Games People Play.* New York: Grove Press, 1964.

BLAKE, R.R., personal communication, June 1979.

BLAKE, R.R., and J.S. MOUTON, *The Managerial Grid.* Houston, Tex.: Gulf Publishing, 1964.

BLAKE, R.R.; SHEPARD H.A.; and MOUTON, J.S.; *Managing Intergroup Conflict in Industry.* Houston: Gulf Publishing, 1964.

BLAKE, R.R., and J.S. MOUTON, *Corporate Excellence Through Grid Organization Development: A Systems Approach.* Houston, Tex.: Gulf Publishing, 1968(a).

BLAKE, R.R., and J.S. MOUTON, *Corporate Excellence Diagnosis: The Phase 6 Instrument.* Austin, Tex.: Scientific Methods, 1968(b).

BLAKE, R.R., and J.S. MOUTON, *Building a Dynamic Corporation Through Grid Organizational Development.* Reading, Mass.: Addison-Wesley, 1969.

BLAKE, R.R., and J.S. MOUTON, *The New Managerial Grid.* Houston, Tex.: Gulf Publishing, 1978.

BLAKE, R.R.; J.S. MOUTON; L.B. BARNES; and L.E. GREINER, "Breakthrough in Organization Development," *Harvard Business Review,* 1964, vol. 42, no. 6, pp. 133–155.

BOUCHARD, T.J., Jr., "Field Research Methods: Interviewing, Questionnaires, Participant Observations, Unobtrusive Measures," in M.D. Dunnette (ed.), *Handbook of Industrial and Organizational Psychology.* Chicago, Ill.: Rand McNally, 1976, pp. 363–413.

BOWERS, D.G., "O.D. Techniques and Their Results in 23 Organizations: The Michigan ICC Study," *Journal of Applied Behavioral Science,* 1970, 9, pp. 21–43.

BOWERS, D.G., "Organizational Development: Promises, Performances, Possibilities," *Organizational Dynamics,* vol. 4, no. 4, Spring 1976, pp. 50–62.

BOWERS, D.G., and D.L. HAUSSER, "Work Group Types and Intervention Effects in Organization Development," *Administrative Science Quarterly,* 1977, vol. 22, pp. 76–94.

BROADHURST, P.L., "Emotionality and the Yerkes-Dodson Law," *Journal of Experimental Psychology,* 1957, 54, pp. 345–351.

BRAY, D.W.; R.J. CAMPBELL; and D.L. GRANT, *Formative Years in Business: A Long-Term AT&T Study of Managerial Lives.* New York: Wiley, 1974.

BROWN, D.L., "Alternatives to the Top-Down Approach or If You're Not a Woodcutter, What Are You Doing with That Axe?" in Symposium, *Power and Organization Development: Humanist Babes in the Machiavellian Wood."* Academy of Management Meeting, Kansas City, August 1976.

BRUNS, W.J., JR., "Accounting Information and Decision-Making: Some Behavioral Hypotheses," *The Accounting Review,* 1968, 43, pp. 469–480.

BUCHANAN, P.C., "Crucial Issues in Organizational Development," in *Change in School Systems,* N.T.L. Institute for Applied Behavioral Science, 1967.

BURCK, G., "Union Carbide's Patient Schemers," *Fortune,* December 1965.

BURKE, W.W., "Managing Conflict Between Groups," in J.D. Adams (ed.), *Theory and Method in Organization Development: An Evolutionary Process.* Arlington, Va.: NTL Institute, 1972.

351

BURKE, W.W., "Organization Development in Transition," *Journal of Applied Behavioral Science,* 1976, 12, pp. 22–43.

BURNS, A., and F.L. GREENBERG, "The Entry and Contracting Process," in Symposium of the Division of Industrial Organizational Psychology, American Psychological Association Meetings. New Orleans, 1974.

BURNS, T., and G.M. STALKER, *The Management of Innovation.* London: Tavistock, 1961.

BYHAM, W.C., "Assessment Centers for Spotting Future Managers," *Harvard Business Review* (48), 1970, pp. 150–167.

CAMMANN, C., "The Impact of a Feedback System on Managerial Attitudes and Performance," unpublished doctoral thesis, Yale University, 1974.

CAMMANN, C., and E.E. LAWLER, "Employee Reactions to a Pay Incentive Plan," *Journal of Applied Psychology,* 1973, 58, pp. 163–172.

CAMPBELL, D.T., and D.W. FISK, "Convergent and Discriminant Validity by the Multitrait-Multimethod Matrix," *Psychological Bulletin,* 1959, 56, pp. 81–105.

CAMPBELL, D.T.,and J.C. STANLEY, *Experimental and Quasi-Experimental Designs for Research.* Chicago: Rand McNally, 1966.

CAMPBELL, J.P.; M.D. DUNNETTE; E.E. LAWLER and K.E. WEICK, *Managerial Behavior, Performance, and Effectiveness.* New York: McGraw-Hill, 1970.

CARLSON, H., "Central Foundry Division Parallel Business Planning Organization." Unpublished paper, General Motors Corporation.

CARROLL, S., and H. TOSI, *Management by Objectives.* New York: MacMillan, 1973.

CHANDLER, A., *Strategy and Structure.* Cambridge, Mass.: MIT Press, 1962.

CHILD, John, "Organizational Structure, Environment, and Performance—The Role of Strategic Choice," *Sociology,* 1972, 6, pp. 1–22.

CHIN, R., and K. BENNE, "General Strategies for Effecting Changes in Human Systems," in W.G. Bennis; K.D. Benne; R. Chin; and K.E. Corey (eds), *The Planning of Change,* 3rd ed. New York: Holt, Rinehart and Winston, 1976, pp. 22–45.

COCH, L., and J.R.P. FRENCH, JR., "Overcoming Resistance to Change," *Human Relations,* 1948, 1, pp. 512–533.

COLEMAN, J.S., "Conflicting Theories of Social Change," in G. Zaltman (ed.), *Process and Phenomena of Social Changes.* New York: Wiley, 1973.

CORNING GLASS WORKS (A), (B) & (C) cases. Boston, Mass.: Graduate School of Business Administration, Harvard University, 1976.

CROCKETT, W.J., "Introducing Change to a Government Agency," in P.H. Mirvis and D.N. Berg, *Failures in Organization Development and Change.* New York: Wiley-Interscience, 1977.

DATAVISION case. Boston, Mass.: Graduate School of Business Administration, Harvard University, 1978.

DAVIS, L.E., "Job Design and Productivity: A New Approach," *Personnel,* 1957, 33, pp. 418–430.

DAVIS, L.E., "The Design of Jobs," *Industrial Relations,* 1966, 6, pp. 21–45.

DAVIS, S.M., and P.R. LAWRENCE, *Matrix.* Reading, Mass.: Addison-Wesley, 1977.

DAYAL, I., and J.M. THOMAS, "Operation KPE: Developing a New Organization," *Journal of Applied Behavioral Science,* 1968, 4, pp. 473–506.

DEARBORN, D.C., and H.A. SIMON, "Selective Perception: A Note on the Departmental Identifications of Executives," *Sociometry,* vol. 21, no. 2, June 1958, pp. 140–144.

DICKSON, W.J., and F.J. ROTHLISBERGER, *Counseling in an Organization: A Sequel to the Hawthorne Researchers.* Boston, Mass.: Division of Research, Harvard Business School, 1966.

DRISCOLL, J.W.; M.J. ISRAELOW; and P.D. McKINNON, "Cooperative Problem-Solving Behavior Between Union and Management: An Exploratory Study." Presented at the Academy of Management Meetings, San Francisco, California, August 1978.

DRUCKER, P.F., *The Age of Discontinuity.* New York: Harper & Row, 1969.

DRUCKER, P.F., "What We Can Learn From Japanese Management," *Harvard Business Review,* March–April 1971.

DUNNETTE, M.D., "Fads, Fashions, and Folderol in Psychology," *American Psychologist,* vol. 21, 1966, pp. 343–352.

DUNNETTE M.D., Symposium on Evaluating Psychological Programs in Industry. Bowling Green, Ohio: Bowling Green University, 1970.

DUNNINGTON, R., personal communication, 1978.

DYER, W.G., *Team Building: Issues and Alternatives*. Reading, Mass: Addison-Wesley, 1977.

DYER, W.G.; R.F. MADDOCKS; J.W. MOFFITT; and W.J. UNDERWOOD, "A Laboratory Consulting Model for Organization Change," *Journal of Applied Behavioral Science,* 1970, 6, pp. 211–227.

FAYOL, H., *General and Industrial Management*. New York and London: Pitman, 1949.

FESTINGER, L.A., *A Theory of Cognitive Dissonance*. Evanston, Ill.: Row Peterson, 1957.

FIEDLER, F.E. *A Theory of Leadership Effectiveness*. New York: McGraw-Hill, 1967.

FIRST NATIONAL CITY BANK (A) & (B). Boston, Mass.: Graduate School of Business Administration, Harvard University, 1975.

FLAMHOLTZ, E.G., *Human Resource Accounting*. Encino, Calif: Dickinson, 1974.

FLEISHMAN, E.A., "Attitude Versus Skill Factors in Work Productivity," *Personnel Psychology,* 1965, 18, pp. 253–266.

FLEISHMAN, E.A.; E.F. HARRIS; and H.E. BURTT; *Leadership and Supervision in Industry*. Columbus, Ohio: Ohio State University, Bureau of Educational Research, 1955..

FORBES, "Corning Glass: On the Way Up," vol. 120, no. 3, 1977, pp. 33–37.

FORD, R.N., *Motivation Through Work Itself*. New York: American Management Association, 1969.

FORDYCE, J.K.,and R. WEIL, *Managing With People: A Manager's Handbook of Organization Development Methods*. Reading, Mass.: Addison-Wesley, 1971.

FOURAKER, L.E., and J.M. STOPFORD, "Organization Structure and the Multinational Strategy," *Administrative Science Quarterly,* 1968, vol. 13, pp. 47–64.

FRANKLIN, J.L., "Characteristics of Successful and Unsuccessful Organization Development," *Journal of Applied Behavioral Science,* 1976, 12, 4, pp. 471–492.

FRENCH, J.R.P., JR., "A Formal Theory of Social Power," *Psychological Review,* 1956, vol. LXIII, no. 3, pp. 181–194.

FRENCH, W.L., and C. H. BELL, *Organization Development: Behavioral Science Interventions for Organization Improvement*. Englewood Cliffs, N.J.: Prentice-Hall, 1978.

FRENCH, W.L., and R.W. HOLLMAN, "Management by Objectives: The Team Approach," *California Management Review,* 1975, vol. XVII, no. 3, 1977.

FRIEDLANDER, F., "The Impact of Organizational Training Laboratories Upon the Effectiveness and Interaction of Ongoing Work Groups," *Personnel Psychology,* 1967, 20, pp. 289–307.

FRIEDLANDER, F., "A Comparative Study of Consulting Process and Group Development," *Journal of Applied Behavioral Science,* 1968, 4, pp. 377–399.

FRIEDLANDER, F., "Congruence in Organization Development," *Proceedings of the Academy of Management,* Atlanta, Georgia, 1971, pp. 153–160.

FRIEDLANDER, F., and L.D. BROWN, "Organization Development," *Annual Review of Psychology,* 1974, 25, pp. 313–341.

FROHMAN, M.A., "An Empirical Study of a Model and Strategies for Planned Organizational Change." Unpublished doctoral dissertation, University of Michigan, Ann Arbor, 1970.

FROST, C.; J. WAKELEY; and R. RUH, *The Scanlon Plan for Organization Development: Identity, Participation, and Equity*. East Lansing, Michigan: Michigan State University Press, 1974.

GALBRAITH, J., *Designing Complex Organizations*. Reading, Mass.: Addison-Wesley, 1973.

GARDNER, J.W., *Self-Renewal: The Individual and the Innovative Society*. New York: Harper & Row, 1963.

GLASSER, W., *Reality Therapy*. New York: Harper & Row, 1965.

GOLEMBIEWSKI, R.T., and A. KIEPPER, "MARTA: Toward an Effective Open Giant," *Public Administration Review,* January–February 1976.

GREINER, L.E., "Patterns of Organization Change," *Harvard Business Review,* May–June 1967, pp. 119–128.

GREINER, L.E.; D.P. LEITCH; and L.B. BARNES, "The Simplest Complexity of Organizational Climate in a Governmental Agency." In R. Tagiuri and G.H. Litwin (eds.), *Organizational Climate*. Boston, Mass.: Harvard University, Graduate School of Business Administration, Division of Research, 1968.

GUEST, R.H., *Organizational Change: The Effect of Successful Leadership.* Homewood, Ill.: Dorsey Press and R.D. Irwin, Inc., 1962.

GYLLENHAMMAR, P.G., *People at Work.* Reading, Mass.: Addison-Wesley, 1977.

HACKMAN, J.R., "Group Influences on Individuals in Organizations," in M.D. Dunnette (ed.), *Handbook of Industrial and Organizational Psychology.* Chicago, Ill.: Rand McNally, 1976.

HACKMAN, J.R., "Work Design;" in J.R. Hackman and J.L. Suttle, *Improving Life at Work: Behavioral Science Approaches to Organizational Change.* Santa Monica, Calif.: Goodyear, 1977.

HACKMAN, J.R., and E.E. LAWLER, "Employee Reactions to Job Characteristics," *Journal of Applied Psychology,* 1971, 55, pp. 259–286.

HACKMAN, J.R., and G.R. OLDHAM, "Development of the Job Diagnostic Survey," *Journal of Applied Psychology,* 60, 1975, pp. 159–170.

HACKMAN, J.R.; G.R. OLDHAM; R. JANSON; and K. PURDY, "A New Strategy for Job Enrichment," *California Management Review,* Summer 1975, pp. 57–71.

HALL, D.T., *Careers in Organizations.* Santa Monica, Calif.: Goodyear, 1976.

HALL, J., "The Use of Instruments in Laboratory Training," *Training and Development Journal,* 1970, 24, 5, pp. 48–55.

HALPIN, A.W., and D.B. CROFT, *The Organizational Climate of Schools.* Washington, D.C.: U.S. Office of Education, Department of Health, Education, and Welfare, Contract No. SAE 543 (8639), 1962.

HAMNER C.W., and F.J. SMITH, "Work Attitudes as Predictors of Unionization Activity," *Journal of Applied Psychology,* 1978 63(4), pp. 415–421.

HARRISON, R., "Choosing the Depth of an Organizational Intervention," *Journal of Applied Behavioral Science,* 1965, 1, pp. 409–432.

HARRISON, R., "Understanding Your Organization's Character," *Harvard Business Review,* 1972, vol. 5, no. 3, pp. 119–128.

HARRISON, R., "Role Negotiation: A Tough Minded Approach to Team Development." In W.G. Bennis; D.E. Berlew; E.H. Schein; and F.I. Steele (eds), *Interpersonal Dynamics* (3rd ed.). Homewood Ill.: Dorsey Press, 1973

HARRISON, R., "Strategy Guidelines for an Internal Organization Development Unit," *O.D. Practitioner,* vol. 4, no. 3, pp. 1–4, undated.

HAVELOCK, R.G., and M.C. HAVELOCK, *Training Change Agents.* Ann Arbor, Michigan: Institute for Social Research, 1973.

HELLER, F.A., "Group Feedback Analysis: A Method of Field Research," *Psychological Bulletin,* 1969, 72, 2, pp. 108–117.

HERMAN, S., and R. PHILLIPS, "Application of Gestalt in OD." Workshop presented in Fall National OD Network Conference. New York, October 1971.

HERZBERG, F.L., *Work and the Nature Man.* Cleveland, Ill.: World Publishing, 1966.

HERZBERG, F.L.; B. MANSNER; and B. SNYDERMAN, *The Motivation to Work.* New York: Wiley, 1959.

HILGARD, E.F., and G.H. BOWER, *Theories of Learning* (3rd ed.). New York: Appleton-Century-Crofts, 1966.

HINRICHS, J.R., *Practical Management for Productivity.* Unpublished manuscript, 1978.

HORNSTEIN, A., and N. TICHY, *Organization Diagnosis and Intervention Strategies: An Instrumental Individual and Group Approach.* Hopewell Junction, N.Y.: Behavioral Science Associates, 1973.

HOUSE, R.J., "T Group Education and Leadership Effectiveness: A Review of the Empiric Literature and Critical Evaluation," *Personnel Psychology,* 1967, 20, pp. 1–32.

HOUSE, R.J., "A Path Goal Theory of Leader Effectiveness," *Administrative Science Quarterly,* 1971, 2, pp. 321–339.

HOUSE, R.J., and J. RIZZO, "Role Conflict and Ambiguity as Critical Variables in a Model of Organizational Behavior," *Organizational Behavior and Human Performance,* 1972, 7 (3) pp. 467–505.

HUSE, E.F., *Organizational Development and Change.* St. Paul, Minn.: West Publishing, 1975.

HUSE, E.F., and C.A. BAREBO, personal communication, 1970.

HUSE, E.F., and M. BEER, "Eclectic Approach to Organizational Development," *Harvard Business Review,* 1971, 49 (5) pp. 103–112.

JACQUES, E., *The Changing Culture of a Factory.* London: Tavistock, 1951.

JAMES, L.R.; E.A. HARTMAN; M.W. STEBBINS; and A.P. JONES, "Relationship Between Psychological Climate and a VIE Model for Work Motivation," *Personnel Psychology,* 1977, 30(2), pp. 229–254.

KAST, F.S., and J.E. ROSENZWEIG, *Organization and Management: A Systems Approach.* New York: McGraw-Hill, 1970.

KATZ, D., and R.L. KAHN, *The Social Psychology of Organizations.* New York: Wiley, 1978.

KELEMAN, H.C., *A Time to Speak: On Human Values and Social Research.* San Francisco, Calif.: Jossey-Bass, 1968.

KELEMAN, H.C., and D.P. WARWICK, "Bridging Micro and Macro Approaches to Social Change: A Social Psychological Perspective." In G. Zaltman (ed.), *Processes and Phenomena of Social Change.* New York: Wiley, 1973.

KEPNER, E.H., and B.B. TREGOE, *The Rational Manager.* New York: McGraw-Hill, 1965.

KLEIN, S.M.; A.I. KRAUT; and A. WOLFSON, "Employee Reactions to Attitude Survey Feedback: A Study of the Impact of Structure and Process," *Administrative Science Quarterly,* 1971, 16, pp. 497–514.

KOTTER, J.P., "The Psychological Contract: Managing the Joining-Up Process," *California Management Review,* 1973, XV (3), pp. 91–99.

KOTTER, J.P., *Organization Dynamics: Diagnosis and Intervention.* Reading, Mass.: Addison-Wesley, 1978.

KOTTER, J.P.; V.A. FAUX; and C.C. McARTHUR, *Self-Assessment and Career Development,* Englewood Cliffs, N.J.: Prentice-Hall, 1978.

LAWLER, E.E., *Pay and Organizational Effectiveness: A Psychological View.* New York: McGraw-Hill, 1971.

LAWLER, E.E., *Motivation in Work Organizations.* Monterey, Calif.: Brooks Cole, 1973.

LAWLER, E.E., "Reward Systems," in J.R. Hackman, and L.J. Suttle (eds.), *Improving Life at Work: Behavioral Science Approaches to Organizational Change.* Santa Monica, Calif.: Goodyear, 1977.

LAWLER, E.E., "The New Plant Revolution," *Organizational Dynamics,* vol. 6, no. 3, Winter 1978, pp. 2–12.

LAWLER, E.E., and C. CAMMANN, "What Makes a Work Group Successful?" *The Failure of Success.* New York: Amacon, 1972.

LAWLER, E.E., and J.R. HACKMAN, "The Impact of Employee Participation in the Development of Pay Incentive Plans: A Field Experiment," *Journal of Applied Psychology,* 1969, 53, pp. 467–471.

LAWLER, E.E., and J.G. RHODE, *Information and Control in Organizations.* Santa Monica, Calif.: Goodyear, 1976.

LAWRENCE, P.R. *The Changing of Organizational Behavior Patterns.* Boston, Mass.: Division of Research, Harvard Business School, 1958.

LAWRENCE, P.R., "How to Deal With Resistance to Change," *Harvard Business Review,* January–February 1969, pp. 4–12, and 166–176.

LAWRENCE, P.R. and J.W. LORSCH, *Organization and Environment.* Boston, Mass.: Division of Research, Graduate School of Business Administration, Harvard University, 1967(a).

LAWRENCE, P.R., and J.W. LORSCH, "New Management Job: The Integrator," *Harvard Business Review,* 1967(b), 45, 6, pp. 142–151.

LAWRENCE, P.R., and J.W. LORSCH, *Developing Organizations: Diagnosis and Actions.* Reading, Mass.: Addison-Wesley, 1969.

LEAVITT, H.J., "Applied Organizational Change in Industry: Structural, Technological and Humanistic Approaches," in J.G. March (ed.), *Handbook of Organizations.* Chicago, Ill.: Rand McNally, 1965.

LESIEUR, F.G. (ed.), *The Scanlon Plan: A Frontier in Labor-Management Cooperation.* Cambridge, Mass.: MIT, Industrial Relations Section, 1958.

LEVINSON, H., *Organizational Diagnosis.* Cambridge, Mass.: Harvard University Press, 1972.

LEWIN, K., "Group Decision and Social Change." In E.E. Maccoby, T. Newcomb, and E. Hartley (eds.), *Readings in Social Psychology.* New York: Holt, Rinehart and Winston, 1947.

355

LIKERT, R., *New Patterns of Management.* New York: McGraw-Hill, 1961.

LIKERT, R., *The Human Organization: Its Management and Value.* New York: McGraw-Hill, 1967.

LIKERT, R., and S.M. FISHER, "MBGO: Putting Some Team Spirit into MBO," *Personnel,* January–February 1977.

LIPPITT, R.; J. WATSON; and B. WESTERLEY, *The Dynamics of Planned Change.* New York: Harcourt, Brace & World, 1958.

LITWIN, G.H., and R.A. STRINGER JR., *Motivation and Organizational Climate.* Boston, Mass.: Graduate School of Business Administration, Harvard University, 1968.

LOCK, E.A., "Toward a Theory of Task Motivation and Incentives," *Organizational Behavior and Human Performance,* 1968, 3, pp. 157–189.

LOCK, E.A.; N. CARTLEDGE; and J. KEPPEL, "Motivational Effects of Results: A Goal-Setting Phenomenon?" *Psychological Bulletin,* 1968, 70, pp. 474–485.

LORSCH, J.W., "A Note on Organization Design." Boston, Mass.: Graduate School of Business Administration, Harvard University, 1975.

LORSCH, J.W., and J.J. MORSE, *Organizations and Their Members: A Contingency Approach.* New York: Harper & Row, 1974.

MANN, F.C., "Studying and Creating Change: A Means to Understanding Social Organization." In *Research in Industrial Human Relations,* Industrial Relations Research Association, Publication No. 17, 1957, pp. 146–167.

MANN, F.C., and R. LIKERT, "The Need for Research on Communicating Research Results," *Human Organization,* 1952, XI, pp. 15–19.

MARCH, J.G., and H.A. SIMON, *Organizations.* New York: John Wiley, 1958.

MARGULIES, N., "Notes on the Marginality of the Consultant's Role," *Social Change.* NIL Institute for Applied Behavioral Science, vol. 7, 1977.

MARGULIES, N., and A.P. RAIA, *Conceptual Foundations of Organizational Development.* New York: McGraw-Hill, 1978.

MARRIS, P., and M. REIN (eds.), *Dilemmas of Social Reform: Poverty and Community Action in the United States* (2nd ed.). Chicago, Ill.: Aldine, 1973.

MARROW, A.J.; D.G. BOWERS; and S.E. SEASHORE, *Management by Participation.* New York: Harper & Row, 1967.

MASLOW, A.H., *Motivation and Personality.* New York: Harper & Row, 1954.

MAY DEPARTMENT STORES (A) & (B) cases. Boston, Mass.: Graduate School of Business Administration, 1976.

McCLELLAND, D.C., "Toward a Theory of Motive Acquisition," *American Psychologist,* 1965, 20, pp. 321–333.

McCLELLAND, D.C., "Managing Motivation to Expand Human Freedom," *American Psychologist,* 1978, vol. 33, no. 3, pp. 201–210.

McCLELLAND, D.C., and D.G. WINTER, *Motivating Economic Achievement.* New York: Free Press, 1969.

McGREGOR, D., *The Human Side of Enterprise.* New York: McGraw-Hill, 1960.

McGREGOR, D., *The Professional Manager.* New York: McGraw-Hill, 1967.

McMANUS, M., and A. BURNES, "The Organizational Image Process." Paper presented at the New Technology in Organization Development Conference, 1975.

MEYER, H.H.; E. KAY; and J.P. FRENCH, "Split Roles in Performance Appraisal," *Harvard Business Review,* 1965, 43, 1, pp. 123–129.

MILES, R.E., "Human Relations or Human Resources?" *Harvard Business Review,* 1965, 43, 4, pp. 148–163.

MILES, R.E., personal communication, 1972.

MILES, R.E., "Organization Development," in G. Strauss (ed.), *Organizational Behavior: Research and Issues,* Industrial Relations Research Association, 1974.

MILES, R.E., and C. SNOW, *Organization Strategy, Structure, and Process.* New York: McGraw-Hill, 1978.

MILES, R.H., and K.S. CAMERON, "Coffin Nails and Corporate Strategies." Working Paper, Division of Research, Boston, Mass., Graduate School of Business Administration, Harvard University, 1977.

MINER, J.B., "Bridging the Gulf in Organizational Performance," *Harvard Business Review*, July–August 1968.

MIRVIS, P.H., and E.E. LAWLER, "Measuring the Financial Impact of Employee Attitudes," *Journal of Applied Psychology*, 1977, 62 (1), pp. 1–8.

MOORE, B., and P. GOODMAN, *Factors Affecting the Impact of a Company-Wide Incentive Program on Productivity*. Report submitted to the National Commission on Productivity, January 1973.

MORRIS, R., (ed.), *Centrally-Planned Change: Prospects and Concepts*. New York: National Association of Social Workers, 1964.

MORSE, J.J., and J.W. LORSCH, "Beyond Theory Y," *Harvard Business Review*, 1970, 48 (3), pp. 61–68.

MURRAY, H.A., *Exploration in Personality*. New York: Oxford University Press, 1938.

MYERSETH, O., "Intrafirm Diffusion of Organizational Innovations: An Exploratory Study." Doctoral thesis, Graduate School of Business Administration, Harvard University, 1977.

NADLER, D.A., "Using Feedback for Organizational Change: Promises and Pitfalls," *Group and Organizational Studies*, 1976, 1, pp. 177–186.

NADLER, D.A., *Feedback and Organizational Development: Using Data Based Methods*. Reading, Mass.: Addison-Wesley, 1977.

NADLER, D.A.; P.H. MIRVIS; and C. CAMMANN, "The Ongoing Feedback System: Experimenting with a New Managerial Tool," *Organizational Dynamics*, 1977.

NEUSTADT, R., *Presidential Power*. New York: Wiley, 1960.

ORDIONE, G.S., *Management Decisions by Objectives*. Englewood Cliffs, N.J.: Prentice-Hall, 1965.

O'REILLY, C.A., III, and K.H. ROBERTS, "Supervisor Influence and Subordinate Mobility Aspirations as Moderators of Consideration and Initiating Structure," *Journal of Applied Psychology*, vol. 63, no. 1, 1978, pp. 96–104.

OUCHI, W.G., and R.L. PRICE, "Hierarchies, Clans, and Theory Z: A New Perspective on Organization Development," *Organizational Dynamics*, 1978, vol. 7, no. 2, pp. 25–44.

PELZ, E.R., "Some Factors in Group Decision," in E.E. Maccoby, T. Newcomb, and E.L. Hartley (eds.), *Readings in Social Psychology* (3rd ed.). New York: Holt, Rinehart and Winston, 1958.

PETERS, T.J., "Symbols, Patterns, and Settings: An Optimistic Case for Getting Things Done," *Organizational Dynamics*, vol. 7, no. 2, Autumn 1978.

PETTIGREW, A.M., "Strategic Aspects of the Management of Specialist Activity," *Personnel Review*, 1975, vol. 4, no. 1, p. 5–13(a).

PETTIGREW, A.M., "Towards a Political Theory of Organizational Intervention," *Human Relations*, 1975, vol. 28, no. 3, pp. 191–208.(b)

PETTIGREW, A.M., "Conference Review: Issues of Change," in P. Watt (ed.), *Personal Goals and Work Design*. London: Wiley, 1976.

PIETERS, G.R., "Changing Organizational Structures, Roles, and Process to Enhance Integration: The Implementation of a Change Program." In *Improving Integration Between Functional Groups: A Case in Organization Change and Implications for Theory & Practice*. Symposium presented at the American Psychological Association, Washington, D.C., September 1971.

PLOVNICK, M.; R. FRY; and I. RUBIN, "New Developments in O.D. Technology," *Training & Development Journal*, April 1975.

PORTER, L.W., and E.E. LAWLER, *Managerial Attitudes and Performance*. Homewood, Ill,: Irwin-Dorsey, 1968.

PORTER, L.W.; E.E. LAWLER; and J.R. HACKMAN, *Behavior in Organizations*. New York: McGraw-Hill, 1975.

REDDIN, W.J., "My Errors in O.D." Paper presented to the Organization Development Division of the Thirty-sixth Annual Meeting of the Academy of Management, August 11–14, 1976.

ROBERTS, E.B., and A.L. FROHMAN, "Internal Entrepreneurship: Strategy for Growth," *The Business Quarterly*, vol. 37, no. 1, Spring 1972, pp. 71–78.

ROGERS, C.R., *Counseling and Psychotherapy: Newer Concepts in Practice*. Boston: Houghton Mifflin Co., 1942.

ROGERS, C.R., *Client Centered Therapy*. Boston: Houghton Mifflin, 1951.

ROGERS, E.M., "Effects of Incentives on the Diffusion of Innovations: The Case of Family Planning in Asia." In G. Zaltman (ed.), *Processes and Phenomena of Social Change*. New York: Wiley, 1973.

ROGERS, E.M., and E.F. SHOEMAKER, *Communication of Innovations: A Cross Cultural Approach*. New York: Free Press, 1971.

ROTHLISBERGER, F.J., and W.J. DICKSON, *Management and the Worker: An Account of a Research Program Conducted by Western Electric Company, Hawthorne Works, Chicago*. Cambridge, Mass.: Harvard University Press, 1939.

RUSH, H.M., *Counseling and Psychotherapy: Newer Concepts in Practice*. Boston: Houghton Mifflin, 1973.

SCHEFLEN, K.; E.E. LAWLER; and J.R. HACKMAN, "Long-Term Impact of Employer Participation in the Development of Pay Incentive Plans: A Field Experiment Revisited," *Journal of Applied Psychology*, 1971, 55, pp. 182–186.

SCHEIN, E.H., "Management Development as a Process of Influence," *Industrial Management Review*, 1961, II (2), pp. 59–77.

SCHEIN, E.H., "Organizational Socialization and the Professional Manager," *Industrial Management Review*, 1965, 1–15.

SCHEIN, E.H., *Process Consultation: Its Role in Organization Development*. Reading, Mass.: Addison-Wesley, 1969.

SCHEIN, E.H., *Organizational Psychology* (2nd ed.). Englewood Cliffs, N.J.: Prentice-Hall, 1970.

SCHEIN, E.H., *Career Dynamics*. Reading, Mass.: Addison-Wesley, 1978.

SCHNEIDER, B., "Organizational Climate: Individual Preferences and Organizational Realities," *Journal of Applied Psychology*, 1972, 56, pp. 211–217.

✓ SCHNEIDER, B., *Staffing Organizations*. Santa Monica, Calif.: Goodyear, 1976.

SCHNEIDER, B., and C.J. BARTLETT, "Individual Differences and Organizational Climate: I. The Research Plan and Questionnaire Development," *Personnel Psychology*, 1968, 21, pp. 323–333.

SCHNEIDER, B.; J.K. PARKINGTON; and V.E. BUXTON, "The Climate for Service in Banks: A Study in Organizational Climate." Mimeographed Report, College Park, Maryland: University of Maryland, undated.

SEASHORE, S.E., and D.G. BOWERS, *Changing the Structure and Functioning of an Organization: Report of a Field Experiment*. University of Michigan, Institute for Social Research, Survey Research Center, 1963, Monograph No. 23.

✓ SHAW, M.E., and J.M. WRIGHT, *Scales for the Measurement of Attitudes*. New York: McGraw-Hill, 1967.

SHMUCK, R.A.; P.J. RUNKEL; and D. LANGMEYER, "Improving Organizational Problem Solving in a School Faculty," *Journal of Applied Behavioral Science*, 1969, 5, pp. 455–490.

SKINNER, B.F., *The Behavior of Organisms: An Experimental Analysis*. New York: Appleton-Century-Crofts, 1938.

SKINNER, B.F., *Contingencies of Reinforcement: A Theoretical Analysis*. New York: Appleton-Century-Crofts, 1969.

✓ STARBUCK, W.H., "Organizations and Their Environments," in M.D. Dunnette (ed.), *Handbook of Industrial and Organizational Psychology*. Chicago, Ill.: Rand McNally, 1976, pp. 1069–1124.

STEELE, F., *Physical Settings and Organization Development*. Reading, Mass.: Addison-Wesley, 1973.

STEELE, F., and S. JENKS, *The Feel of the Work Place: Understanding and Improving Organization Climate*. Reading Mass.: Addison-Wesley, 1977.

STOGDILL, R.M., *Individual Behavior and Group Achievement*. New York: Oxford University Press, 1959.

SYKES, A.J.M., "The Effect of a Supervisory Training Course in Changing Supervisors' Perceptions and Expectations of the Role of Management," *Human Relations*, 1962, 15, pp. 227–243.

TAGIURI, R., and G.H. LITWIN, *Organization Climate: Explorations of a Concept*. Boston, Mass.: Graduate School of Business Administration, Harvard University, 1968.

358 TAYLOR, F.W., *Scientific Management*. New York: Harper & Row, 1911.

TAYLOR, J., and D. BOWERS, *Survey of Organizations: A Machine Scored Standardized Questionnaire Instrument.* Ann Arbor, Mich.: Center for Research on Utilization of Scientific Knowledge, Institute for Social Research, University of Michigan, 1972.

THOMAS, R.R., "Managing the Psychological Contract." Boston, Mass.: Graduate School of Business Administration, Harvard University, 1974.

THOMPSON, J.D., *Organizations in Action.* New York: McGraw-Hill, 1967.

THURBER, J.A., "The Corning Glass Works Outplacement Center." An internal company document, Corning Glass Works, Corning, New York, 1975.

TICHY, N.M., "Agents of Planned Social Change: Congruence of Values, Cognitions and Actions," *Administrative Science Quarterly,* 1974, 19, pp. 164–182.

TICHY, N.M.; H. HORNSTEIN; and J. NISBERG, "Organization Diagnosis and Intervention Strategies: Developing Emergent Pragmatic Theories of Change," in W.W. Burke, *Current Issues and Strategies in Organization Development.* New York; Human Science, 1977.

TICHY, N.M., and J.M. NISBERG, "Change Agent Base: What They View Determines What They Do," *Group and Organization Studies,* September 1976, (3), pp. 286–301.

TIME MAGAZINE, February 12, 1973, p. 73.

TOFFLER, A., *Future Shock.* New York: Random House, 1970.

TORNATZKY, L.G., "Implications of the MSU-NIMH Innovation Diffusion Project: Towards an O.S.P.E.D." Symposium, *The Diffusion of Innovation.* American Psychological Association, Washington, D.C., September 1976.

TRIST, E.L., and K.W. BAMFORTH, "Some Social and Psychological Consequences of the Long Wall Method of Goal Getting," *Human Relations,* 1951, 4, pp. 3–38.

TRIST, E.L.; G.W. HIGGINS; H. MURRAY; and A.B. POLLOCK, *Organizational Choice.* London: Tavistock, 1963.

TRW. Boston, Mass.: Graduate School of Business Administration, Harvard University, 1979.

TURNER, A.N., and P.R. LAWRENCE, *Industrial Jobs and the Worker.* Boston, Mass.: Harvard University, Graduate School of Business Administration, 1965.

TUSHMAN, M., *Organizational Change: An Exploratory Study and Case History.* Ithaca, N.Y.: New York State School of Industrial and Labor Relations, Cornell University, 1974.

URWICK, LYNDALL F., *Notes on the Theory of Organization.* New York: American Management Association, 1953.

VROOM, V.H., *Some Personality Determinants of the Effects of Participation.* Englewood Cliffs, N.J.: Prentice-Hall, 1960.

VROOM, V.H., *Work and Motivation.* New York: Wiley, 1964.

VROOM, V.H., and P.W. YETTON, *Leadership and Decision Making.* Pittsburgh, Pa.: University of Pittsburgh Press, 1973.

WALTON, R.E., *Interpersonal Peacemaking: Confrontations and Third Party Consultation.* Reading, Mass.: Addison-Wesley, 1969.

WALTON, R.E., "Frontiers Beckoning the Organizational Psychologist. Invited address presented at the 79th Annual Meeting of the American Psychological Association, Washington, D.C., September 1971.

WALTON, R.E., "Innovative Restructuring of Work," in J.M. Rosow (ed.), *The Worker and the Job: Coping with Change.* Englewood Cliffs, N.J.: Prentice-Hall, 1974.

WALTON, R.E., "The Diffusion of New York Structures: Explaining Why Success Didn't Take," *Organizational Dynamics,* Winter 1975, pp. 3–22.

WALTON, R.E., "The Topeka Story: Part II," *The Wharton Magazine, Winter 1978,* pp. 36–41.

WALTON, R.E., and J.M. DUTTON, "The Management of Interdepartmental Conflict: A Model and Review," *Administrative Science Quarterly,* 1969, 14, pp. 522–542.

WALTON, R.E., and L.A. SCHLESINGER, "Do Supervisors Thrive in Participative Work Systems?" *Organizational Dynamics,* vol. 7, no. 3, 1979, pp. 24–38.

WEBER, M., *The Theory of Social and Economic Organization,* (translated by A.M. Henderson and T. Parsons), T. Parsons (ed.). New York: Free Press, 1947.

WEICK, K.E., "Systems Theory of the Middle Range," in *Systems Theory and Organizational Research.* Symposium, Eastern Academy of Management, Philadelphia, Pa., 1973.

WEICK, K.E., "Enactment Process in Organizations," in B.M. Staw, and G.R. Salancik (eds.), *New Directions in Organizational Behavior.* Chicago, Ill.:St. Clair Press, 1977, pp. 267–300.

WHITMORE, K.R., "Matrix Organizations in Conventional Manufacturing-Marketing Companies." Master's Thesis, Cambridge, Mass: Sloan School of Management, MIT, June 1975.

WHYTE, W.F., *Money and Motivation.* New York: Harper & Row, 1955.

WOODWARD, J., *Industrial Organization: Theory and Practice.* London: Oxford University Press, 1967.

WORK IN AMERICA. Report of a special task force to the Secretary of Health, Education, and Welfare. Cambridge, Mass.: MIT Press, 1973.

ZALTMAN, G., *Processes and Phenomena of Social Change.* New York: Wiley, 1973.

ZAND, D., "Collateral Organizations: A New Change Strategy," *Journal of Applied Behavioral Science*, 10, (1), 1974.

INDEX

A

Action planning, 101–102
Adaptability
    of individuals, 187–189
    of organizations, 4, 16–17
Argyris, Chris, 90–91
Attitudes, employee, 24–25

B

Beckhard, R., and Harris, R.,
    116–117
Behavior
    reinforcing, 68
    role of leader in changing, 67
    theory in Grid OD, 208
Behavorial change, 194–196
    fade-out, 196
Blake, Robert and Jane Mouton, 6,
    205–211 *passim. See also* Grid
    Organizational Development
Bottom-up change, 54–55, 59–61

C

Career development strategies, 201
Change
    approaches effectiveness criteria,
      65–67
    causes of, 47–50
    follow up, 105–108
    initiating, 227–228, 230
    leadership role in, 66–69
    support for, 229–230, 234–236
    sustaining, 232–234
Change agent, 9, 76–78, 218–255.
    See also Consultant
    characteristics of effective agent,
      222–223
    counseling, 191
    external, 257
    in formal systems, 64–65
    internal, 257
    maintaining motivation, 103–104
    role in interventions, 75
    role in new policies, 51–52
    solution development, 100–101
    and structural change, 157, 159